DÜRRENMATT

Dürrenmatt

A STUDY IN PLAYS, PROSE, THEORY

BY TIMO TIUSANEN

PRINCETON UNIVERSITY PRESS

Published by Princeton University Press, Princeton, New Jersey
In the United Kingdom:
Princeton University Press, Guildford, Surrey

Library of Congress Cataloging in Publication Data will
be found on the last printed page of this book

Publication of this book has been aided by a grant from
The Andrew W. Mellon Foundation

This book has been composed in Linotype Times Roman

Printed in the United States of America
by Princeton University Press, Princeton, New Jersey

Contents

IIIIIIIIIIIIIIIIIIIIIIIIIIIIIIIIIIIIIIIIIIIIIIIIIIIIIIIIIIIIIIIIIIIIIIIIIIIIIIIIIIIIIIII

CONTENTS

Preface

‖‖

"Modern drama": we usually think of the drama since Henrik Ibsen. As time proceeds, a subdivision will grow in scope and significance: drama since World War II. This study concentrates on a playwright who began his career in the late 1940's, and who is by many taken to be the most important living playwright writing in German. My acquaintance with his art began simultaneously with my work in the professional theater: *The Visit* by Friedrich Dürrenmatt was the first play I directed, together with Sakari Puurunen. After that experience, I also wrote a seventy-page essay on his work up to 1963. In my mind, Dürrenmatt and the stage belong together. This book reviews his entire work up to 1977.

The Academy of Finland has financed this research project in two decisive phases. First, my appointment as Research Assistant enabled me to concentrate on gathering additional materials on Dürrenmatt during most of the year 1970. Second, my term as a Senior Research Fellow of the Academy since April 1974 helped me to complete the book. I also gratefully acknowledge smaller grants given by the Academy to people who have assisted me.

I remember well the excitement with which I studied the reviews and other materials gathered by Dürrenmatt's theatrical agency, Reiss AG, Basle, Switzerland, in spring 1971: thirteen big portfolios. Mrs. Elke Bernard was most helpful to me both then and later on. Every scholar is dependent on libraries; I mention with special gratitude Deutsche Bibliothek, Helsinki, and the British Library, London, both of which have furnished me with pleasant working surroundings.

Dr. Hansres Jacobi deciphered a great number of abbreviated names for me. Dr. Balz Engler, my "secret agent" in Switzerland, Professors Irma Rantavaara, Hans Fromm,

George E. Wellwarth, and Joseph Strelka have all helped me with their constructive criticism.

Mr. Kingsley Hart, Senior Lecturer in English at the University of Helsinki and my former teacher, kindly worked on my language. Mrs. Marjorie Sherwood, of Princeton University Press, took care of the editing job with concern for every detail. Mrs. Ritva Käki worked on the index, and Miss Rauha Riihinen typed a part of the manuscript. My very best thanks to all of them.

Chapter 15 ("Strindmatt or Dürrenberg?") is based on a paper I read at the Strindberg Symposium in Stockholm in 1973; it was later published in *Strindberg and Modern Theatre* (Strindberg Society, 1975).

Grateful acknowledgment is made to the following publishers for permission to quote from copyrighted works:

Copyright for almost all works by Friedrich Dürrenmatt in German: Verlags AG "Die Arche," Peter Schifferli, Zürich—with the exception of *Die Ehe des Herrn Mississippi* (© Europa Verlag, Zürich) and *Der Richter und sein Henker* © 1952, *Der Verdacht* © 1953 by Benziger Verlag Zürich, Köln.

To Alfred A. Knopf, Inc. and Random House, Inc. for permission to quote from *Traps, Once a Greek*, and *The Pledge*, all translated by Richard and Clara Winston, and from *The Visit*, translated by Maurice Valency.

To Jonathan Cape Ltd. for permission to quote from *The Judge and His Hangman*, translated by Cyrus Brook; from *A Dangerous Game, Once a Greek*, and *The Pledge*, each translated by Richard and Clara Winston; from *The Visit*, translated by Patrick Bowles; from *The Quarry*, translated by Eva H. Morreale; and from *The Four Plays*, translated by Gerhard Nellhaus, Michael Bullock, William McElwee, and James Kirkup.

To Grove Press, Inc. for permission to quote from *Four Plays*, translators as above.

To New York Graphic Society for permission to quote from *The Quarry*, translator as above.

PREFACE

To *Schweizer Illustrierte* for permission to quote a poem originally published by it. To Hope Leresche & Sayle, Dürrenmatt's agent. Schauspielhaus Zürich (under the management of Mr. Harry Buckwitz), Suomen Kansallisteatteri, Helsingin Kaupunginteatteri, Tampereen Teatteri, and Tampereen Työväen Teatteri have kindly made a selection of their production photographs available for publication.

"Der Rest ist Dank," Dürrenmatt says: "the rest is thanks."

At Pälkäne, Finland, February, 1977
Timo Tiusanen

ix

Abbreviations

The titles of Dürrenmatt's works not translated into English are given in two languages in the list below.

ANTHOLOGIES

DK   *Dramaturgisches und Kritisches* (Dramaturgic and Critical Writings)
FP   *Four Plays*
GH   *Gesammelte Hörspiele* (Collected Radio Plays)
K I-II *Komödien I-II* (Comedies I-II)
S   *Die Stadt* (The City)
TS   *Theater-Schriften und Reden* (Writings and Lectures on the Theater)

PLAYS AND ADAPTATIONS

B   *Der Blinde* (The Blind Man)
EAE   *Episode on an Autumn Evening*
Esg   *Es steht geschrieben* (It Is Written)
FV   *Frank V* (not translated)
H   *Herkules und der Stall des Augias* (Hercules and the Augean Stables)
KJ   *König Johann* (King John)
M   *Der Meteor*
Miss *Die Ehe des Herrn Mississippi*
Mit   *Der Mitmacher* (The Partaker; acting edition)
PeP   *Porträt eines Planeten* (Portrait of a Planet)
Ph   *Die Physiker*
PS   *Play Strindberg* (not translated)
TA   *Titus Andronicus* (not translated)
TV   *The Visit*
W   *Die Wiedertäufer* (The Anabaptists)
Wk   *Woyzeck* (not translated)

PROSE

DG   *A Dangerous Game* (title in the U.S.: *Traps*)
G   *Gespräch mit Heinz Ludwig Arnold* (Interview with H.L.A.)

x

GsG   *Grieche sucht Griechin*
GuR   *Gerechtigkeit und Recht* (Justice and Human Rights)
JHH   *The Judge and His Hangman*
OG   *Once a Greek . . .*
P   *The Pledge*
Pa   *Die Panne*
Q   *The Quarry*
RsH   *Der Richter und sein Henker*
SaA   *Sätze aus Amerika* (Sentences from America)
Sz   *Der Sturz* (The Fall)
Z   *Zusammenhänge* (Connections)

DÜRRENMATT'S SOURCES

DoD   *Dance of Death* (Strindberg)
Re   *Urfaust* (Goethe, Reclam edition)
TR   *The Troublesome Raign* (anonymous)

These abbreviations are used when Dürrenmatt's works or sources are quoted. Page numbers are given immediately after the abbreviation. If there are several short quotations from nearby pages within a paragraph, page numbers are given after the last quotation. For fuller details of these volumes, see Bibliography and Appendix, pp. 443, 441.

Where English translations of Dürrenmatt's works exist, the translation, not the original text, is generally quoted. There is a translation of *Der Meteor* (The Meteor); I found it too late to use it. In the discussion I employ mainly English titles, no matter whether the work in question is translated or not. There are abbreviations for German titles when their original versions are referred to. Quotations from untranslated works by Dürrenmatt or from studies in languages other than English have been translated by the author of this study.

The line numbers in two plays by Shakespeare (*King John* and *Titus Andronicus*) are given in the traditional way (e.g., II.i.370).

List of Illustrations

||||||||||||||||||||||||||||||||||||||||||||||||||||||||||||||||||||||||||||||||||||

1. *It Is Written.* Dürrenmatt's first world première was directed by Kurt Horwitz at the Zurich Theater (Schauspielhaus).

2. *The Marriage of Mr. Mississippi.* Anastasia and Mr. Mississippi drinking a friendly cup of coffee; the play was directed by Mikko Majanlahti at the Tampere Theater. Photograph by Pertti Räsänen.

3. *The Visit.* Claire Zachanassian dressed for her eighth wedding. Play directed by Eugen Terttula at the Workers' Theater of Tampere in 1963.

4 and 6. *The Visit,* directed by Sakari Puurunen and Timo Tiusanen at the People's Theatre–Workers' Theater of Helsinki in 1963. Ill's family, from left to right: Anja Haahdenmaa, Stig Fransman and Martta Kontula. The Guelleners playing trees: Eino Kaipainen, Sasu Haapanen and Veikko Sorsakivi. Photographs by Pentti Auer.

5. *The Visit.* World première in Zurich in 1956, directed by Oskar Wälterlin, stage design by Teo Otto. Group in the center of the picture, from left to right: Ill's wife (Traute Carlsen), Ill (Gustav Knuth) and Claire. Photograph by W. E. Baur.

7. *Frank V.* World première in Zurich in 1959, directed by Wälterlin.

8. *The Physicists.* Helge Hansila (in the middle) in the Tampere Theater production of 1963, directed by Kalervo Nissilä. Photographs 3 and 8 by Juhani Riekkola.

9. *The Physicists.* The play directed by Jack Witikka at the Finnish National Theater in 1963. Photograph by Pertti Jenytin.

10. *The Physicists.* World première in Zurich, directed by Kurt Horwitz in 1962.

xii

xiii

DÜRRENMATT

Introduction

A HOST OF DÜRRENMATTS

||||||||||||||||||||||||||||||||||||||||||||||||||||||||||||||||||||||||||||||||||||||||

Friedrich Dürrenmatt. A Protestant or a nihilist? A child of nature or a penetrating theoretician of the theater? A profound moralist or a charlatan? The variety of opinion is wide indeed; the point most generally agreed upon is that this Swiss author is one of the most important European playwrights to have emerged since World War II.

Dürrenmatt's rise to fame began in the early 1950's. The German-speaking countries were the first he conquered. Siegfried Melchinger was the first but not the last scholar to characterize him as "the greatest power among living playwrights in the German-speaking theater."[1] He said this in 1957; Bertolt Brecht had died in 1956. From the point of view of Germany, Dürrenmatt is both an in- and an outsider. This is the first paradox inherent in his work; it is not the last one.

The great tradition in Swiss literature has been in the novel rather than in drama. In fact, Dürrenmatt (born 1921) and Max Frisch (born 1911) are the first Swiss dramatists ever to have made European and world reputations. Their sudden and almost simultaneous emergence was prompted by a combination of favorable circumstances, in addition to their talents. The continuity of German drama was broken; Dürrenmatt and Frisch stepped in to fill the gap.[2]

Dürrenmatt was born in the village of Konolfingen, close to Berne, as the only son of a Protestant minister; he has a younger sister.[3] Friedrich seems to have enjoyed a peaceful,

[1] Melchinger, *Drama zwischen Shaw und Brecht*, 1957, p. 66.
[2] Hans Bänziger, *Frisch und Dürrenmatt*, 1967 (1960), p. 206, and Rolf Kieser, "Gegenwartsliteratur der deutschen Schweiz," *The German Quarterly*, *41*, 1 (Jan. 1968), p. 72.
[3] Bänziger, p. 122.

3

protected childhood, yet the fairy tales and history books he read and the glimpses of reality he saw when playing games with the village children included macabre, terrifying elements. This can be read from "Dokument," a piece of childhood memoirs written down in 1965. A one-handed greengrocer splitting heads of lettuce; an underpass, "a dark cavern" (TS 32), where the boy went astray when three years old; looking at butchers slaughtering animals:

> Terrible-beautiful land of childhood: the world of experience was small, just a silly village, nothing more, the world of tradition was enormous, swimming in a mysterious cosmos, pervaded by a wild fairy-tale world of heroic battles, unfathomable. One had to accept this world. One was delivered to faith, defenceless and naked (TS 37).

Dürrenmatt *in nuce* is here: his Swiss home milieu, elements of the absurd and grotesque, of fantasy and everyday life, of microcosm and macrocosm, of religion and of the fear caused by it. Are his works at least partly rationalizations or fabrications into art of some early experiences of horror and insecurity?—a question that does not mean denying Dürrenmatt his individuality, his somber and hilarious creative fantasy.

"Such influences form us; what comes later, only confirms what was formed before. . . . The village brought me forth, and so I am still a villager," Dürrenmatt writes (TS 30).[4] What came later included living and going to secondary school in Berne, absent-minded studies at the universities of Zurich and Berne (philosophy, literature, and science), starting to paint and write, floating around in Bohemian circles. His efforts as a painter were doubtless important to the would-be playwright: he grew used to thinking in pictures, to seeing his scenes on the stage. The drawings he has published prove him to be a not uneven caricaturist. Walter Jonas, an artist,

---

[4] "I think that a great many things taking place in one's youth, before a literary phase, are very important," Dürrenmatt says in Sauter, "Gespräch mit F.D.," *Sinn und Form, 18*, 4 (Fall 1966), p. 1228. Real-life experiences figure behind his work (G 59).

remembers youthful Dürrenmatt as an incessant debater on thousands of subjects and as an inventive story teller: he could improvise a short story or a fairy tale on any subject given him.[5] Dürrenmatt did not change as a writer. His polemical fireworks and his immense delight in story telling are among the most characteristic features of his varied work.[6] It is as if he needs a "subject given" to start his imagination working; this starting-point may be an earlier play or a school of playwriting—or it may be one of his own sudden inspirations. What is in this way beginning to take shape is by Dürrenmatt called "Stoff." "Stuff, material, subject-matter"—the implication is that Dürrenmatt works at something concrete and non-esoteric. And he needs a concrete opponent, as it were, to be at his best, offensive and defensive at the same time. The polemical urge to rearrange, to reshape, not only to shape, seems to be an innate quality in him. When he starts theorizing, he sees himself surrounded by ready-shaped material, and ponders "still possible stories"—as if nothing would be impossible for this imagination embracing heaven and hell.

Dürrenmatt's formative years: a great variety in living surroundings, an abundance of contradictory impulses. Dürrenmatt himself: a Renaissance figure. His works were bound to be anything but dry or monotonous.

Some clues to Dürrenmatt's work can be found in his early experiences and personal qualities. His *Writings and Lectures on the Theater* seems to contain several other clues. Yet combining Dürrenmatt the practicing playwright and Dürrenmatt the theoretician of the theater is a far from simple undertaking. We are, in fact, approaching the most controversial areas in Dürrenmatt research.

[5] Peter Wyrsch, "Die Dürrenmatt-Story," part two, *Schweizer Illustrierte*, 52, 13 (March 25, 1963), pp. 23–24.
[6] Urs Jenny speaks of Dürrenmatt's "elementary delight" in comedy (*F.D.*, 1965, p. 11), Elisabeth Brock-Sulzer finds pages in which Dürrenmatt is "a master in polemics" (preface to TS, p. 19). Cf. TS 56: "I write, . . . because I love to tell stories."

5

INTRODUCTION

The situation is further complicated by the richness and variety of Dürrenmatt's total output. He plays several contradictory roles with equal gusto. He is a comedian, a religious meditator, a moralist; a child of nature and a theoretician of literature; a dramatist and a prosaist. There is not just one Dürrenmatt, there is a host of them. All this, no doubt, adds to the density of problems, to the *Problemträchtigkeit* of his works. It also limits the argumentative force of any statement found in his essays.

Moreover, Dürrenmatt has been changing within each of his roles. What he said about the situation of the modern playwright in 1955 has not necessarily preserved its validity up to the 1970's. *Theaterprobleme* (Problems of the Theater), the most important and consistent of Dürrenmatt's treatises, has been translated into English and included in a great many anthologies, among them Dürrenmatt's own *Four Plays*. Its formulations about tragicomedy and the grotesque are sometimes taken as authoritative maxims: this is what Dürrenmatt is about, this is what modern drama at large is about.[7] The essay was, however, originally intended to be only a personal statement, and did not include a guarantee for a year or for twenty years. There are also Dürrenmatt's other treatises to help us to qualify our impressions.

Dürrenmatt's theoretical writings do not form any monolithic whole. They hardly could, written as they were mostly as afterthoughts during thirty years of continuous and capricious development.[8] "A writer not contradicting himself will never be reread" (TS 8) is the motto of *Writings on the Theater*. The result is that any scholar in Dürrenmatt has to keep reading these pieces over and over again.

[7] *Problems of the Theater* is seen in a critical perspective, e.g., by Karl S. Guthke: "by no means cogently and lucidly reasoned" (*Modern Tragicomedy*, p. 129). Cf. Murray B. Peppard, *F.D.*, p. 126.

[8] To refer to just one complete reversal of direction: Dürrenmatt began his literary career as a Kafkaist, yet later turned into an "Anti-Kafkaist" (Hans Mayer, *Zur deutschen Literatur der Zeit*, p. 281).

6

Dürrenmatt also engages in polemics. "Most difficult of all: not to exculpate oneself" (TS 89), he once wrote. This difficulty proved to be insurmountable. Dürrenmatt is no exception to the general tendency of writers to speak about their intentions rather than about their achievements when defending themselves. He once teased his critics by refusing to lay "the egg of explanation" "in the henhouse of his plays" (TS 108); yet *Theater-Schriften* includes not fewer than sixty-five items, its sequel *Dramaturgic and Critical Writings*, twenty-seven.[9] Dürrenmatt has laid so big a basketful of eggs that one does not know how to make an omelette of them. Teasing his critics and interviewers is part of Dürrenmatt's publicity game. He "tells one critic something, another something else, emphasizing every time different things, speaking ironically, dialectically, indifferently, bitingly, exaggerating or playing down according to his whims."[10] A sure way of losing oneself in the wonderland called Dürrenmattiana is to take him over-seriously or to be devoid of sense of irony. All a critic without the compass of irony will see is a glimpse of Dürrenmatt's cloak disappearing around the next bend in his path.

The truths offered to the readers of Dürrenmatt's theories are to be taken "with a grain of salt" (FP 11). A chapter and a part of another will later be devoted to sorting out these statements, with their plentiful inner contradictions and just as numerous interesting revelations. In addition, Dürrenmatt's plays will be compared with his prefaces and other contemporary statements on the craft of playwriting. It is not self-evident that all sayings by Dürrenmatt the essayist

---

[9] Cf. Mandred Züfle, "F.D.," *Schweizer Rundschau, 66*, 1–2 (Jan.–Feb. 1967), pp. 29–30.
[10] Werner Oberle in Grimm et al. (eds.), *Der unbequeme Dürrenmatt*, p. 10. Cf. Brock-Sulzer's preface to TS, p. 25, Margareta Deschner, "F.D's Experiments with Man," diss., University of Colorado, 1966, p. 22, and Manfred Durzak's critical remarks on Dürrenmatt's theory in *D., Frisch, Weiss*, pp. 31–34, 38.

and polemicist can be verified even if one devotes the closest of readings to his plays.[11] In the final accounting, it is the play that matters.

The plays are ambiguous. This is a result of Dürrenmatt's Renaissance dimensions, and of his conscious choice, not of any deficiency in his talent. "It happens to be my passion, not always a happy one perhaps, to want to put on the stage the richness, the manifold diversity of the world" (FP 22), he wrote in *Problems of the Theater*. To qualify this statement: it was so at least up to the early 1960's. At about that time he started condensing and eliminating his richness.

The bigger part of Dürrenmatt criticism has thus to face considerable difficulties.[12] Blasphemous or pious? Parodic or serious? Profound or shallow? What are the central themes in a given play? So much energy is needed to answer these simple questions that scholars seldom pursue the case to an equally important question: how far is Dürrenmatt successful in dealing with these matters? They are not helped by Dürrenmatt's impatience with any and all interpretations trying to catch him as a propagator of a 'message.' His starting-point is a conflict, not a soluble problem. George E. Wellwarth has characterized Dürrenmatt, with good reason, as a man "with something to say who does not wish to be caught saying it."[13]

Dürrenmatt is fighting a two-front war. On one hand, he is waging the battle for independence of any artist against the over-eager searchers for messages. For them, a work of art is something neatly solved at the end; the world is like an arithmetical problem solved without a remainder. "We have got

[11] Cf. Herbert Madler, "Dürrenmatts mutiger Mensch," *Hochland*, 62, 1 (Jan.–Feb. 1970), p. 45.
[12] Claus Drese ("F.D.," *Eckart*, 28, 4, 1959, p. 385) and Hans-Jürgen Syberberg ("Zum Drama F.Ds," diss., München, 1963, p. 106) have emphasized the equivocal character of Dürrenmatt's plays.
[13] Wellwarth, "F.D. and Max Frisch," *The Tulane Drama Review*, 6, 3 (March 1962), p. 14. Cf. TS 208.

to be poets (*Dichter*) for them, that is the difficulty, resolvers of world riddles, exhibitors of prescriptions for living, or even magicians" (TS 147). On the other hand there is Dürrenmatt's paradoxical and polemical attitude to all kinds of formulas of thought. He needs them—to reject them, to rebel against them, to establish a creative tension between them and his own ideas. They may be religious, dramaturgic or social formulas; they are there to balance the second basic feature in Dürrenmatt. There is an endless richness of artistic invention, of *Einfälle*,[14] and a boundless freedom in him, as there was the mysterious and unfathomable world of fairytales in the child Friedrich.

The real danger in interpreting Dürrenmatt is in trying to catch him with the help of too narrow a formula.[15] He may be caught once, quite precisely, with nothing left over; yet the same formula may be inadequate when used next time. Moreover, finding a pattern of thought in a play does not necessarily mean that Dürrenmatt is behind it; he may have needed it just to fight against it.

This brings us right into the middle of a controversy. Is Dürrenmatt a devout product of his religious background or a rebel against it? The critical opinions are far apart. For Elisabeth Brock-Sulzer, Dürrenmatt's works are "without the Christian paradox not at all conceivable"; Robert Holzapfel finds "a divine plan" in all of his plays; and Fritz Buri "the artistic invention of 'grace' " just as widely, at least "in a

[14] According to Deschner, p. 28, *Einfall* "has been variously rendered in English as 'inspiration,' 'artistic invention,' 'brainwave,' etc."; she also quotes the preface by Robert E. Helbling to *The Physicists* recommending "invention" in "its original Latin meaning . . . 'to come on' or, more freely, 'to stumble on' something." Peppard's contribution is "scurrilous inspiration" (p. 23); those of Gerhard Nellhaus in his rendering of *Theaterprobleme* are "flash of idea" (FP 27), "conceit," "inventive idea," and "invention" (FP 33). I shall use "artistic invention."

[15] "He does not fit in any framework" (Marcel Reich-Ranicki, *Literatur der kleinen Schritte*, p. 241).

pious mockery."[16] On the other hand, Ruth Blum remarks that Dürrenmatt only reveals the work of Satan and fails to bring forth the positive Christian message, and Hans Mayer says that Dürrenmatt bases his work on a "theology without God."[17]

The strongest support for these conflicting opinions on Dürrenmatt's religiousness, whether pro or con, is to be found in his early works.[18] Young Dürrenmatt employed many Christian symbols and concepts. Yet this is not, as such, any proof of a more or less orthodox Protestant faith expressed in his art. The decisive question is how and to what purpose these symbols are employed. A comparable case is Luis Bunuel, the remarkable Spanish-born film director, who has used Catholic symbols to give expression to his doubts and disbelief. Dürrenmatt's attitude will have to be scrutinized case by case; religious formulas of thought or "divine plans" may be among those "subjects given" he needs to start his imagination working.

In his childhood Dürrenmatt felt "delivered to faith." He was so before and during World War II. His religious background can be connected with another central concern: justice. If there is a God, how could He permit World War II? What kind of justice is administered by God? The image of a cruel, torturing God is clearly recognizable in Dürrenmatt's early writings. As a Swiss citizen sensitive to what happened in all of Europe, Dürrenmatt also developed a typical guilt complex—for having been saved, for having

[16] Brock-Sulzer, "F.D.," *Der Monat, 15,* 5 (May 1963), p. 56: reprinted in Nonnenmann (ed.), *Schriftsteller der Gegenwart.* Holzapfel, "The Divine Plan Behind the Plays of F.D.," *Modern Drama, 8,* 3 (Dec. 1965), pp. 237, 245. Buri in Grimm et al. (eds.), *Der unbequeme D.,* p. 59.

[17] Blum, "Ist F.D. ein christlicher Schriftsteller?" *Reformatio, 8,* 8 (Sept. 1959), pp. 538–39. Mayer, "F.D.," *Zeitschrift für deutsche Philologie, 87,* 4 (Fall 1968), p. 483; cf. p. 485.

[18] Marianne Kesting has spoken about Dürrenmatt's "religious question that is later secularized into a humanistic and moral one" (*Panorama des zeitgenössischen Theaters,* p. 225).

"endured peace."[19] Max Frisch has described the situation of the postwar Swiss generation: "We lived at the brink of a torture chamber, we heard the shrieks, yet we were not among those who screamed; we remained without the depth of suffering endured, yet were too close to suffering to be able to laugh."[20]

Switzerland, a neutral country on the roof of Europe, has been right in the middle of fighting armies in two world wars, yet it has preserved its borders intact. This is one side of the coin: Dürrenmatt and Frisch were able to grow up in peace. The other side is that the forces behind the Swiss "hedgehog position" and "mental self-defense" turned out to be a petrifying influence in the postwar years.[21] Switzerland is not only the home of many a global organization, and the refuge for Lenin and James Joyce, for Thomas Mann and Brecht, for the Dadaists and anti-Fascists,[22] it is also a country of solid and self-satisfied prosperity, of petty bourgeois, of bank and office clerks. Its vices and virtues are those of the middle class: preference for stability and security over intellectual daring, for common sense over sensitivity, for careful handling of public and private funds over financial and spiritual encouragement to the arts and artists.[23] Cleanliness of public buildings and of the mind, of clothes and literature, characterize this mountain and garden state for tourists. These features can be called virtues—hardly, however, from the point of view of a creative artist.

[19] Siegfried Kienzle in his article on Dürrenmatt in Dietrich Weber (ed.), *Deutsche Literatur seit 1945 in Einzeldarstellungen*, p. 362. Cf. H. F. Garten, *Modern German Drama*, 1964 (1959), pp. 249–50, and Hans Weigel, *Lern dieses Volk der Hirten kennen*, p. 18.

[20] Frisch in his *Tagebuch 1946–1949*, quoted by Kurt Marti in *Die Schweiz und ihre Schriftsteller*, pp. 39–40.

[21] Marti, pp. 27–30, 56, speaks of a "neurosis of self-defense," described by Dürrenmatt in *Romulus the Great*; cf. Peter Dürrenmatt, *Schweizer Geschichte*, pp. 710–11.

[22] Marti, p. 22; Sakari Saarikivi, *Aikamme maalaustaide*, pp. 232–33.

[23] Herbert Lüthy, *Die Schweiz als Antithese*, 1969 (1961), p. 25.

INTRODUCTION

The consecutive generations of postwar Swiss writers and critics have tended to grow increasingly critical of their home country.[24] The term "Swiss malaise" has been coined to describe this disaffection, whose symptoms are irritating uneasiness, even before World War II; efforts to fly from the narrowness of Swiss circumstances, abroad or into fantasy; later, returns to home. Dürrenmatt is not a severe case, though his criticism and satire have grown sharper since the late 1960's. To him Switzerland is a convenient place to live, not a trauma or a problem.[25] Yet the small village community of his masterpiece *The Visit* (Der Besuch der alten Dame) is a critical picture of his environment, both universal and Swiss in its implications. Its starting-point is an ironical variation of an archetypal event in Swiss literature: the homecoming of a native.

Dürrenmatt's theoretical and practical thinking in matters of the state is basically Swiss. The state exists to serve the people, cabinet ministers are civil servants in the original meaning of the word.[26] He is afraid of modern giant states, with powers "too vast, too complex, too horrible, too mechanical" (FP 31) to be controlled by an individual. By contrast, Switzerland is a "community of tiny cantonal and communal democracies";[27] it is probably the country in the modern world where direct, non-representational democracy has its greatest say, not always to the good of efficiency. Several religious denominations, four language groups and cultural spheres exist side by side; peace is preserved through

[24] E.g., Hans Zbinden and Werner Weber in Bruno Mariacher and Friedrich Witz (eds.), *Bestand und Versuch*, pp. 767–77 and 840–47; Max Wehrli, "Gegenwartsdichtung der deutschen Schweiz," in Kayser, ed., *Deutsche Literatur in unserer Zeit*, 1966 (1959), pp. 119–22; Peter Bichsel, *Des Schweizers Schweiz*, 1969, pp. 12–14, 27, 29.
[25] Karl Schmid, *Unbehagen im Kleinstaat*, 1963, pp. 192–93, 197; cf. Bänziger, p. 197, Kieser, p. 79, and Thorbjörn Lengborn, *Schriftsteller und Gesellschaft in der Schweiz*, pp. 18–21, 27, 257–58.
[26] Bernardo von Brentano, *Schöne Literatur und öffentliche Meinung*, p. 111.
[27] Lüthy, p. 16; cf. p. 7.

a policy of mutual tolerance, or of mutual indifference. Dürrenmatt also belongs to the generation of European writers who suspect that the stem word for "nationalism" is "Nazi."

A Swiss author writing in German has better reasons than most for such a suspicion. He speaks and hears German with a difference: Swiss German. He has a kind of dress-circle view of Germany in the center of the stage in the latest world tragedy; he understands the language spoken and the psychology of the acting; he has critical distance by not being one of the actors.[28] Swiss writers and critics are well aware of the dangers of provincialism, yet they also know that the Swiss-German paradox opens the first doors toward an international theater and reading public.[29] Besides, one of the best routes into universality seems to go through the local rather than around it. There is nothing so English as Shakespeare, nothing so Russian as Dostoevski, yet these two speak to all nations and ages.[30] They have filtered the world through their personal and national experiences and in so doing succeeded in giving it a concrete form, the form of art.

A writer belonging to a small nation may go astray along either of two roads. He may drown in the minutiae of his surroundings and end up in regional literature. Or he may run dry in the desert of the abstract generalities belonging to an adopted, non-personal internationalism.[31] Dürrenmatt has tried both—and the middle road, too, leading to the goal.

[28] The metaphor of a stage is employed by Bänziger, loc. cit., p. 21, and in his article "Kurze Startbahnen," *Merkur*, *11*, 10 (Oct. 1957), pp. 992–93.

[29] Cf. Hugo Leber, "Gewandelte Perspektiven," *Welt und Wort*, 24, 10 (Oct. 1969), pp. 312–13, Gian Paolo Tozzoli, "Gefahren und Chancen," ibid., p. 320; Heinz-Peter Linder, "Die schweizerische Gegenwart im modernen Roman der deutschen Schweiz," diss., Bern, 1957, p. 8.

[30] Similar comparisons and conclusions are presented by Zbinden in "Zur Situation der Literatur in der Schweiz," *Welt und Wort*, 1969, pp. 308–09.

[31] Cf. Witz in Mariacher and Witz, p. 9.

Sometimes through Germany, sometimes through other regions on the map or of the mind.[32]

Dürrenmatt has shown an all-pervasive interest in justice, in judges and judgments, in death at the hands of an executioner. Its origins are in his early religious conviction, in the historical situation during his formative years, or perhaps in an innate inclination like color blindness. When he follows his theme of justice to its logical end, the results are often powerful and grotesque. Prominent examples are the ritual murder at the end of *The Visit*, or the unnecessary suicide of the traveling salesman in *A Dangerous Game*, a major story. With the word "grotesque" we seem to have found a useful clue to Dürrenmatt's world, and a clue to modern literature as a whole.

"The grotesque" has been a relevant concept ever since Wolfgang Kayser published his widely influential book *Das Groteske* in 1957. Not only has this study had an influence on Dürrenmatt research; it was also influenced by one of Dürrenmatt's theoretical statements about the grotesque as a specifically modern form of expression.[33] A few years later Reinhold Grimm was able to prove, point by point, that all the typically grotesque phenomena listed by Kayser are to be found in Dürrenmatt. As Kayser puts it, they express a breakdown in the categories we need for finding our way in the world. Grotesque disharmonies include the mixing up of separate conceptual spheres, abolition of the laws of statics, loss of identity, deformation of natural proportions or historical chronology.[34] According to Grimm, these phenom-

[32] The possibilities of combining the local with the universal are mentioned also by Wehrli, pp. 122–24; Joachim Kaiser praises Dürrenmatt's and Frisch's ability to make their plays both profoundly symbolic and thoroughly Swiss: "Grenzen des modernen Dramas," *Theater heute*, 5, 12 (Dec. 1964), p. 12.

[33] Kayser, *Das Groteske. Seine Gestaltung in Malerei und Dichtung*, p. 11.

[34] Kayser, p. 199; Grimm in *Der unbequeme Dürrenmatt*, 1961, pp. 72–83.

ena belong to "the demonic grotesque"; in addition, there are numerous examples of Dürrenmatt's vital and playful grotesqueries, for example in his numerous parodies, those "grotesque and provocative mixtures between separate spheres." Dürrenmatt's self-expressed desire to give shape to the unshaped leads to the demonic grotesque, while his inclination to reshape ready-made formulas leads to the parodic grotesque.[35] Grimm calls the grotesque "the basic structure" in Dürrenmatt,[36] and his conclusions have been accepted, with some shifts in emphasis, by a great many other Dürrenmatt scholars.[37] Yet the problem needs some further probing.

Before Kayser, the word "grotesque" was a concept in stylistics. The first merit of his book was that he was able to show how widely grotesque elements have figured in Western art throughout the centuries, especially during the Renaissance and the Age of Romanticism, and in our age. The second merit, not so indisputable, is that he tried to give the word a completely new meaning, no longer limited to stylistics. He wanted to probe deeper, to the contents of grotesque works of art, to the philosophy of life behind them. There is in fact a dichotomy in the way Kayser uses his central con-

[35] Grimm, p. 94; cf. TS 33, 38, and especially 136–37: Dürrenmatt's definition of the grotesque as "one of the great possibilities to be precise" and his rejection of nihilism.

[36] Grimm, p. 91.

[37] Christian M. Jauslin, *F.D.*, 1964, p. 124, chooses provocation as "the basic structure" in Dürrenmatt, the grotesque and parody as the most essential means toward this end. The central position of the grotesque is emphasized, e.g., by Günter Waldmann, "Ds paradoxes Theater," *Wirkendes Wort, 14*, 1 (Jan. 1964), p. 22, by Adolf D. Klarmann, "F.D. and the Tragic Sense of Comedy," *The Tulane Drama Review, 4*, 4 (May 1960), p. 81, and by Volkmar Sander, "Form und Groteske," *Germanisch-Romanische Monatsschrift*, Neue Folge, *14*, 3 (1964), pp. 308–10. Werner Mittenzwei connects the grotesque with "the capitalistic society" [*Gestaltung und Gestalten im modernen Drama*, Berlin und Weimar, 1969 (1964), p. 39], Erich Kühne with "bourgeois literary research" ("Satire und groteske Dramatik," *Weimarer Beiträge, 12*, 4, 1966, p. 549). A recent theory by Arnold Heidsieck interprets the grotesque as a distortion of human values (Robert E. Helbling in *F.D.*, ed. by Gerhard P. Knapp, pp. 234–36).

15

cept. He finds two kinds of the grotesque, genuine and less genuine.[38] "Echte Groteske" is a work of art giving full expression to a grotesque view of the world, with elements of fear, metaphysical anxiety, and black humor. Our familiar and safe world is suddenly revealed to be "alien and weird." A precipice opens, "demons" or "animals of apocalypse" break into our everyday existence: "grotesque means giving shape to 'Id,' to that ghastly 'Id.' "[39] Kayser's "genuine grotesque" might also be called "absolute grotesque," absolute in the sense that it is not submitted to any other artistic aims or philosophical considerations.

Kayser's reasoning somehow captured the spirit of the late 1950's. So did Dürrenmatt in *The Visit*. Yet during the very years Kayser was working on his book, there was a group of playwrights busy writing plays that Kayser might have called "genuinely grotesque." This group was later to be subdivided into the absurdist and the grotesque playwrights. *Sinn oder Unsinn?*, published in 1962, is an anthology of studies, with the subtitle "The Grotesque in Modern Drama." Its discussions cover a wide field, extending from the Italian "Teatro grottesco" to Harold Pinter, from Antonin Artaud to Eugène Ionesco, from Georg Büchner to Wolfgang Hildesheimer.[40] The separation into different schools of playwriting had not yet taken place, at least in the critical practice of the contributors. In 1961 Martin Esslin, one of the co-authors of *Sense or Senselessness?* had, however, published the first edition of his remarkable study, *The Theater of the Absurd*. With its publication, if not earlier, our second term was coined.

The border line between these terms is not clearly drawn. "Absurdism" is a term with strong philosophical connotations, denoting the work of a group of playwrights expressing

[38] Examples of the "genuine grotesque" e.g. on pp. 128, 142, 154, 175 in Kayser.
[39] Ibid. pp. 198–99.
[40] Grimm et al. (eds.), *Sinn oder Unsinn?*, 1962.

a basic experience of the senselessness of human life. This definition brings us into the vicinity of Kayser's "genuine grotesque," also called "absolute grotesque" in my discussion above. Yet things are hardly clarified by the observation that many absurdists use grotesque exaggeration or distortion to express their absurdist philosophy. Furthermore, since the early 1960's it has not been possible to call a situation in drama "absurd," in the original sense of the word, without beginning to wonder whether we have not unwillingly implied that the situation in question or the entire play belong to "the theater of the absurd." Or we cannot use the word "grotesque" without suspecting that we are perhaps hauling behind our ship the whole net of meanings associated with "the theater of the grotesque." And remembering Kayser, Bosch and Brueghel, too.

Drama nach Brecht (1968) by Rainer Taëni is an effort to clean up this mess by building up a systematic framework of thought. Taëni distinguishes three recent possibilities of theatricalism, the Brechtian epic theater, absurdism, and the theater of the grotesque. Playwrights of the epic theater believe in the changeability of the world and aim at making social relationships conceivable to the public.[41] Absurdists proclaim the world not only unchangeable but basically senseless, and let the form of their plays reflect this interpretation of the state of affairs. The world of a grotesque play may be out of joint; it is not totally unreal, as is frequently the case in absurdism. The possibility that a grotesque play deals with specific social circumstances, rather than with life in toto, brings it close to the satiric end of the epic theater. Thus grotesque playwrights take a kind of middle position

[41] The controversy between "Aristotelian" and "epic" theater has lost impetus in recent years; they are now widely seen as two possible alternatives. Anni Carlsson comments on recent changes of taste: morally engaged documentary plays or contemporary period plays were completely passé in the late 1950's—to be resurrected during the 1960's (*Die deutsche Buchkritik*, 1969, p. 363). Cf. Hans Christoph Angermeyer, *Zuschauer im Drama*, p. 29.

17

in making the existence of a sensible world order question-able.[42] For them, the world is self-evidently neither rational nor senseless; they are social and metaphysical agnostics.

It seems to me questionable that there are weighty enough reasons to go on speaking about the theater of the grotesque as a clearly definable school in playwriting—although Taëni is by no means the only one to do so. The place of the theater of the grotesque in Taëni's total pattern could be given to an established dramatic genre: tragicomedy. It is a genre speaking specifically to the audiences since World War II; it is an expression of basic uncertainty; it combines comic and tragic elements, as Taëni's theater of the grotesque does.

These three features of tragicomedy are strongly emphasized by Karl S. Guthke in his study *Modern Tragicomedy*, 1966. Guthke follows the theory and practice of tragicomedy from the seventeenth century to the present day, not ignoring Dürrenmatt's contributions as a practicing and theorizing playwright. In his concluding chapter, "The Philosophy of the Tragicomedian," Guthke makes distinctions that help us to place tragicomedy between absurdism and the epic theater, exactly where Taëni located the theater of the grotesque: "Asking questions is in essence what the tragicomedian attempts to do in our time. He is—knowingly or unknowingly —far from asserting that 'meaninglessness' is the last word. He does know, however, that he cannot 'save the world.' That is his wisdom and his despair—which drives him on to literary creation." In his next sentence Guthke quotes Dürrenmatt: "And thus we should not try to save the world, but to bear it. That is the one real adventure which remains possible for us in this late time."[43]

After this replacing operation, what senses are there left to the term "grotesque" in modern drama? If not valid as the distinguishing characteristic in a school of playwriting, where is it valid? We can certainly think of tragicomedies

[42] Taëni, *Drama nach Brecht*, pp. 13–17.
[43] Guthke, *Modern Tragicomedy*, pp. 171–72; *The Quarry*, p. 161, and p. 141 below include slightly different translations.

devoid of the grotesque: plays by Molière, Shakespeare, Chekhov or Ibsen (*The Wild Duck*). Grotesque tragicomedy is a subdivision of tragicomedy, and a specifically modern way of voicing tragicomic uncertainties, though not the only type of tragicomedy in our age. This means that we need not return the term "grotesque" to stylistics, to its pre-Kayserian usage. There are both valid and questionable observations about the contents of the grotesque in Kayser.

Kayser emphasizes the mysterious, inexplicable features of the grotesque: "the formations of the grotesque are a play with the absurd."[44] Is it necessarily so? Does this not refer to an extreme form of the grotesque, to be called "absolute grotesque" for example, as suggested above? "Absolute grotesque" means that the tension between the disharmonious or conflicting elements within the grotesque grows to its extreme limits, to a question of life and death, of the existence of a just or sensible world order. This need not, however, bring us into the unreal world of absurdism; it may take place in modern tragicomedies still creating an impression of reality. It takes place in Dürrenmatt's *Visit*. An "absolute grotesque" is a work of art not submitted to any other messages or aims: it is an answer in itself. "Absolute grotesque" approaches the position of an independent aesthetic category like "tragic" or "comic."

On the other hand, there is also the playful or "parodic grotesque." It creates tensions between earlier works of art and new modifications. Third, we can speak of the grotesque without any qualifying adjective and still connect it with certain contents. We can experience the fear or confusion caused by a mixture in the familiar categories of our thought without being shaken in our fundamental beliefs. A definition of this "normal" grotesque is formulated by Lee B. Jennings: "the fearsome made ludicrous in freakish form."[45] There is

[44] Kayser, p. 202; there are other references to the absurdity of the grotesque e.g. on pp. 31, 34, and 64.
[45] Jennings, "Gottfried Keller and the Grotesque," *Monatshefte für deutschen Unterricht, 50*, 1 (Jan. 1958), p. 9. In his introduction to

no reason to give up using "the grotesque" as a stylistic concept; there can thus be grotesque elements within absurdism and the epic theater. It is in its stylistic sense and in these three meanings that the word "grotesque" will be used in this study.

Dürrenmatt's position in the total pattern of postwar drama is somewhere in the middle field. He is neither an absurdist, nor an epic playwright, nor an honorary member in the nonexistent theater of the grotesque. Again, he does not believe in formulas of thought; the world is neither completely senseless nor rational and easily changeable. Dürrenmatt is a tragicomedian and a comedian employing grotesque and other stylistic elements to question the world order, sometimes with the implication that the world is more empty of meaning than is commonly assumed. He flourishes in the grotesque, and this leads him both into easy mannerisms and into final touches of a master's hand. It will be a fascinating aspect of our research to see how far the plays and other works of Dürrenmatt can be called "absolute grotesques," how far the conflicts he experiences in this world of ours release other reactions in him.

All the various forms of the grotesque have something in common. The contrast or conflict inherent in them is unsolvable. The grotesque is not to be made harmless. It is to be experienced. The grotesque is an adequate concept in a discussion of modern literature, with its inner contradictions, stratified structures and elusive contents.

Dürrenmatt is primarily a playwright. He is also a writer working in the closest cooperation with the theater; he was permanently employed as a dramaturge at the Basle City

---

The Ludicrous Demon, 1963, Jennings approaches my "absolute grotesque," in a way, yet prefers "preserving the unity of the concept 'grotesque'" (p. 17; cf. pp. 25–26). *The Grotesque*, 1972, by Philip Thomson distinguishes the grotesque from a great many related phenomena, and defines the grotesque as "the unresolved clash of incompatibles in work and response" (p. 27).

Theater in 1968–69. Twenty years before, at the beginning of his playwriting career, he had jotted down in his notebook: "Writing a play also means directing it" (TS 87).

It was natural for a would-be painter to visualize his scenes: "It is impossible for me to write a play, if I do not know what the scenes will look like on the stage. I often sketch designs for the setting before starting to write, and during the writing I sometimes outline even the movements of the actors."[46] It is customary for Dürrenmatt to take quite an active part in the rehearsals before the world première of a new play, occasionally also later on. He has himself directed at least *The Visit* and the original productions of two classic plays adapted by him, *Woyzeck* and *Urfaust*. There are problems that are solvable for him only while he is working on the stage and with the stage, not at his desk.[47] This has resulted in several versions of most of his plays. Dürrenmatt keeps rewriting his scripts, in a notable case for twenty years: *It Is Written*, his firstling from 1946, was reshaped and rechristened as *The Anabaptists* in 1967.

Consequently, Dürrenmatt's plays must also be seen in their relation to the stage. To read these contradictory and elusive works of art we need all possible help, all available criteria. How far is Dürrenmatt successful in handling his themes? The stage will answer: if not in the form of a new stage interpretation, then in the form of a critical interpretation paying due attention to Dürrenmatt's stage language.

To take an example, the final scene in *It Is Written* has given rise to several contradictory interpretations. The pious merchant Knipperdollinck and his nihilistic counterpart John Bockelson are dying on the wheel of torture, the former proclaiming God's grace and man's submission to God's will. This scene has been taken as evidence of the profound Christianity in Dürrenmatt: God's grace is victorious, even

---

[46] Wyrsch, "Die Dürrenmatt-Story," part five, *Schweizer Illustrierte*, 52, 16 (April 15, 1963). Cf. Sauter, p. 1230.

[47] Horst Bienek, *Werkstattgespräche mit Schriftstellern*, p. 110. Cf. TS 156–57, 204.

at the cost of Knipperdollinck's life. Yet can we forget the grotesque scenic form given to this climax, can we release its inner tensions? Hardly; instead, we should experience it as it is, as a grandiose dramatization of a conflict, full of inner contradictions, ironies, and parodies. It is a stratified scenic image.[48]

This finale is constructed with the help of several scenic means of expression; it does not consist of words alone. The setting is there, the wheels of torture are placed against a wall, the lights are concentrated on Knipperdollinck alone— after a series of short scenes has been played around him (Esg 107–11). The actors contribute to the impact of the scenic image. This is what happens everywhere in drama; a playwright uses *scenic means of expression*, including

> dialogue, setting, properties, costumes, sound and light- ing effects, music, groupings, the actor's individual ex- pression, his gestures, movements, make-up, vocal and facial expressions.

The closing scene in *It Is Written* is of great significance for our total impression of the play. No interpretation can ignore it. We have thus found the second sign of a scenic image:

> A *scenic image* is a scene (or, more often, part of a scene) in which several scenic means of expression are used to achieve an effect charged with thematic signifi- cance.[49]

---

[48] Syberberg sees a Dürrenmatt play as a stratified system of ten- sions "between antinomies and polarities, such as high and low, banality and greatness, comic and tragic" (p. 126). Cf. the discussion below of the religious interpretations of this scenic image, pp. 53–56.

[49] There is a detailed discussion of this concept in my previous study, *O'Neill's Scenic Images*, 1968, pp. 11–19. Since formulating it I have attended hundreds of rehearsals and performances of the most varied plays, yet not found anything that would gainsay using it to illuminate a play or a performance. The present discussion includes only a few major arguments for using it.

22

A scenic image is a rhythmic entity, a pregnant moment in the continuous flow of visual and auditive images filling up the stage.[50]

What to call a "scenic image" in a given play depends ultimately on a critic's individual judgment. Or on a stage director's: two directors of the same play will probably construct scenic images at different points in their productions. Drama research or practical theater work are hardly imaginable without personal points of view. "Personal" is not, however, synonymous with "arbitrary." On one occasion Dürrenmatt allowed quite a lot of creative freedom to the stage director, but not to the point of arbitrariness: different conceptions should strive to "strike the tone set by the author."[51] Listening to the tone is the aim of our scenic analysis, too. If convincing enough arguments are given by the scholar, the concept of scenic image may be a valuable tool in developing drama research toward greater exactness. It can add a decimal fraction to our approximate values. It might also be a worthwhile effort to connect this concept with the general lines of thought prevailing in gestalt psychology.

Analyzing plays with the help of scenic images does not favor any -ism or school of playwriting over other schools. All it presupposes is an imaginative use made of the possibilities of the stage. Any full-length masterpiece will probably

[50] Guthke speaks of "certain moments of heightened intensity" during which "specific tragicomic essence" or any other tone may become "clearly appreciated" (p. 144). Esslin describes Ionesco's "stratified images" that are "not only verbal but also concretely in situation, decoration, movement, gesture and light before our eyes and ears," and Beckett's archetypal images that "*are* his message, not only *symbols* for this message" (*Sinn oder Unsinn?*, pp. 110–11, 121; cf. *Theater of the Absurd*, p. 18). Syberberg mentions certain situations as "essential moments in the dramatic series of events" (p. 13; cf. pp. 65, 119). "Pregnant moment" is a term quoted by Syberberg (p. 48) from Emil Staiger. These are all parallel cases to the concept of scenic image.

[51] Dürrenmatt when interviewed by Leland R. Phelps, "D's *Die Ehe des Herrn Mississippi*," *Modern Drama*, 8, 2 (Sept. 1965), p. 158.

turn out to be a conglomerate of several scenic images, all interacting, all throwing each other into relief, and placed at certain intervals, to make the rhythm of the play and of the performance breathe. Using this concept means analyzing a play in depth; it will not be resorted to if it is possible to describe a play along more general lines, with due concern for its scenic qualities. From the point of view of literary analysis, a scenic image effects a crystallizing moment in the developing themes of a play: a character may be revealed, an idea evaluated anew, the general validity of the events established, or an impression of completeness achieved. Such a moment presupposes coordination between several scenic means of expression.[52]

When constructing his images, a playwright will resort to similar scenic means of expression over and over again. These favorite means are called *scenic units*. Dürrenmatt loves to duplicate his figures; there are, e.g., the two eunuchs in the grotesque escort of Claire Zachanassian in *The Visit*. Using double figures is one of Dürrenmatt's scenic units.

Scenic analysis is there to complete other methods available for a scholar in drama, not to throw them overboard. In fact, several methods or approaches have already been used in this introduction. Dürrenmatt has been seen from social and psychological points of view, and the literary contents or the themes of his plays have been subjected to a preliminary analysis. It will be so throughout this study. The literary side will have to be thoroughly dealt with for the reason that I cannot suppose American readers to be familiar with Dürrenmatt's works—with the possible exception of *The Visit* and *The Physicists*. Having quite an arsenal of different approaches is certainly no drawback in the case of Dürrenmatt, a many-sided and capricious author. Modern literary and drama research as a whole keeps absorbing the results of philosophy, linguistics, sociology, social history,

---

[52] Oberle remarks on the importance of interaction between several scenic means of expression (*Der unbequeme Dürrenmatt*, p. 28). Cf. E. E. Stoll, *Art and Artifice in Shakespeare*, p. 132.

psychology, etc. into its own constructions of thought. This is all fine and sounds up-to-date; yet there are so many interdisciplinary ideas in circulation that scholars in drama are running the risk of neglecting their own discipline.

It is easy to outline the contents of two additional scenic studies in Dürrenmatt. One of these would deal with his dramaturgy, comparing the numerous versions of his plays, noting deletions, additions, and rewritten scenes, and making a concentrated effort to describe his adaptations of classic plays. The other would be a history of his plays on the stage, starting with the world première, paying attention to the first production in Germany, then to a few major interpretations in other languages. These areas will not be ignored in the following discussion, yet the emphasis will be on giving a critical picture of the most important printed versions of his own plays.

Reviews of Dürrenmatt show a clear line of development since the late 1940's. The writings assume a more matter-of-fact tone, and grow richer in ideas and critical standpoints.[53] After the première of *The Visit* in 1956 the attitude to Dürrenmatt changes sharply: instead of being one of a great many promising playwrights he is from now on taken to be one of the masters of the modern stage, and every world première of his becomes a major publicity event within the German-speaking world. Since the late 1960's, expressions of disappointment have grown in volume. Dürrenmatt's position is thus still controversial,[54] and even as a celebrity he has been true to his reputation as a nuisance. Some of the un-

[53] In the archives of Reiss AG, Basle, I went through a considerably greater number of reviews and playbills than those mentioned in the Bibliography.

[54] Oberle speaks of the contradictory reactions to Dürrenmatt: on one hand, he is taken as a talented routinist; on the other, his opinions are mistrusted. For some, he is a "theological poet," for others, a "cynical buffoon" (*Der unbequeme D.*, p. 10). Helmut Prang compares Dürrenmatt with the greatest writers of comedy, e.g., Aristophanes and Shaw (*Geschichte des Lustspiels*, 1968, pp. 19–20, 104, 193, 297).

favorable reviews he receives can be taken as expressions of hurt feelings; his arrows often strike home. Dürrenmatt's defenders favor this explanation, declaring it as his aim to arouse violent reactions from his audiences—pro or con— and this indeed is his achievement. Yet he can hardly be granted a position outside and above all critical standards; his work includes its highs and its lows, its masterpieces and its failures. They should be judged coolly, without prejudice.

An overeagerness to defend Dürrenmatt against any and all critical attitudes somewhat mars the expert publications of Elisabeth Brock-Sulzer. In her preface to *Friedrich Dürrenmatt* she openly confesses to be *pro* the subject of her study; as a polemical attitude this is understandable, yet we may wonder whether a scholar should not rather be for the good works of an author, against his poor ones.[55] There are two book-length studies published in America, both of them useful and soundly critical. Murray B. Peppard is illuminating and careful, especially in his discussion of *The Visit*; his book is rich in viewpoints. The study by Armin Arnold is at its best when dealing with Dürrenmatt's early works. The main interest in *Frisch und Dürrenmatt* by Hans Bänziger lies in its varied background materials. Valuable points of view, partly also scenic, are included in the books by Christian M. Jauslin and Urs Jenny, and Hans Mayer has made interesting comparisons between Brecht and Dürrenmatt. Three major studies were published while the present work was in progress: Peter Spycher discusses the stories and novels thoroughly, Ulrich Profitlich concentrates mainly on Dürrenmatt's characterization, and Manfred Durzak on his concept of history.[56] Numerous shorter studies published mostly in American, Swiss, or German scholarly periodicals will be

[55] Brock-Sulzer, *F.D.*, 1964 (1960), p. 19; cf. critical remarks in Jauslin, p. 15, and in Kienzle (Weber, ed., *Deutsche Literatur seit 1945*, p. 385).

[56] Peppard, *F.D.*, 1969; Arnold, *F.D.*, 1969; Bänziger, *Frisch und D.*, 1967 (1960); Jauslin, *F.D.*, 1964; Jenny, *F.D.*, 1965; Mayer, *D. und Frisch*, 1963; Spycher, *F.D.*, 1972; Profitlich, *F.D.*, 1973; Durzak, *D., Frisch, Weiss*, 1972.

mentioned as the argument proceeds. They will be needed: we are hunting for a host of Dürrenmatts.

One of these once put the following sigh into the mouth of Mr. Korbes, the author:

> I've been interpreted in terms of depth psychology, Catholicism, Protestantism, Existentialism, Buddhism and Marxism, but never before in the manner you've undertaken (EAE 28).

Why not interpret Dürrenmatt, for a change, in terms of the art he practices: as a writer for the stage?

|||||||||||||||||||||||||||||||||||||||||||||||||||||||||||||||||||||||||||||||||

PART ONE
ENTERING THE STAGE

|||||||||||||||||||||||||||||||||||||||||||||||||||||||||||||||||||||||||||||||||

The world is resting in the mirror.
It has a headache.
God is sitting in the middle.
He is asleep.
His hair is white light.
A snake winds itself round His neck.
It strangles.
God is stifled to death.

(Dürrenmatt, 1943)

1   Early Prose Works

A DEAD END

||||||||||||||||||||||||||||||||||||||||||||||||||||||||||||||||||||||||||||||||||||

The poem quoted is probably the earliest piece of literary writing extant by Friedrich Dürrenmatt. It was written during the night between January 13 and 14, 1943. Dürrenmatt and his artist friend Walter Jonas created a whole picture book on that night, with Dürrenmatt writing the poems, Jonas drawing the pictures.[1] The enterprise was more or less a joke; the book was never published. Though casually sketched, the poem contains several interesting facets: a macabre basic idea, preoccupation with God, a simplistic style continued in Dürrenmatt's early prose. This exercise is a starting-point for his long journey into the absolute grotesque. Dürrenmatt is an author with world-wide ambitions; it is fitting that the first word we have from him is "the world."

Both God and the world are dead in our next piece of evidence. *Die Stadt* (The City), published in 1952, is a collection of short stories and prose exercises, mostly from the years 1943–46.[2] Its first two pieces are from 1943, a year of severe headache for the world, and of growing pains for Dürrenmatt, then a twenty-two-year-old would-be writer—or painter? That year he also wrote his first play, later destroyed, discussed in our second chapter. In "Weihnacht" ("Christmas"), placed as the opening piece in *The City*, he sends his nameless alter ego walking into a world so completely dead and frozen that one cannot hear one's own voice: even the echo is silent. In the snow the "I" of the story

[1] The poem is published and the history of its birth reported by Wyrsch, "Die Dürrenmatt-Story," part two, *Schweizer Illustrierte*, 52, 13 (March 25, 1963), p. 23.

[2] See Appendix, A List of Works, for the years of writing and publication: pp: 441–42.

finds the Christ-child, with no eyes under the lids, and eats up its halo: "It tasted like stale bread. I bit its head off. Old marzipan. I walked on."[3]

According to Fritz Buri there is an old German saying calling the taste of Christ and his grace "old marzipan."[4] Buri does not specify the tone of that saying; the context in Dürrenmatt hardly gives the expression any positive connotations. The air, the stars, the moon, the sun, the echo, the Christ-child, are all dead, and the only living particle in the mysterious endgame landscape does not get any revelation after having tasted Christ's body: "I walked on." God is stifled to death, or Christ is stale bread and old marzipan; if there is a general atmosphere to be read from the matter-of-fact tone of these two exercises, it is that of utter disappointment, of the death of hope, of all human emotions. Dürrenmatt tells his stories of minimum length and maximum chilliness without bringing any moral comments of his own into them.[5] He is dramatizing conflicts, not solving problems, and his dramatics take the form of a few barren verbal images.

There is a more active attitude in favor of man, against God, in the next exercise. "Der Folterknecht" ("The Torturer," 1943) is a series of visions of terror, emotionally highly charged, though stylistically simple and rhythmically monotonous. In the middle of a concrete description of a torture chamber, the reader is suddenly confronted by human emotion: "the pains cling to the walls" (S 15). There is more of a plot than before, including suggestions of a Dr. Jekyll

---

[3] The entire text, half a page, is published in English in "F.D's 'Weihnachten': A Short, Short, Revealing Story," by Edward Diller, *Studies in Short Fiction*, 3, 2 (Winter 1966), p. 138.

[4] Grimm et al. (eds.), *Der unbequeme Dürrenmatt*, p. 62.

[5] Diller (p. 139) tries to read a Christian message about man's thirst for God's warmth into "Christmas." Arnold compares it with the "Grandmother's Story" in Büchner's *Woyzeck*, a play Dürrenmatt was to adapt thirty years later, and finds in the story man's criticism against God who "has not treated him in a fairer way and given him a better chance" (*F.D.*, p. 11). Spycher, sensing a conflict rather than a message, says that the story-teller experiences a world void of "a childlike belief in Christ" (*F.D.*, p. 41).

and Mr. Hyde theme, or of a kind of Faustian pact between man—and a Devil-like, sadistic God.[6] "The Torturer" is comparable with a medieval copperplate engraving, drawn with a crude technique and dealing with a terrifying subject. Living close to a torture chamber was a simile Max Frisch employed to describe his Swiss experience of World War II in a fragment quoted above. At the end of the story, when the torturer is tortured to death, the central idea is expressed with world-wide, as well as religious, implications: "The torture chamber is the world. The world is pain. The torturer is God. He tortures." (S 20)[7]

The style of these three early exercises is simple, in fact, elementary. Yet their explosive religious ideas make them sound less derivative than the next or middle group of short stories in *The City*, written in 1945–51. With them we enter a Kafkaesque world of nightmare and guilt. In only a few years, Dürrenmatt had grown more conscious of belonging to a literary tradition.[8] There are clear thematic cross-references; two of the stories, "Die Falle" ("The Trap") and "Der Hund" ("The Dog") can be called variations of themes handled in "The Torturer." Feelings of erotic guilt and death wishes are combined with suggestions about the existence of divided or duplicate personalities.

It is not necessary to give a detailed account of these stories. They or their lonesome heroes show no interest in the usual activities of life; the storytellers just walk around, get

[6] The story is not easily decipherable: "Dreadful things are asserted and hinted at, but not concretely enough portrayed to be visualized" (Peppard, *F.D.*, p. 19).

[7] In a way, Dürrenmatt starts from the core of a modern tragicomic vision of life, not far from Beckett's absurdism. Guthke speaks of God as "the supreme nihilist," enjoying a "puppet show," with men as his puppets (*Modern Tragicomedy*, pp. 118–19, 169). Referring to a private letter of Dürrenmatt's, Spycher concludes that the young would-be writer read philosophy in order to contend with the religious faith of his father, yet rejected nihilism in favor of thinking combined with belief (pp. 17, 24–25, 33, 372).

[8] There is a careful discussion by Brock-Sulzer on "Dürrenmatt and the Sources" in *Der unbequeme D.*, pp. 117–36.

33

engaged in strange undertakings, and see macabre nightmares or visions.[9] The border line between reality and dream is blurred. The surroundings are highly romantic: houses like labyrinths, sometimes as hopelessly fallen down as Poe's house of Usher, rooms or cells below the surface of the earth, moonlit or foggy nights, lighting conditions abruptly changing between glaring sunshine and menacing darkness, fires glowing red as in hell itself. The executioner, a favorite ghastly figure to Dürrenmatt ever since the slaughterers of his childhood, makes his entrance a few times, as he did in "The Torturer," too. The total effect might be grotesque—yet the other half, the normal everyday life, is lacking. There is no tension between conflicting elements, because the stories dive headlong into the mysterious underworld of crime and punishment, guilt and innocent suffering. The fearsome is not made ludicrous; the texts are chemically pure of humor.[10]

It is surprising that the writer of these stories was ready to establish himself as a comedian in his next phase. Dürrenmatt began his work as a heavyweight Kafkaist, not as a realist.

Three stories are worth closer analysis, for various reasons. "Der Theaterdirektor" ("Theater Manager," 1945) moves closer to recent historical reality than any other story in the collection. It is a parable of Hitler's Germany, projected into a sphere of life Dürrenmatt felt tempted to enter, the world of the theater. Its villain is a spider-like theater manager, using his art as a steppingstone to further his political aspirations.[11] He reduces the actors to marionettes, the stage to a prison cell without any dimension of depth; all

[9] Cf. Spycher's summary (pp. 34–36) of Dürrenmatt's themes in *The City*.

[10] Peppard, p. 20, makes a similar reservation.

[11] The story "Der Alte" ("The Old Man"), published in the *Bund* in 1945 yet not included in *The City*, is discussed by Spycher, pp. 48–52. Its central character is an early portrayal of a nihilist, thus foreshadowing both "Theater Manager" and Dürrenmatt's detective fiction.

accidental and individual features are cut away from the plays, until there is just one message left, a collectivistic proclamation against human freedom. Dürrenmatt's simile works on two levels: it corresponds to what happened in German theater life in the 1930's and to what was taking place on the political stage.

What Dürrenmatt criticized in this early story is in harmony with his later antipathies as a practicing playwright. There is, however, one notable exception: in his story he sternly rejects the idea of mixing up contradictory tones of voice, a mark of his own later style. "Most devilish of all was that . . . the genres began to intermingle, so that tragedy was turned into comedy, comedy forged to resemble tragedy" (S 62). Brock-Sulzer tries to explain away this surprising attitude by referring to the "extra-theatrical aims" of this theater manager.[12] A more probable interpretation is that mixing the genres was an inborn inclination in Dürrenmatt, and he wrote down that condemnation when caught by a puritan fit of self-doubts. He has his caprices, his path its twists.

The climax of "Theater Manager" takes place during the festive inaugural performance of a new theater. The supreme theatrical manipulations of the manager deify the audience, until anybody daring to contradict the collective ecstasy is found to be guilty of sacrilege. There is such an individual, an actress unwilling to submit to the measured steps of the ensemble. She is literally torn to pieces, in front of the audience, and this scene charged with mass hysteria marks the outbreak of a political revolution. Though the climax is unnecessarily violent and the execution of the story not flawless, Dürrenmatt's metaphor develops, for the first time, the dimensions of an artistic symbol with a multiple motivation. This happens, symptomatically enough, in a story placed in the theater. "Theater Manager" is truthful both as a description of Hitler's gradual stealing into power and as a commentary on the world of the theater.[13]

[12] Brock-Sulzer, *F.D.*, pp. 235–36.
[13] Cf. Arnold, p. 15.

35

"Der Tunnel" ("The Tunnel"), both begun and completed in the early 1950's, is no longer an exercise. It is the strongest link between Dürrenmatt's short prose pieces and his novels; it is an achievement that would defend its place in any anthology of short fiction published in German since World War II. The entire story grows into a poetic metaphor of the world suffering from headache. Both its narrative details and its total structure are rhythmically well mastered; the ticktack rhythm of Dürrenmatt's first exercises is left miles behind, as the writer sends his train into a tunnel not far from his home town. The train is never to emerge from the tunnel.

Dürrenmatt is conscientious in creating an atmosphere of everyday life in the first pages of the story. The normal is emphasized as a contrast to the abnormal that is soon to break into it. The precarious balance between the contradictory elements in the grotesque, lacking in *The City* so far, is now firmly established. Dürrenmatt sketches a hilarious self-portrait to function as the third-person hero of the story: a fat twenty-four-year-old undergraduate engaged in nebulous studies and having the ability to see the terrible behind the scenes (S 151). Before this ability is put to the test, the other passengers in the compartment are outlined with a light hand and with a curious interest in life new to the readers of *The City*.

Then the train passes into the tunnel, and the landscape, golden in the light of the sinking evening sun, is wiped away by the darkness of the tunnel walls. There are no signs of alarm, not even after there should be: the student knows the location of the tunnel well enough, and his watch tells him that the train should already have passed out of the tunnel. He dismisses the possibility that he might have taken the wrong train, then starts pressing the conductor. There must be some explanation for the overlong journey in the tunnel, mustn't there? Yet people everywhere in the overcrowded train go on with their business as if nothing had happened—and Dürrenmatt goes on furnishing his story with touches of humor: "In a second-class compartment an Englishman, beaming with peace, stood at the window of the corridor and tapped the windowpane with the pipe he was smoking. 'Simplon,' he said" (S 157).

After a daring climb over the locomotive, the student and the conductor arrive in the driver's cabin, only to find it empty. Something abnormal has taken over. With accelerating speed, not controlled by the levers and switches of the engine, the train is rushing toward the center of the earth, toward a vacuum, "racing madly with the speed of a star through a world made of stone" (S 161). The situation is hopeless, yet the student preserves his calmness of mind and even gives the closing line of the story "not without ghostly hilarity": " 'What shall we do?' . . . 'Nothing. God let us fall and thus we are rushing up to him' " (S 167).[14]

"The Tunnel" is not only a remarkably well-rounded short story, it is also characteristically Dürrenmattian. One of the aims of his art is to show us the wild and chaotic underworld beneath the surface of our clean, safe, and bourgeois Swiss, European, and Western way of living.[15] Dürrenmatt is an artistic reconnoiterer penetrating into that world, into Hermann Hesse's "other reality." He believes in the existence of such a world of unmotivated guilt, of alienation, and of constant disorder. We may, as mankind, be rushing headlong toward our destruction.[16] As individuals, we are rushing toward our death.

[14] Peppard (p. 20) sees in this hilarity "a token of inner religious faith," Brock-Sulzer a kind of rescue: the student is the only brave and clear-sighted person in the train (p. 247). Diller senses in the closing words an admission of "absolute dependence on God" ["F.D's Chaos and Calvinism," *Monatshefte*, *63*, 1 (Spring 1971), p. 30].

[15] Esslin has spoken about Dürrenmatt's "neurosis of the neutrals," leading "to a relentless probing of the guilt . . . behind the safe and bourgeois façade of his well-ordered world" (*The Guardian*, Jan. 10, 1963).

[16] Werner Zimmermann emphasizes the nature of the story as a parable in which the train represents mankind as a whole (*Deutsche Prosadichtungen unseres Jahrhunderts*, volume II, pp. 62–63). Cf. Hans Ulrich Voser, "F.D., das 'enfant terrible'," *Ex Libris*, *13*, 7 (July 1958).

37

The above is a general justification for Dürrenmatt's artistic symbol, absurd as it is. There are also more specifically personal features in the story. Dürrenmatt has his world-wide ambitions, he wants to cover this planet of ours with the results of his thinking; yet he has to admit that the position of writers and other artists is not what it used to be. Science is there, too; minds schooled to think only in figures and formulas, only in terms of facts and columns, are unwilling to give any factual value to the fears and apprehensions of the individual. "The Tunnel" is directed against this line of thinking. The fundamental idea of *The Physicists*, Dürrenmatt's protest against the hydrogen bomb, is already here, as a seed. Dürrenmatt sends his train toward the center of the earth, through solid rock or whatever science knows is there. The fall is not to be stopped with the levers and switches of science.[17]

"The Tunnel" shows symptoms of scientophobia. Dürrenmatt is also sensitive to the bacilli of scholarophobia, as we shall see. Living in the middle of a world full of ready-made formulas, he defends his own freedom of movement. He does this with defiance and polemical gusto. In "The Tunnel" he takes a commonly accepted truth, a law of nature, and mishandles it until we are ready to approve its direct opposite. There is nothing so unequivocal as the railroad, a direct line of communication between two points. This is the formula of thought Dürrenmatt twists and bends until we are ready to believe that the railroad between Berne and Zurich leads toward the middle of the earth. Or into nowhere.

In this artistic miracle he is helped both by his own growing skills and by a nightmare or irrational fear shared by many. "The Tunnel" is built as a trap for the reader; before he even notices what the writer is about to do, safely identifying himself with the ignorant passengers of the train, he is

[17] By making the machine disobey orders, "Dürrenmatt wants to express the menace to the world caused by mechanization" [Karl Moritz, "F.D.: Der Tunnel," *Der Deutschunterricht, 12,* 6 (Dec. 1960), p. 76].

tempted to put some faith in the symptoms of the abnormal. The scenes and what is behind them are shaped with equal persuasiveness. In all of its illogicality, the story proceeds just as logically as the most convincing creations of Kafka, Dürrenmatt's master par excellence. At the same time, the pupil is proving his independence by his "ghostly hilarity." And "The Tunnel" is an artistic equivalent to that odd claustrophobic feeling at the bottom of one's stomach when the train, any train, rushes into a tunnel, and the safe world of sunshine is left behind. Depending on one's habits, this feeling is perhaps more terrifying in the Alps than on the metros of man-built cities: there the huge mass of the mountains, untamed nature, rises above one. After a passing moment of apprehension one resorts, of course, to one's reason. There is nothing so safe as a railroad, a direct line of communication between two points. . .

Urs J. Baschung draws the conclusion that in Dürrenmatt's work as a whole there is a belief in a Christian world order.[18] On the other hand, Hans Mayer speaks of Dürrenmatt's "theology without God"; "God has thus let us fall. . . . God is there, but useless for the human condition."[19] The calmness of mind or "ghostly hilarity" experienced by the student is achieved only at the expense of total disaster for Dürrenmatt's symbol of mankind. Calmness of despair or serenity caused by complete trust in God? Or an absolute grotesque? A matter of faith? "Pilatus" ("Pilate"), the last story in *The City*, includes Dürrenmatt's next word on the relations between God and man; it was not to be his last.

Dürrenmatt's message is hardly consoling. "Pilatus," written as early as 1946, is the other important achievement in the volume, and masterly in every detail. Attaining a style suited to the period was no problem for Dürrenmatt, later a writer of several historical plays. The story of Christ's last

[18] Urs J. Baschung, "Zu F.Ds 'Der Tunnel,'" *Schweizer Rundschau*, 68, 10–11 (Oct.–Nov. 1969), pp. 480–90.

[19] Mayer, "F.D.," *Zeitschrift für deutsche Philologie*, 87, 4 (Fall 1968), pp. 483–84.

days is told from the point of view of Pilate, largely as a stream of his perceptions. When he sees Christ, Pilate immediately recognizes him as God, and his first reaction is a fear of God. "Fear" in the original meaning of the word: terror. "The chasm between man and God had been infinitely wide, and now, as God had built a bridge over this chasm, and had become man, he [Pilate] had to perish, be shattered by Him like one thrown by waves against a cliff" (S 177–78). Looking at the scene of the scourging of Christ from a dark corner, Pilate knows that "there existed between God and man no understanding except death, no grace except damnation, and no love except hatred" (S 184). Then he rides to the cross, through a landscape grotesquely distorted by the earthquake mentioned in the Bible. The entire world is alienated and weird; in this story Dürrenmatt has created a demonic absolute grotesque, devoid of the humor balancing "The Tunnel." At the foot of the cross, Pilate sees above his head, as the last horror of the day, "the dead face of God" (S 192).

Pilate à la Dürrenmatt: a strange executioner, suffering in the role he is compelled to play to the death at the end, a substitute torturer. The scourging scene toward the end of the story: a scenic image hidden in narrative prose, visualized in its every detail, with exactly coordinated, purposeful lighting effects.[20] The religious attitudes in Dürrenmatt's firstling: ambivalent and somber, with emphasis on suffering and torture. According to Arnold, the collection is a circle starting from Christmas and the Christ-child and closing on the day of Christ's resurrection. Both of these God-figures "abandon man, they do not care for him, one has to write them off as consolation and hope."[21] *The City* as an artistic whole: interesting evidence of Dürrenmatt's fight to "achieve dis-

[20] Spycher (pp. 116–17) mentions the whipping scene as a powerful example of the marked visual character of this story.

[21] Arnold, p. 11; cf. pp. 19–20. Joachim Bark interprets "Pilatus" as a parable told to doubting modern readers (Knapp, ed., *F.D.*, p. 65).

tance from the picture that possessed" him, through studies in philosophy, through these exercises (S 197). A portrait of the writer as a young painter.

Dürrenmatt's visual talent can be seen on every page of his firstling. Yet there is also a clear line of development in employing this talent for literary aims. The first exercises proceed as a gradual and rather painful piling up of images, word by word, detail by detail. These prose pieces are monotonous strings of similar metaphors, little else. All of a sudden, however, dynamic images appear among the static ones, images full of tension, caught, as it were, right on the verge of a leap forward: "The towers rise arrowlike into the sky" (S 19). These images are, as Deschner says about another pair of examples, "pregnant with dramatic action."[22] Or, still further from the very beginning, Dürrenmatt's images grow into inexplicable scenes in miniature, with actors and an atmosphere. On the last page of "The Dog" this beastly incarnation of evil is seen walking in the rain, side by side with the vanished heroine of the story: "a dark shadow, gentle and noiseless as a lamb . . . with yellow, round, sparkling eyes" (S 34). Always Dürrenmatt thinks in images.

In the best achievement of *The City*, Dürrenmatt creates an artistic whole that is a dynamic, stratified image in its entirety: the train rushing through an endless tunnel. The relation of the writer toward his materials is growing flexible. He takes the narrative details in "The Tunnel" either seriously or, alternately, from a comic distance, and with the purpose of the whole firmly in his mind. Comedy creates distance from the picture. As Bänziger puts it, in this story we experience a fracture between "black literature," not in harmony with Dürrenmatt's personal qualities, and many-colored literature, right in the direction of his talents.[23] Dürrenmatt was, especially when writing the derivative middle section of his collection, running toward an artistic and philo-

---

[22] Deschner, "F.D's Experiments with Man," p. 41.
[23] Bänziger, *Frisch und D.*, p. 131.

sophical dead end,[24] finding an expression for his youthful *Weltschmerz* only in Kafkaesque, self-centered prose. In his next phase he found a new arena to fill up with the grotesquely contradictory images his phantasy kept creating. He did not have to fight against his innate inclination to think in images; he could use it. "Images are answers to reality," is one of his mottos (G 80). In the enclosing wall of his dead end Dürrenmatt found the stage door.

[24] The expression "dead end" is also used by Peppard, p. 24. "Throughout my literary career I have only landed in dead ends," Dürrenmatt remarks (G 44).

2 Poetry in Picture Books

IT IS WRITTEN, THE BLIND MAN

|||||||||||||||||||||||||||||||||||||||||||||||||||||||||||||||||||||||||||||||||||||||||||||||||||

"I presented scenes from uncertain times, especially the great adventures of mankind" (S 113). The storyteller in Dürrenmatt's short story "The City" fills the walls of his attic room with drawings, thus outlining the program of Dürrenmatt the dramatist for a long time to come. Four early plays take place during adventurous, uncertain periods in the history of mankind; he needed some practice before directly approaching the turmoils of our own time. In the far-away past, there was expanse enough for Dürrenmatt's grotesque imagination, and for the abrupt changes of tone and style he favored from the very beginning of his playwriting career. Distance in time helped him to achieve distance from the picture. When choosing historical backgrounds for his artistic inspirations he was able to rely on a sense of history, highly developed in Central Europe, and on a tradition of producing period plays, firmly established in the German-speaking world.

Yet Dürrenmatt's very first effort, written before "The City," dealt with the present—or, rather, with the future. *Der Knopf* (The Button), also known simply as *Comedy*, was finished on October 2, 1943, but was never to be published. According to the report of a friend it included "terrible fantasies of hell, with whores, drunkards, technicians, mutilated people," Adam, and a rapist-killer called Nabelpfiff. One of its scenes was dedicated to Kafka. The play as a whole dealt with the atom bomb—two years before Hiroshima. This is how we can interpret Dürrenmatt's central idea of a destructive machine powerful enough to bring doomsday upon us. The fears are concentrated on the button starting

43

the machine, and at the end, of course, somebody sits on it by accident. Knells for the world.[1]

Dürrenmatt did not make his stage début with this highly explosive script reminiscent of the films of Stanley Kubrik or of *Eh?*, a farce by Henry Livings. Two and a half years later, in March, 1946, Dürrenmatt finished his first produced play, *Es steht geschrieben* (It Is Written). The play had nothing to do with science fiction, quite a lot with history and religion. Kafka exerted a decisive influence on Dürrenmatt's non-dramatic prose; his models as a dramatist are to be found elsewhere.

Aristophanes, Nestroy, Wedekind, and Brecht are the names most commonly mentioned as Dürrenmatt's sources, by critics and by the playwright himself. What this varied lot perhaps have in common is an emphasis on freedom and unorthodoxy, not on the schematization prevalent in their own times. Aristophanes encouraged Dürrenmatt to rely on his scurrilous and parodical inspirations and his rough sense of humor.[2] Johann Nestroy (1801–62) was a master of the *bon mot*, a schooled practitioner of the theater, and a satirist; Dürrenmatt has seen his Viennese folk comedies as a colorful and fantastic continuation of the metaphysical world theater of the baroque (TS 142–45). There is a baroque abundance and a coexistence of extreme contrasts in Dürrenmatt; there is his ambition to create the whole world on the stage.[3] In the overlong monologues of his first play he is drunk with words —as German expressionism was in the 1920's.[4] Frank Wede-

---

[1] Bänziger, *Frisch und D.*, pp. 125–26; Wyrsch, "Die Dürrenmatt-Story," part two, *Schweizer Illustrierte*, March 25, 1963, p. 24.

[2] Therese Poser in Rolf Geissler, ed., *Zur Interpretation des modernen Dramas*, p. 71; Sauter, "Gespräch mit F.D.," *Sinn und Form*, 18, 4 (Fall 1966), p. 1228.

[3] Clifford A. Barraclough, "Nestroy, the Political Satirist," *Monatshefte für deutschen Unterricht*, 52, 5 (Oct. 1960), pp. 253–57; Kienzle in Weber, ed., *Deutsche Literatur seit 1945*, p. 374; Brock-Sulzer in Nonnenmann, ed., *Schriftsteller der Gegenwart*, pp. 86–87.

[4] Wolfdietrich Rasch, *Zur deutschen Literatur seit der Jahrhundertwende*, pp. 225–26; Mayer, *Zur deutschen Literatur der Zeit*, p. 304.

kind (1864–1916), a pre-expressionist, will become a topical name in our discussion later on. So will Bertolt Brecht; at the moment suffice it to say that *It Is Written* is full of characters breaking away from their roles, reminding us of the alienation effect à la Brecht and Thornton Wilder.[5]

Both Brecht and Wilder were played at the Zurich Theater (Schauspielhaus) during the war years. It is worth emphasizing that the theater, partly financed from public funds, is an esteemed cultural institution throughout the German-speaking world. Repertory companies are placed on the same level with public libraries and museums: all help to keep the past alive and furnish the present with a perspective of cultural tradition.[6] Under these circumstances Dürrenmatt has been able to follow his twofold ambition of writing plays with a wide popular appeal and of indulging in the delicacies of parody, which presupposes sophisticated audiences conscious of a literary and theatrical tradition. He has also established himself as a dramaturge, as an adapter of classic plays, since the late 1960's.[7]

In 1960, there were over three hundred subsidized repertory companies in the Federal Republic of Germany. In 1947, the year of Dürrenmatt's stage début, these cultural institutions were undergoing repair. Houses were being restored and new companies started in temporary buildings; the time for constructing magnificent new theater buildings was yet to come. To heal the spiritual and intellectual scars left by many years of seclusion and Nazi general and cultural policies, quite a number of foreign plays were being played.

[5] Joseph Strelka, *Brecht, Horváth, Dürrenmatt*, p. 115, remarks that Dürrenmatt is a follower of Brecht's only in the details of his stage technique.

[6] *Deutsches Theater heute*, an anthology of articles published originally in *Theater heute*, p. 117.

[7] The German word "Dramaturg" has also another meaning: in a repertory company his position is mainly "that of literary director of the theater" (William R. Ellwood, "Preliminary Notes on the German Dramaturg," *Modern Drama, 13*, 3, Dec. 1970, p. 254). Cf. Antony Price, "The Freedom of the German Repertoire," ibid., pp. 242–45.

Swiss plays did not create any translation problems. With the exception of *Draussen vor der Tür* (The Man Outside) by Wolfgang Borchert, there were no remarkable new German plays written for a long while; the creative energies of a great many German writers, as well as Dürrenmatt's, were partly channeled to radio theater.[8] The stage was set for the Swiss, for Frisch and Dürrenmatt.

The Zurich Theater had been a center of lively activity during the squalid war years. Prominent artists of the stage joined the originally Swiss company as refugees from Hitler's Germany. Theater manager Oskar Wälterlin, stage directors Kurt Hirschfeld, Leopold Lindtberg, and Kurt Horwitz, stage designer Teo Otto, actors Therese Giehse, Ernst Ginsberg, and Leonard Steckel all helped the Zurich Theater to achieve its high position as the leading free stage in the German-speaking world—and all were to have a role to play in Dürrenmatt's success.[9]

There were also small cabaret theaters. Dadaism was born in Cabaret Voltaire, Zurich, in 1916,[10] and the critical political circumstances preceding World War II provided plenty of material for its successor, Cornichon, founded in 1933. Dürrenmatt was engaged to write sketches for this company in the late 1940's, after his first play, but his contributions were limited to four brief scripts.[11] Though his contact with the cabaret was short-lived, there are elements in his style that speak of a natural inclination towards the cabaret: reliance on improvisation, on surprising repartee, on verbal

[8] *Deutsches Theater heute*, p. 51; Ernst Johann–Jörg Junker, *Deutsche Kulturgeschichte der letzten hundert Jahre*, pp. 198, 206; Martini in Kayser, ed., *Deutsche Literatur in unserer Zeit*, pp. 81, 84–88; Henry Beissel, "Between Two Nightmares," *Seminar*, 1, 2 (Fall 1965), pp. 56–57; Michael Patterson, *German Theatre Today*, pp. 2–14.

[9] Cf. Brock-Sulzer in *Schweizer Theaterbuch*, pp. 46–47, and Guido Calgari, *Die vier Literaturen der Schweiz*, p. 244.

[10] Herbert Read, *Vuosisatamme maalaustaiteen historia* (A Concise History of Modern Painting), p. 117.

[11] Wyrsch, part three, *Schweizer Illustrierte*, April 1, 1963, p. 25; Heinz Greul, *Bretter, die die Zeit bedeuten*, p. 439.

and scenic jokes, and on an immediate contact between the performer and the audience.[12]

A remarkable period in Swiss theatrical life preceded an internationally remarkable period in Swiss drama. Brecht and other refugees not only helped the willing Swiss artists and audiences to raise the standard and importance of the Zurich Theater; they also created a need for native plays. Switzerland was long taken to be too idyllic a country to produce dramatists of stature, and this prejudice may have contributed to the disappointments of Cäsar von Arx, the best-known Swiss playwright of the interwar years, who died embittered in 1949.[13] Dürrenmatt certainly had his share of critical and audience resistance, beginning with the scandal caused by his first play. It is, however, of greater significance that he also had his friends and supporters among the stage artists, especially in the Zurich Theater,[14] and among the critics looking for promising Swiss playwrights. He was given a chance to school himself, and he had wider horizons across the border, in Germany. Dürrenmatt's stage début was well timed.

The first word of Dürrenmatt the playwright is God, the first idea developed is that of the world turned upside down. *It Is Written* begins with a textbook example of the absolute grotesque, or with a verbalization of a painting by Bosch or Brueghel: "God revealed his face, and the sun was extinguished in the sea, and the ships were burnt above the waters./The whales were washed ashore./The mountains sank and the forests opened, fire broke out from the depths" (Esg 9). The diction echoes the Bible, the free verse employed

---

[12] A great many "avant garde" solutions (songs, raisonneurs, playing directly to the public) were transferred from the urban style of the cabaret to the established theaters of the postwar years (Bänziger, p. 21).

[13] Arnold, *Die Literatur des Expressionismus*, pp. 162–74; cf. Peter Seidmann, "Modern Swiss Drama," *Books Abroad*, 34, 2 (Spring 1960), p. 112.

[14] Cf. Brock-Sulzer in *Schweizer Theater*, pp. 48–50, and TS 157–58: Dürrenmatt's confession of love for the Zurich Theater, written in 1951.

has been compared with that of Christopher Fry, T. S. Eliot, and Paul Claudel, all prominent writers of poetic plays during the 1940's.[15] The character uttering this somber description is Dürrenmatt's own.

He is an anabaptist. In his search for adventurous times Dürrenmatt turned to the age of the Reformation, and to a unique rebellion in the German city of Münster. Between the years 1533 and 1536 the city was governed by an extreme sect of Protestants, consisting "of bakers, goldsmiths, furriers and confused preachers" (Esg 12), and claiming to follow God's will exactly as "it is written" in the Scriptures. Their fanatical self-reliance soon led to terrorism, which made the Catholics and Lutherans join forces in besieging and conquering Münster. In the prologue of the play, grotesque visions of doomsday end in a justification of violence. God orders the anabaptists to commit atrocities on their enemies.

These materials might well be utilized for a streamlined, sinewy tragedy. This was, however, far from Dürrenmatt's intention. *It Is Written* is a kind of picture book for the stage, a series of static scenes interspersed with long monologues and spiced with grotesque and parodical tones. Instead of a continuous line of action, Dürrenmatt shows glimpses of individual fates, more or less loosely tied together. The play lacks a clear focus; neither is it a social drama, a description of the community of the anabaptists. For the most prominent characters, there are Bernhard Knipperdollinck, a rich merchant; Johann Bockelson, an unscrupulous pseudo-prophet; and Franz von Waldeck, a ninety-nine-year-old Catholic bishop. Kniperdollinck is a personification of genuine religious humility, Bockelson his complete antithesis, a sensual atheist using the anarchistic state of affairs to grasp pleasure for pleasure's own sake. It is the unwelcome duty of the worldly-wise and acquiescent Bishop to judge both of them. His judg-

[15] E.g., Jauslin (*F.D.*, p. 32) makes these comparisons; he mentions, more specifically, Luther's translation of the Bible and its Book of Psalms. Cf. Bänziger, p. 134.

ment is identical in both cases: pious or profane, man dies on the wheel of torture.

A conspicuous feature in *It Is Written* is a surplus of monologues. Their first function is to disrupt the credibility of the stage figures. "I am not historical, I have never lived and never felt sorry for it" (Esg 13), one of the characters says. Stepping aside from a role has no Brechtian functions; it serves only as a cabaret-like joke, a further parodical element among an abundance of others.[16] Monologues also include quite needless descriptions. When surrounded by a group of attending maids, Bockelson keeps telling the spectators what they are in fact seeing on the stage (Esg 40). Otherwise the scene is quite cleverly constructed: funny, satiric, hitting the mark. In another scene Dürrenmatt gets so excited by his bright (and Shakespearean) idea of letting a night-watchman appear drunk that he makes the man talk about his drunkenness, instead of acting it (Esg 71). In these examples the words are taken to be an addition to the stage situation—a caption as it were—or a stanza of poetry written for a drawing already finished by a cooperating painter. These details, like messages in a logbook, tell us that a painter is on his way toward the stage. Dürrenmatt had, in this early phase of his career, quite a lot to learn about fusing his scenic means of expression together.

Some of the descriptive monologues are more functional, and there are also soliloquies of meditation, spoken by the Bishop. Still another group of monologues or long speeches grows into exuberant, expressionistic "word arias"[17] with a lyrical function. Again, these passages are mainly recited by Bockelson. He has an inclination to fall into poetic, strictly materialistic raptures: "Night! Night! Cool, infinite night!

[16] Heinrich Henel calls the alienation effects in *It Is Written* merely amusing "theater effects" (Grimm, ed., *Episches Theater*, p. 390).

[17] This term is used by Brock-Sulzer, not, however, in connection with *It Is Written* (*F.D.*, p. 99). Cf. Mayer: "All expressionistic drama tended . . . toward word oratory" (*Zur deutschen Literatur der Zeit*, p. 48). The quotations in this paragraph are in prose.

Full of whistling storm, falling stars and floating clouds!"
(Esg 61). On one hand, these passages remind us of *Baal*,
Brecht's first play, which also included expressionistic elements;[18] on the other, they form a contrast to Knipperdollinck's religious ecstasy at the end of the play. Bockelson's
declaration of faith states his belief "in the empty sky, in this
wall, in legs and arms, in face and hands and in the earth,
lying down below everything like the body of a woman! There
is nothing else!" (Esg 62). When at their best, these outpour-
ings include glimpses of genuine poetry; when at their worst
and longest, they reveal Dürrenmatt's intoxication with words.
It Is Written is a curious mixture of elements of undeniable
talent, perhaps even of genius, and embarrassing defects.

Before knocking at the stage door, Dürrenmatt was "possessed by the picture." Now he is a prisoner of the word.[19]
His inspiration is basically lyrical.[20] "It is a prejudice that
drama must be absolutely dramatic," he wrote in a manuscript from the years 1947–48 (TS 87). The characters of
It Is Written keep addressing the moon, the earth, the roof
ridge, the head of their executed adversary, or an off-stage
character; details of the setting or pieces of property are
called "you." "Moon! Moon in the sky! Why are you round
and bright and pure?" (Esg 102). The actors stand, as it
were, sidelong on the stage, speaking neither across the stage
to their fellow actors nor to the audience. When they start
calling one another "you" the play, especially its ideological
discussion, begins to live and take shape.

The next to last climax in the play is a crucial test for
Dürrenmatt's stage lyrics. The reign of the anabaptists is
moving toward its end. Knipperdollinck and Bockelson get

[18] According to Deschner, both Baal and Bockelson are "grotesque
experiments" and "amoral characters." Their difference is that Baal
is "coarse and repulsive" even in his humor, whereas Bockelson "has
true picaresque blood in his veins" ("F.D's Experiments with Man,"
pp. 59–60).

[19] Bänziger, p. 134.

[20] Cf. the critical remarks in Deschner, p. 62, and in Garten,
Modern German Drama, p. 256.

the inspiration to go dancing over the moonlit roofs of Münster. Dürrenmatt the painter gives them a magnificent background, "a giant moon, with craters and seas clearly visible. It is hanging on an infinite, deep blue and starless sky" (Esg 102). Dürrenmatt the playwright aims at a grotesque and poetic scenic image: the unscrupulous tyrant and the humble penitent, the king and his clown, one in his royal cloak and crown, the other in rags, are dancing against an infinite background. The setting, used with ambition and skill, and the stage action are fused together. Yet this scenic image does not grow from the themes handled before, nor does the text carry the burden placed on it by the setting.

It is probably a part of Dürrenmatt's conscious strategy to neglect the motivation of dance scene.[21] Knipperdollinck and Bockelson are just given the artistic invention, and off they dance. Dürrenmatt is demonstrating his creative freedom—to the disadvantage of his play. The scattered structure of *It Is Written* led the playwright to avoid a real encounter of his two protagonists in dialogue. Instead, he constructs a predominantly visual scene to prove the similarity of his antipodes. He is aiming at a paradox, and at a Christian or Calvinistic paradox: penitent or sinner, man has no value before almighty God. Paradox is a demanding pirouette in the figure skating of a thinker; it must stand analysis. Dürrenmatt's paradox has no strong links to his story. The moon dance does not bring together the divergent themes carried by Knipperdollinck and Bockelson; it is at most a picture of their lunacy.

Moreover, there are deficiencies in the dialogue of the scene. The early lines are a string of exclamations, amounting to "O moon!" and little else. As poetry this is hardly adequate; as a script for the stage, the passage is marred by the characters' descriptions of what they are doing: "I shall wander over the roof with you like a cat! Light as she, quick as she, hot as she" (Esg 102). Later in the scene, Dürrenmatt's

[21] In an interesting reading of the play, Durzak connects the scene with Dürrenmatt's concept of history as a senseless chaos of events (*D., Frisch, Weiss*, p. 50; cf. pp. 45–48).

verbal images grow more pregnant; there is a touch of poetry in this over-long scene. If not a crystallization of the themes of *It Is Written*, the moon-dance scene is a summary of the most characteristic vices and virtues in its dialogue and total conception.

It was during the moon-dance scene that the public lost its patience at the world première and started a noisy demonstration against the performance. The reviews include somewhat contradictory reports about the seriousness of the episode and the reasons for it.[22] This theater scandal, a rare phenomenon in Swiss theater life (at least before Dürrenmatt), was perhaps a result of accumulated boredom during the three-hour performance, perhaps a protest against Dürrenmatt's "extremely grotesque provocation" in equating the sinner and the penitent,[23] or a refusal to accept the abrupt changes of tone and the parodical elements of the play. Dürrenmatt had in any case hit his mark. He went backstage beaming with satisfaction.[24]

The religious themes of *It Is Written* were brought center stage toward the end of the play. Knipperdollinck and the Bishop are its key religious figures, along with Jan Matthisson, the fanatical prophet of the anabaptists, and Judith, Knipperdollinck's daughter. In his blind faith in God's will and ability to guard Münster, Matthisson strides singlehanded against the enemy: a clown of faith, killed immediately (Esg 55). Judith is used to construct rather a distracting parallel to her namesake in the Bible.

The encounter between Knipperdollinck and the Bishop

[22] According to the murderous review by Willy Zimmermann, Dürrenmatt was "a young elephant in a china-shop," his play only "richly chaotic and very undisciplined puberty fevers of a certainly highly talented beginner" (*Neue Zürcher Nachrichten*, April 21, 1947). Brock-Sulzer is, with a few reservations, on Dürrenmatt's side (*Die Tat*, April 24); middle positions are taken, e.g., in the *Neue Zürcher Zeitung* (April 21: Jakob Welti) and *Die Weltwoche* (April 25: Georgine Oeri).

[23] Arnold, p. 26.

[24] Wyrsch, "Die Dürrenmatt-Story," part three, *Schweizer Illustrierte*, April 1, 1963, p. 24.

early in the play is a Shavian scene of clear argumentation not disturbed by self-centered lyricism. The Bishop, an old and resigned figure, is conscious of the dichotomy in the ranks of the anabaptists. There are genuine Christians and erring fanatics among them: "the blood of the innocent will run for the purest of aims." Human minds cannot interpret God's will: "It is written, he who has ears shall hear, and he who has eyes shall see. But who has eyes and ears!" In these formulations the Bishop sounds very much like the humble later heroes of Dürrenmatt. He is the one-eyed bishop in the country of the blind.[25] His humility has a religious motivation: "Before God we are both wrong, the anabaptist and the bishop." And when Knipperdollinck asks whether the baptists and Christ are not the same when saying the same, we reach the core of Dürrenmatt's vision: "Nothing is the same with him. He is the sword, and we are the body that will be killed" (Esg 32–33).

Dürrenmatt, a writer in extremis, has given an extreme and grotesque expression to his idea. God and man are totally incommensurable. The antithesis striking enough for Dürrenmatt is that between the sword and the body. In his scenic language the sword is replaced by the wheel of torture. Dürrenmatt's God is the cruel God of a writer in love with grotesque contrasts; it is the same God that died on the cross to the wonder and bewilderment of Pilate in Dürrenmatt's short story.

The origins of this image of God have been found in Kierkegaard and Karl Barth. Dürrenmatt was supposed to write a dissertation on "Kierkegaard and the Tragic"; instead, as he has told, he wrote *It Is Written*.[26] Barth, a Swiss-born Protestant theologian and a personal friend of Dürrenmatt's,[27] starts in his book *Der Römerbrief* from a concept of God as "totali-

---

[25] Jenny (*F.D.*, p. 20) points out that the Bishop is the only figure in the play not distorted or made ridiculous.

[26] Wyrsch, part two, March 25, p. 25.

[27] Barth lost his professorship in Hitler's Germany (Johann–Junker, *Deutsche Kulturgeschichte*, p. 175). His importance as a theological writer is emphasized by Gisbert Kranz, *Christliche Literatur der Gegenwart*, pp. 237–38.

ter aliter," as "wholly other." God is separated from man
"by an endless qualitative distinction"; he is "beyond the
reach of man's most fervent religious efforts. God's 'no' has
to strike down everything that has originated in man before
God's gracious 'yes' can reach him."[28]

This may well be how we are supposed to experience and
interpret Knipperdollinck's fate. The merchant makes a
"most fervent effort" by following the humble teachings of
the Bishop and throwing away everything he has; he loses
his family and lives among rats. He does all this, because he
takes with deadly earnestness the Bible's word about the
difficulties of the rich: deadly in the literal sense of the
word. Struck down by God's "no" Knipperdollinck is
reached by God's "yes" on the wheel of torture. Just before
his death he has an exalted experience of God's grace:

> The depth of my despair is but a sign of Thy justice,
> and my body lies in this wheel as in a cup
> which Thou fillest now with Thy grace to the brim!
>
> (Esg 111).[29]

These are the concluding lines of *It Is Written*. With them,
we are facing the last scenic image of the play, preliminarily
discussed in the introduction (pp. 21–22). Seeing this image
against the background of the entire play, we have still better
reasons to emphasize its ambiguous and grotesque character.
Is Knipperdollinck, like Matthisson, a clown of faith? Or
is he the only one in the play saved by God's grace? He calls
himself Bockelson's clown and speaks about his holy folly
(Esq 100, 104); at the end, he sees God's justice affirmed.

For Dürrenmatt's critics, Knipperdollinck has been quite
a problem. Most critical formulations recognize the self-
contradictory nature of the scenic image.[30] It is not the final

---

[28] Deschner, p. 53; cf. ibid., pp. 15, 48, and Eberhard Busch, *Karl Barth*, p. 350: Dürrenmatt's attitude to life seemed to Barth "like that of my 1921 *Romans*" in January, 1948.

[29] Translation by Peppard, p. 30.

[30] Peppard (p. 35) states that Knipperdollinck's final speech "emerges from a setting that destroys its impact," whereas Allemann

result of a logical development, preceded as it is by the moon-dance scene, which is loosely connected to the rest of the play. Dürrenmatt gives an image, a momentary glimpse, not a view of the world complete and solid. All interpretations are thus running the risk of being after-rationalizations, descriptions of a theme not consistently handled by the playwright. Keeping this reservation in mind, we must start adopting a critical distance to Dürrenmatt's religious ideas, or to their religious interpretations by the critics. Knipperdollinck is proclaiming a religion of complete submission to God's will; human efforts are of no value, God is "totaliter aliter." How far are we to take Dürrenmatt's image literally, how far as a symbol of a mental or spiritual condition? If God's grace can reach man only when he lies on the wheel of torture, with his joints crushed, then we are at a point where religion denies the value of human life, in favor of God's values. We can question whether this is a correct interpretation of the Scriptures, as they are written.

The readers or spectators have to decide whether to follow Dürrenmatt into these extremes of Barthian Protestantism. *It Is Written* is clearly the work of a young and austere writer; it does not radiate the strange mixture of pity and sympathy emerging from, for example, the clear-sighted, anything but belletristic major novels of Graham Greene: *The Power and the Glory* (1940), *The Heart of the Matter* (1947). Dürrenmatt is not interested in describing the sinners—or, rather, he is interested only in those committing the sin of pride, in those who claim that they have interpreted God's will, as it is written, and as it should be lived.

---

finds in that self-revelation "a last and concluding folly" of an existence limited to an untragic and fanatic search for God; his death is ludicrous, meaningless and tragicomic (von Wiese, ed., *Das deutsche Drama*, II, p. 437). Brock-Sulzer balances precariously between calling the end "consoling" and "a scandal" (*F.D.*, p. 25). Bänziger (p. 135) has a presentiment that there is genuine faith behind Dürrenmatt's parody of faith. Cf. Durzak, pp. 51–52. Buri recognizes only God's grace (*Der unbequeme D.*, pp. 40–41); his interpretation is refuted by Knapp (*F.D.*, 1976, ed. by Knapp, pp. 23–24).

Knipperdollinck on the wheel of torture: the image is
charged with contradictory impulses. Other self-contradictory
details include Dürrenmatt's sudden twist from the discussion between the merchant and the Bishop into the grotesque
execution scene with colorful costumes (Esg 34).[31] Instinc-
tively or consciously, Dürrenmatt tried to achieve rhythm in
the happenings on the stage as early as in his first play. This
mass scene introduces one of Dürrenmatt's scenic units or
"figures in the carpet," comparable to O'Neill's moonlight
monologues and carried by an actor's individual expression:
an executioner. He is an athletic figure, eagerly admired by
the mob, or by a girl: "Such an executioner is like God!"
(Esg 38). In *The Visit*, the executioner was to be a gymnast
(TV 97), and the death sentence was to be confirmed by a
chorus of everybody present. The mob in *It Is Written* repeats a key phrase, with ironic overtones, and the falling
heads are identified with a reminiscence from Dürrenmatt's
youth, with heads of lettuce. See Fig. 1.

All kinds of heads are handled with equal ease by another
grotesque figure in the scene, a vegetable woman, Dürrenmatt's Mutter Courage. Her anachronistic shouts foretell the
twelve world wars to come and drown the farewell speech
of a monk who is about to be executed: "Onions! . . . Eat
onions!" (Esg 37). When Knipperdollinck starts throwing
his money to the mob, the monk escapes in the ensuing
tumult. Dürrenmatt thus gives a parodical finishing touch
to this grotesque, broad, and memorable scene, with quite
a lot of action inherent in the situation itself.

In his stage directions Dürrenmatt gives precise instructions about the lights. He uses a wide scale of expression,
from near darkness to the full glare of projectors. He needs
these effects in order to avoid constant changes of scenery
and to keep his freely constructed sequence of scenes fluc-
tuating and moving; he is not far from a kind of film montage, or from the scattered structure of a "storm-and-stress"

[31] Klarmann calls this shift too abrupt ("F.D. and the Tragic Sense
of Comedy," *The Tulane Drama Review*, 4, May 1960, p. 84).

play. Dürrenmatt's lighting scheme grew from expressionism, or from the wartime style in the Zurich Theater, accustomed as it was to making a virtue out of necessity under the leadership of Teo Otto, a creative stage designer.[32] The static impression left by *It Is Written* arises from lack of movement and interaction within the individual scenes rather than between them. Dürrenmatt knows how to create tension between his consecutive scenic images, yet he keeps each of them relatively motionless. He sees each scene as a 'still' or as a painting, not as a smoothly moving fragment of continuous action.

However, Dürrenmatt expects a flexible reaction from his audience. The spectators are supposed to be sensitive to delicate changes between seriousness and parody. The playwright is leaving Kafka behind and proceeding at full speed toward the parodic grotesque. Parody offers him another possibility to stylize reality, to exaggerate and move beyond the realm of everyday life. The jokes in *It Is Written* include quotations from Goethe or Schiller,[33] parodic notes from the orchestra pit (Esg 12), and quasi-Biblical *bons mots*: "for he who wants to have a sword puts iron into the fire" (Esg 10). Or a new variation of Descartes: "Judico, ergo . . . dumm" (Esg 15)—"I judge, therefore I am stupid." Judging the success of these and other parodic details is difficult; *It Is Written* is an early play in which the playwright is less sure of himself than he later is, and less clear-headed. He is in love with minor parodic details.

According to Beda Allemann, parody is for Dürrenmatt "a means of defending himself against literary history," his first play "an act of parodic despair and despairing parody." Dürrenmatt tries to make the whole concept of tragedy look ridiculous by replacing the heroic concluding scenes of trag-

---

[32] Cf. Allemann, p. 422. If Dürrenmatt's stage directions are taken without excessive literalness, they are hardly as impractical as Jauslin (p. 30) and Peppard (pp. 29–30) suppose.

[33] Jauslin (p. 36) catalogues quotations from Goethe and Schiller, e.g., in the jargon of the two scavengers (Esg 14) or in the final words of the judge (Esg 108).

57

edy with "death by hanging." "The horizontal tension of
tragedy leading toward disaster gives way to a vertical tension
within the individual scenes."[34] These observations reveal
Dürrenmatt's polemical relation to his materials and his liking for grotesque discords. He is "an anti-Schiller" and "an
anti-Brecht";[35] in *It Is Written* he is also an anti-tragedian,
writing a Brechtian counter-sketch ("Gegenentwurf"), a
new variation close to an established form of art.[36]

Being so much "anti," being against so many phenomena,
is apt to arouse antagonism. Dürrenmatt's comic relief is too
insistent, "undercutting more often than underscoring the
potential pathos."[37] Yet we can also hear another tone of
voice in *It Is Written*, that of despair, that of *The City*. The
trouble with the play is that these conflicting elements are
not in balance. Dürrenmatt's genuine compassion for the
sordid state of affairs during and after World War II is
expressed in an excessively literary and derivative form.
Without knowing it, our budding playwright dances along
the roof of high romanticism: there is an unmotivated murder
scene, there are moonlit nights, court scenes with dozens of
extras in delightful groupings, etc. Dürrenmatt does not quite
get rid of the things he is parodying; he is a prisoner of tragedy, too. *It Is Written* moves somewhere between full-scale
parody and deep seriousness, between Aristophanes and
Kafka.

Parody is a quizzical confession of love for the beloved of
yesterday. Dürrenmatt is only courting tragedy; he has not
yet made love to it, nor learnt to know it thoroughly. He is
also a novice in the precarious art of making love to tragedy
on the stage and through the stage.

In spite of his inexperience and uncertainty, Dürrenmatt
has a firm grip of a character type that was to remain with

[34] Allemann, pp. 421–35.
[35] Brock-Sulzer in Grimm, ed., *Der unbequeme Dürrenmatt*, p. 125.
[36] Grimm in ibid., p. 87. Profitlich (*F.D.*, p. 57) remarks that this
presupposes a public conscious of earlier literary habits.
[37] Peppard, p. 27; cf. p. 30, and Arnold, p. 24.

him for some time to come. Bockelson and Matthisson are megalomaniacs. The former elects himself as the sovereign ruler of a godless universe; the latter considers himself and his city to be elected by God. These two proud sinners are compared with Knipperdollinck, a monomaniac in humility. All three are caricatures drawn by a writer favoring exaggeration. They are judged by the Bishop, who understands everything yet cannot help anybody. His situation is not far from Dürrenmatt's own in his later plays, which are peopled by mono- and megalomaniacs.

Dürrenmatt's Münster fresco is an exercise for the village of Guellen in *The Visit*: now a city of anabaptists, later a village of materialists. Guellen has far wider implications; anyone can find his own portrait in this village. Yet already in *It Is Written* Dürrenmatt gathers a community at meetings of the city council or in mob scenes, and emphasizes the role of its leaders. In so doing he aims at laying bare its mechanics—and does this over-eagerly rather than with caution. Münster is from the very beginning without any mask of respectability, without the realistic veils that could have been removed for dramatic effect.

When the curtain rises, an important dramatic event has already taken place. The conventions have been eliminated. The anabaptists have broken the social and religious order of both Catholics and Lutherans. "A fundamental blowing up of conventions takes place in every play of Dürrenmatt's," Allemann writes. In Dürrenmatt's stage début the community itself "effects this, by establishing the rule of the anabaptists." His farces move within a field of tension existing between order and chaos, conventions and freedom, formulas and arbitrariness.[38] Or, from an artistic point of view: between total plans and sudden inspirations. Which of his effervescent inventions is he to reject? Which to develop further? Is the sum total of a great many small ideas equal to one great idea? Does dropping several minor details lead to

[38] Allemann, p. 429. Cf. Neumann et al., *Dürrenmatt, Frisch, Weiss*, pp. 33–34.

simplification pushed too far? Every time Dürrenmatt fights a round with his materials, his critics must consider these points. Abundant or meager? Scattered or condensed? A combination of richness and compactness? *It Is Written* is amply provided rather than spare, scattered rather than logical, rich rather than compact. It is both unconventional and a typical first play, including the sum total of its writer's ideas.

It is to the credit of the Zurich Theater that Dürrenmatt was young enough when the play was produced. He had time to learn his craft. He was also humble and resilient enough to admit that he needed the cooperation and advice of the stage artists. *It Is Written* is awkward *and* promising; that is its final paradox. Its most promising feature is intensity.[39] Stark expressive power is gathered in the long lines of the free verse, proceeding like the swell of an ocean. There are powerful visions of doomsday, of execution, of torture. The separate scenic images do not form a continuous line of action. Yet the play conveys the impression of a rich talent behind all the inexperience and uncertainty. The writer of this immature play is a victim of his own diversified, not yet coordinated abilities as a painter, a meditator, a parodist, a budding poet, a writer of monologues—and as a meteor falling unexpectedly amidst life regulated by conventions. A minor playwright does not begin his career with so untamed and wild a play as *It Is Written*. It will be interesting to see what Dürrenmatt as an experienced dramatic craftsman was to make out of these materials when writing his new version of the play, *The Anabaptists*, in 1967.

The world première of *It Is Written* was directed by Kurt Horwitz, artistic director of the Basle Theater. The first night was in Zurich on April 19, 1947: the date of Dürrenmatt's

[39] The power of Dürrenmatt's first play is noticed, e.g., by Karl Schmid in the playbill of the world première, p. 6, and by Jenny, p. 24. The first reactions of Wälterlin, Horwitz and Hirschfeld were similar (Wyrsch, part three, April 1, p. 23).

birth as a playwright. He devoted the rest of the year 1947 to writing his second play, this time tailored to meet the needs and possibilities of the Basle Theater. *Der Blinde* (The Blind Man) had its première in Basle on January 10, 1948. Horwitz chose to act: he interpreted the focal role of Negro da Ponte, and Ernst Ginsberg was the stage director.

Stage history helps us to follow Dürrenmatt's "zigzag line of development."[40] Compared with *It Is Written, The Blind Man* is technically less demanding. Instead of the thirty-six actors used in Zurich, it manages with eleven actors and a few extras; instead of over twenty different sets, *The Blind Man* employs just one basic setting, with a few changeable details. The play is thematically concentrated, too: everything in it is connected with the central theme of blind faith. The story woven around a blind duke proceeds mostly in one tone of voice, the shrill pitch of despair. In some respects, the play is a step forward; in others, it leads backward to the Kafkaesque world of the middle stories in *The City*, written in 1945–46.[41]

The basic idea of *The Blind Man* flashes past in two scenes of *It Is Written*. A blind anabaptist tries in vain to warn his brethren: "It is terrible to know that an old man without eyes is the only one seeing" (Esg 90).[42] In *The Blind Man* a blind duke sitting in front of his destroyed castle is the only one seeing; at the end of the play, he sees his faith confirmed. The time chosen as his background is, again, a turbulent one: the Thirty Years War (1618–48) is ravaging Germany, the troops of Wallenstein and those of Sweden have spread destruction in the dukedom. The Duke knows nothing of this; he is recovering from an illness that has blinded him.

---

[40] Jenny, p. 24; he also speaks of Dürrenmatt's inclination "to fall from one extreme to another," e.g., from the explosive spectacle of *It Is Written* to the strong concentration of *The Blind Man*.

[41] Arnold (p. 29) remarks that the play belongs to the same world of thoughts and feelings as Dürrenmatt's early prose.

[42] Cf. Bänziger, p. 135. Matthisson's last speech includes a reference to the miracles in the Bible: "Have not Thou also said to the blind man: let it happen to you according to your faith" (Esg 55).

61

His son Palamedes and his daughter Octavia have not the heart to tell him.

Negro da Ponte, an Italian nobleman and officer passing through, has no such scruples. The Duke makes Negro the governor of his possessions, and Negro starts a cruel game to show the Duke that his blind faith is groundless. The helpless old man is led around his castle, as though on an endless flight from the enemy. Negro's retinue, a grotesque collection of wartime parasites, acts suitable roles in this play within the play staged by Negro: a whore plays abbess, a black servant is introduced as Wallenstein. The end of the play leaves the Duke sitting where he was at the beginning, with both of his children dead, his faith unshaken.

The dialogue is more agile and speakable than in *It Is Written*. Much of it is in one-line speeches, so that the monologues and other long speeches are conspicuous. It is quite natural that the Duke speaks in monologues. He is a solitary figure, out of contact with his surroundings, and apt to describe his own feelings. His safe and peaceful inner world is contrasted with that of those with sight. This ironical conflict is a central factor in the play, for the Duke is entirely dependent on what he hears others saying. Just as "it is written" was the only guideline for the anabaptists, so "it is said" is for the Duke. A case of monomania again.

This leads to another use of monologues. As in *It Is Written*, the characters tend to describe the setting and the situation on the stage. This time their procedure is more natural, as they are speaking to a blind man. Yet the final effect is tiresome for the spectator; the last long speech in the play is a clear case of over-use of this type of monologue (B 73–75). Negro tells the Duke what the audience has seen and known all through the performance. Also elsewhere, it is no trouble at all for Dürrenmatt to shake two-page monologues out of his sleeve, including lyrical monologues à la Bockelson, spoken by Negro to his retinue, or monologues of introspection. The characters of *The Blind Man* have a marked tendency to speak about their interrelations rather than act them. They also exert a mysterious influence over one another, especially over the Duke. Negro is a megalomaniac reveling in man's power over his neighbor. One word from him, and the Duke loses his happiness: "This is the power that one man can have over another,/a proof that there is nothing besides man" (B 33). Dürrenmatt is attaching metaphysical implications to his pattern of characters. He deals with blind faith, not only in the surrounding reality, but also in God. His Duke is a metaphor of religious faith; destroying his faith in "it is said" means also destroying belief in God and proving that "there is nothing besides man." This is what Negro is after.

Faith is an abstract concept, and Dürrenmatt has worked hard to give it a concrete form on the stage. But unfortunately his lines are full of other abstractions, too.[43] Truth, delusion, love, death, freedom, blindness: these are big words denoting important ideas, which Dürrenmatt does not make concrete; he merely plays ball-games with them.[44] He tries to be profound; he succeeds in being vague. There are only tenuous ties between these abstractions and the stage situations. Matters are not helped by worn-out poetic metaphors: "As a steep flame I am shooting up to the infinite" (B 58). Dialogue in drama does not necessarily convince simply because the characters are convinced of their own general validity: "My despair is yours now, for it is the despair of all people" (B 60). It is easy to state such a thing, difficult to make an audience experience it.

[43] Jenny finds fault with Dürrenmatt's language: it does not support his idea. "Where it looks for greatness, it often retails only big words (curse and grace, life and death, truth and lie); where it should express the 'Credo quia absurdum,' the paradox of faith, it often resorts only to the paradox as a rhetorical figure" (p. 26).

[44] Erich Brock sees Dürrenmatt's dialectic ball-games mainly as a laudable contrast to the word arias, yet remarks that his language tends to start running idle ("F.D.: 'Der Blinde,'" *Schweizer Monatshefte*, 27, 1947–48, p. 746). The simile of a ball-game is also employed by Werner Weber in his review of the première: "But a play is not playing with words" (*Neue Zürcher Zeitung*, Jan. 12, 1948).

Dürrenmatt's own afterthoughts were critical. *The Blind Man* was a "play with verbal arias," its roles were "hardly hinted at," because the playwright had fled from his stage figures "into poeticism" (TS 205).[45] In Dürrenmatt's picture book there is quite a lot of poetry, yet only one drawing. This time he had seen the play as a single still: the Duke in front of his castle, a prisoner of his faith, with Negro as his tempter and Palamedes as a helpless and despairing bystander. The individual scenes are not too long; what is prolonged is the total structure of the play. *It Is Written* was scattered, *The Blind Man* is too narrow, too strictly concentrated, and over-obvious in its repetitions. The monomaniacal will of the Duke is so pervading an element that it prevents Dürrenmatt from varying his theme: monomania turns into monotony. Whatever happens, the Duke is unflinching in his faith, and testing his faith is a matter mainly of words, not of deeds.

The abstract problem of delusions has been concretized with consummate skill by Henrik Ibsen in many of his major works, by Eugene O'Neill in *The Iceman Cometh*, and by Arthur Miller in *The Death of a Salesman*. In spite of Dürrenmatt's efforts, the problem remained abstract in his treatment. He did not dramatize life, he dramatized the theater. He achieved this by playing the dialogue and the setting, the audible and the visible, against one another. The spectators are asked to keep two settings constantly in mind: one they see in front of them on the stage, the other is painted for them by the words.[46] Dürrenmatt wrote his second play *about* his most burning artistic problem—word versus picture (FP 20).[47] He did not try to solve this problem while treating any other topic.

[45] "Language can lead a writer astray," Dürrenmatt writes in another comment on *The Blind Man*. "The joy of being able all of a sudden to write . . . can make an author talk too much" (FP 27).

[46] Jauslin, p. 42: "This means quite simply making too great demands on the spectator."

[47] *The Blind Man* is admired by Frisch as a "model example of a theatrical situation," based as it is on "the opposition between per-

Dürrenmatt's interest in the dramatics between dialogue and setting led him to neglect other essential elements. There is little suspense in *The Blind Man*. The audience is told too much too early; the tricks of Negro and the faith of the Duke just go on filling the stage scene after scene. In *Hamlet*, the "mousetrap" play within the play adds greatly to the suspense; in *The Blind Man*, Negro's play is too dominating an element. It discharges tension, it does not generate it.

The Blind Man is a less promising play than *It Is Written*. It is more literary and less powerful; though it is better controlled, on the surface at least, the control brings with it an element of baroque-like schematization and allegory. This time Dürrenmatt is following a formula of thought, not rebelling against it. The characters represent certain concepts —faith, disbelief, doubt, or life—and their collision leads to extreme consequences, in a good Dürrenmattian manner.[48] Suspecting Palamedes to be a traitor, the Duke yields his son to the executioner and strangles the court poet with his own hands: quite a murderous criticism of his poor lines. Octavia commits suicide off-stage. Negro gives orders that the poet's body, covered with a cloak, be brought back to the stage, and leads the blind man into thinking that he is standing in front of his dead daughter. It is Negro's intention to shatter the Duke's blind faith once and for all, first by stating that Octavia is dead, then by showing her alive. Negro does not

---

ception and imagination" ("On the Nature of the Theatre," *The Tulane Drama Review*, 6, 3, March 1962, p. 6). This reveals Frisch's interests rather than the merits of Dürrenmatt's play. The worlds of an apparently blind man and of the seeing are contrasted in a later novel by Frisch, *Mein Name sei Gantenbein*, 1964.

[48] Though there is interaction and confrontation between the characters to a certain degree, the play "remains basically allegorical and the demonstration of an abstraction," failing to create "a meaningful dramatic conflict" (Peppard, p. 32). According to Robert B. Heilman, Brecht, Frisch, and Dürrenmatt bring to the stage "a part of a man— a mood, a need, a passion, an obsession," not "a fully developed personality" (*The Iceman* . . . , p. 167).

know about Octavia's suicide. When the cloak is removed in the focal scenic image of the play, Octavia's body is revealed. The Duke has been right; what happens to him is in accordance with his faith. Negro goes away, "staggering like a blind man" (B 77).

Grotesque religious imagery created by a writer in love with the grotesque? Certainly. What about the story leading to this happy catastrophe? The motivations of the characters do not fit the twists of the plot. Octavia, representing life or Sartrean existentialism, is full of animal spirits—yet in her last scene she suddenly turns desperate. Jenny comments on this contradiction, then calls the final twist merely a "coup de théâtre" in which Dürrenmatt's courageous parable between religious faith and faith in something's being true falls apart.[49] The decisive scene between Palamedes and the Duke (B 51–54) is a result of certain dramaturgic arrangements. The playwright has made up his mind beforehand that the father must condemn his own son to death. He can attain this goal only through some surprising somersaults of thought.[50]

The Duke has been seen as one of Dürrenmatt's "men of courage." According to Dürrenmatt's own definition, "the lost world order is restored within them" (FP 34). Yet the Duke is in an emergency situation, in a dead end, as Herbert Peter Madler has stated. His blind faith in what is said is not the result of a revelation showing the world in a new light;

[49] Jenny, pp. 29–31.

[50] There is a sophisticated Christian interpretation presented by Deschner. The Duke is being tested "in a world of visible absurdity," where the "vertical relationship between man and God is broken" (p. 66); he chooses to have "faith in man" and "faith in God" (p. 69). The relation between the Duke and Palamedes is a symbolic representation of man's relation to God: "the Duke as a father-figure . . . becomes a veiled embodiment of the 'wholly other' God" (p. 83). Deschner is ready to admit that these "multiple levels of meaning . . . make strenuous demands on the audience" (p. 75). They do; a stage production does not allow for several careful readings: Dürrenmatt has not given his religious ideas a clear scenic form. He clashed with religion and his father, he says (G 19).

it is his only chance to go on living. This makes him into an obstinate and dangerous opponent. Negro, a fanatical man of action typical of Dürrenmatt, is provoked by the solitary Duke to act as the tester of his faith.[51]

The Duke is the ambiguous protagonist of a grotesque play. Christian interpretations tend to ignore or minimize the atrocities committed or caused by the Duke and his blind faith. Right at the moment when he is strangling his court poet he says that he is offering him "the only truth that does not kill, that is not from the hand of man" (B 68). Yet he is only defending his faith from the truth offered him by the poet. Exactly like Knipperdollinck, exactly like Romulus the Great in Dürrenmatt's next play, the Duke exceeds all limits, and sacrifices those closest to him to his idiosyncracies. The merchant loses his wife and daughter, the Duke his daughter and son.

A Christian paradox of love again? Rather, a continuation of the youthful austerity that dictated the solution of *It Is Written.* And the paradox of a writer of grotesqueries who wants to give the maximum amount of weight to the arguments of his imagined opponent—only to overweigh them. To prove his faith the Duke is permitted to kill, to yield his son to the executioner, and to cause the suicide of his daughter. Presupposing the existence of a God "wholly other," so far above and outside man's reach that these deeds become acceptable or recommendable, means introducing a deus ex machina, in the literal sense of this term, to defend the play. In this secularized age of ours, Christian-minded critics tend to applaud when a remarkable writer speaks about God and seems to postulate the existence of God. It is not emphatically enough asked what kind of God he is creating; any God will do.[52]

[51] Madler, "Ds mutiger Mensch," *Hochland, 62,* 1 (Jan.–Feb. 1970), pp. 36–45, 47–48. The article is republished in *Schweizer Rundschau, 69,* 5 (Sept.–Oct. 1970), pp. 314–25.

[52] Arnold (pp. 30–32) connects *The Blind Man* with Dürrenmatt's earlier accusations against God ("one has to be blind to believe in God"), and sees only a grotesque delusion in the end of the play.

With these two plays Dürrenmatt tried his hand at two basic dramaturgic models that were to continue to appear in his works. His first experiment was a panoramic play, a new variation of the world theater typical of the Baroque: *It Is Written*. This colorful fresco in Brueghel's or Bosch's vein abounded in the parodic and absolute grotesque dappled with paradoxes in the richly effervescent chaos of the play. As his second experiment, Dürrenmatt made a charcoal drawing dramatizing just one basic paradox, a study of an individual that is limited in its scale of colors and narrow in scope: *The Blind Man*. *It Is Written* is abundant, scattered, and wild, *The Blind Man* monotonous, schematic, and compact. What these plays and Dürrenmatt's early prose have in common is an emphasis on religious problems, with God portrayed as a cruel and inexplicable force, alien to man.

The three works of Dürrenmatt's apprenticeship grow from one root. They are written by a religious-minded youth in love with grotesque contrasts, by a reader of Kafka and Kierkegaard, and by a student in philosophy, examining our concept of reality.[53] There is a clear line of development in the artistic standard of these works, from the first prose exercises to "The Tunnel," from the lyrical and descriptive monologues of *It Is Written* to the agile dialogue of *The Blind Man*. Dürrenmatt the painter was brimful of visions easily translated into stage pictures; but Dürrenmatt the young playwright did not as yet know how to turn them into a continuous flow of stage action. What he was not sure about was how to construct scenic images, with a fusion of a great many scenic means of expression, and with a cluster of themes going through these scenic images as beams of light pass through a lens. He saw picture and word as enemies, not as two elements of equal importance. If there is a relation

---

Brock recognizes the cruelties caused by the Duke and calls the victory of faith "purely poetic, floating," not to be brought in harmony with "the dogmatic faith of the church" (p. 746).

[53] Dürrenmatt writes about his starting-points: "My education was philosophical, the theater was something unfamiliar, . . . my writing hardly more than an attempt to clear out a chaos of thoughts, to establish a bit of order" (TS 204–05).

between his pictures and words, it is not organic. His plays are like picture books by a painter, with poems by someone else.

Fortunately, Dürrenmatt's relation to the word was far from settled. He was young and flexible enough when entering the stage; he was open to new stimuli. They led him into another dead end, into over-emphasized poeticism, as he later admitted. Yet his dead ends are only apparently closed by walls: throughout his career Dürrenmatt has been obstinate and powerful enough to clear away all kinds of obstacles. Defying conventions, going through dead ends, is a favorite pastime for Dürrenmatt. Sometimes he has successfully made a new breakthrough; at others he has banged his head against the wall.

The most interesting aspect of the young Dürrenmatt is the abundance of his talents, the apparently endless variety of roads open to him. He might have turned into a writer of cabaret plays, into an established Kafkaist, into an epic playwright, or into a Protestant Claudel. His tones of voice range from that of youthful and pathetic *Weltschmerz* to the urbane and ribald. There are influences from Aristophanes and Brecht, from Nestroy and Wedekind, from Swift and Shakespeare, from Wilder and Rabelais, in Dürrenmatt's early works. He is a meeting-place for half the classics of world literature. This company, boisterous rather than refined, not only is a sign of Dürrenmatt's youthful dependence on his models, it also bears testimony to his rich talents, to all kinds of tensions and seeds in him. Having convinced even his cruelest critics of his seriousness of purpose with *The Blind Man*,[54] Dürrenmatt was ready for the next turn in his path. He was to write what he calls "a comedy," dealing with the last days of the Roman empire, subtitled "An Unhistorical Comedy." He was to write one of his most charming and important works, *Romulus the Great*.

[54] There are surprisingly positive comments on *The Blind Man*, e.g., by W. Jäggi in *Basler Volksblatt*, Jan. 12, 1948. The critics were perhaps eager to compensate Dürrenmatt for the scandalous reception of *It Is Written*.

|||||||||||||||||||||||||||||||||||||||||||||||||||||||||||||||||||||||||||||||||||||||||||||||

PART TWO
A CREATIVE OUTBURST

|||||||||||||||||||||||||||||||||||||||||||||||||||||||||||||||||||||||||||||||||||||||||||||||

Amazing. A world goes up in flames and you make silly jokes (FP 62).

3 A Judge of His Own Case

ROMULUS THE GREAT

‖‖

With *Romulus the Great* (Romulus der Grosse), we meet a new Friedrich Dürrenmatt. An amazing metamorphosis since *The Blind Man*: not only has he changed from a gloomy religious ponderer into a hilarious comedian, he has also turned into a full-fledged writer for the stage— overnight, as it seems.[1] The first version of *Romulus the Great* had its world première in Basle on April 23, 1949, fifteen months after the previous play. There were, however, difficulties behind Dürrenmatt's apparent ease in learning stagecraft. In 1948 he had devoted much time and energy to a serious play dealing with the history of Babylon and written in the same vein as his first two dramas, only to lose his faith in it and burn the script. On the same day he got the basic idea for *Romulus* as a sudden artistic invention, and wrote it with speed and enjoyment.[2] Out of the ashes of Dürrenmatt's destroyed script arose his fifth play, *An Angel Comes to Babylon*, 1953, the first and only part of a projected trilogy.

An incessant flow of new works, interrupted endeavors, several versions of each completed play for its various productions: Dürrenmatt is at the beginning of his most enterprising creative period. He advances on a wide front. His creative outburst lasts about a decade, from 1948 to 1957, and results in four stage plays, four novels and a long story, most of his remarkable radio plays (which fill a fairly substantial volume), theoretical treatises, theater and book re-

---

[1] This is where Brock-Sulzer places the most conspicuous caesura in Dürrenmatt's career: he turns into a writer of comedies, he becomes a "man of the theater" (*F.D.*, p. 42). Cf. Arnold, *F.D.*, p. 33.

[2] Deschner, "F.D's Experiments with Man," p. 94; Wyrsch, "Die Dürrenmatt-Story," part four, *Schw. Illustrierte*, April 8, 1963, p. 23.

views, and so on. Yet his main target is tragicomedy. At the beginning of this decade Dürrenmatt was a promising local talent; at the end of it he was known all over the world. Not only was he prolific, but he also maintained a high level of distinction. There are not many comparable creative outbursts in the work of other European writers since World War II.

It all begins with *Romulus the Great.* So do our textual headaches. There are four main versions of this play, the first one finished in 1948–49, but not published; the second version is dated 1957—that is, at the end of Dürrenmatt's great period; the latest are from 1961 and 1964. The most significant changes take place between versions one and two, and, as the second version is the one translated into English, I use it as my basic text and compare it with other versions at some points. This procedure makes Dürrenmatt's step forward look even greater than it actually was. The 1957 version takes advantage of his stage experiences during the interim years. These experiences are the fundamental reasons for the new versions. He knows that casting and staging a play in cooperation with a new theater company and in a new social and cultural situation usually leads to a need for changes, and he has been willing to execute these changes himself in the case of major revivals of his plays. Dürrenmatt is one of those flexible playwrights who experiment with and learn from the stage (TS 155–57, 171–72).

"After a lost war one has to write comedies." Guthke quotes this saying by Novalis with the implication that in the chaos that follows a lost war the rigid scale of values presupposed by tragedy does not exist. Comedy and tragicomedy have been the prevalent dramatic genres after both world wars.[3] Dürrenmatt's first "comedy" begins with a desperate and exhausted messenger from the front arriving

[3] Guthke, *Geschichte und Poetik der deutschen Tragikomödie*, p. 361. Dürrenmatt calls his play a "comedy"; as we shall see later on, "tragicomedy" is an apter definition of it.

at the country estate of Romulus, the last Roman Emperor. The messenger is a traditional figure in classical tragedy; in Dürrenmatt's world of comedy he is not even granted admittance. The Teutons are coming, the mighty Roman Empire is falling apart. Spurius Titus Mamma, Captain of Cavalry, finds himself with this urgent news in the middle of "a huge flock of cackling chickens," in a desolate setting with "a few wobbly, half-broken chairs," and with rows of "the venerable busts of Rome's statesmen, thinkers and poets" (FP 47) upon the walls. In the middle of this chaos, age-old court ceremonies are respectfully carried on by two over-dignified chamberlains: "Patriotism which conflicts with cultivated behaviour is undesirable" (FP 48).

This expository scene brings us right into the heart of the matter. Dignity and pomp are contrasted with decay and indolence: "An organization as immense as the Roman Empire simply cannot totally collapse" (FP 48). The first targets for Dürrenmatt's arrows are those who cling to the remnants of the world order soon to be demolished.[4] They include the Empress Julia, a flock of cabinet ministers, and Zeno, the Isaurian, Emperor of the Eastern Roman Empire, now a refugee at Romulus' estate. They do not include Romulus. Zeno is a slave to his court ceremonies and their custodians, the chamberlains; Romulus is a sovereign ruler over *his* chamberlains, over every situation up to the end of the play. He does not obey any formulas of thought; he is surrounded by prisoners of convention. Having just received the news that his Minister of Finance has fled, Romulus sits down at his breakfast table and enters upon a long and detailed discussion on the abilities of his hens to lay eggs. The hens are named according to emperors or statesmen. Romulus has great admiration for Marcus Aurelius, a civilized ruler, and Odoaker, the present chief of the Teutons; he refuses to eat

---

[4] "The breakdown of a world order and the ordered world is the theme of the play. The Roman Empire stands here symbolically for Western civilization" (Peppard, *F.D.*, p. 37). Cf. Deschner, pp. 101–03.

the eggs of Domitian, an energetic Emperor of Rome, and he has just eaten up Caracalla, another effective administrator (K I 15).[5] Raising poultry is the favorite business of the last Emperor of Rome in this unhistorical comedy.

An emperor in a chicken yard: a joke fit for cabaret? Not only that; Dürrenmatt's caprice has a multiple motivation. It helps him furnish his discursive comedy with substitute action: when the cook of the imperial court chases hens for dinner, it is both a joke and a macabre reminder of the danger threatening Romulus and the entire empire. Similarly, the substitute action of hunting for the panther of Claire Zachanassian is to hang over Ill's head like Damocles' sword in *The Visit*.[6] When chatting about his favorites, Romulus reveals to the unwitting audience something about his own attitudes. It is a part of Dürrenmatt's careful total plan that the audience is to remain unaware of Romulus' real character for a long time—not, however, uninterested in the stage action. This is why Dürrenmatt uses all kinds of jokes, verbal and scenic. The audience is misled into thinking that Romulus does not want to hear bad news from the front because of his indolence, because of the corruption prevailing in the court. Yet there is a plan in his chaotic behavior, morality behind his apparent immorality.[7] Romulus is dressed in the motley attire of a clown, to be removed during the second half of the play.

So far, Dürrenmatt had thought in separate pictures. In *It Is Written* the span of his thoughts was at most two consecutive scenes. Or, rather, that was what he was able to control successfully, in a way that guaranteed that his ideas

[5] The translation gives the better-known Caligula (FP 51) instead of Caracalla (A.D. 186–217); though the difference is not great, it is more in line with Romulus' way of thinking that he eats up a cruel and resolute emperor.

[6] The hens and Claire's panther are associated also by Joseph Strelka, *Brecht, Horváth, D.*, p. 130, and by Kienzle in Weber, ed., *Deutsche Literatur seit 1945*, p. 378.

[7] The foreshadowing features in Acts I–II can be utilized by the actor. Ignoring them, Durzak does not find the coordinating factors between Romulus' various roles (*D., Frisch, Weiss*, pp. 61, 66–67).

were conveyed to the audience. If *It Is Written* is an unor-
ganized collection of static scenic images, and *The Blind Man*
just one image stretched out beyond its durability, then
Romulus the Great is the first play by Dürrenmatt consti-
tuting an organic whole with strong interaction between its
various scenic images. *The Blind Man* is over-obvious and
lacking in suspense; *Romulus the Great* is an ideological
thriller, full of twists of plot, full of red herrings swimming
across the stage. Though a discursive comedy, *Romulus the
Great* is not devoid of action. It is Dürrenmatt's first successful synthesis of richness and compactness, of detail and a
controlling basic idea. All minor paradoxes help to build up
a central one: a pacifist as the Emperor of Rome.

The hens of Romulus also assist the playwright in following the Aristotelian unities. The hen is the domestic animal
obeying the unity of time closest of all by laying an egg every
twenty-four hours; in commenting on this, Brock-Sulzer
doubtless presents an observation in accord with the play.[8]
Marcus Aurelius & Co. make it possible for Dürrenmatt to
open acts I and IV of his comedy with a commentary on the
hens, and with Romulus at his breakfast table. At the same
time the hens sketch a picture of everyday life in the shadow
of world history. The result is grotesque incongruity, a parody of ancient Rome as we know it from history books or
from classical or pseudo-classical plays. Dürrenmatt, a victim of scholarophobia, is writing a counter-sketch to the findings of historians. The pomp of the empire is nullified in
several ways: its glorious past is reduced to a collection of
busts, quite disrespectfully sold by Romulus to a Greek art
dealer, its inglorious present is accompanied by the cackling
of the hens, and by news of defeats on the battlefield. The
brightest plan for its future is to marry Romulus' daughter
Rea to Caesar Rupf, a manufacturer of trousers.

---

[8] Brock-Sulzer, p. 48. Frisch calls the cackling hens completely
theatrical metaphors in the playbill of the Zurich première in December 1949. Unity of time with the help of the hens means also parodying the unity, Jauslin remarks (p. 55).

77

Captain Mamma's desperate and unsuccessful efforts to get some sleep after his exhausting ride are a reminder that Rome is fighting a losing war. These repetitions are also another trick à la cabaret. An entirely serious exponent of the same fact is Emilian, Rea's "bridegroom" (FP 81), returning home after three years as a prisoner of war. Rea is rehearsing patriotic lines from Sophocles' *Antigone* under the guidance of her imperial teacher when Emilian suddenly stands in front of her: "Not one of the living, not one of the dead!" (FP 80).[9] According to his own words, Emilian comes "from the world of reality, straight to this farce of an imperial residence" (FP 78). Dishonored and scalped by the Teutons, Emilian is Romulus' only opponent of stature. His sufferings have made him swear resistance to the enemy at any price. He is even ready to sacrifice his beloved Rea for the good of his native country. The plan to marry Rea to Rupf compels Romulus, for the first time, to put aside his mask of indolence and take the initiative. Those favoring resistance are ready to sacrifice an individual for the common good, as the community of Guellen is in *The Visit*. Romulus disagrees.

He does so in the climactic scenic image of Act II. Hopes of saving Rome by the marriage are running high, Zeno recites ecstatic lines from the Byzantian court ceremonies, and an order is given to stop the burning of the imperial archives. As the smoke clears away, Romulus appears surrounded by his court (FP 86). His short scene with Emilian is built up with the help of lighting effects, groupings, and an abrupt change in the general atmosphere of the act. Though Dürrenmatt worked on the scene even after version two, and gave Emilian more concrete arguments, it is Romulus who says the last word in the scenic image, and does so with the full authority of a ruler: "The Emperor will not permit this marriage. . . . The Emperor knows what he is

---

[9] In the third version Emilian appears on Rea's line "For see, I am betrothed to Acheron" (FP 79; K I 42). Rea is betrothed either to a man half dead or to a tributary of the river in Hades.

doing when he throws his empire to the flames, when he lets fall what must break, when he grinds under foot what is doomed." And off he goes, "scattering chicken feed," to the impotent fury of Emilian: "Down with the Emperor!" (FP 88).

As a contrast to this scene acted in public, Act III begins with a series of intimate scenes. They take place in Romulus' bedroom, near midnight, with two candelabras as the only sources of light. In a farewell scene with his empress Julia, Romulus reveals that he married her only to become the Emperor of Rome. During his reign he has done nothing to prevent his empire from collapsing, because he doubts the necessity of Rome's existence: "Our state has become a world empire, an institution officially engaged in murder, plunder, suppression, and oppressive taxation at the expense of other people—until I came along" (FP 94). When Julia accuses Romulus of being Rome's traitor, Romulus gives a name to his secret role: "No, Rome's judge" (FP 95).

In his second farewell scene Romulus encounters Rea, who is still eager to sacrifice herself for Rome: "My country, above all."

ROMULUS: No, one should never love [one's country] as much as one loves other human beings. . . . Every state calls itself "country," or "nation," when it is about to commit murder (FP 96–97).

We meet here Dürrenmatt's very Swiss suspicion of modern giant states, of states using more emotional names for themselves only as propaganda weapons (cf. Introduction, pp. 12–13 above). And we meet two variations of Dürrenmatt's attitude to marriage and love. The marriage between Julia and Romulus, based only on their ambitions, has been "horrible" (FP 92); this theme, only touched here, was to be more fully developed in *The Marriage of Mr. Mississippi*, Dürrenmatt's next play.[10] Rea's and Emilian's love story

[10] Brock-Sulzer, p. 50, remarks on this.

is not given emphatic treatment, though their first meeting in the play is a delicately written scene. As a whole, Dürrenmatt is quite an unerotic writer. He is interested in love only as an axis for his plots.[11] Romulus is no Romeo.

In the next scene Romulus grows to his full stature. The process of removing the attire of the clown, begun at the end of Act II, is now completed. Paradoxically enough, a deepening of Romulus' characterization is achieved after a farcical sequence parodying the murder scene in Shakespeare's *Julius Caesar*. A serious discussion between Romulus and Emilian is interrupted by a group of murderers emerging from all possible hiding places on the stage—from the wardrobes and from under the couches and beds. Caesar's classic ejaculation "Et tu, Brute?" is rendered as "You, too, Cook?" (FP 102). Dürrenmatt turns his discursive comedy into a horror farce—only for a moment, however. Dressed in his imperial toga and wreath, surrounded by a circle of his cabinet ministers and friends with daggers in their hands, Romulus is ready to make his great speech, in his private bedchamber now turned into a political arena:

I didn't betray my empire; Rome betrayed herself. Rome knew the truth but chose violence. Rome knew humaneness but chose tyranny. Rome doubly demeaned herself: before her own people and before the other nations in her power. You are standing before an invisible throne, Emilian; before the throne of all the Roman Emperors, of whom I am the last. Shall I touch your eyes that you may see this throne, this pyramid of skulls down whose steps cascade rivers of blood in endless waterfalls, generating Rome's power? . . . Rome has grown weak, a tottering old hag, but her guilt has not been expiated and her crimes not erased. . . . The Teutons are coming; we have spilled the stranger's blood; we must now pay back with our own. . . . Do we still have the right to be more than victims? (FP 104–05).

[11] Cf. Philipp Wolff-Windegg, *Basler Nachrichten*, April 13, 1964.

This is a tense scenic image. Tense because of the thriller-like situation; tense because Romulus' words are charged with thematic significance. It forms a pregnant moment in the constant flow of stage action, a moment full of outer or 'plotty' tension—and inner, thematic tension. Moreover, Dürrenmatt's language employs effective, unadorned rhetoric. So does his stage language. The lonely figure of Romulus, the night lighting, the circle of conspirators, the tension carefully built up toward this climactic moment: Dürrenmatt is in control of his scenic means of expression; he knows how to coordinate them. The stage picture and the dialogue do not conflict. Dürrenmatt the painter and Dürrenmatt the writer have merged in Dürrenmatt the dramatist. Or in Dürrenmatt the tragicomedian: the tone of the scenic image is not only deeply serious, it is also gently mocking, because of its parodical elements. Dürrenmatt has constructed a stratified, self-contradictory scenic image.

The tension is heightened and relieved. In spite of Romulus' rhetoric, Emilian gives the sign to the conspirators by shouting "Long live Rome!" The daggers are drawn—then "a horrifying cry of fright" interrupts the murder scene before our Caesar is stabbed to death: "The Teutons are coming!" (FP 105). The brave murderers fly in panic; only Romulus stays. It turns out that the cry is a false alarm, and Romulus closes the act with a wry remark to his chamberlain: "When the Teutons arrive, let them come in" (FP 106).

Interrupting murder at the last moment: a coup de théâtre? Of course; yet this twist is motivated by its location in the action of the play. Our interest in Romulus has been awakened during Act III from a new angle; we are itching with curiosity. How will our clown, now turned into a political philosopher, cope with the Teutons? The playwright cannot have another trick up his sleeve, can he?

He can, and it appears in the second version of the play. When revising the script in 1957, Dürrenmatt added yet another somersault of thought to his thriller. At the beginning of Act IV Romulus takes things very calmly; he is the only one who has not fled. His presence of mind has been interpreted in various ways, as an expression of his stoic inclinations, or as something typical not only of this imperial chicken farmer but also of the peasants from the Berne region, Dürrenmatt's native canton.[12] Romulus eats his last breakfast, a ritualistic meal before execution.[13] Food is served on a cheap tin plate and a cracked bowl: "Never mind. Indeed, perhaps these old dishes are more fitting for my last meal" (FP 109). Two favorite rituals of Dürrenmatt's seem to follow one another: meal and execution.

The entrance of the first Teuton has been awaited with terror throughout the play. When he finally enters, "there is nothing about him except his trousers that is barbarian. He looks at the room as if he were walking through a museum, and indeed, makes notes now and then on a small pad" (FP 111). He is Odoaker, ruler of the Teutons. His favorite pastime: raising poultry. "I am a peasant and I hate war. I sought a human way of life not to be found in the primeval Teutonic forests. I found it in you, Emperor Romulus" (FP 116). Instead of power politics, these two talk about trousers, about wine and beer, and about breeding chickens. At first, tension is once again relieved by laughter. Deadly enemies are bosom friends. Then anxiety darkens the atmosphere of this hearty encounter.

Odoaker wants to submit his nation to Romulus, "the only man who knows how to rule this world" (FP 117). If Romulus refuses, the world will fall to Odoaker's nephew Theodoric, a personification of the warlike virtues of the Teutons—or of the Hitler Youth. "He is ruining my people with his way of life," Odoaker complains. "He never touches girls, drinks nothing but water, and sleeps on the bare ground" (FP 115). The two rulers find themselves in a vicious circle, not to be broken by any rash acts. Romulus has miscast himself in the role of Rome's judge: "I took it

[12] Jenny, *F.D.*, p. 39, Poser in Geissler (ed.), *Zur Interpretation des modernen Dramas*, p. 83, and Bänziger, p. 139.
[13] Deschner, p. 143.

upon myself to be Rome's judge, because I was ready to die. I asked of my country this enormous sacrifice because I, myself, was willing to be sacrificed" (FP 116). Instead of sacrificing himself to Rome's guilt, Romulus "has sacrificed Rome to himself."[14] His latest victims include his wife and daughter, Emilian, and the cabinet ministers, all drowned during their flight to Sicily. Romulus has been afraid of Rome's past, Odoaker of Germania's future; now they have to state: "Reality has put our ideas right" (FP 119).

Romulus, this charming, humane, and courageous pacifist, is in fact a megalomaniac, a kinsman of Knipperdollinck or of the Duke. Like them, he sacrifices those closest to him to his idée fixe;[15] more clearly than the earlier characters, he is put right by reality. Unlike his predecessors in Dürren-matt's gallery of characters, Romulus is ready to resign to the sentence passed on him by unfathomable reality. After a crisis, after several plans made together with Odoaker to break their common vicious circle, Romulus is ready to accept retirement as his final destiny, even if for him it is the worst "of all possible fates" (FP 118). For Dürrenmatt, Romulus is "a dangerous fellow, a man determined to die," "a human being who proceeds with the utmost firmness and lack of consideration for others. . . . His tragedy lies in the comedy of his end; instead of a sacrificial death he has earned for himself retirement. But then—and this alone is what makes him great—he has the wisdom and the insight to accept his fate" (FP 123).

All there is for the unwilling Odoaker to do is to rule over the Teutons and Romans—until he is killed by Theodoric. The years of his reign will be forgotten in world history, yet "they will be among the happiest this confused world has ever lived through." So these two imperial chicken farmers decide to play their comedy "once more and for the last

14 Waldmann, "Dürrenmatts paradoxes Theater," *Wirkendes Wort*, *14*, 1 (1964), p. 25.

15 Wellwarth, "F.D. and Max Frisch," *The Tulane Drama Review*, *6*, 3 (March, 1962), p. 19.

time" (FP 119). Pacifism is possible only in "anti-history," only outside the official record of historians, in the world of a playwright's imagination; this is one of the final messages of this comedy, subtitled in German "ungeschichtlich" ("unhistorical"). With a group of Teutons standing at attention, in a scenic image acted in public and closing this comedy dealing with the users and use of public power, Romulus resigns in favor of Odoaker; the translation suggests that he plays with a bubble. As happens so often in Dürrenmatt, when poetry is demanded by the stage situation, Romulus' farewell speech is poetry of the stars:

> The Emperor is dissolving his Empire. Look, all of you, once more upon this tinted globe, this dream of a great empire, floating in space, driven by the slightest breath of my lips. Yes, look once more upon these far-flung lands encircling the blue sea with its dancing dolphins, these rich provinces golden with wheat, these teeming cities overflowing with life; yes, this empire once was a sun warming mankind, but at its zenith it scorched the world; now it is a harmless bubble and in the hands of the Emperor it dissolves into nothing (FP 120).

Romulus the Great has been called, quite correctly, Dürrenmatt's "most Shavian play . . . clever, witty, graceful, full of fine repartee and irony."[16] Like Shaw in so many of his plays, Dürrenmatt is hunting and killing the mythical and pathetic stories of world history.[17] In so doing he uses the technique of a mock-serious thriller, twisted so that everything is turned upside down at regular intervals. During the action of the play the clown Romulus turns out to be "a wise judge over the world"—until the final twist proves

[16] Klarmann, "F.D. and the Tragic Sense of Comedy," *The Tulane Drama Review*, *4*, 4 (May 1960), pp. 87–88; cf. Prang, *Geschichte des Lustspiels*, p. 354, and Wellwarth, pp. 17–18.
[17] Drese, "F.D.," *Eckart*, *28*, 4 (1959), p. 387. Margret Eifler connects the play with *Marius und Sulla* by Christian Dietrich Grabbe: "Romulus as a parodied Sulla" (Knapp, ed., *F.D.*, pp. 46–47).

this wise judge to be, after all, a clown.[18] When piloting his ship along the winding fairway into the harbor, Dürrenmatt introduces or implies several concepts which were to play focal roles in his later practice and theory as a tragicomedian.

These concepts are "absurd," "chance," and "the worst possible turn." Both Romulus and Odoaker find themselves in an absurd situation, as the calculations on which they have based their entire line of action prove to be wrong. Romulus' lifelong ambition has been to be a judge of his own case, the case of the other nations of antiquity versus the empire of Rome. He has condemned to death both the empire and himself. On the other hand, Odoaker has given in to his belligerent nephew and started the war against Rome only to submit his Teutons to Romulus, an avowed pacifist. Both find themselves in an utterly absurd situation. Romulus has to beg Odoaker to kill him (FP 117)—yet this is only a panic reaction, for killing Romulus would not deter Theodoric from entering into power, it would only smooth his path. The situation questions man's ability to reason: "man's every planned, that is sensible, line of action, must fail."[19]

This absurd situation is brought about by chance. It was pure chance, not included in Romulus' calculations, that his adversary would also be a chicken farmer and a pacifist. Nor did Odoaker suppose that his adversary would expect him to act the role of executioner. Dürrenmatt has called chance an ambiguous concept, open to several interpretations. One of his own definitions is that chance is "what limits man."[20] It also drives Dürrenmatt's plots into their "worst possible turn" (TS 193). This is stated in the oft-quoted point 4 in Dürrenmatt's afterthoughts, or "Twenty-one Points," to *The Physicists*.

Retirement is for Romulus, as mentioned above, the worst

[18] Syberberg, "Zum Drama F.Ds," p. 70.
[19] Waldmann, p. 29.
[20] Deschner, p. 120, footnote 45; cf. all of pp. 119–22.

"of all possible fates." Yet he resigns himself to it, not as a proud hero of tragedy, but as a humble hero of modern tragicomedy. Dürrenmatt's protagonists, both on the stage and in the novels, are over and over again brought to a breaking-point, where they have to admit that human reason is not in control over this world of ours. A genuine tragicomedian, Dürrenmatt is questioning the existence of a world order. "The absolute grotesque," as the problem of the sense or senselessness of our lives, can be seen behind the constellation of *Romulus the Great*. There is an absurd, incalculable element in life, there is chance as a limit to man. Dürrenmatt needs this limit; his own relation to chance is ambiguous. The positive side of chance is that it means a gap in the chain of logic, and a weapon to fight formulas with. Whether for good or bad, chance has a role on Dürrenmatt's stage. The train may rush into a vacuum, the ruler of the Teutons may prove to resemble a peace-loving Swiss farmer. Not to despair in the absurd situations caused by chance, not to give in when facing the worst possible turn in their fate, is the solution for Dürrenmatt's "men of courage."[21] Romulus and Odoaker are men of courage. In *Romulus the Great* there is courage in the middle of quasi-courageous attitudes, and real heroism behind the masks of clowning and mockheroism. There is a kind of world order re-established in Romulus' and Odoaker's minds—an order including the possibility of blind and absurd chance.

The paradoxical close of *Romulus the Great* corresponds to Dürrenmatt's basic views. A tragic, self-sacrificing end would be a relief; *Romulus* is "an obstructed tragedy." "Instead of a terrible end," there is "an endless terror."[22] Nonheroic retirement is both in harmony with Romulus' nonheroic outer behavior and in tragic conflict "with his inner heroism." Romulus emerges "as neither a positive nor a nega-

[21] Syberberg, p. 80; Jacob Steiner, "Die Komödie Dürrenmatts," *Der Deutschunterricht*, *15*, 6 (Dec. 1963), pp. 87–88. Madler denies that Romulus is a "man of courage"; Madler's arguments are not quite convincing ("Ds mutiger Mensch," *Hochland*, *62*, 1, pp. 45–46).

[22] Brock-Sulzer, p. 54.

tive hero, but as a tragicomic figure who engages the spectator's sympathy to the same degree that he deserves condemnation."[23] *Romulus the Great*, though subtitled "a comedy," was in fact reshaped into a tragicomedy in 1957, after Dürrenmatt had formulated his practice and theory as a tragicomedian, in *The Visit* and in *Problems of the Theater*. The change was fundamental; it affected not only the plot of the play.

The most careful comparison of the various versions of *Romulus* has been published by Jauslin. The dialogue was tightened; in addition to less remarkable changes concerning Zeno's two chamberlains and Emilian's speeches at the end of Act II, the end of the play was made "totally different." The first Romulus wins the Teutons to his side by granting them various offices and honors in the service of Rome, as soon as they appear on the stage.[24] He accepts retirement quite happily, as a full-fledged character in comedy would. Romulus the Second is the protagonist of a tragicomedy, with a streak of darker color in his portrait.

Romulus, whether he moves in the world of comedy or in that of tragicomedy, is a stage personification of Dürrenmatt's polemical talents. He is an invincible debater, formulating his arguments with wit and Shavian splendor. He is also a solitary figure, like the Duke or the lonely heroes of Dürrenmatt's short stories; yet he is firmly rooted in his own sphere, the field of political tension. His role is a rewarding one; playing the clown, he can always bring his opponents down to earth. When his Minister of War speaks of "total mobilization," the phrase is an easy target for Romulus: "Purely stylistically, I do not like that" (FP 64). Sometimes his lines reach the status of *bons mots*:

ZENO: We must save our culture.
ROMULUS: Why? Is culture something anyone can save? (FP 61).

[23] Peppard, pp. 38–39, 43. Cf. Syberberg, p. 108.
[24] Jauslin, pp. 46–55; cf. Jenny, p. 36.

In the two focal scenic images of the play, Romulus leaves his "cool, sober, ironical" way of speaking, and achieves a genuinely rhetorical effect. His self-defensive answer to the conspirators in Act III, quoted above, proceeds through a series of antitheses, as a variation of the language of the Bible; his farewell speech, also quoted, rises to the level of poetry with its metaphors.[25] These speeches resemble Dürrenmatt's earlier prose style, and provide the only evidence of his old inclination to write "word arias."[26]

Around Romulus, the figures of the play are, moreover, characterized by their way of speaking. This is a remarkable step forward for Dürrenmatt as a playwright. He is now achieving by means of dialogue and action what he tried to do with over-long monologues in his previous plays.[27] The various strata in the dialogue have been analyzed by Syberberg: there are elements of slang, of the language of the business world, and of the conversational and bureaucratic language of the court. When these strata are placed side by side, when the discussion changes from one level to another, the results can be either comic or serious.[28] Dürrenmatt is eager to show the hollowness of late Roman phraseology, which is associated with the inflation of phrases during Nazi times in Hans Zbinden's essay published in Dürrenmatt's formative year, 1943.[29] There are also many anachronisms, now handled with more discretion than in *It Is Written*.

[25] Poser, pp. 84, 86–87.

[26] Brock-Sulzer has a remark on this in her review in *Die Tat*, Dec. 14, 1949.

[27] Arnold, p. 33; Brock-Sulzer, *Dürrenmatt in unserer Zeit*, p. 25.

[28] Syberberg, pp. 81–82, 86.

[29] Zbinden wrote in 1943: "We are today witnesses to such a depreciation, to such a degradation of the word, that there are not many examples of it in the history of various cultures. The closest parallels are perhaps to be found in the verbosity of the Alexandrian age or in the bombastic language of late Roman emperors." Is this one of the seeds of *Romulus*? On the level of an unconscious impression of memory? In Dürrenmatt's play the picture of a late Roman emperor is completed with Zeno, a representative of Byzantine culture, which is a continuation of the Alexandrian tradition. Zbinden's essay has been republished in Bruno Mariacher and Friedrich Witsch (eds.), *Bestand und Versuch*, 1964, pp. 840–47.

A manufacturer of trousers in Roman antiquity is, of course, a walking anachronism; he speaks in the manner of a typical self-made man: "Business is business" (FP 53). On a great many occasions, Dürrenmatt shoots his arrows at clearly recognizable targets in Germany: if the Teutons "remain in Germania, they will civilize themselves and that will be ghastly" (FP 53). Or, to take an example from recent times, from Nazi jargon: "Our strategic position grows more favourable . . . from defeat to defeat" (FP 75).[30]

There is another movement in the dimension of time when Rea recites *Antigone*. The periods mixed up are not modern times and antiquity, but Greek and Roman antiquity. The empires of Romulus and Zeno are both dying out, and, as the chamberlain Pyramus points out, "the darkness of the Middle Ages" (FP 108) is about to fall on the world. Sophocles' lines serve Dürrenmatt's parodical aims: on the eve of a real world catastrophe, people do not speak in neatly tailored verse. To appreciate these parodical details, the audiences must be conscious of a common European cultural heritage. More easy-going cabaret tricks are served up by Dürrenmatt as combinations of verbal and scenic jokes: "Now I have stepped on another egg! Isn't there anything here but chickens?" (FP 73).

The Blind Man was abstract and lacked action; *Romulus* is concrete and full of action. Part of the action is woven around the felicitous invention of the hens, part around other caprices. Mamma, the sleepless messenger, is such a caprice. The general atmosphere of decay is accentuated by the collection of busts in the background. In Act II, after Romulus has sold everything to his Antique Dealer, porters keep carrying the busts away, as a stream of background action to be utilized according to the judgment of the stage director. At the beginning of Act IV, there is only one bust left, that of Romulus, the first King of Rome: a long perspective in time is opened with this simple means of expression. As a whole, the setting of the play is not conspicuous, yet it helps to concretize the themes of the play. Since *It Is Written*

[30] Cf. Deschner, p. 101.

Dürrenmatt has learnt to coordinate his ideas about the setting with the rest of the play.

When turning his plentiful ideas into an abundance of stage-filling action, Dürrenmatt uses some familiar scenic units, such as doubling his figures. There are two emperors, both with two chamberlains, there are two anachronistic businessmen. Repetitions are employed for comic effect, for example in the repeated entrance of the murderers in Act III.[31] With an amazingly sure hand, Dürrenmatt keeps these plentiful ideas together: "an organized, carefully calculated action is placed against a background of cackling hens, people rushing in and out, climbing . . . from under beds, and antique salesmen carrying away the flotsam of an over-ripe empire."[32] Dürrenmatt never loses sight of his aim: all details help him to build up a play with a rich dramatic texture—and a play in which the themes are firmly gathered together in the scenic images described above. Dürrenmatt's abundance is turned to advantage for the first time; he succeeds in combining the universal implications of his theme with a tight total structure and with an improvising, cabaret-like tone.[33] The result is one of Dürrenmatt's very best stage plays, comparable with *The Visit* and *The Physicists*.[34]

[31] Wolff-Windegg, loc. cit.
[32] Peppard, p. 33; ibid., p. 40: "Much of the slapstick comedy . . . is visual and forms an essential part of the setting and scenery."
[33] After the success of the first two versions (see, e.g., Welti, *Neue Zürcher Zeitung*, Dec. 12, 1949), the subsequent ones have fared surprisingly badly with the critics. Each critic has his own personal view of how to handle the precarious balance between farce and a play of ideas (Wolff-Windegg, loc. cit.; Manuel Isler, *National-Zeitung*, April 14, 1964; Günther Rühle, *Frankfurter Allgemeine*, March 8, 1965). Gore Vidal's adaptation of *Romulus* opened in New York in January, 1962; according to the adapter, Dürrenmatt "had neglected to dramatize his situation" ("Comment: Turn left," *Esquire*, May, 1962). What Vidal did to dramatize the situation is rejected by John Simon: "Excised . . . was any sign of Dürrenmatt's sturdy masculinity of approach" (*The Hudson Review*, *15*, 2, Summer 1962, pp. 264–65).
[34] Brecht liked *Romulus* but was not permitted to produce it (Esslin, *Brief Chronicles*, p. 123).

With *Romulus the Great*, Dürrenmatt completed a kind of trilogy. His first three historical plays are all grotesque visions against the background of warfare. From this point of view, Dürrenmatt can be seen as an exponent of postwar skepticism, perhaps with a touch of disappointment because of the cold war just beginning.[35] The arrival of the Teutons does not change anything. Theodoric, not Romulus, has been called "Great" by the historians. Dürrenmatt not only describes the devastation of human and material values caused by the war, he also criticizes the wartime ideals of resistance at any price and of personal sacrifices demanded by one's native country.[36] He does so more clearly than before in his third play, in which religious problems are retreating from the center of the stage, and his comic talent is given free space to move. When *Romulus the Great* was brought over to Germany as the first Swiss theater visit since the war, the defeatism of its hero caused a shock to spectators and critics.[37] "The Man Outside," a suffering soldier returning from the front, was the loser in Dürrenmatt's play.

Yet Dürrenmatt saw both sides of the coin. He gave valid arguments to both Emilian and Romulus, and described their conflict as an insoluble one. In an interesting passage in his memorial speech on Ginsberg, Dürrenmatt reminisces about the time he was writing *Romulus* and saw Ginsberg as Hamlet in a production directed by Horwitz. Like Hamlet, Romulus faces the problem of judging an unjust world, and what Dürrenmatt learnt from Ginsberg's Hamlet was that it is not necessarily the playwright's business to solve the universal problem of a just world order, or to solve any problems at all. It is enough for a playwright to describe a conflict, to see

[35] Henning Rischbieter sees the play primarily as a criticism of attitudes prompted by the cold war, neglecting its parallels with Hitler's Germany (Karlheinz Braun, ed., *Deutsches Theater der Gegenwart*, I, pp. 631–32).

[36] Dürrenmatt disagrees with the Swiss wartime "mental self-defense" and its remnants, as is pointed out by Marti, *Die Schweiz und ihre Schriftsteller*, pp. 28–29, 47–48.

[37] Wyrsch, "Die Dürrenmatt-Story," part four, April 8, 1963.

91

and show that man lives in a world full of conflicts (TS 206-08). Romulus certainly does.[38] It is through steps like this that Dürrenmatt arrives at his tragicomic vision. It is through the Reformation, the Thirty Years War, and a third endgame, played at the close of the Roman Empire, that Dürrenmatt approaches his own age. Having rid himself of his most urgent need to describe World War II in the disguise of history, he is now ready to face the postwar world, in a new variation of his world theater.

[38] Jan Kott has written an imaginative piece of criticism on *Romulus*, taking into account all possible reactions to the approaching catastrophy. His conclusion is that "there are situations in which one can choose only between grotesque attitudes, for other attitudes have not been provided by the scenario." Disillusionment caused by recent historical events may be a partial explanation of Dürrenmatt's early and lasting popularity in Poland. Kott's essay was written in 1959, republished in *Theatre Notebook 1947–1967*, London, 1968. Cf. Syberberg, p. 76.

4 Don Quixote in a Broken Mirror

THE MARRIAGE OF MR. MISSISSIPPI

||||||||||||||||||||||||||||||||||||||||||||||||||||||||||||||||||||||||||||||||||||||||||

When the Swiss production of *Romulus the Great* visited Germany its audience included Hans Schweikart, director of the Münchener Kammerspiele. A few years later Schweikart was to help Dürrenmatt several steps forward toward a real international breakthrough by presenting three of his plays for the first time. This happened in Munich between March, 1952, and December, 1953, and the plays produced were *The Marriage of Mr. Mississippi* (Die Ehe des Herrn Mississippi), *Nocturnal Conversation with a Despised Person* (stage adaptation of a radio play), and *An Angel Comes to Babylon*. It was of special significance for Dürrenmatt that Schweikart had confidence in *Mississippi*, a script rejected by Dürrenmatt's closest friends and collaborators in the Swiss theater.[1] From now on, he had direct connections with the theater in Germany.

The collaboration with Schweikart resulted in the first published version of *Mississippi*. The second or 1957 version is included both in *Four Plays* and in *Komödien I*; it is our basic text. There is a third version, published together with the film script, also by Dürrenmatt, in 1961. In 1969, twenty years after he had started working on the project, Dürrenmatt still planned a new production of the play in Basle; he had to give up this idea when he resigned from his position as dramaturge.[2] *Mississippi* is a dear and misshapen child.

Here you have its first cry, the opening moments of stage action:

[1] Wyrsch, part four, *Schweizer Illustrierte*, April 8, 1963, pp. 24–25; Jauslin, *F.D.*, p. 17.

[2] Melchinger, "Ein Kommentar," *Theater heute*, 10, 12 (Dec. 1969), p. 34. Dürrenmatt directed the play in Berne in 1954; its second version was directed in Zurich by Leopold Lindtberg in 1957.

THE FIRST OF THE THREE IN RAINCOATS: You have been condemned to death, Saint-Claude. Put your hands behind your head.

(SAINT-CLAUDE *obeys.*)

Go and stand between the windows.

(SAINT-CLAUDE *obeys.*)

Turn your face to the wall. That's the simplest way to die.

(SAINT-CLAUDE *turns his face to the wall. The ringing [of the church bells] dies away. A shot.* . .) (FP 130).

This is Dürrenmatt's idea of how to open a comedy—a very Dürrenmattian comedy, of course. He has looked at the turmoils of the recent European past through the lens of history. Now he creates distance from his subject-matter by using a theatricalistic machinery and shrill comic overtones. Saint-Claude does not even fall down when shot to death. He just keeps standing and starts describing the route of the bullet through his shoulder blades and heart: "My death, which you have just witnessed . . . really takes place at the end of the play. . . . But for what I might call therapeutic reasons we have shifted my murder to the beginning; this enables us to get one of the worst scenes over quickly" (FP 131). We are thus back at the epic stage techniques of *It Is Written*. The characters step out of their roles and start commenting on the action, addressing the audience directly. They even resort to the old Dürrenmattian mannerism of painting with words what is simultaneously seen on the stage.

An effort is made to achieve a kind of general relevance through the setting. This is what Dürrenmatt achieved in *Romulus* by means of his choice of period and by means of the entire action of the play. Instead of describing the fall of an empire the playwright now concentrates on destroying pieces of furniture. They are carefully chosen to build up a museum of European history. There are "Louis Quatorze chairs" and a "Louis Quinze" table, there is a plaster Venus and a Gothic grandfather clock, there are both southern and northern views opening from the windows of Dürrenmatt's

94

living room. Busts and pictures descend from above and disappear again: Dürrenmatt's bust phase, begun in *Romulus*, is not yet finished. In the center of the stage there "stands a round Biedermeier coffee table; this is really the main character in the play, upon which all the action centres, and the production should make this clear" (FP 129–30).

These stage directions belong to the second version of the play, not as fantastic as the first, or Schweikart, version. Dürrenmatt no longer demands that the house look as if it were inhabited by giants at the top, by dwarfs at the bottom.[3] "The unreal and fantastic may safely be left to the text, to the author" (FP 205), he remarks in his note, warning against the dangers of over-abstraction. We can thus concentrate on the action revolving around that Biedermeier table and on the dialogue spoken while the violent stage events shatter this neatly arranged miniature of the common European cultural heritage.[4] "All the world is a room," Dürrenmatt says. "Inhabited by fanatics," he adds.

There is, first of all, Florestan Mississippi himself, a Public Prosecutor in favor of the Law of Moses. Anastasia, a femme fatale, favors nothing but her own pleasure. Frédéric René Saint-Claude, shot to death in such a pleasant way, is a childhood friend of Mississippi's; their divergent careers began in the same gutter. Mississippi found and read the Bible and was converted; so was Saint-Claude after having read *Das Kapital* by Karl Marx. When the two meet again during the action of the play, Mississippi is the Public Prosecutor with more than two hundred death sentences to his credit in an undefined European country, and Saint-Claude is a Cominform agent determined to provoke a communist revolution

---

[3] Leland R. Phelps, "D's *Die Ehe des Herrn Mississippi*," *Modern Drama*, 8, 2 (Sept. 1965), p. 158, and Jenny, *F.D.*, pp. 113–14; cf. Bänziger, *Frisch und D.*, p. 142, Brock-Sulzer, *F.D.*, p. 60, and Jauslin, *F.D.*, p. 57.

[4] Jenny, p. 40, Wellwarth, "F.D. and Max Frisch," *TDR*, 6, 3 (March 1962), p. 20, Diller, "D's Use of the Stage," *Symposium*, 20, 3 (Fall 1966), pp. 201–02, and Bänziger, p. 143.

in the same country. The complicated action of the play also involves Diego, a Minister of Justice always ready to compromise for the good of the changing political situation, and Count Bodo von Übelohe-Zabernsee, an unhappy idealist and Don Quixote, in love with mankind. According to a monologue of Bodo's, Dürrenmatt did not create these characters light-heartedly, but was "concerned to investigate what happens when certain ideas collide with people who really take them seriously and strive . . . with insane fervour and an insatiable greed for perfection to put them into effect" (FP 162). What happens is told in a series of violent scenes.

The pomposity of the above reflects the general quality of the dialogue. There are echoes from Dürrenmatt's early prose in the diction and vocabulary of the play. Samples taken from one page only include phrases like "monstrous," "unimaginable suffering," "an awful destiny," "our mutual torment," or "dreadful" (FP 135). The playwright employs them, no doubt, with his tongue in his cheek, as a mock-serious and parodical alienation effect.[5] Mississippi & Co. are not only fanatics; they are caricatures of fanatics, with their extreme and uncombinable views on how to improve our world. Yet their inflated expressions lead to monotony and over-obviousness. Dürrenmatt seems to enjoy himself while listening to these parodical overtones; it is doubtful whether the spectators take a similar delight in them. Parody is a good spice but a poor dish. In *Mississippi* comedy rests on a shallower basis than in *Romulus*—on overstatements in dialogue and characterization, on Dürrenmatt's theatricalistic tricks, and on sudden reversals in the plot.

Jauslin has described the confusing shifts between Bodo's role as a stage character and as a speaker addressing the audience directly. He draws the conclusion that Dürrenmatt reveals not only his characters but the theater itself, parodying

---

[5] "The constant use of hyperbole . . . helps to underline the hollowness of the convictions behind the words" (Peppard, p. 47). Cf. Brock-Sulzer, p. 59: a confession of love of these parodical "big words in this play."

the theatricalistic machinery he is employing, his own scenic means of expression.[6] This feature is intimately bound up with the twisted plot line of the play.

The first line of development is straight—for a while. After the theatricalistic opening ceremonies we meet Mr. Mississippi in Anastasia's living room; he introduces himself to her as the Public Prosecutor investigating the sudden death of her husband. Her nervous reactions build up a suspicion in the minds of the spectators; she even "drops her coffee cup in terror" (FP 135). We are following a scene from a realistic play, with one of the actors gaining the upper hand and forcing his antagonist against the wall; there are sinister overtones à la Ibsen or Strindberg. The formal, somewhat stiff conversation leads to a series of small revelations climaxing in a moment in which the woman is dumbfounded when Mississippi formulates a direct accusation of murder; she denies the accusation, yet the audience cannot help knowing the truth now. Three tense moments, three scenic images, follow close on one another: the moment of Anastasia's confession to the murder, carefully prepared by the playwright, then Mississippi's proposal of marriage to her, totally unprepared for—and *his* confession. Both have murdered their spouses. Dürrenmatt is having fun and games with his plot; he is out-Strindberging Strindberg.

In the sequence described above there are three total reversals of the plot within two pages, or a few minutes of stage action. The most surprising of these is doubtless Mississippi's proposal: having just squeezed a confession of murder from his victim, our prosecutor, "correct as always" (FP 133), goes on to ask for her hand. "It is like pulling a string that brings the whole structure tumbling down, jerking everyone . . . back to a startled and shocked attention."[7]

[6] Jauslin, pp. 69–72; Wellwarth states that "it seems as if Dürrenmatt is stepping aside and mocking his characters, the audience and— necessarily—himself as well" (p. 27).

[7] Wellwarth, *The Theater of Protest and Paradox*, p. 140; the proposal scene and several others are mentioned as examples of how Dürrenmatt employs "this enormously effective" surprise technique.

The marriage of Mr. Mississippi is not intended to be bliss; it is punishment, "hell for both parties," and "a triumph of justice" (FP 146). Confronted with Mississippi's threat to expose her crime, Anastasia can only consent. As a continual penitence she is to watch every execution driven through by her prosecutor-husband. During five years of married life she establishes herself as the Angel of the Prisons, to the complete satisfaction of Mississippi, brilliantly confirming his "thesis that strict laws strictly obeyed are alone capable of making man a better, nay a higher being" (FP 149). Dürrenmatt is experimenting with his characters, Mississippi with his marriage.

Dürrenmatt has explained this strange union as a variation of the imperial liaison in *Romulus the Great* (TS 243). There is a difference in the motivation of the murders: Anastasia kills her first husband in a fit of jealousy, Mississippi his first wife as a just punishment for her infidelity, according to him. He is firmly determined to bring back the Law of Moses, because the present laws are "miserably degenerated," so that "only idealists out of touch with reality can still imagine that the cheque paid by Justice is covered" (FP 144). Mississippi is "a rigid, merciless Puritan, punitive, and . . . given to quantitative standards of moral improvement." His conception of guilt and penance leads to "a magnificent parody of tragic sensibility and action" in the proposal scene.[8] What is needed to make Mississippi a parodical figure later is proof positive that he has not been able to educate Anastasia into becoming "a higher being." Toward the end of the play it becomes a decisive question whether Anastasia has been faithful to her husband or not.

She has not, of course. Anastasia is the mistress of every male character in the play. Her power to attract men is the only coordinating factor in this "confused and tangled melodrama deliberately presented out of its temporal and causal

[8] Heilman, "Tragic Elements in a Duerrenmatt Comedy," *Modern Drama*, *10*, 1 (May 1967), pp. 15–16.

sequence."[9] Dürrenmatt is practicing a dramaturgy of caprice and freedom; he is giving in to his sudden artistic inventions, and constructing a play without a preconceived total plan. As he puts it himself, he is writing at random (TS 240). The result is that the characters are shuffled back and forth according to the demands of the changing situations. Each of the men suffers from an irresistible passion for Anastasia, and each is planning to elope with her. The action is not motivated by psychological or, indeed, any other probabilities. Dürrenmatt even marshals a communist revolution only to build up more twists in his twisted plot, and lets his Mississippi be confined in a mental hospital for a while. In *Romulus the Great* the many turns of the plot led to a bravura performance; now there is an over-indulgence in them, e.g., in the expository scene. On one hand, this leads to parody;[10] on the other, to hollow scenic images not sustained by themes significant enough. There are lots of moments tense only because of their outer, or 'plotty' tension.

There is little point in summarizing the entire action of the play; it would be more profitable to concentrate on the role of Bodo and on the last moments of the stage action. The Count, an unlucky aristocrat and humanitarian founder of hospitals, is ruined by his passion for Anastasia; so are Mississippi and Saint-Claude. Diego, the master-politician, is the only one to rise undamaged from the ashes of his passion. Bodo, although a self-parodical mouthpiece of the author, is "almost carelessly linked with the rest of the play."[11] He

[9] Peppard, p. 44.
[10] *Mississippi* includes, e.g., a parodical version of a recognition scene between two lovers long departed, modish in old melodrama:
ANASTASIA (*cries out*). Bodo!
ÜBELOHE (*stands motionless for an instant, then he too gives vent to a blood-curdling cry*). Anastasia! . . . Some black coffee, please. (FP 167).
Jenny (pp. 40–44) catalogues further objects of Dürrenmatt's parody: salon plays, Wedekind, Claudel, and the Brechtian alienation effect.
[11] Peppard, p. 46.

makes his entrance late in the play, arriving from his jungle hospital in Borneo; his genuine love for Anastasia, or his achievements as a patron of hospitals, are not demonstrated by stage action, but just mentioned in the monologues pouring fluently from Dürrenmatt's pen. As in *The Blind Man*, Dürrenmatt is guilty of his old sin of abstraction; as in *It Is Written* he is offering his audience an overdose of monologues.

What is made very concrete for the spectators is Mississippi's failure in his educational efforts. Both he and Anastasia murdered their first spouses with the help of a sugar-like poison; drinking coffee from that all-European Biedermeier table is a pleasant reminder of this early in the play and a new variation of Dürrenmatt's last meals before execution. The feast is repeated in the end; there is poison in both cups, yet neither Anastasia nor Mississippi knows that their own cups are poisoned. See Fig. 2. We are thus witnessing a scene full of tragic irony, climaxing in Anastasia's death with false assurances of innocence on her lips. Mississippi dies shortly afterwards, firm in his belief in her innocence. When the opening scene of the play has been repeated and Saint-Claude has met his journey's end for the second time, all there is left of the play is a song proclaiming the eternal recurrence of these mad idealists, a finale not without its poetic and summarizing values. The lines are recited by the three principal male characters, including Bodo in the grotesque attire of a Don Quixote, "submerged in the circling shadow of a windmill":

Again and again we return, as we have always returned
In ever new shapes, yearning for ever more distant
    paradises
Ever and again thrust out from among you
Nourished by your indifference
Thirsting for your brotherhood
We sweep by above your cities
• • •
Forward then! (FP 203–04).

100

Mississippi is not a straightforward description of the war or its aftermath. It is an analysis of its causes in the recent European past and in the future. Dürrenmatt's basic theory is that the violence inhabiting our living rooms is caused by a collision between fanatical believers in various formulas of thought. Mississippi believes in divine justice, as formulated in the Law of Moses; Saint-Claude in earthly justice, as verbalized in the doctrine of communism. Their strivings to change the world are nourished by the indifference of the spectators, or ordinary citizens, and followed with amused detachment by Anastasia and Diego, "a whore who passes unchanged through death" and a politician desiring "power and nothing else," embracing "the world" (FP 203). In this eternal comedy Bodo or a genuine lover of mankind is capable of only a futile gesture of defiance:

> I gallop on my sorry jade
> away over your greatness
> into the flaming abyss of the infinite (FP 204).

These meanings can be read into the last scenic image of *The Marriage of Mr. Mississippi*. So it was before World War II, so it was in the early 1950's, so it will be in the future, according to Dürrenmatt's sinister prophecy: "Again and again we return." This last image is an entirely successful dramatization of Dürrenmatt's ideas; it is, as it were, the largest splinter in his broken mirror reflecting Don Quixote and the world.[12] With its scenic arrangements, it speaks a language in harmony with its poetic diction and with the rest of the play. The self-depreciation of Bodo is visualized by means of his attire and situation, whereas the circling shadow of

[12] Grimm takes the grotesque figure of Don Quixote in this scene as an example of how an image borrowed from literature is used as "a unifying symbol for the entire work of art," not parodied or alienated as a counter-sketch (*Der unbequeme Dürrenmatt*, p. 89). As to the title of this chapter, cf. H. F. Garten, *Modern German Drama*, p. 257, using the simile of "a distorting mirror." Gerwin Marahrens reveals the weakness of Bodo (Knapp, ed., *F.D.*, pp. 102–06), opposes Christian interpretations of the finale (pp. 106–08), and sees the play as a criticism of ideologies (pp. 109–16).

the windmill is a concretization of his powerlessness. And physical death on the stage is not the end of the Mississippis, Saint-Claudes, and Anastasias of this world. If they die, they are resurrected.

Throughout the play Dürrenmatt works hard to give universal relevance to his characters. The emphasis in the play is not on the characterization of the individual figures, but on the total pattern formed by them. It is easy to accept Saint-Claude or Mississippi in the terms intended, as caricatures of fanatics; it is possible to see a vista of depth behind the Don Quixote-like figure of Bodo in the last scene. It is more difficult to accept Anastasia, for reasons stated below. The characters of *Mississippi* have been criticized as being only concepts;[13] this remark is not only justified, it even corresponds to Bodo's phrasing that it was Dürrenmatt's intention to investigate the collision between ideas and characters.

While working on *Mississippi* in February, 1951, Dürrenmatt criticized a play by Max Frisch, *Graf Öderland*, for being limited to the sphere of the private. Its hero, a public prosecutor, remained a special case, never acquiring dimensions of universal validity (TS 257–59). This was a pitfall Dürrenmatt decided to avoid when finishing *his* play about a public prosecutor. Moreover, in his witty answer to Tilly Wedekind, widow of the playwright, Dürrenmatt denies her accusation of plagiarism, confessing at the same time that he was influenced by Wedekind in an entirely different way. In Wedekind's *Marquis von Keith* there is a proletarian playing the role of an aristocrat, and his reflection in the mirror, an aristocrat disguised as a proletarian.[14] This gave Dürren-

---

[13] See, e.g., Jauslin, pp. 63, 72, Brock-Sulzer, pp. 64–66, and Rivers Carew, "The Plays of F.D.," *The Dublin Magazine*, 4, 1 (Spring 1965), p. 59.

[14] Mayer has emphasized Wedekind's influence on the early works of Dürrenmatt and found the character constellation from *Marquis von Keith* already varied in *It Is Written*, in the contrast between Knipperdollinck and Bockelson ("F.D.," *Zeitschrift für deutsche Philologie*, 87, 4, Fall 1968, pp. 482, 494).

matt the basic idea of "dialectics *with* characters." He made up his mind to "write inductively" and to outline his five main characters "by developing one from the others and so on" (TS 244–45). In the same paragraph he also mentions the pair Don Quixote and Sancho Panza.

Taking the characters of *Mississippi* as thinly disguised ideas brings us to a crucial point in our evaluation of the play. It has been stated above that Bodo is only loosely connected with the rest of the play; only in the last scenic image is he in focus. Conversely, Anastasia is constantly in focus: all threads of action run through her. These two major characters are not in balance,[15] nor is a balance reached between the foreground and background in the entire play. The narrative foreground—the constant amorous adventures around Anastasia—steals too much attention. A group of characters are developed dialectically from one another; the action woven around them should be more directly developed from the same dialectics. The eternal fight between the representatives of law and order, of social equality, of Christian faith, and of political flexibility should be directly reflected on the level of action. Instead, Dürrenmatt uses the circumlocution of symbolic action around Anastasia; his Mississippi and Saint-Claude confront one another only as rivals for her favors. She is, of course, a symbol herself, a personification of the world, Frau Welt or the Whore of Babylon, adopted from old allegories. Yet she is introduced to the audience as a murderess out of jealousy, with a real past and several real-life suitors. The greater part of Dürrenmatt's energies goes into winding these threads into new twists.

It is as if Dürrenmatt had tried to combine two uncombinable elements. There is his dramaturgy of freedom and artistic inventions, of surprise and chance. Second, there is

[15] Bodo's relation to Anastasia "remains tenuous and conversational rather than functional." As Bodo is connected with Mississippi and Saint-Claude only through Anastasia, "the play suffers from an underlying duality without a happy synthesis either of style or message" (Peppard, p. 45).

103

DÜRRENMATT

a group of characters growing out of a political dialectic and demanding action based on this dialectic. The first of these elements is expansive, if not explosive; the second presupposes concentration. Only in the finale of *Mississippi* does Dürrenmatt reach a balance between these centrifugal and centripetal forces, only during the last moments of stage action does the background pattern reach the forestage. The result is a grotesque and memorable scenic image. "Scattered or compact?" is a stock question to be asked every time a play of Dürrenmatt's is discussed. *Mississippi* is scattered most of the way.

Parody belongs to the foreground of *Mississippi*. Once again, Dürrenmatt is balancing precariously between comic and serious tones of voice. Parodical details tend to get the upper hand, until the final solutions, even before the last scene, help a more somber tone emerge from among the shrill sounds of the composition. When revising his script for version two Dürrenmatt eliminated some of his religious metaphors, such as an identification between Mississippi and Judas, Bodo and Christ. What is left of these elements is included in some of Bodo's lines and in a meeting of Mississippi and Bodo under the Biedermeier table and under machine-gun fire. "Are you a Christian?" Mississippi asks. "I am a Christian," Bodo answers (FP 183). Jenny comments: "It is unique in Dürrenmatt's work that a new version does not mean a clarification, an increase of dimensions, but a reduction, a moderation."[16] This reduction can only be interpreted as an additional proof that Dürrenmatt was moving away from the religious problems of his early career. "The emphasis is no longer on the way to God, but on the

[16] Jenny, p. 46. According to Deschner, retaining the scene in its original form would have made the play "too explicit for the author's taste. . . . Dürrenmatt offers in Übelohe a human alternative to man's attitude to the world" ("F.D's Experiments with Man," p. 153). On the other hand Blum calls Bodo "a misconstruction from the Christian point of view"; his philanthropic deeds are not consecrated by any Christian doctrine, by "Liturgia" ("Ist F.D. ein christlicher Schriftsteller?" *Reformatio, 8,* 8, Sept. 1959, pp. 536–37).

104

way of the individual in the world."[17] That way led toward
the windmills and through many a strange adventure, to be
seen in the light of parody.

Even if the constellation of characters in *Mississippi* was
developed inductively, Dürrenmatt could not help returning
to his earlier interests. He is a critic and a parodist of those
who believe in formulas of thought. His Mississippi is just as
blind in his reliance on Anastasia as the Duke in his faith—
or as Bodo in his belief in love. What makes Bodo, however,
a sympathetic fanatic, is that he "deals in particulars," tries
to help individual people, whereas "Mississippi, Saint-Claude,
and Romulus deal in generalities."[18] Bodo is "unheroicized"
and parodied by his author, yet he belongs to Dürrenmatt's
men of courage.[19] Diego has been called "an amoralist of
Bockelson's kind,"[20] and Anastasia is both a Super-Lulu from
Wedekind and a figure foreshadowing Claire Zachanassian in
The Visit. Claire shares Anastasia's profession and Mississippi's inflexible entanglement with justice. Like Claire, Anastasia should be one of the Norns, immortal; Jenny is doubtless right when criticizing the final solutions in *Mississippi.*
Anastasia dies without confessing her infidelity: Dürrenmatt
makes her give up her last triumph over the credulity of her
husband, and sacrifices her immortality to a Grand Guignol
effect with three bodies on the stage.[21] The conflict between
the demands of the plot and those of the background pattern
is solved in favor of the plot.

There are also other details revealing the continuity in
Dürrenmatt's works. *Mississippi* is the most typical example
of his unerotic comedies, using love only as an axis for its
complicated plot. This time Dürrenmatt's attachment to

---

[17] Robert Holzapfel, "The Divine Plan," *Modern Drama, 8,* 3
(Dec. 1965), p. 240.

[18] Wellwarth, "F.D. and Max Frisch," *TDR, 6,* 3 (March 1962),
p. 22.

[19] Heilman, p. 12.   [20] Deschner, p. 140.

[21] Jenny, pp. 48–49. The similarities between Mississippi's and
Claire's conceptions of justice are pointed out by Helmut Prang,
Geschichte des Lustspiels, p. 355.

abundance makes him double action: Mississippi and Anastasia are to perform "the movements involved in drinking coffee . . . very precisely: e.g., both lift their cups to their mouths at the same time" (FP 134). In another scene three clerics, "one Protestant, one Catholic, one Jewish," sing Anastasia's praises, partly in chorus (FP 172–73), thus losing their individuality and acting like grotesque marionettes.[22] Mississippi is a grotesque mixture of judge and victim;[23] he belongs to the long series of Dürrenmatt's unwilling executioners and judges of themselves, paying at least lip service to the strain of their harassing job: "But it is better to be guilty than to see guilt. Guilt can be repented; the sight of guilt is fatal" (FP 145).

From the neutral Swiss point of view Dürrenmatt's concern for justice is well motivated. For years, the well-equipped armies of World War II had been killing and destroying, and there was every reason to inquire whether "the cheque paid by Justice" was covered at all, and whether murdering would be justified under any circumstances. In an interesting scene Dürrenmatt combines a claustrophobic situation with his sciento- or medicophobia: "Through all the doors . . . and through the windows . . . and also from the grandfather clock, doctors in white coats and thick horn-rimmed spectacles throng onto the stage" (FP 187). They come to take Mississippi to an enclosed place, to an asylum. Entering through windows is a whim of Dürrenmatt's to be found later on, too.

The changes Dürrenmatt made in the dialogue of *Mississippi* between the first and second stage versions concentrated mainly on tightening it and on suppressing the religious elements.[24] The same line of development is continued in stage version number three; the changes are not very remarkable.[25]

---

[22] Jauslin, pp. 123–24.

[23] Oberle in *Der unbequeme Dürrenmatt*, p. 18.

[24] Jauslin, pp. 57, 119.

[25] In version three there are some additions, deletions, and rearrangements of speeches, especially at the end of Saint-Claude's and

The additions made were more fully developed in the film script.

Interpreting the qualities of a ready-made film from its script sounds to me a difficult task—and a task outside the field of this study. I am confining myself to a few comments. The script makes slick, clever, and technically smooth reading; the parodical elements of the stage version seem to be replaced by rather obvious satire. It is, of course, impossible to deduce from the written page whether it was Dürrenmatt's or the director's (Kurt Hoffmann) intention to parody the cinematic style of some well-known directors. Dürrenmatt was not satisfied with routine work: with turning narrative passages in the stage version into action in the film, and with dispersing the scenes all around Europe City, as the milieu was called, thus translating his work to fit the new medium. His never-resting imagination, gormandizing with the pictorial possibilities of film, kept creating fresh grotesqueries: wedding guests in deep snow; the conditions of the strange marriage explained only before the altar; Anastasia at an execution. Mississippi proclaims his belief in the Law of Moses in a public speech made in the chapel of a prison: general chaos of rioting prisoners follows, preparing the way for the revolution stirred up by Saint-Claude. This revolution and Diego, rechristened Sir Thomas, play a much more prominent role on the screen than on the stage; Bodo and Mississippi's house retreat from the center of interest.[26] Anastasia leaves the impression of being just an ordinary film vamp, not a symbol of the world—if she ever succeeded in being one.

Mississippi's first meeting (FP 120–22; Miss 37–39). Bodo's and Anastasia's scene in Act II finishes with Bodo's outburst of feelings in free verse; when deleting its last ten lines Dürrenmatt cleaned out some religious images, among them Bodo's line of self-recognition: "a last Christ" (FP 189; Miss 67).

[26] Cf. Bänziger, p. 147. Dürrenmatt has himself said that he "varied his own theme," making "a political farce" out of a religious comedy (Bienek, *Werkstattgespräche mit Schriftstellern*, p. 109).

One cannot help suspecting that Dürrenmatt is replacing the misleading foreground of the stage versions with a foreground of another type, precisely as misleading. Instead of blurring his background pattern with a series of love affairs, he now indulges in a criminal melodrama—not without its comic and picaresque elements. "The three in raincoats" get names and roles; they lodge in Anastasia's bedroom on the morning of revolution, while the house is surrounded by police. New surprising twists of the plot are developed (as if there had been any lack of them). In a curious way Dürrenmatt shows a minimum amount of interest in developing further his main intellectual argument, the political and religious ideologies of his characters.[27] Perhaps the trouble with *Mississippi*, whether on the stage or on the screen, is that Dürrenmatt solved this part of the problem too early. He knew exactly, right from the beginning, what kinds of figures he was going to create.[28] The result was a mechanization of the characters, and a plot without living, changing, and shifting interaction with the characters. The plot does not change the characters: it just follows their dictates, in ever new yet basically similar situations.

The Marriage of Mr. Mississippi, Dürrenmatt's fourth stage play, was both a partial success and an important event in his career. It helped him establish himself in Germany; it created an aura of daring avant-gardism around his name; it was produced in Chile, in Israel, and in New York.[29] Its intellectual background pattern was hardly given an adequate scenic form; yet sensitive critics and audiences in a great

[27] Ulrich Gregor calls the film "a commercial vulgarization of the intellectual acrobatics that make up the charm of the stage play" ("Verfilmtes Theater," *Theater heute*, 2, 8, Aug. 1961, p. 44).

[28] According to Durzak, the collision between the characters and reality was a clear enough starting-point, yet "the real difficulty" was in executing the experiment with the help of "a definite action" (*D., Frisch, Weiss*, p. 73). Dürrenmatt drifted to more and more artificial entanglements toward the end of the play (p. 78).

[29] Wyrsch, "Die Dürrenmatt-Story," part five, *Schw. Illustrierte*, April 15, 1963, p. 37.

many countries seemed to register the existence of Dürren-matt's concern for contemporary issues of worldwide signifi-cance. A writer of historical plays known only within the German-speaking world, and to a limited extent even there, took his first steps toward global reputation. Dürrenmatt and his *Mississippi* were helped by the fact that the German drama of the early 1950's seemed to be lagging behind inter-national, especially French, creativity; Dürrenmatt and Frisch created hopes that German drama would rapidly catch up and overtake it.[30] The ultimate message of the play also corresponded to the contemporary feeling of hostility toward all ideologies,[31] especially toward their fanatical variations.

[30] Koebner, *Tendenzen der deutschen Literatur seit 1945*, pp. 348–49, Marti, *Die Schweiz und ihre Schriftsteller*, p. 14.

[31] Cf. Mayer, *Zur deutschen Literatur der Zeit*, pp. 301–20, espe-cially pp. 304–05.

5   To Whom Grace Belongs

AN ANGEL COMES TO BABYLON

llllllllllllllllllllllllllllllllllllllllllllllllllllllllllllllllllllllllllllllllllll

"What we have to find out now is what Heaven really intended, haven't we?" (FP 280). This puzzled question is prompted by the central artistic invention in *An Angel Comes to Babylon* (Ein Engel kommt nach Babylon), Dürrenmatt's fifth stage play. Kurrubi, a girl "created by our Lord . . . a few moments ago," comes to Babylon, escorted by an angel who has the task of delivering this personification of God's grace to the lowliest of men. Heaven is there, as the background of the entire play—and as the background of its first stage picture. "A vast sky is suspended over the whole scene. In its midst hovers the Andromeda Galaxy, seeming oppressively close, as it might look through the telescopes of Mount Wilson or Mount Palomar." The foreground is occupied by man's world, by the banks of the Euphrates, by "the maze of the streets which make up the giant city with its millions of inhabitants, a mixture of magnificence and filth" (FP 211). Like a chemist, or like an artist practicing his own alchemy, Dürrenmatt is observing the reactions started by his invention. Grace touches filth.

We are thus back in the religious concerns of Dürrenmatt's youth. The first version of *Angel* was sketched in 1948, after *The Blind Man* and before *Romulus*, but destroyed. The two produced and published versions date back to 1953 and 1957; the latter of these is translated into English and subtitled "A Fragmentary Comedy," a definition referring to Dürrenmatt's abortive plan to write a trilogy, of which *Angel* was to be the first part.[1] The subject, the building of the Tower of Babel, had occupied Dürrenmatt's mind since his

---

[1] Brock-Sulzer, *F.D.*, pp. 74–75; Wyrsch, part four, April 8, 1963; Deschner, "F.D's Experiments with Man," pp. 158–59.

110

childhood (K I 258). When treating it, he created a synthesis between his earliest stage style and his somewhat later tone of comedy.

As in the moon-dance scene in *It Is Written*, man is seen against the background of the sky; again, a whole world is brought onto the stage.[2] The list of characters ranges from King Nebuchadnezzar to lepers, pickpockets, and beggars. The setting is not limited to the confines of a country estate, as in *Romulus*, nor to the walls of a single room, as in *Mississippi*. Dürrenmatt's Babylon is a wide and anachronistic city, a kind of urban milieu through the ages[3]—just as the setting in *Mississippi* was an all-European museum. There are "old-Babylonian gas-lamps," bicycles, and trams among Dürrenmatt's props and sound effects, as well as remnants from still earlier periods in the history of mankind: "sarcophagi, heathen idols, an ancient royal throne" (FP 211, 239). All through history, Dürrenmatt implies, the grace of God may fall upon man, to his bewilderment.

An unconventional triangle is the basis of *An Angel Comes to Babylon*. Its most conventional member is King Nebuchadnezzar, a personification of worldly order, who has just established a "Welfare State" and "a faultless empire" (FP 215–16) in Babylon. In this perfect state there is no place for beggars. The King is "a young man still, rather nice and somewhat simple-minded" (FP 214); at the beginning of the play we meet him on the banks of the Euphrates, firmly determined to compel Akki, the last beggar in his realm, to

---

[2] Dürrenmatt calls this his first question: "Where does the play take place? . . . In Dürrenmatt the boards of the stage mean the world in a specific way. . . . In [his] grotesque work the world of man appears small compared with God's world" (Oberle in *Der unbequeme D.*, ed. by Grimm et al., pp. 11, 15).

[3] "The setting of the play in a vague time and place . . . allows Dürrenmatt much freedom in the use of anachronisms," yet it also makes the play entirely dependent on "its own self-contained symbolism. As in *The Blind Man*, the lack of specific setting involves a tendency to be allegorical" (Peppard, *F.D.*, p. 50). Cf. Garten, *Modern German Drama*, p. 257, and FP 21.

111

enter the service of the state. Akki, the second member in Dürrenmatt's triangle, is many things: a charming rogue, a storyteller, an artist in the difficult art of living, a patron of dozens of poets, a social anarchist. The triangle is completed by the Angel, an absent-minded representative of Heaven and a scientist who sees only the wonders of nature on earth, not its human misery.[4] He is portrayed with delicate touches of humor and lyricism.[5]

Akki is thus placed between two believers in formulas of thought. The Angel is completely adjusted to creation: "What is created is good, and what is good is happy" (FP 213). This satisfaction with God's order is contrasted with an equally strong belief in man's order, as represented by Nebuchadnezzar and his perfect state. Phrases used by the King echo the name of *It Is Written*: "What is just is just. . . . Everybody should be who he is." Against these maxims Akki raises his bravado, his belief in freedom: "I'm who I please" (FP 215, 218).

To whom does grace belong? Nebuchadnezzar is the mightiest of men, Akki the lowliest. If a popular vote were to be arranged among the spectators of *Angel*, they would no doubt yield Kurrubi, or God's grace, to Akki.[6] Moreover, the Angel has a map specifying Akki as the addressee of the heavenly parcel. Things are, however, complicated by the fact that King Nebuchadnezzar has assumed the disguise of a beggar. Ever since his early stories Dürrenmatt has liked telling Cinderella stories the other way around: there are many rich men as paupers in his works. Contrary to the information that has reached the far-away lookouts of Heaven, there are thus two beggars surviving on earth. The

[4] Cf. Wellwarth, "F.D. and Max Frisch," *TDR*, 6, 3 (March 1962), p. 24; Erwin Leiser, "Den fromme nihilisten," *Bonniers Litterära Magasin*, 25, 2 (Feb. 1956), pp. 127–28.

[5] Bänziger is disturbed by the comic elements in Dürrenmatt's portrayal of the Angel (*Frisch und D.*, p. 149).

[6] Otto Mann has referred to an old motive, handled, e.g., by Hofmannsthal: "the beggar is the genuine man" (Friedmann and Mann, eds., *Deutsche Literatur im 20. Jahrhundert*, I, p. 158).

Angel is no expert in human beings; he is a physicist, and a specialist in giant red suns (FP 233). In his dilemma he chooses to wait for the results of a competition in begging between Akki and Anashamashtaklakou, alias Nebuchadnezzar.

A charming expository scene, in which Kurrubi and the Angel enter the stage from the Andromeda Galaxy, is followed by this competition: a sequence of action effective on the stage.[7] Comedy is also created by minor interludes of anxious or wrathful pantomime by the members of the royal retinue following the competition from their hiding place. They come forward, one after another: the Prime Minister, the Senior Theologian Utnapishtim, the General, and the Hangman. The King, nicknamed Nebby by Akki, is an amateur in begging, and of course no match for Akki, who adapts his technique according to his victims. So the Angel deviates from his instructions and delivers Kurrubi to Nebuchadnezzar, the loser in the match, and obviously the lowliest of the low.

Kurrubi has fallen in love with Nebby. Not with the King, but with the helpless beggar. She is a girl created "a few moments ago"; yet she is somewhat surprisingly guided by maternal instincts. This is another example of Dürrenmatt's love relationships' being dictated by the demands of the plot and little else.[8] Nebuchadnezzar, also in love, is eager to make her his queen, yet unwilling to give up everything he has and follow her as a beggar, as she insists. These complications bring us to the close of Act I, to Nebuchadnezzar's fit of rage against the insulting gift of Heaven: "When will Heaven ever learn to give each man what he needs? . . . Nebuchadnezzar hungers for a human being, so Heaven ought to give him you" (FP 236). Kurrubi, the gift of God trampled underfoot by the King, finds temporary lodgings with Akki. This is a

[7] The begging competition has been called particularly fit for the stage, e.g., by Brock-Sulzer (*Die Tat*, Feb. 2, 1954).

[8] Kurrubi's love for the King is "a pure abstraction" (Georg Hensel, *Spielplan*, p. 1026).

result of chance and Akki's cleverness rather than of any divine plan.

Each of the characters in this triangle has his own act. Act I was the Angel's, Act II is Akki's, Act III is to be the King's. This does not only apply to the stage pictures, but also encompasses the action and the central field of problems in each of the acts.[9] The sky and the problem of God's grace were focal in Act I; now we are to become more closely acquainted with the teachings of Akki. In a way, this means a digression from the straightest line of development: a discussion of the conflict between God's order and man's is postponed until Act III. The opening act of the play, "with its delicately ironical atmosphere of fairy tale," is "wonderfully rounded, having only one flaw" in being too self-contained.[10] It is a reproduction of Act I from the destroyed first version. The anger of Nebuchadnezzar might have led into the building of the Tower right away, at the end of Act I. Instead, there follows an act-long circumlocution. Dürrenmatt almost succeeds in telling the essential contents of his planned trilogy in its opening act.

The setting of Act II is grotesquely cluttered. We are brought into Akki's lodgings "beneath one of the Euphrates bridges," into "a wild hotch-potch of various objects of every period," "with parchments and clay tablets closely written with poetry" hanging everywhere. Romulus had his henhouse; Dürrenmatt's Hercules will be placed in the midst of a dungeon enveloping the whole country of Elis. Akki and his followers move about "on an enormous rubbish dump" (FP 239). Ruling over this ample setting, Akki behaves as if he were a Renaissance prince, feeding fifty poets, and throwing away his day's haul into the Euphrates: "pearls, precious stones, pieces of gold." Prodigality is essential to maintain

---

[9] These connections are also seen by Therese Poser in her enlightening analysis of the play (Geissler, ed., *Zur Interpretation des modernen Dramas*, p. 89).

[10] Jenny, p. 52; he also points out Dürrenmatt's difficulties in developing his materials after Act I (pp. 53–54). Cf. Deschner, p. 168.

"a really high standard in beggary" (FP 240). When Akki's poets leap up from a great many sarcophagi, we can register another item in the long list of Dürrenmatt's surprising entrances.

Kurrubi is studying man's world: "With every step I see more injustice, more sickness, more despair around me" (FP 240). The Angel, on the other hand, falls into raptures at the wonders of nature—"I tremble with awe in every limb. Wonder upon wonder glows within me and I am shaken through and through by the knowledge of God"—until he cannot help bursting into a poem:

> Over the continents, over blue seas,
> Dazzled, my silver way I thread;
> Over the hills and the fields and the trees
> Soaring through clouds or gliding under,
> Moving softly on wings outspread,
> Absorbed in Earth's unceasing wonder (FP 252–54).

It is easy to recognize Dürrenmatt's familiar poetic idiom here: as in *Mississippi*, as in *Romulus*, he is writing swift-moving valedictory poetry and poetry of the stars.

Akki speaks in prose. When Dürrenmatt wants to give a condensed picture of Akki's observations of life, he makes his hero speak in rhymed prose. Akki's stories are *maqamat*, following a traditional form in Arabic literature, and describing man's world in the tone of picaresque fiction, not nature in a tone of exaltation, as the verse spoken by the Angel does.[11] Akki has no illusions; he is wise in the ways of the world, or else he would not be able to practice his begging profession.[12] His longest *maqamat* reflects the topsy-turvy

[11] In his clever translation into English, William McElwee renders Akki's first three stories without rhyme (FP 245–46), yet uses rhyme fairly widely in the longest and most important story (FP 263–65). He calls the stories, somewhat misleadingly, "sagas"; the word "maqamat" ("Makame") occurs in Dürrenmatt's own text (K I 207, 225).

[12] Akki, compared with Brecht's Azdak from *The Caucasian Chalk Circle*, e.g., by Bänziger, p. 150, is "one of the great creations of

115

world, a motif occurring in folk poetry in various parts of the world. As a millionaire he was a spendthrift, as a general he "omitted to send out orders for the attack"; for him, "hanging means letting go" (FP 263–64).

Akki's stories and the whole of Act II climax in a passage revealing his philosophy of life. It consists of a gospel of craftiness for the weak: "If you wish to grow old pretend to be stupid. Attack from within. Be already in the cells before the trials begin."[13] Persecuted by the King, the last beggar in Babylon chooses the only way to survive: "He pulls the black mask over his face and stands there, a red-cloaked hangman" (FP 265). *Angel* is a comedy abounding in masks and disguises: grace is disguised as Kurrubi, the King as a beggar, and now, in the last scenic image of Act II, Akki is concealed behind the mask of a hangman. Dürrenmatt gives his hero one of his favorite grotesque attires.

With his hangman's black mask, Akki is ready to enter Act III. Another forward-pointing element in Act II is the fate of Kurrubi. Everyone keeps wooing her, from the poets to banker Enggibi, from the wine-merchant Ali to the two workmen. She even turns the banker into a guitarist and singer. There are signs of a general unrest, caused by Kurrubi and the appearance of the Angel, until the assembled crowd makes up its mind to "invest her with the greatest honour that we have in our power. . . . Let us enthrone her as our Queen" (FP 255). Kurrubi agrees to say good-bye to Akki, praising him in Christian terms: "You gave me food when I hungered and drink when I was thirsty. . . . I love you as I would love a father" (FP 256). Akki is left in the hands of "The Formal One," the King's hangman—only to escape

---

Dürrenmatt," "endowed with wit, intelligence, charm and humor, and an unquenchable love of freedom and independence" (Peppard, p. 49).

[13] According to Klarmann, Akki "represents Dürrenmatt's true hero —the non-hero. . . . Unless the unheroic Akkis survive, there will be no happiness, no beauty, no poetry, no refuge for Divine grace, only grim pursuit of duty" ("F.D. and the Tragic Sense of Comedy," *TDR*, *4*, 4, May 1960).

through a clever trick that compares in ingenuity with Macheath's in *The Threepenny Opera*. Akki gives the hangman a secondhand bookshop in exchange for his life and his new disguise.

In King Nebuchadnezzar's throne room in Act III there is "an element of cruel and bestial barbarity." There are also "giant stone statues," reminding one of Dürrenmatt's bust phase; and there is the King himself, "with his feet resting on Nimrod's shoulders" (FP 266). Dürrenmatt takes literally the current definition that "the King's feet must rest on the shoulders of his predecessor," otherwise "all five hundred thousand paragraphs of the Babylonian legal code would become worthless" (FP 268). Nebby and Nimrod have lived thousands of years, alternating on the throne, without any real change in the government. Their excessively great ages (also Akki's) are perhaps a reference to and a parody of the novels about Jacob published by Thomas Mann in 1933–43. The King is made a grotesque and mechanical figure by being doubled and by being given lines to be said simultaneously with Nimrod's.[14] Doubling his characters is one of Dürrenmatt's scenic units. Nebby and Nimrod are interchangeable. Kurrubi is unique.

In this setting visualizing man's earthly power we are back in the central concern of the play. The Senior Theologian Utnapishtim is ready to explain why Kurrubi was first given to Nebuchadnezzar. "Heaven is always right. . . . All men are pretty equally lowly if we remember the enormous differences in outlook with which Heaven regards events here below" (FP 271). A rebellious mob brings Kurrubi in, wanting to crown her as their queen. The girl recognizes the King as her beloved beggar: "Let us get out of this stone house and this city of stones. I will beg for you and care for you" (FP 279). Utnapishtim interferes with a theology of relativism. Heaven does not demand "absolute obedience from us," it only demands "what is possible. . . . Men want to see

---

[14] Jauslin remarks of this (*F.D.*, p. 81).

117

grace bestowed upon their Kings, not on their beggars. . . .
And you can be a help to men, my child, for they need your
help" (FP 280–81).[15] All seems prepared for a union of
heavenly and earthly powers—contrary to Dürrenmatt's total
plan aiming at the building of the Tower of Babel.
Dürrenmatt can save his plan only through another reversal of the plot. As in *Mississippi*, he employs a revolution
as a deus ex machina. A few moments earlier the mob was
demanding a marriage between Kurrubi and Nebuchadnezzar; now they start throwing stones at the statue of Nebby.
The Angel is made guilty of disturbing the prevailing order
of things: "A State and sound government are only possible
if earth remains earth and Heaven Heaven" (FP 283). This
interpretation, presented by the Prime Minister, certainly
touches an important theme; yet a statement in the dialogue
is hardly enough to motivate a total off-stage reversal in the
action of the play. Shortly before, the Prime Minister was
beaming with satisfaction; now he has only "a dull joke"[16]
to offer: "The more often a politician contradicts himself,
the greater he is" (FP 283). Contradicting himself is not
necessarily a mark of greatness in a playwright.

In the next scenes Dürrenmatt's dramaturgic manipulations lead into one more somersault of thought. The King is
immediately successful in his efforts to incite the mob against
Kurrubi, its idol: "She bewitched us" (FP 290). When the
absolute demands of God's grace are made public, every
suitor gives her up. A political give-and-take deal results in
a plan to deny the celestial origin of Kurrubi in order to save
the state. The Angel is to be explained as an actor from the
court theater. Kurrubi does not consent to this plan, and she
is rejected by everyone. The time is ripe for Nebuchadnezzar's great final speech proclaiming the building of the Tower

[15] Dürrenmatt once called Utnapishtim "the most tragic and painful
character" in the play (Bänziger, p. 151). He has also been taken
as an exponent of an "untruthful theory of grace" (Buri in Grimm
et al., *Der unbequeme Dürrenmatt*, p. 50).

[16] Jenny, p. 57: there follows a clear-headed analysis of Dürrenmatt's dramaturgic contrivances.

of Babel: "Is Heaven so high that my curses cannot reach it? . . . I will oppose to the Creation out of the void the creation of the spirit of man, and we shall see which is the better: my justice, or the injustice of God." The magnificence of this speech is annulled by a grotesque scenic image. Inconsequential bad news is brought onto the stage, and the idiot son of both Nebuchadnezzar and Nimrod, a hopeless picture of the future, "walks across the stage on a tightrope. Nebuchadnezzar covers his face in helpless rage—in helpless sorrow" (FP 293).[17]

Kurrubi is delivered up to the King's hangman, alias Akki, to be killed. In the last scenic image of *An Angel Comes to Babylon* we see Akki and Kurrubi "disappear, followed, it may be, by a few poets leaping through the sandstorm." This poetic image of valediction is preceded by Akki's love song to this life of ours: "And I love an earth which still exists; an earth of beggars, lonely in its happiness, and lonely in its dangers, colourful and wild, wonderful in all its possibilities; an earth which I conquer again and again, maddened by its beauty, entranced by its face, ever oppressed and never defeated" (FP 294). Between the Scylla of celestial order and the Charybdis of man's order, there is a narrow route of escape through which Akki and Kurrubi direct their journey into the promised land of ambiguity and abundance.[18] Behind their backs Dürrenmatt's triangle of characters dissolves. Akki and Kurrubi leap out of a trilogy never completed— taking their author with them.

As in *The Marriage of Mr. Mississippi*, Dürrenmatt closes his play with a poetic scenic image; as in *Mississippi*, he resorts to an over-complicated plot. *An Angel Comes to Baby-*

[17] "The sublime and the ridiculous blend in a grotesque way," Grimm says of this scenic image (*Der unbequeme D.*, p. 78).

[18] Sister Corona Sharp calls Akki "the grave-merry man," invited "to be the guardian of God's gift to the world"; he "affirms the world and sees it as his plaything," thus realizing "the spirit of play," a valuable and liberating idea ("D. and the Spirit of Play," *University of Toronto Quarterly*, *34*, 1, Oct. 1969, pp. 73–74).

Ion is perhaps his richest stage play. It is rich in a great many respects—rich in characters, in comic details, in witty aphorisms, in verbal and scenic jokes, in settings and properties, in its crisscrossing themes. It is anything but compact. There are several layers in the dialogue of the play. The one that dominates consists of concrete dialogue in the tone of comedy, handled with ease, completed by fairly frequent *bons mots*: "The more perfect a State, the more stupid officials it needs" (FP 243). As in *Romulus*, Dürrenmatt "has found a light and cheerful tone. As a stylistic achievement, the play ranks among his very best."[19] Stylistic variety is furnished by occasional touches of parody, especially of Hölderlin;[20] by Nebuchadnezzar's outbursts of rhetoric; by Akki's *maqamat*; and by the psalm-like verse spoken by the Angel. His last departure from Earth is adorned with an anthem of praise, expressive in its pregnant images and its heaving rhythm:

The unreal miracle amidst the noble deserts of the stars.
The blue of Sirius, the whiteness of Vega, the roaring
    Pleiads
in the blackness of night of the universe—
so exciting in their form and their strength,
winnowing with their breathing great sheaves of light
    in space,
the bellows of the universe.
All these weigh nothing against this tiny grain of matter,
    this minute ball,
chained to its sun, encircled by its little moon,
enclosed in ether,
breathing amidst the green of its continents and the
    silver of its seas (FP 291).[21]

[19] Peppard, p. 52. Dürrenmatt's rich range of language is appreciated by Poser, pp. 93–94.
[20] These parodical elements are carefully analyzed by Jauslin, pp. 79–80.
[21] There is a printing error: all of this poem is not set in separate lines (FP 291–92). It is compared with Claudel's long verse by Jauslin, p. 78.

An Angel Comes to Babylon is a play rich in verbal poetry
—if by poetry we mean passages distinguished by a dense-
ness of metaphors and by a freedom of the diction from the
strictest rules of sentence logic.

Dürrenmatt uses these poetic highlights to express a focal
theme. There is a discrepancy between God's and man's
worlds; the former is "beautiful beyond all measure," yet
man does not see this beauty, being imprisoned in his own
"shabby, dissolute world."[22] Act III includes a description of
the endless pettiness of power politics; for Dürrenmatt, it is
entirely irrelevant whether man's world is governed by
Nebuchadnezzar or Nimrod, with their alternating reform
programs. This, or any other theme, runs the risk of being
drowned in a Dürrenmattian abundance of materials, particularly in Act III. "Accounts are settled with approxi-
mately everything to be called man's world: politics, theology, poetry, democracy, dynasty, the common people, the
monarch—not to speak of the Angel."[23] An effort to avoid
Brechtian over-emphasis on economic reasons leads Dürrenmatt into mirroring all mankind, and into "abandoning a
simple story-line."[24] *Angel* is confusing in its richness.

This is the more surprising because it was Dürrenmatt's
original idea "to do a piece of deductive playwriting"[25]—
as a contrast to his inductive experiment in *Mississippi*.
Everything had to lead to the building of the Tower of Babel.
Inadvertently, Dürrenmatt got carried away by the colorful
figure of Akki, and by his own enthusiasm for his sudden
artistic inventions. He was caught in his basic dilemma be-

[22] Oberle in *Der unbequeme D.*, p. 12.
[23] Brock-Sulzer, *F.D.*, p. 77. "As so often with Dürrenmatt, the
central theme . . . is blurred by a profusion of bizarre detail" (Garten, p. 258).
[24] Jauslin, p. 84.
[25] Deschner, p. 169: the expression is used to describe Dürrenmatt's task in rewriting the script while retaining the Act I of the
destroyed version. The play was to be "well-rounded, rigorously
straight-lined and colorful"; yet the story was not "thought to an end"
(Jenny, p. 58).

121

tween compactness and abundance. This time he chose abundance.

Angel leaves the impression that it consists of small bits of action. There is no great sweep of action, no grand design behind the play—or, if there is such a design, it is concealed behind all kinds of surface phenomena. There is quite a lot of movement back and forth, onto and from the stage: entrances and exits of the King's retinue, of the poets, or of Akki. Orders for hanging are given and cancelled, characters move quickly across the stage. Then there is a return to the static basic situation; everyone sits down to ponder once again to whom grace belongs. It is as if a sprinter were training for a marathon race, with minor spurts of activity as his only result. He also runs the same lap twice, in Acts I and III. The play is fragmentary also in the sense that its various parts are not well knit together.[26] The poetry of the play is verbal, not a poetry of stage architecture, not leading into a memorable string of interacting scenic images. The concluding scenic images stand in isolation.

Moreover, there is confusion about Akki's function and position. This patron of fifty poets, a man of Renaissance dimensions, is not a beggar out of social necessity; he is the embodiment of a philosophic or religious attitude to life. "Ruling the world is Heaven's business and begging is mankind's" (FP 234), the Angel once states. "Secret teachers, we are, educators of the people. . . . We obey no law, that freedom may be held in honour" (FP 231), Akki says, thus confirming that he is quite a specific kind of a beggar. Once again, Dürrenmatt is concretizing an abstract concept, turning a metaphor into a character. Akki is the lowliest of the low, yet his human stature far exceeds this definition. Kurrubi is delivered twice to him, once "in a chance bargain" (FP 256), once by mistake. Is Heaven's will fulfilled when Akki receives Kurrubi? Yet Kurrubi loves Nebuchadnezzar, mis-

---

[26] After a detailed comparison with Brecht's *The Good Person of Szechwan*, Durzak finds confusion in the way Dürrenmatt combines his acts (*D., Frisch, Weiss*, pp. 84–90).

led by his disguise as a beggar. Why?[27] Is this just a whim of the playwright?

Here we are, in the many disguises and false bottoms of *Angel*.[28] To whom does grace belong? The play does not give any unambiguous answer. If the final impression is that of confusion, it is not only because our world is rich, confused, and without contour. The play is muddled also because of Dürrenmatt's dramaturgic manipulations. Akki calls Kurrubi "a chance bargain," employing a central concept in Dürrenmatt's dramaturgy discussed above, on pp. 85–86. In *Romulus* chance was an essential theme; in *Angel* it has a function only in the plot of the play. It drives the plot into its best possible turn, a happy end, not into its "worst possible turn." The latter was to be the function of chance, according to Dürrenmatt's formulation somewhat later, in 1961.

Every time "chance"—that is, something not to be concluded directly and logically from the action—appears in the plot of a play, there is reason to ask whether this "chance" is not in fact a contrivance of the playwright. This question becomes the more urgent the closer we move toward traditional dramaturgy based on impeccable logic. There may be absurdist plays based entirely on a dramaturgy of chance; *Angel* is not one of them. Its essential contention seems to be that the acts of Heaven are incomprehensible to human beings, and that only "chance," or a contriving playwright, can assure us that God's grace sometimes falls into the hands of a man worthy of receiving it. This is a contention directly in line with Dürrenmatt's earlier and later findings emphasizing the role of chance in life—e.g., in the novel *The Pledge*. Yet he seems to have found more indisputable artistic equivalents to this idea in his works not set in ancient Babylon.

[27] Similar questions are asked by Poser, p. 89.
[28] "Dürrenmatt works too much with false bottoms. . . . His angel is not an angel, nor his King Nebuchadnezzar a king, nor his beggar a beggar" (Karl August Horst, "Humoristische Brechung und Trickmechanik," *Merkur*, *10*, 8, Aug. 1956, p. 595).

DÜRRENMATT

On the credit side of *An Angel Comes to Babylon* there is a charming central character, an unconventional basic idea, many stylistic felicities and comic situations. Yet these merits can hardly conceal the debit side: an entangled story line, an overdose of distracting materials, and high intentions not fully realized.[29] *Romulus the Great*, until *The Visit* Dürrenmatt's best play, has splendid artistic invention well executed; *Angel* has a comparable basic idea, yet the execution lags behind. It is easy to approve of Dürrenmatt's *angelus ex machina*: he is a catalyst, an ingredient starting an interesting experiment in artistic alchemy.[30] It is more difficult to accept the later complications. Chance or a miracle feeds our curiosity at the beginning of a play; chance introduced later on may feed our disbelief.

Another central invention in *Angel* is the building of the Tower. According to Dürrenmatt, it is "one of the most grandiose though most absurd undertakings of mankind; the more important because we see ourselves mixed up with similar undertakings today. . . . All are against the Tower and yet it comes about" (K I 258). Dürrenmatt alludes to the atom bomb or to the release of nuclear power, a contemporary theme to which he was to give a straightforward treatment in *The Physicists*.[31] What he would have made of this subject in its Babylonian disguise is an open question, as his trilogy was never completed. According to an outline dating back to 1948, Nebuchadnezzar's revenge on Heaven was to lead to a duel between the King and the builder of the Tower. The latter wanted to enslave mankind with the Tower, yet he was to die with a proclamation of freedom on his lips.[32]

29 Even plays that do not completely deliver Dürrenmatt's message, among them *Angel*, prove his "mastery of the stage," thanks to his plentiful detail inventions (Steiner, "Die Komödie Ds," *Der Deutschunterricht*, *15*, 6, Dec. 1963, pp. 97–98).

30 The Angel is an irresponsible power coming and crushing "a world of conventions" (Allemann in Wiese, *Das deutsche Drama*, II, pp. 428–29).

31 Cf. Kesting, *Panorama des zeitgenössischen Theaters*, p. 225.

32 Brock-Sulzer, *F.D.*, pp. 74–75.

Akki and Kurrubi escape to freedom through a narrow pass between various systems of thought. In the same way Dürrenmatt was to choose his own way between absurdism and the epic theater. *An Angel Comes to Babylon* is a step toward a colorful theater with a wide popular appeal, influenced by cabaret and the Viennese folk comedy, by Nestroy and Raimund.[33] Thus far, Dürrenmatt has already used a great many of his scenic units in his stage plays, creating settings showing man against the sky or in the middle of grotesque abundance, giving his heroes last meals, hangman's attire, or surprising entrances, doubling his figures or making them speak in chorus, and furnishing his dialogue with touches of parody, his action with interludes of pantomime. His individualistic heroes or non-heroes are often placed in the middle of a group of characters, and these social pressures result in displays of rhetoric. When leaving their oppressive or even claustrophobic stage situations, they burst out into valedictory poetry and poetry of the stars.

A grotesque disharmony is the greatest common denominator in these scenic units. They and other units were to go on appearing in Dürrenmatt's plays. Up to this point, the most memorable string of scenic images constructed with their help occurs in *Romulus the Great*. Elsewhere, as in *Angel*, Dürrenmatt's scenic images, striking as they may be, have tended to remain isolated, without intricate interrelations with the rest of the play. His poetry has been verbal rather than a poetry of stage architecture, his stage pictures have been paintings rather than frames for scenic images. Most of his scenic images have been lacking in depth and in interaction with other scenic images for the eye, ear, and mind.

In his constant quest for new formulas to demolish, Dürrenmatt was next to use the central artistic invention of *Angel* turned upside down. When God's grace touches man's filth, it creates only disaster. When a compulsion to revenge, disguised as justice, touches man's world, it creates only

[33] Bänziger, p. 151.

125

prosperity.[34] In Dürrenmatt's next stage play, not a single feather of the Angel remains. Before approaching the village of Guellen, we need, however, a more complete account of Dürrenmatt's journey toward his masterpiece, *The Visit*. We need to follow his steps through his novels, his radio plays, and his theoretical writings up to the late 1950's.

[34] This paradoxical connection between *Angel* and *The Visit* is seen by Neumann (*D., Frisch, Weiss*, p. 49).

6   Nature Behind the Scenes

THREE NOVELS

||||||||||||||||||||||||||||||||||||||||||||||||||||||||||||||||||||||||||||||||||||||||||||||

Dürrenmatt began his career as a writer of prose fiction, then turned to the stage. After he had finished *Romulus the Great*, and while he was struggling with the rich and many-faceted materials of *Mississippi* and *Angel*, he wrote two detective stories for serial publication in a periodical. No doubt lack of money provided the incentive: yet these novels are worth serious consideration. Their names and dates are *The Judge and His Hangman* (Der Richter und sein Henker, 1950) and *The Quarry* (Der Verdacht, 1951). Together they form the second group of Dürrenmatt's prose works; the third consists of *Once a Greek . . .* (Grieche sucht Griechin, 1955), a novel of entertainment; the fourth and most successful group, to be discussed in a separate chapter, includes the short story *A Dangerous Game* and Dürrenmatt's third detective story, *The Pledge*. Early in the 1950's Dürrenmatt also launched out on the air, writing most of his radio plays; these are the years marking the core of his creative outburst. There were several parallel lines in his work, followed for a while, then dropped.

It is a sign of Dürrenmatt's growing international reputation that all five of these works have been translated into English. Or it is a sign of "an Anglo-Saxon streak in Dürrenmatt as well; he owes much to the English detective novel which also takes murder for granted in the most well-ordered of middle-class societies."[1] Contrasting an existing order of things with an underlying chaos is one of the main sources of Dürrenmatt's grotesqueries—and of his detective stories. When turning to detective fiction Dürrenmatt found an established literary genre, a formula to employ and to

[1] Esslin, *Brief Chronicles*, p. 118.

127

grapple with. He found a mold to fill up with another kind of metal, a metal of his own.

The shape of the mold is most easily recognized behind the fabric of *The Judge and His Hangman*, Dürrenmatt's earliest detective story. It is a straightforward narrative, atmospheric, like the corresponding products of Georges Simenon or Graham Greene;[2] it is not particularly rash or violent in its action. The first deviation from the rules of the game takes place in the opening chapter. When a country constable finds the body of a police lieutenant collapsed over the wheel of a car by the roadside, he does not leave everything as it is. He covers the pistol wound in the temple with the dead man's felt hat, binds the body into an erect position, and drives off, with the corpse sitting "motionless at his side, except that now and then, when they came to a rough bit of road, its head nodded like a wise old Chinaman's" (JHH 7).[3] Dürrenmatt sacrifices a rule of procedure to a grotesque effect.

The case of Lieutenant Schmied is turned over to Commissioner Bärlach from the Berne police (JHH calls him "Inspector"). He is Dürrenmatt's detective in two stories. Bärlach is a grumbling old man who has served in Turkey and Germany before returning to his native canton; he is urgently in need of a cancer operation and knows that his life expectancy is at most a year. Modern criminology, as represented by Bärlach's chief Dr. Lutz, is despised by our Commissioner, who relies on his "hunch" and on his sure sense of human character.[4] Chanz, another police officer, is chosen by Bärlach as his assistant on the case.

[2] The following names have been connected with Dürrenmatt's detective stories: E.T.A. Hoffmann, Poe, Chesterton, Greene (Klarmann, *TDR*, 4, 4, May 1960, p. 79), Hammett, Stout, Chandler, and Simenon (Arnold, *F.D.*, pp. 48–49). Spycher compares them with Friedrich Glauser, a Swiss novelist, and his detective Studer (*F.D.*, pp. 128–29).

[3] Eugene E. Reed sees in this "stylistic grotesquerie" a device making the readers "feel more keenly the absence of the commonplace, the presence of evil" ("The Image of the Unimaginable," *Revue des Langues Vivantes*, 27, 1961, p. 119).

[4] Cf. Peppard, *F.D.*, p. 110.

Following a lead, Bärlach and Chanz find themselves outside the house of Gastmann, a big-time businessman and an acquaintance of Bärlach's since the days of his youth in Turkey. A lonely house in the countryside where an evening party is going on: a setting not unusual in a detective story. Bärlach is suddenly attacked by a huge dog, leaping, as it were, from an early story of Dürrenmatt's, called "The Dog."[5] Chanz saves Bärlach by shooting the dog to death, and the two policemen have to face a group of Gastmann's guests in evening dress. This is a crowd scene typical of Dürrenmatt in its combination of everyday reality and social nightmare: "It was embarrassing to stand there as though before a crowded grandstand" (JHH 33). Later on that same night Bärlach and Chanz have a strange and decisive meeting on the scene of the murder itself, looking "into each other's faces. Those few seconds seemed to last for hours. Neither spoke and their eyes were like stones" (JHH 41). This is a meeting between the judge and his hangman.

Gastmann is the prime suspect for having arranged the murder of Schmied. While developing his plot in this direction Dürrenmatt tries his hand at a few scenes belonging to the mold of detective fiction: there is Gastmann's influential advocate trying to tamper with the investigation, there is an attack on Bärlach in his home in the middle of the night. The former of these scenes includes dialogue that sounds somewhat stiff and artificial, perhaps because of paradoxical circumstances in Dürrenmatt's relation to the language. His mother tongue, learnt before school-age, is "Schwyzerdütsch" or Swiss German; according to his own confession, this is "the language of his emotion." High German is taught at school; it is his "father tongue," the language "of his intel-

---

[5] The English translation by Cyrus Brooks omits a few very Dürrenmattian points, e.g., in the description of the attack: "the old man did not utter anything, not a cry of fear, it all seemed to him so natural and so fully integrated into the order of this world" (RsH 39). Another detail cut out is a satiric passing shot at eclecticism: a political party is called "Conservative Liberal Socialist Coalition of the Independents" (RsH 53).

lect, of his will, of his adventure"[6]—and of his books. Dürrenmatt's all-pervading abundance includes two "parent-
tongues," one heard everywhere, the other the language of
literature. His High German includes Swiss elements: in
grammar and vocabulary. Dissonances between these two
layers of language are bound to strike the ear of native
speakers of German; suffice it to refer to these circumstances
and to state that the advocate scene in *Judge* is dictated by
Dürrenmatt's intellect and by the demands of the plot rather
than by emotion. The dialogue of the scene aims at being
spoken High German, yet does not quite succeed.

There is a scene in the novel using the language of emotion. Schmied's funeral takes place in pouring rain, with the
municipal band "trying desperately to keep their brass instru-
ments under their coats," with policemen in civilian clothes,
"all with the same raincoats, the same black bowler hats,
holding umbrellas aloft like sabres, fantastic mourners . . .
unreal in their probity." This grotesquely uniform crowd is
disturbed by the arrival of Gastmann's gangsters, two "great
loutish fellows, butchers in evening dress, so drunk that they
were always on the point of falling." Singing bawdy songs
written in the Berne dialect, the language of Dürrenmatt's
emotion, they throw a laurel wreath on the coffin, and stumble away "through the wet grass, holding each other up,
clinging to each other, falling over graves and overthrowing
crosses in the violence of their intoxication" (JHH 57–59,
RsH 72–74).[7] They come and go unexpectedly, as meteors
might, perturbing the sacred peace of the graveyard; they
are elements in an unconventional, completely personal scene
to be called absolutely grotesque. Chaos breaks up order.
No detail in the exact description of the events is without its
significance in this masterfully controlled scene.[8]

[6] Dürrenmatt in *Allemanisch-welsche Sprachsorgen und Kultur-fragen*, ed. by Roberto Bernhard, p. 38, reprinted in DK 87.

[7] I have added two phrases omitted or misinterpreted in the translation: "unreal in their probity," "butchers in evening dress."

[8] There are two details also occurring in Dürrenmatt's memories of
childhood: "the graveyard was without fear," while the village butch-

"Death, the relatively stable eye of the storm of life, the justice which the dead Schmied has served—these are alike made to seem obscenely ridiculous," Eugene E. Reed writes in his analysis of the graveyard scene. He also finds a new dimension behind this scene, "a once abstract evil now made palpable."[9] Gastmann is the representative of evil; having seen his emissaries in the graveyard we are now prepared for a meeting between Bärlach and Gastmann to start two pages later. Their first encounter, in Turkey, had resulted in a lifelong bet. Bärlach, a representative of law and order, claimed that the criminal had always to pay for his crime, "because no man can calculate exactly and on every occasion the ever-present element of chance." Gastmann, on the other hand, maintained that "it is just this chaos in human relationships that makes it possible to commit crime and get away with it." There are lots of crimes "incapable of solution because the world never even knows they have been committed" (JHH 63).

We have now arrived at the central idea of *The Judge and His Hangman.* Both Bärlach and Gastmann recognize the role of chance in life, yet the conclusions they base on their identical observations are diametrically opposite. For Bärlach, chance means a regrettable hole in the inscrutable chain of logic supporting a moral world order; for Gastmann, chance guarantees a freedom to do whatever one pleases, whether good or evil, without any moral scruples at all. They have lived accordingly: Gastmann committed a murder in the presence of Bärlach, yet got away with it, and since those days he has crossed Bärlach's path "again and again, committing . . . bolder, madder, badder crimes" (JHH 65), yet avoiding punishment each time. On the other hand, he is also free to do good, as stated by Dürrenmatt's half-humorous self-portrait in the novel, who is an author inter-

---

ers at their work made the onlooking children think that there was nothing human in the beast of prey called man (TS 34–35).

[9] "The Image of the Unimaginable," p. 121. Cf. Brock-Sulzer's appreciative description of the scene (*F.D.*, pp. 184–86).

ested in Gastmann as "a genuine nihilist."[10] If ever Gastmann "does good it is out of pure caprice, on the spur of the moment. . . . He is not the man to do evil for the sake of gain. . . . He will do it for no reason at all" (JHH 77). Gastmann is the antithesis of a monomaniac.

Dürrenmatt, a former student of philosophy, had been preoccupied with the philosophic problem of freedom for quite a while. In the concluding pages of *Angel*, Akki and Kurrubi fled into a freedom to be enjoyed with one's good deeds and with God's grace. Gastmann represents a nihilistic freedom not at all related to a scale of good and evil. All his life, he has had the upper hand in his fight with Bärlach. During the action of the novel Bärlach, a man mortally ill, beats Gastmann by manipulating chance, the ingredient in life that had guaranteed Gastmann victory for a lifetime. Bärlach's last chance is Chanz (spelled in German Tschanz). The Commissioner has known all the time that Schmied was murdered by Chanz out of rivalry. Unable to condemn Gastmann for crimes he has really committed, Bärlach executes him for a murder he did not commit.[11] Chance plays into Bärlach's hands. Its personification Chanz is the ordinary criminal doing "evil for the sake of gain"; he lacks the nihilistic and metaphysical dimensions of Gastmann, and it is possible for Bärlach to manipulate him. He is fit to be Bärlach's hangman.

Bärlach started recruiting Chanz as his hangman at their

[10] Dürrenmatt's attitude to the modish nihilists of the postwar years is marked with ambiguity and self-irony. His Gastmann is a seeker "still greedy to find out the meaning of [his] own existence and this mysterious world" (JHH 62). Bockelson turns nihilism into an alluring temptation. In his student years Dürrenmatt had the words "a nihilistic poet" written on his door (Wyrsch, *Schw. Illustrierte*, part two, March 25, 1963, p. 23). Cf. Bänziger, *Frisch und D.*, pp. 152–53.

[11] Spycher takes Bärlach quite critically: our detective has accepted a Mephistophelian pact with the evil and uses highly questionable means to win his bet with Gastmann (*F.D.*, pp. 140, 159, 161–62). On the other hand, these two represent contending forces within Dürrenmatt himself (p. 156). Cf. Arnold, p. 49.

very first meeting, by employing hints and double-talk. " 'I'm a big, black tom-cat'—Bärlach said the words quite seriously —'and I have an appetite for mice' " (JHH 19). Dürrenmatt also reports the reactions of Chanz with great care—greater than would be motivated by his role as a Watson. Toward the end of the novel Bärlach says a word of forewarning to Gastmann: " 'I'm the only man who knows you, and am therefore the only man who can judge you. I *have* judged you, Gastmann, and I've sentenced you to death. . . . Today the executioner will come to kill you' " (JHH 95). And there follows a long and detailed description of Chanz's journey into the place of execution, Gastmann's house—a telling description, speaking with its pregnant nature images, telling in the same way as the description of Ill's farewell drive in *The Visit.*

Chanz as the surprise murderer fits the formula of a detective story. At the same time, this solution carries Dürrenmatt's deeper concerns, his interest in the problem of freedom and in the role of chance in life. We meet a paradoxical constellation of characters, a triangle of the judge, his hangman, and the condemned. Romulus and Mississippi were judges of themselves; there is a strange alliance between Bärlach and Gastmann, the judge and the condemned. " 'We liked each other at first sight' " (JHH 62). Not only do they share a considerable part of their past (as Saint-Claude and Mississippi do), there are even suggestions of a Jekyll-and-Hyde theme, figuring also in Dürrenmatt's early story "The Torturer." This theme is touched when Bärlach looks at the dead body of Gastmann, knowing well that his life, too, is played out:

> As Bärlach stood there, the dim light of the mortuary fell on his face and hands and played over the corpse, the same for both, created for both, reconciling them. The silence of death fell on the old man, crept into him, but did not bring him the peace it had brought the other. The dead are always right (JHH 103).

133

Hinting at an identification between the judge and the condemned: is this a Christian line of thought? Should one judge oneself? Another pair consists of Schmied and Chanz (JHH 16). Dürrenmatt's interest in double figures is persistent; in this case his antipodes find a conciliation in death.

Accounts have been settled between the judge and the executed; they have still to be settled between the judge and his hangman. Dürrenmatt is moving outside the sphere of the legal machinery set up by society, yet he tries to give an atmosphere of ritual to the closing scene of the novel. Bärlach invites Chanz to a terrible last meal, described as a textbook example of the grotesque. Bärlach "began on his third pie, never pausing, greedily consuming the good things of this world, crunching them between his jaws like a demon intent on satisfying a boundless hunger. His figure threw a grotesque and enormous shadow on the wall behind him. The vigorous movements of his arms, the rise and fall of his head resembled the dance of some triumphant negro chieftain" (JHH 105–06). Between the various courses of the drawn-out meal he explains his every move in checkmating Chanz, then sends his hangman to death, to suicide.

As so many times in Dürrenmatt, justice is done in a ghastly atmosphere. For him, human justice is a cruel, terrifying, inhuman phenomenon. The impact of the scene is heightened by the fact that Bärlach is now "strong and masterful, the picture of unchallengeable superiority" (JHH 107), yet he has been suffering from stomach pains throughout the novel and knows well enough the verdict of the doctors. First the operation, after that twelve more months to live.[12] Having a gorgeous meal and judging over Chanz takes his last physical and mental powers. He is old and dying, like the Bishop in *It Is Written*, another judge over his neighbors.

Neumann has remarked that a pun is an additional motiva-

---

[12] Reed (pp. 122–23) remarks that Bärlach is "mortally ill": a grotesque contrast to his role as a winner. The scene is a "triumphant counterpoint to the funeral scene in which evil made mock of those very qualities which here emerge victorious."

tion for Dürrenmatt's dinner-table trials. The German word "Gericht" means both "tribunal" and "dish."[13] Having a friendly dinner together is one of the very last rituals existing within our Western culture; Dürrenmatt employs it when needing a rite. More specifically, he makes use of it because of the grotesque contrasts that can easily be built on it. Here we are, happily consuming "the good things of this world"; the next moment we shall be dying.

Dürrenmatt's most spectacular last meal takes place in his short story *A Dangerous Game*. As we shall see, it takes us outside the limits of detective fiction. *The Judge and His Hangman* moves mostly within the limits of this genre; in spite of certain philosophical overtones described above, this novel can be read as a detective story proper. Dürrenmatt is by and large in control of the technical side: he gives his story a strong sense of authenticity, he knows how to handle motivation, opportunity, and proof.[14] He also furnishes his novel with touches of satire and local color. Gastmann's guests, for instance, include "small-time home-bred artists," "only interested in art and themselves" (JHH 48, 51).[15]

More interestingly, Dürrenmatt devotes quite a lot of his attention to descriptions of nature. On the stage, nature is compelled to figure mainly behind the scenes; it can be displayed behind the scenes of a novel, in a different meaning of the phrase. Dürrenmatt follows the variations of light in his Swiss scenery with special care. He places his crimes between the mountains, he shows nature behind the scenes.

[13] Neumann et al., *D., Frisch, Weiss*, p. 56, note 7.

[14] Spycher finds, however, several "undeniably clumsy, improbable and inconsistent features" in the deeds of Chanz (pp. 145–48).

[15] Bänziger has mentioned Dürrenmatt's patches of local color (pp. 153–54), while Brock-Sulzer stresses the importance of parody in these detective stories (pp. 181–82). Cf. Arnold, p. 52, and Spycher, p. 132. It is perhaps a parodical detail that Chanz beats three professionals in a gunfight, receiving bullets exactly in those parts of the body where the detectives are always hit: left shoulder and forearm (JHH 93, 99–100).

After the graveyard grotesquerie, before the first meeting between Bärlach and Gastmann, our Commissioner

> was bathed for a few seconds in dazzling light as the sun burst through the clouds, vanished again, and came back a second time—all part of the wild game of elements. Monster clouds came hurtling from the west, banked up against the mountain-sides, throwing fantastic shadows across the town which lay by the river between forest and mountains. . . . The world was so beautiful (JHH 60).

When trying to bring nature onto the stage, Dürrenmatt often sees man against the background of the sky, in a way one might call typically Swiss.[16] Switzerland is a vertical country: in the mountain district one looks at the landscape from below, seeing it against the background of the sky, and if the sky is half-covered with clouds, this may result in most dramatic changes of light, between glittering sunshine and ominous darkness, as in the passage quoted. So it is in Dürrenmatt, too: the contrasts are violent, the sky is there. Without speculating any further about the connections between a country and its literature, I find it somehow impossible to imagine that Dürrenmatt would live and write in the Netherlands.

The Judge and His Hangman, Dürrenmatt's first detective story, can be seen as a string of fairly short scenes placed against varied backgrounds, against nature. The novel is crisp, compact, relatively rich in materials, and without major flaws; most of the scenes have thematic significance and can thus be called scenic images embedded in narrative prose. In scenes dictated by the demands of the plot and little else, Dürrenmatt becomes less inspired and intensive. There are two grotesque and wildly inspired scenes as the highlights of the novel, those at the graveyard and at Chanz's last dinner table. In them the corners of the mold are filled with Dürrenmatt's own metal up to the brim.

[16] Dürrenmatt's Swiss qualities have been pointed out by his publisher Peter Schifferli (Wyrsch, part four, April 8, 1963).

According to legend, Dürrenmatt did not know beforehand what was going to happen from one installment to the next in his detective stories.[17] In the case of *The Judge and His Hangman* the legend is refuted by the name of the story, by its careful total structure, and by Bärlach's systematic procedure in recruiting Chanz as his hangman. In the case of *The Quarry* the anecdote may have some relevance. Dürrenmatt's opus two about Commissioner Bärlach is a thriller, repetitious, artistically uneven, and not fully concretized. Its style bears close resemblance to that of his early prose.

The action of the novel begins from the final chord of *The Judge and His Hangman*. Bärlach is operated on; as a convalescent in a Berne hospital he finds a lead pointing toward a Swiss-born doctor Emmenberger as a previous Nazi torturer. In the concentration camp of Stutthof Emmenberger used to operate without anesthesia; he had his first sadistic experience when he and Bärlach's doctor friend Hungertobel witnessed an accident in a hut on the Alps. A medical student had to be operated on with a pocketknife:

> The evening sun . . . made the scene all the more frightful, since a strange deep-red light settled for an almost unbearable length of time on this empty world of ice and stone. It was a deathly illumination.
>
> . . . And when Emmenberger made that cut, my God, Hans, his eyes were wide open, too, and his face distorted. All of a sudden it seemed as if something satanic broke out of those eyes, a kind of overwhelming joy of torture— or whatever you want to call it (Q 26, 28).

Again, Dürrenmatt is following closely the light in a Swiss mountain landscape; again, he is painting the portrait of a nihilist. A devil is born in an "empty world of ice and stone," in a world without God.

There is not much of a riddle involved. Bärlach is quickly convinced that the Nazi doctor Nehle is in fact Emmenberger

---

[17] Brock-Sulzer, p. 181. Spycher, p. 136, disagrees with the legend in the case of JHH.

who still practices in his private clinic for the rich in Zurich. The Commissioner is transferred to that hospital, has interesting discussions on the state of affairs in our world with Emmenberger and his mistress Dr. Edith Marlok,[18] runs the risk of being operated on again, this time without anesthesia, and is rescued by Gulliver, a gigantic Jew, the only one to survive an operation à la Emmenberger in Stutthof, and a "judge with his own laws" (Q 39).[19] This is a thriller plot, not searching for the identity of a murderer, but asking whether the detective will win and how.

The novel has a clear-cut structure: its first part takes place within the walls of a normal hospital, its second part is a descent into hell. The latter part opens with a chapter called "The Abyss"; on his way to Emmenberger's clinic Bärlach reaches the center of Zurich in Hungertobel's car on New Year's Eve and has an experience of death crystallized in a cool and precise prose:

> You will die, he thought . . .—and the earth will still revolve around the sun, in the same undiscernibly wavering course, rigid and without mercy, fast and yet so quiet, all the time, all the time. What does it matter whether this city here is alive or whether the gray, watery, lifeless plain covers it all—the houses, the towers, the lights, the people —was it the lead waves of the Dead Sea I saw shimmer through the darkness of rain and snow when we drove across the bridge?
>
> He felt cold. The coldness of the universe, an ominous, large, stony coldness enveloped him for the fleeting trace of a second, for an eternity (Q 81).

These two quotations include the poetic highlights of *The Quarry*. They are images included in two scenes completely

---

[18] Dr. Marlok, a Stutthof prisoner, is Dürrenmatt's first sketch of a female monster, a line continued in *The Visit* and in *The Physicists*. There is a careful discussion on the characters of the novel in Leonard Forster's introduction to *Der Verdacht*, pp. 15–19.

[19] Akki, Gulliver, or King Augias are not fanatics in search of absolute values: their aims are partial and "within their reach" (*Profitlich, F.D.*, pp. 50–53).

138

concretized, placed against wider backgrounds, and written in a rhythmical diction echoing Dürrenmatt's Kafkaesque early prose, yet with a fresh and final sound. Dürrenmatt's social nightmares place an individual in the middle of a hostile or indifferent crowd; his metaphysical nightmares envisage man in the middle of a stony and frozen universe. In Emmenberger's claustrophobic hell Bärlach is mainly a listener. The novel is doomed to little action and movement by Bärlach's condition: all the time he is a helpless patient in two hospitals. Dürrenmatt has taken the virtuoso task of making the long discussions live by the force of their arguments alone. He does not quite succeed: they tend to be verbose and repetitious. The special qualities of Emmenberger as a nihilist are approached by Hungertobel, Gulliver, Marlok, and the doctor himself. There is not enough narrative tension, the tension of a fully concretized thriller; yet several of Dürrenmatt's intellectual tensions are discernible. Interestingly enough, Marlok and Emmenberger, Dürrenmatt's ambivalent nihilists, develop lines of thought figuring later on in his theory and practice as a tragicomedian. They do so in long monologues, not energetically interrupted or gainsaid by our weakening knight of justice.[20] When they dig at the roots of our modern disbelief, they certainly make their points:

> One believes in something—even though it's quite vague, as if an uncertain fog hung over it all. One believes in something like humanity, Christianity, tolerance, justice, socialism, and love for one's neighbors—things that sound a little bit empty. People admit it, too, but they also think the words don't matter. What matters is to live decently

[20] Peter B. Gontrum makes quite a lot of Dürer's painting "Knight, Death and Devil" as a symbol in the novel. Bärlach asks it to be brought into his room; he is himself "less well equipped . . . than Dürer's Knight to fight evil. . . . As Dürrenmatt proceeds from one novel to the next, he places more and more limitations on the effectiveness of his Knights." In *Judge*, Bärlach "is able both to control circumstances and to destroy evil"; in *The Quarry* "this is accomplished by Gulliver, a figure totally unrelated to Bärlach" ("*Ritter, Tod und Teufel,*" *Seminar, 1,* 2, Fall 1965, pp. 92–93).

and according to one's best conscience. And that they all try to do—partly by struggling for it, partly by just drifting. Everything we do, deeds and misdeeds, happens by chance. . . . By chance you become good and by chance you become evil (Q 143).

Drawing ultimate conclusions from this doctrine of chance, Emmenberger denies the value of justice and sees man's freedom in his "courage to commit crime": "For when I kill another human being . . . when I put myself outside all the order of this world, erected by our weakness—I become free, I become nothing but a moment. But what a moment! In intensity as gigantic, as powerful, as unjustified as matter" (Q 147).

Like a preacher, Dürrenmatt is driving his readers toward a point where they have to make a clear-cut choice, where they are standing in front of two alternatives, mutually exclusive. We can complain at the vagueness of our beliefs, we can state that our guilt is shared by so many that we do not know "what crime sticks to the fruit we eat" (Q 118); yet we do not necessarily develop into sadistic mass murderers. The Nazi doctor is no longer free to do good, as Gastmann was. The Duke in *The Blind Man* was an exponent of blind belief; his actions led to death, murder, and destruction. Emmenberger is a blind disbeliever—and a murderer. Dürrenmatt's position is in between; we should neither believe nor disbelieve blindly. The world is neither the creation of an omnipotent, man-loving God, nor a product of blind chance. Or we should not, as monomaniacs do, base all our deeds on either of these views.

Yet Dürrenmatt proceeds quite cautiously in developing his positive answer to the accusations presented by his nihilists. Bärlach does not say a word: "The old man was silent" (Q 148).[21] The impression one receives from the last en-

[21] Spycher sees Marlok's and Emmenberger's philosophies as "variations of negative possibilities within Bärlach's view of the world." Bärlach keeps quiet because he does not want to compete with a devil like the Nazi doctor (pp. 189–95). Marlok and Emmen-

counter between Bärlach and Emmenberger is that Bärlach resists the last temptation to state his faith, to say something he did not know to be true for sure. Emmenberger does his very best to make the old man speak. The doctor is so superior, so certain of himself in his role as torturer, that he wants to lose; for him, there is the irrational temptation to think that he may be wrong, after all.[22] This can be concluded from his behavior when Bärlach has been silent for the last time: "Then Emmenberger's face—which had been greedy for an answer—became cold and relaxed. . . . It was as if disgust shook him when he turned away from the sick man, tired and indifferent" (Q 151).

Dürrenmatt's last word is reserved for Gulliver. There has been quite a lot of abstract discussion, partly pathetic, because it is not furnished with the counterweight of irony or sarcasm. As in his youthful prose, Dürrenmatt fails to achieve the balance inherent in the grotesque; instead he achieves pathos.[23] In the concluding chapters of the novel there is, however, a motif well developed in terms of the thriller. The hands of a clock approach the moment of operation, of death: "There was no longer an outside world, no earth that revolved, no sun, and no city. There was nothing but a greenish round disk with hands that moved, overtook each other, covered each other, tore away from each other" (Q 153–54). And then Gulliver arrives, this figure cut directly from a fairy tale, as a trumpeting deus ex machina: "We as individuals cannot save this world, that would be so hopeless a task as that of poor Sisyphus. . . . Therefore, we ought not to try to save the world but to get through it— the only true adventure that remains for us at this late hour" (Q 161). In the last glimpse we have of him, he is framed by

berger think Dürrenmatt's thoughts, yet he rejects their deeds (Arnold, pp. 54–55).

[22] Cf. Gontrum, p. 91.

[23] Brock-Sulzer finds fault with Dürrenmatt's impatience when dealing with his materials, and the resulting schematism and pathos (pp. 195–96).

a window,[24] with Emmenberger's dwarf against his left cheek, "while the almost full moon appeared on the other side of his majestic head, so that it seemed as if the Jew carried on his shoulders the whole universe, earth and humanity" (Q 162).

The Quarry, this uneven but interesting thriller, closes with a painting. There are both deeply personal and contemporary tones vibrating in Dürrenmatt's somber melody: Sisyphus is a figure actualized by Albert Camus, and Dürrenmatt is playing with the Swiss guilt complex caused by the war. One can read the novel as a thriller, not to one's complete satisfaction: why does Bärlach, for instance, reveal himself right after his arrival at the clinic?[25] His only trump card is that Emmenberger does not know anything about his suspicion. Is it played because Dürrenmatt had no other cards in his hands or up his sleeve? Or did he play it because the installment had to be delivered to the periodical at the right time? Gulliver and Minotaur, the giant and the dwarf, are figures from literature rather than from concentration camps. Against the dark background formed by the moral bankruptcy of World War II Dürrenmatt builds a narrow narrative in which the results of his theoretical and practical thinking are seen in a fluid state. Concretizing his abstracts is a constant problem for Dürrenmatt. This time theoretical elements are disproportionate: they spill over the brim.

The intrusion of chaos was repelled in *The Quarry* at the last moment. Dürrenmatt begins his next novel *Once a Greek. . .* by building up a moral cosmos too well-ordered

[24] John R. Pfeiffer has paid attention to the repeated occurrence of windows in Dürrenmatt's prose: 24 times in *Judge*, 26 in *The Quarry* etc. They are theme-bearers: "the windows symbolically admit the influence of the 'unimaginable.' " Gulliver comes and goes through the window; at the end of the novel he bends its bars apart. When Gulliver is framed by the window, it is "like a painting," reminiscent of the legend of St. Christopher ("Windows, Detectives, and Justice," *Revue des Langues Vivantes*, *33*, 5, 1967, pp. 454, 458).

[25] Bärlach's plan to go into Emmenberger's hospital is "wrongheaded" and "surprisingly dilettante" (Spycher, p. 185).

to last. He calls his novel "a comedy in prose" (GsG 3); it is a satiric fairy tale, partly hilarious and fast-moving, yet not quite thought through to a logical conclusion. Its near-sighted hero is Arnolph Archilochos, an Assistant to an Assistant Bookkeeper in the enormous Petit-Paysan Engineering Works: a forty-five-year-old bachelor, teetotaler, nonsmoker and vegetarian. His world is "fixed, punctual, ethical, hierarchic" (OG 6).

The summit of Arnolph's "ethical cosmos" is occupied by the President of the country, "a sober man, a philosopher, almost a saint" (OG 6). Number Two is Bishop Moser, "head of the Old New Presbyterians of the Penultimate Christians" (OG 8), not to be mixed up with the Old or with the New PPC. Number Three is Petit-Paysan, Arnolph's employer; Number Four Passap, a well-known abstract painter; and so on down to Number Eight, Arnolph's brother Bibi, father of an amorphous family with clear criminal tendencies and a chronic need of money. The lowest place in Arnolph's cosmos is reserved for "the negative principle," for the Communist Fahrcks (OG 11). This is, of course, the kind of order Emmenberger or Marlok would have smashed with a subordinate clause. For greater safety Arnolph keeps the pictures of his top eight in his garret, and tries his best to get a few of the topmost hung on the walls of Chez Auguste where he takes his meals.

This is a milieu of a new kind in Dürrenmatt: the world of the nondescript. It is sketched with warmth and humor, until a cooler wind of satire begins to blow through it, through Dürrenmatt's amalgamation of Paris and some Swiss city.[26] Arnolph puts a "wanted" advertisement in "Le Soir": "Greek seeks Greek wife." He gets an answer from a girl called Chloé Saloniki, and meets her in Chez Auguste. Chloé is too charming to be true, a "good fairy," a "vision of loveliness and grace" (OG 21). From the very beginning she takes it

[26] Archilochos lives in "a provincial, fabulous Paris" (Brock-Sulzer, p. 210); "bistros à la Paris are visited by people from Seldwyla" (Bänziger, p. 155).

for granted that Arnolph will marry her. These two take a long walk "through deserted suburban streets" (OG 25), through the landscape of Dürrenmatt's early prose. Rain and fog, used to paint a hazy, melancholy background for the early chapters, are retreating: "Blue sky shimmered between masses of fog, delicate and elusive at first, a mere hint of spring . . . , faintly tinged by sunlight, then clearer, brighter, stronger" (OG 28). To Arnolph's amazement he is benevolently greeted by all the top men in his ethical cosmos, from Number One down to Number Seven, while the weather was growing "steadily warmer and more brilliant, the sky steadily bluer and more unreal. . . . He was more than an Assistant Bookkeeper now. He was a happy man" (OG 32).

The miracles of nature and of Sunday are continued on Monday. Archilochos finds himself climbing the long ladder of bureaucratic hierarchy in Petit-Paysan Engineering Works with breathtaking speed. He has a discussion with a Bookkeeper, a Chief Bookkeeper, and then with Petit-Paysan himself, meeting him in the cool and high air of an industrial heaven cluttered with classic works of art.[27] When trying to remember the name of our hero, Petit-Paysan enumerates, in a regal manner, a considerable part of the letter A in a *Who's Who* of ancient Greece: Anaximander, Agesilaus, Aristippus, Artaxerxes, Agamemnon, Anaxagoras. Just to add to Dürrenmatt's fun and games with names, Directors Zeus and Jehudi, bypassed by Archilochos on his upward journey, have nervous breakdowns, and the whole sequence of hilarious satire is finished with Arnolph as the newly appointed General Director of the Atomic Cannon and Obstetrical Forceps Division, with two years' salary in his pocket, ready to start his honeymoon.

Dressed up appropriately to his new position Arnolph is nominated a member of the Old New Presbyterian World Church Council, and painted in the pose of a raging Ares by

[27] Petit-Paysan is Bührle in Swiss German: the name of a well-known industrialist (Bänziger, p. 156).

Passap—abstractly of course.[28] In a rococo palace given to
him as a wedding present by an unknown donor, he is about
to embrace Chloé in her bedchamber, when they are disturbed by Nadelör, an art dealer, first wet through, then
frozen stiff,[29] so that he rings "like a glockenspiel" when he
walks (OG 107). This is a typical example of the grotesque
detail swarming in this abundant extravaganza;[30] Nadelör is
used as a surprise moment beyond credibility, and, what is
worse, beyond fun.

Obviously, this line of development cannot be sustained
any longer. Our Cinderella (Cinderellus?) has to be brought
down. Dürrenmatt gathers his whole cast together in a culminating scene, set in the Héloïse Chapel, and rhythmically
well mastered. This is a wedding scene in which two worlds
meet—and crash. There is the world of the underdog, represented by Arnolph, and by the "barren, poverty-stricken air"
of the chapel itself (OG 135). There is the sophisticated
world of Chloé, and of Arnolph's dignitaries, from Number
One down: "the sparkle of jewelry and pearl necklaces filled
the room; shoulders and breasts glowed, and fumes of the
finest perfume rose upward into the half-charred rafters."
These are existing worlds; they meet mainly in fairy tales.
When Bishop Moser lays "the Bible with its bright gilt edging
on the cracked wood of the lectern" (OG 136), these two
worlds touch one another; and when Arnolph has said his
"I do", and turns to face the dignified congregation, he suddenly understands: "I HAVE MARRIED A COURTE-
SAN!" (OG 140).

So Arnolph wakes up at long last—in the middle of a
social nightmare. Dürrenmatt's starting-point has been to

[28] Passap's chaotic studio may be a reminiscence from Dürrenmatt's youth; he was to use a similar milieu in his play *The Meteor*.
Cf. Spycher, note 79, p. 381.
[29] "Hyperbole in visual imagery" leads to "numerous comic effects."
"The phrase 'frozen stiff' " is taken literally (Peppard, p. 118).
[30] These grotesque elements are carefully described by Peter
Marxer ("Literarischer Humor," *Volkshochschule*, March 1963, pp.
77–88), many of them also by Grimm (*Der unbequeme* D., pp. 74–
75, 81–82).

take the phrases "pure fool" and "city-wide prostitute" literally; once more, he is concretizing abstracts.[31] This artistic invention carries him up to the climax of the novel, not any further. Arnolph's ethical cosmos breaks into splinters, and so does the novel, more or less. From now on Dürrenmatt's problem is to develop his plot situation by situation, without any precise direction. Fahrcks saves Arnolph on the verge of suicide and sends him to assassinate the President with a hand grenade. The life of an anarchist has its darker side, our Greek finds out, when climbing up the facade of the President's palace, decorated with an abundant collection of sculpture, making "his way between enormous breasts and thighs." Archilochos has his precarious moments in the middle of "a battle with Amazons" (OG 153)—as Dürrenmatt has been sighing among other remnants of our ancient heritage, in *Romulus*, in *Angel*, as a tragicomedian.

The President receives Archilochos in a grand way, chats about his own escapades, and offers our vegetarian and teetotaler some chicken:

"Ludwig, pour us the champagne."
"Thank you," Archilochos said. "But I'll kill him nevertheless," he thought.
. . . And so Archilochos ate and drank, in the first place in order to gain time and adjust to the novel circumstances, and then because he was enjoying it (OG 159–60).

That ends his career as an anarchist; and a speech by the President makes his adjustment to the novel circumstances complete:

"A grace has been conferred upon you. . . . There are two possible reasons for this grace, and it depends upon you which of them is the valid one: love, if you believe in that love, or evil, if you do not believe in that love. Love is a miracle that is eternally possible; evil is a fact that is eternally present. Justice condemns evil, hope longs to reform

[31] These phrases are mentioned, e.g., by Peppard, p. 117.

it, and love overlooks it. Only love is capable of accepting grace as it is" (OG 164–65).

When listening to this speech, plentifully scattered with the central concepts of Dürrenmatt's literary cosmos, one cannot avoid the lurking suspicion that the writer is quite in earnest.[32] It would seem to be so even against the background of the final developments in the novel. Archilochos returns to his palace, full of tender feelings for Chloé, only to find his rascal of a brother there, with family, relatives, and friends, celebrating a medium-sized Bacchanalia. That is enough to turn him into "Ares, a Greek god of war, as Passap had predicted" (OG 168). In the ensuing stage-filling battle "Arnolph swung, choked, scratched, struck, smashed, pounded heads together, raped a mistress while wooden legs, brass knuckles, rubber truncheons, and bottles hailed down on him. . . . Finally, when they were all outside, he threw the hand grenade after the howling crew, and the explosion illuminated the garden along with the first light of morning" (OG 169–70). In the last phrase of this first ending, we see him bloodstained, purged of feelings of pity and fear, with his glasses lost.

There follows ending number two, written for "public libraries" (GsG 142). Arnolph finds his Chloé in Greece, returns to his rococo palace, and establishes a boarding house, with the whole cast of the novel as his boarders. Then, finding their virtuous world a little dull, Arnolph and Chloé Archilochos decide to go back to Greece in search of the statue of Aphrodite. " 'We must never stop seeking the goddess of love,' she whispered. 'Otherwise she will abandon us' " (OG 180). Second curtain.

Without doubt, Dürrenmatt is entertaining both his readers and himself. He is employing another formula, writing his love story, yet not proceeding very far into the jungle of

[32] The scene is taken in earnest, e.g., by Arnold, p. 61; Peppard, p. 116; and Brock-Sulzer, p. 214. A saying by Dürrenmatt himself points in the same direction (Wyrsch, part five, *Schw. Illustrierte*, April 15, p. 37).

eroticism. At least the second end of *Once a Greek.* . . is to be taken as a parody;[33] it might have been better to leave it out. Chloé is an earthly angel, bringing the grace of erotic love to our teetotaler; losing his glasses means for Archilochos gaining a new vision of our world, a more honest one, a more disillusioned one.[34] Dürrenmatt's artistic alchemy compels his readers to follow vigilantly the developing story, until its early climax makes the total structure totter. Arnolph Archilochos is both a cog in a big industrial machine and raging Ares; his story is both a hilarious satire and a sentimental novel of entertainment.[35]

Certainly, the role of nature is conspicuous in *Once a Greek.* . . . When the fog lifts, our nondescript anti-hero sees and can be seen clearly—until the sun brings with it coldness and frost, which turns into a thaw in the first ending of the novel.[36] Background and plot are intimately interwoven also in Dürrenmatt's two first detective stories. When nature in her changing colors and lights is actively present, Dürrenmatt's scenes—or, if we can use our theater terminology— his scenic images, gain additional depth. They are placed within a wider frame of reference; that extra dimension makes their structure more intricate, more stratified. Dürrenmatt is on his way toward many-dimensional, stratified scenic images. This is perhaps the most important new feature in this group of three novels, all varying Dürrenmatt's central themes of justice, chance, and conflict between chaos and order. After these three more or less successful exercises Dürrenmatt was ready to write his most significant stories, *A Dangerous Game* and *The Pledge.*

[33] Cf. Neumann et al., p. 50; Grimm in *Der unbequeme D.*, p. 89.

[34] Arnolph had seen everything "false and distorted" through the glasses (Brock-Sulzer, p. 215).

[35] Archilochos could be either a genuine office worker or a reborn Ares, "yet he is neither of these, or he is it alternately, as the writer wants to have it" (Horst, "Humoristische Brechung," *Merkur, 10,* 8, p. 819). Spycher poses a long series of questions not answered by the story: who and why arranges Arnolph's sudden rise? "It all remains undecided" (pp. 211–13).

[36] Peppard (p. 115) remarks about the connection between the weather and the spiritual atmosphere of the novel.

7 The Absolute Grotesque Takes Over

A DANGEROUS GAME,
THE PLEDGE

||||||||||||||||||||||||||||||||||||||||||||||||||||||||||||||||||||||||||||||||||||||||

Dürrenmatt's alter ego in the short story "The Tunnel" had a special ability to see "the terrible behind the scenes" (S 151). A major representative of this ability of Dürrenmatt's is *A Dangerous Game* (Die Panne, 1956), a longish story. With it and with the novel *The Pledge* (Das Versprechen, 1957) we are in the very years that indicate the highest peak in Dürrenmatt's creative work; *The Visit* was finished in 1955. These three works are connected by a network of cross-references, and they are also related to Dürrenmatt's central theoretical writings. Facing this field of problems, we can note with interest that Dürrenmatt begins the prose version of *A Dangerous Game* with a short theoretical treatise.[1] Its position is emphasized by calling it the "First Part" of the story.

"Are there any feasible stories left, stories for writers to write?"[2] This is the question raised by Dürrenmatt, and he answers it by using a method of elimination. He supposes a writer refusing to talk about his own person, "to generalize

[1] There is a radio play version of the story, published in 1961 (GH 245–87) and discussed in my Chapter 8, which deals with all of Dürrenmatt's radio plays. After having weighed quite a lot of evidence, Spycher, contrary to most scholars, is inclined to take the story to be earlier (pp. 260–71). The radio play is earlier, Dürrenmatt says (G 34). There is also a television version by Dürrenmatt and adaptations for the stage made in Italy and the USA (Jenny, *F.D.*, p. 9).

[2] Richard and Clara Winston have succeeded quite well in translating the story itself into English. Their rendering of "First Part" is, however, either based on some earlier version of the text, or a free and abridged interpretation, not a translation. I am using my own translation, except for a few passages taken from DG 9–10, amounting to some six lines. The German original is included in *Die Panne*, pp. 7–12, and in TS 78–80.

romantically, lyrically his ego . . . as if truthfulness would
turn all this into general validity, and not into medical or,
in the best case, into psychological data." This writer, obviously not very far from Dürrenmatt himself, prefers working at his materials as a sculptor might: he cares neither about
a good name in the history of literature, nor about a conspicuous place in mass communication media. He knows
that "the basis of his writing is in himself, in his consciousness and unconsciousness . . . , in his belief and doubts."
Yet he also thinks that this is of no concern to the reading
public: "let it be enough what he writes, shapes, forms, let us
show the surface in an appetizing manner, and only the
surface." Having eliminated these subjects as "feasible
stories" our writer may already consider writing only about
biology or astronomy. The mighty of the world, the presi-
dents, Bulganins and princesses are there for the illustrated
weeklies, for the caprices of fast-changing fashion.

On the other hand, there is "the everyday life of the individual: . . . an average life, subject to changes in the weather
and fluctuations on the stock exchange, beset with minor
trials and tribulations, emotional upheavals attendant upon
personal crises, yet without connection with the totality of the
world." This is a key passage, running parallel with an oft-
quoted sequence in *Problems of the Theater*: "Today art
can only embrace the victims, if it can reach men at all; it
can no longer come close to the mighty. Creon's secretaries
close Antigone's case" (FP 31). Having refused to find general validity in the self-confessions of a writer, having as-
signed the mighty to the weeklies, Dürrenmatt still finds some
hope for the writer in the nondescript, in Arnolph Archilochos, in Alfredo Traps, in Alfred Ill. Yet he also emphasizes the difficulties inherent in taking their stories as feasible
ones: where is the connection with the totality of the world?
"Fate has left the stage on which we play, to lurk behind the
scenes, outside the concept of art valid today;[3] in the fore-

[3] Dürrenmatt's phrase is "ausserhalb der gültigen Dramaturgie,"
translatable also as "outside valid dramaturgy," following the theater
terminology employed in this sentence.

ground everything, the illnesses, the crises, turn into accidents." Human beings are less dangerous than the possibility of a world catastrophe caused by a machine, "a screw coming loose." "We are not any more threatened by God, by justice, by a fate like that in the Fifth Symphony, but by traffic accidents, by dams bursting because of faulty construction."

Dürrenmatt has been writing with his best polemical brio, defending his privacy and his own way of writing, rebuffing other possibilities. There is something not quite consistent in his argument; perhaps he leaves the question open as to how an average life can grow into a universal destiny, in order to answer it in the "Second Part," in the story itself. Or perhaps he does not deny the role of fate altogether, but only modifies it. Fate still lurks "behind the scenes," not "a fate like that in the Fifth Symphony"; if we cannot call it "fate" any more, than there is something inexplicable and terrible behind the scenes, outside our concept of art. There are still "feasible stories left," there is still universal significance to be achieved. This is stated in Dürrenmatt's credo, placed at the end of his "First Part":

> Our way leads into this world of breakdowns in which there still emerge a few feasible stories on the dusty wayside, sharing company with billboards for ballet shoes, Studebaker and ice cream, and with cairns commemorating victims of accidents. In these stories an ordinary face looks like the whole of humanity, bad luck expands unwittingly into universal dimensions, righteousness, justice, and perhaps even grace, are still made manifest, caught by chance for a fleeting instant in the monocle of a drunken old man.

The story begins with a breakdown. Forty-five-year-old Alfredo Traps, a sales manager in textiles, is on his way home when his new Studebaker breaks down. He might go home to his wife and four sons by train, yet prefers staying overnight in a country village, tempted by the possibility of

151

an amatory adventure. He has an ordinary face; his morals are those prevailing among businessmen in those postwar years, in the middle of an all-European boom.[4] Dürrenmatt takes his time in revealing Traps' morals: at the beginning he draws an idyllic picture of a harmless and enjoyable night in the company of four retired servants of justice. In the village "everything was solid and clean; even the manure heaps in front of the farmhouses were carefully layered and neatly squared off" (DG 14). Throughout the story Dürrenmatt is a master in creating atmosphere with the help of short and poignant descriptions of scenery and of the company celebrating an enormous meal.

The inns of the village are fully occupied, so Traps is directed to a private house behind a sizable garden of flowers, mainly roses. His host, a retired judge, is not in the habit of charging for a night's lodging, yet expects his guest to join the company of his habitual visitors. Traps says good-bye to his amatory adventure, and gets "quite a jolt" when seeing the "old codgers," "like monstrous" ravens in their frock coats. They look "slovenly, superannuated, untidy" (DG 19); their ages are seventy-seven, eighty-two, eighty-six, and eighty-seven,[5] their professions judge, prosecutor, defending counsel. And executioner—though this is revealed to Traps much later during the course of the evening. Every night these four "play at holding court" (DG 23). All they need is a defendant.

Traps has "a liking for crude practical jokes. He would be glad to play, he said" (DG 24). Having thus been assured of a defendant and their evening's fun, the old men are ready to start their supper: " 'A crime can always be found' " (DG 25). In a subtle way Dürrenmatt keeps vacillating between bad omens and feelings of reassurance, registered by

[4] Cf. Mayer, *Zur deutschen Literatur der Zeit*, p. 322.

[5] According to Lutz, Bärlach relied on "a rustic gendarmerie of trustworthy granddads" (JHH 102). Here we have their court. Dürrenmatt's figures are often of a great age; this gives them sharp contours, compels them "to that extreme form of their character which is hardly distinguishable from madness" (Brock-Sulzer, *F.D.*, p. 223).

Traps and, more alertly, by the reader, proceeding "with growing enjoyment to the series of inadvertent confessions which Traps makes."[6] Before these confessions start slipping out, Traps is warned by his defending counsel: " 'It is sheer recklessness . . . to feign innocence before our court' " (DG 27). Yet this is exactly what Traps maintains, achieving an effect of horror: " '*Innocent?*' . . . The sudden silence was frightening. Not the clink of a fork or spoon could be heard, not a heavily drawn breath or sipping of soup" (DG 29).

It is quickly established that Traps used to be "just a plain ordinary traveller in textiles" (DG 30). Now he is a sales manager and a privileged agent for Hephaeston. It is easy for the learned judge to recognize in this trade mark Hephaestos, a Greek god, "and a great and subtle smith, who trapped the goddess of love and her lover . . . in a net forged so fine as to be invisible" (DG 34). Transparent Hephaeston, "the greatest synthetic of all" (DG 35), grows into a symbol of the double plot in the story. Traps managed to ensnare his tyrant of a boss Gygax in an invisible net (at least he thinks so), and before long he is trapped in a net of jurisdiction by his newly-won friends.[7] Traps had to cut "old Gygax's throat" (DG 36), to use an expression current in business circles, in order to get on. Gygax died at the age of fifty-two, shortly before Traps took his job. Comments the prosecutor: " 'We've turned up a corpse, and that is the main thing, after all' " (DG 39).

[6] Peppard, *F.D.*, p. 103. He leads the name Traps back into the German words "trapsen," "to stumble or stagger," or "der Taps," "an awkward fellow" (p. 105). With the name Tschanz in mind we can also refer to an English stem word: Alfredo certainly falls into a series of "traps." Bänziger refers to "die Trappe," "trap for an animal" in Grimm's dictionary, and a word in the Berne dialect (Knapp, ed., *F.D.*, p. 218).

[7] Gontrum sees both sides of this matter ("*Ritter, Tod und Teufel*," *Seminar*, *1*, 2, Fall 1965, p. 94), while J. F. Alexander lists several meanings for "breakdown": the accident that makes Traps stay in that house, his "mental collapse," his behavior toward his boss, what happened to Gygax, and the end of the story ("Introduction" to *Die Panne and Der Tunnel*, p. 25).

Ingeniously enough, Dürrenmatt lets the interrogation take place in a friendly atmosphere. "A cosy intimacy, a warmth and fondness of each for all, spread through the company, and with it a relaxation of manners and a greater informality" (DG 40). In fact Traps is so credulous that he has not even noticed that the interrogation has already started. As in *Judge*, as in *The Quarry*, we are moving outside the official legal machinery, "free from needless red tape of forms and verbatim reports and documents" (DG 41)—so much the worse for our defendant. Ominous details and key questions are served just as suavely as the numerous dishes at the company's supper table. Yet Traps is enjoying the time of his life, for "the particular beauty of this game of ours . . . is the way it gets under one's skin and gives one the shivers. The game threatens to turn into reality" (DG 49). It certainly does.

In an interim discussion with his defending counsel Traps learns that the fourth officer of law present is a former executioner. The name of this sturdy and silent gentleman is Mr. Pilet, perhaps an echo from Dürrenmatt's early story "Pilate." Traps also hears that his amiable companions have reinstated the death penalty in their "own private brand of justice": " 'It is precisely the risk of death penalty that makes our game so exciting and unique' " (DG 45). The warmth of the summer night in the rose garden and "the greater warmth of the wine" consumed in considerable quantities help Traps overcome these shocks: "he was a man who had seen a good deal . . . not some timorous, strait-laced, small-minded prig" (DG 47). Back in the villa he goes to Mr. Pilet, presses his hand, and calls it a pleasure "to have so fine and upstanding a man to dine with." Pilet blushes and murmurs in embarrassment: " 'Delighted, delighted, will do my best' " (DG 50).

Traps is not making the job of his defending counsel any easier by insisting on his innocence, and by excluding the counsel from his confidence. When the interrogation is reopened, he tells that Gygax died of a heart attack: " 'He'd had one years before and had to be careful' " (DG 53).

154

Traps learnt this secret from Mrs. Gygax, a wife cruelly neglected by "the old bastard," and "a cute little piece" consoled by Traps "in Gygax's living room and later on . . . in the Gygax marital bed" (DG 54). Not seeing how far these revelations are likely to compromise him, our defendant is somewhat amazed at the excitement they cause. Pilet calls it a confession, the counsel for the defense protests that his client has "lost his mind." A loud and heated argument on some technicality leads to a question put by the prosecutor: " 'Are you still on friendly terms with Frau Gygax?' " When Traps explains that he has "kept away" from her "since Gygax's death" (DG 55–56), this is enough to release another outburst of merriment, with everybody shouting with glee:

> The midget judge blew out all the candles except one; then, bleating, hissing, and growling a wild accompaniment, he held his hands behind the flame of this single candle and deftly threw a shadow-play upon the wall: he crooked his fingers this way and that to make goats, bats, devils and goblins. Pilet drummed on the table until the dishes and glasses danced, chanting: "We'll have a death sentence, we'll have a death sentence" (DG 56).

In this key phase of his plot, Dürrenmatt piles grotesque details upon one another: the animal-like noises, the shadows and darkness, the distorted figures on the wall, the bats and devils. "This is in fact an invasion of spirits from hell under a comic disguise, thus according to Kayser purest grotesque."[8] Dürrenmatt is building up his absolute grotesque.

Then follows the summing up of the case. The prosecutor, speaking like Gastmann or an eloquent and smooth-tongued version of Mr. Mississippi, calls Traps' deed "a murder so subtly arranged that of course it has brilliantly escaped the attention of official justice." Traps forgets himself for a moment and starts protesting, then remembers: "Of course—

[8] Grimm in *Der unbequeme D.*, p. 80.

155

what a wonderful joke!" (DG 58). The whole company
drinks to the sales manager's health with a 1914 vintage
wine, "for without a culprit it is scarcely possible to discover
a murder or to make justice prevail" (DG 59). Feelings of
friendship between an officer of law and a condemned man,
hinted at in *Judge*, are now openly expressed: "They embraced, hugged, patted each other on the back, drank to
each other; a tide of emotion washed over them, the joy that
accompanies the blossoming of a new friendship" (DG 60).
In retirement all the old men have learnt to appreciate the
beauty of crime, not only the beauty of justice; justice includes, rather, something "terrifying and beautiful" (Pa 76).
All kinds of paradoxes collide in this speech and in this remarkable scene. There is the very Dürrenmattian idea of
justice as a terrifying phenomenon, there is the over-eager
appreciation of "a beautiful murder" felt by a great many
detectives, in literature and perhaps also in reality, and there
are elements of a parody of Christian forgiveness and of
tragedy, not seldom called "a joyful event" (DG 59).

It is still up to the prosecutor to prove his case, to show
that Gygax was murdered, though he died of a heart attack.
The prosecutor shows his artist's hand by sketching an exact
picture of Gygax: "a vigorous, robust man . . . bristling with
good health" (DG 64), concealing his critical illness, fancy-
ing "himself as being far too extraordinary, too overpowering
a man for the thought of adultery ever to occur to his wife"
(DG 67). Feeling perfectly at ease because of the friendly
ceremonies performed, assured by the bursts of laughter interrupting the "trial" every now and then, Traps lets one
dangerous detail after another slip from his tongue. He brags
about his adulterous liaison with Mrs. Gygax: " 'It finished
him off when he found out.' " And Gygax did find out,
because Traps told one of his enemies, a friend of Gygax's,
all about Mrs. Gygax and himself, thus using this outsider as
a messenger: " 'I really didn't see any reason to be considerate of him' " (DG 69).

The pattern is complete, from the prosecutor's point of

view. Traps is guilty of a murder "*dolo malo,* of having acted with premeditation." On one hand, he "engineered the revelation" to Mr. Gygax, on the other, he ceased to visit Mrs. Gygax after her husband's death, thus proving "that the wife was only an instrument in his bloodthirsty plans." Consequently, the prosecutor demands the death penalty for a murder, "performed by a psychological technique in such a manner that apart from adultery nothing was done contrary to the law—to all appearances, at any rate" (DG 81–82).

Traps has been following the show of the prosecutor "in excellent spirits." Having a murder imputed to him "upset him somewhat and made him a bit pensive," yet in a pleasant way, "for it awakened in him inklings of higher things, of justice, crime and punishment, guilt and atonement, and filled him with amazement at his own capacities." The chilling fear he had felt in the garden and "later during the hilarity at the table, now seemed to him utterly unfounded, part of the joke. It was all so human" (DG 77). In other words, Traps is giving in to the temptation of tragedy, to the temptation of justice. The ancient court with its grotesque servants is now beginning to sit within his mind, inside his head.

So, "sluggish and peaceful from the wine," sipping an 1893 cognac, our commercial traveller approaches a moment of parodical self-recognition, of *anagnorisis*:

He had planned and executed the murder, he told himself. . . . But not so much to further his career . . . —rather, it was in order to become a more...what was the word? ...a *realer* person—deeper, worthier...he fumbled for the thought, having reached the limits of his intellect... worthier of the respect and affection of these educated, cultivated men, who now (even Pilet) seemed to him like the ancient Magi he had once read about in the *Reader's Digest* who had known not only the secrets of the stars but the secrets of justice also. Justice—how the word intoxicated him! . . . It rose like a huge, incomprehensible sun

157

DÜRRENMATT

over his limited horizon, an idea only vaguely grasped and
for that reason all the more able to send shudders of awe
through him (DG 83–84).

It is a tempting role Traps sees in his mind's eye, the role of
a big-time criminal or of a tragic hero. It is all the "worthier,"
all the "realer," because it glimmers so far above his nondescript head, like the stars, like a sun.[9]
No wonder Traps does his best to sabotage the well-mean-
ing speech by his defending counsel, reducing his crime to
the commonplace. A familiar constellation is here turned
topsy-turvy: the accused is so flattered by his portrait as
drawn by the prosecutor that he refuses to believe his de-
fender. Corpulent Mr. Kummer considers his client "not only
innocent, but even incapable of guilt. (Embittered, insulted,
Traps interjected: 'But I *am* guilty, I *am!*')" (DG 84–85).
Interrupted by repeated protests from his client, the defending counsel continues his summary, admitting adultery, swindling ("he has swindled his way through life") and "malig-
nant spite," all faults amounting only to "an unethical taint":

"He is not capable of a culpability that is great and pure
and proud. . . . He is not a criminal, but a victim of the
age, of our Western civilization, which, alas, has fallen
farther and farther away from faith, from Christianity,
from universals, succumbing more and more to the rule
of chaos. . . . This average man of ours, this man in the
street, has fallen unforewarned into the hands of a crafty
prosecutor . . . who has tied together unrelated facts,
forced a logical plan upon the disorganized whole . . . has
read intention where there was only accident, has twisted

[9] In a comparison with *Kleider machen Leute* by Gottfried Keller,
Lida Kirchberger recognizes the false elements in Traps' role. He is
"forced by circumstances to play a part . . . and becomes one with
his assumed personality." "The man with the Studebaker no longer
exists and has been replaced by the hero of a fairy tale in a sphere
where the yearning for justice is fulfilled" ("'Kleider machen Leute'
und Ds 'Panne,'" *Monatshefte für deutschen Unterricht*, 52, 1, Jan.
1960, pp. 6, 8).

158

thoughtlessness into premeditation. . . . As for the heart attack itself, the Föhn that Traps mentioned is the crucial factor. . . . Of course I must admit that there was a certain ruthlessness in my client's behaviour, but ruthlessness is obligatory under the normal laws of commercial life, as he himself repeatedly stressed. Of course he often felt a desire to kill his boss. . . . But only in thought—and that is precisely the point" (DG 85–87).

When listening to this speech, one cannot help recognizing familiar tones of voice. It is as if this speech, made in order to defend Alfredo Traps, were in fact a part of a "J'accuse," of an indictment, written and signed by Friedrich Dürrenmatt and mailed to his own age. A defense as an indictment: another paradox, no doubt.

Then Traps takes the floor, agrees wholeheartedly with the prosecutor, stumbles on the verge of another self-recognition (only that night "had it dawned on him what it meant to lead a true life, to be true to oneself"), and is assured that the sublime ideas of justice and punishment "had resulted in a new birth for him" (DG 88), in a rebirth. Then the tiny judge delivers the verdict, "drunk as a lord," so that only "the general sense of it could be guessed." It is a death sentence, rebuffing mercy, assuring the average man of his fate, so that life is "perfected with logical consistency, like a work of art, and the human tragedy revealed in all its beauty," shining radiantly, "welded into flawless form" (DG 91). And then the evening reaches its climax, with champagne, with the first hint of dawn, with drunken babbling, until Traps, "in the seventh heaven, all his desires satiated" (DG 93), goes upstairs to his room, with dim images floating through his mind. A moment later the rest of the company get the bright idea of bringing his death sentence to him scribbled on parchment, blunder up the stairs, arrive at the door of the guest room, and freeze into immobility.

In the window frame hung Traps, motionless, a dark silhouette against the dull silver of the sky, amid the heavy

159

fragrance of roses floating in through the open window—
hanged so definitely and so finally that the prosecutor,
from whose monocle the gathering morning light was reflected with a brightness that increased every second, had
to gasp for air before he cried in perplexed helplessness
and sadness over the loss of his friend, cried quite grievously: "Alfredo, my good Alfredo! For God's sake what
were you thinking of? You've bedevilled the most wonderful evening we've ever had!" (DG 94–95).[10]

A Dangerous Game ends with its stupefying climax, with
this image. The story is not continued beyond its culminating
scene, as *Once a Greek*...was; moreover, there is a consistent line running through the entire narrative, preparing
for this end.[11] Traps' story is also rich in concrete details:
it is one of Dürrenmatt's best-rounded syntheses of compactness and abundance. One can find in this slender volume
associations with almost every other work of Dürrenmatt's:
another sign of its focal place, and of its highly stratified,
concentrated form. *A Dangerous Game* is a compendium of
the paths and dead ends trodden by Dürrenmatt, with all
kinds of elements brought from his previous works, whether
failures or total or partial successes.

First of all, there is a thick layer of parody in the story,
a parody of tragedy. A few observations have been presented
above; their number can be increased. Hephaestos is the name
of a Greek god, Gygax sounds like one; the image of a net
plays a part in the *Oresteia*. There is a chorus employed; The

---

[10] According to the original text, the prosecutor says his curtain
line "recht schmerzlich," "quite grievously," while Traps "verteufelt,"
or "bedevils" the night (Pa 120). I have inserted these expressions
into the Winston translation. They are of some importance; "quite
grievously" (instead of "griefstricken," DG 95) distorts the image
in a grotesque way (Grimm, *Der unbequeme D.*, p. 79), and both
God and devil are brought into it. Cf. Brock-Sulzer, p. 222, and
Holdheim, *Der Justizirrtum als literarische Problematik*, p. 95.

[11] "Dürrenmatt never ceases to be an exactly calculating artist,"
Marcel Reich-Ranicki writes about *Die Panne* and the radio plays
(*Literatur der kleinen Schritte*, p. 246).

Poultry Farmers' Association is celebrating in the village, singing in chorus: " 'Our life is like a voyage . . .' " (DG 43, 62). When they have finished, the function of the chorus is taken over by "pious sentiments" embroidered on antimacassars in the parlor of the villa: " 'Blessed be he who walks in the ways of righteousness' " (DG 78). The voice of common humanity is expressed in these lines of the chorus, in a parodical vein. At the end of a wine party, Traps experiences rebirth, as Dionysos used to do in Athens; this is another motivation for the ritualistic supper party, celebrated as Traps' Last Supper. More significantly, Traps yields to the subtle temptation of tragedy in his two decisive moments of wrongheaded self-recognition. There are several essential elements of Greek tragedy present in this prose story.

Yet *A Dangerous Game* cannot be taken only as a parody of tragedy. It has been established in the previous chapters that Dürrenmatt needs artistic formulas to employ and to renew, to fill up with his own metal. His talent is essentially polemical; he requires an object for his criticism—and a counterweight for his own creation. Only when there is tension between the model chosen and the piece of art created does Dürrenmatt find that his stories are "still feasible." He thrives in the parodistic grotesque. He likes moving somewhere between his object or model, a downright parody, and a counter-sketch ("Gegenentwurf"), a newly-created subject filled with a fresh kind of significance (cf. p. 58 above). He moves in waters not easily charted. *A Dangerous Game* is one of those works a critic can peel like an onion—only to find out that all its artistry is in the peel itself. Let us call some of it the peel of tragedy.

A Dangerous Game is also a story about a trial. All necessary officers of law are present, a case is tried, a death sentence announced. The prosecutor functions as an ingenious detective, thus establishing a connecting link with Dürrenmatt's detective stories. Yet this trial is only play-acting, "a tragic play with a farcical streak." Hans Mayer continues by stating that the conviction is based on a "theory of conditions," abolished in jurisprudence long ago. Traps only created certain conditions "not precisely salutary for a man suffering from a heart condition." In an ordinary court Traps would not have been tried at all.[12] The defending counsel is quite right, yet he loses his case.[13]

This is enough to disqualify *A Dangerous Game* as a detective story. It was never meant to be a proper one; it just uses the formula of a trial story. This is more of the peel of our onion, and not the last. Mayer remarks that the theory of conditions preserved its validity in the tradition of tragedy up to Hebbel; it has not preserved it any longer, in a society of "total and general irresponsibility" represented by Traps and Gygax. Our two businessmen live through the delirium of the postwar all-European boom which grants them a kind of general relevance as embodiments of our age. "Guilt and atonement? They will do as aesthetic concepts only as long as the aesthetic sphere of play-acting is retained."[14] This is a sphere carefully guarded by our anachronistic officers of law, gathering each night in the villa surrounded by a rose garden. In their aesthetic games they have abolished chance, and with it reality. Condemning Traps to death is for the judge "like a work of art," revealing the human tragedy "in all its beauty." Our old men live in a world of art, in a world without accidents, without chance, without breakdowns. They are apt to approve the fabrications of the prosecutor, exchanging the chaos of life for premeditation and a logical chain of thought. Like Negro da Ponte or Romulus they manipulate reality and are punished. Their gustatory enjoyments symbolize "the aesthetic as a whole."[15] They play a game misunderstood by our lowbrow Traps.

The superannuated world of the villa is also grotesquely distorted. "The old codgers" are like ravens or like characters in a satyr play; their "legal" proceedings are every now and

[12] Mayer, *D. und Frisch*, pp. 23–24.
[13] Holdheim, pp. 88–89.
[14] Mayer, pp. 24, 28. Cf. Neumann et al., *D., Frisch, Weiss*, p. 30.
[15] Holdheim, p. 91.

then interrupted by grotesque interludes, in addition to the shadow-play scene quoted above. The prosecutor stands "on his chair seat, waving his wine-spotted napkin like a banner, flaunting his waistcoat sprinkled with bits of salad and meat and splashes of tomato sauce" (DG 72). Forms of human intercourse are deformed by a slackening of manners, by a Dionysian ritual, by increasing drunkenness.[16] As Holdheim says, there are two processes developed simultaneously: the legal case is under construction, the evening under destruction. "At the moment when the chain of proof is closed, total Pandemonium burst out, and when denouncing his precisely founded verdict, the judge can only mumble."[17]

The grotesque is "the oldest and most spectacular form combining the uncombinable."[18] What is combined here? All kinds of things, including the peel of our onion. *A Dangerous Game* is a collage-like combination of various formulas employed in literature: those of tragedy and of a trial story. It is a comitragedy, a hybrid genre in which the tragic elements predominate, not a tragicomedy in the accepted sense of that term. It is a cross between aesthetic play-acting and reality, between an anachronistic concept of justice and a modern dissolution of morals. It shows a macabre foreground against an idyllic background. All around Traps, there is "a panorama of felicity, divine blessing and cosmic harmony" (DG 32); when Traps hangs from the window frame, an embodiment of gallows humor, he is seen as a silhouette "against the dull silver of the sky, amid the heavy fragrance of roses." In its combination of authentic everyday life and feelings of guilt it is one of Dürrenmatt's deepest dives into "another reality," into an underworld of crime and anxiety, lurking behind the scenes of our well-ordered Western civilization. It is written by the author of "The Tunnel" (cf. p.

[16] "The 'grotesque' party with a total alienation and disintegration into a chaos is a recurrent motif in the history of the grotesque" (Kayser, *Das Groteske*, p. 125). Cf. Peppard, p. 105, and Thomson, *The Grotesque*, p. 56.
[17] Holdheim, p. 93.
[18] Neumann, p. 31; cf. Kayser, p. 126.

37 above). And, to round it all off, it is "a still feasible story," in which "righteousness, justice, and perhaps even grace . . . are caught by chance for a fleeting instant in the monocle of a drunken old man." How is this achieved? How are we to interpret the last image of the story and, with it, the story itself? It is easy to reject the idea that *A Dangerous Game* is a tragedy in prose; rather, it is a countersketch to all kinds of tragedies, and even to Dürrenmatt's own tragicomedy *The Visit*, where the self-chosen death of Alfred Ill is still a conciliatory deed, confirming at least his own sense of justice. Nor can I take the suicide of Alfredo Traps merely as a breakdown, as an accident demonstrating that we live in a world of irresponsibility and chance, though this interpretation seems to be closer to the mark.

The grotesque is not only a principle governing the stylistic details of *A Dangerous Game*. It dictates its final solution, too. The unnecessary and "tasteless" yet happy suicide of our anti-hero is in a profound way grotesque, a disproportionate deed. I cannot submit it to any intellectual analysis, however astute, legally or aesthetically.[19] It is an absolute grotesque. It reveals a conflict, it does not solve any problem. It weighs life and death and registers zero. It includes that inexplicable element mentioned by Kayser as a prerogative of the grotesque.[20] If it proves anything, then it reveals a grotesque fate. A grotesque fate: a contradiction in terms, is it not?

[19] Mayer says that "a culmination of the grotesque is reached by insisting on ancient tragic atonement" in the case of Traps (p. 26); he calls the suicide "tasteless" (p. 28). As shown by my quotations, I go along with the interpretations presented by Mayer and Holdheim, but not as far as their final conclusions. Taking *A Dangerous Game* only as a demonstration of a "breakdown," as Mayer does (pp. 29–31), ignores the character of the story as inexplicable absolute grotesque. Holdheim seems to me to go unnecessarily far in expecting the story to be a tragedy (pp. 95–96).
[20] Kayser, passim, e.g., p. 199. Traps' fall "into a bottomless pit . . . is not to be analyzed rationally" (Werner Kohlschmidt in Albert Shaefer, ed., *Das Menschenbild in der Dichtung*, p. 191). Cf. Spycher, p. 247.

Fate presupposes an ordered world, the grotesque a disordered world, chaos.[21] Is this the fate Dürrenmatt still sees "lurking behind the scenes, outside the concept of art valid today"? Does he want to have both, chaos and order? Are "universal dimensions" attainable through grotesque disharmonies, and only through them? If so, then we should have found the connecting link between the two parts of his story; if so, then the grotesque can be achieved out of comitragedy, as Dürrenmatt believes the tragic can be achieved out of comedy, "as a frightening moment, as an abyss that opens suddenly" (FP 34). And if so, then we should have found a basic and irreconcilable dichotomy in Dürrenmatt's world. On one hand, there is a materialistic world of breakdowns governed entirely by chance, without any justice at all: the world of Dürrenmatt's nihilists. On the other, there is the ironical, self-contradictory, terrifying world consisting of both chaos and order, governed by chance *and* reason, by a grotesque fate, by a grotesque justice, caught "for a fleeting instance" in a grotesque scene. This latter world, the world of Dürrenmatt's "men of courage" and of his own creative imagination, still produces a few "feasible stories" for us, to be read by a dusty roadside.

During the war years Alfredo Traps was an unlicensed peddler, "making his weary way for miles through dark woods to remote farms" (DG 70). Gunten, the prime suspect in a sex murder in the novel *The Pledge*, is a peddler; when making his way through a wood to the village of Mägendorf he finds the mutilated body of a girl. Later on, the third-degree interrogation in the police headquarters makes him confess to the murder, and he hangs himself in his cell. There are thus several connecting links between Traps and Gunten; on the other hand, *The Pledge* continues the discussion of a

[21] Neumann (pp. 32–33) sees in Dürrenmatt "irreconcilable conflicts between finding sense and destroying sense." Fate is sometimes taken as an accident, an accident sometimes as fate: "a symbiosis between chaos and order."

165

theme mentioned and illustrated in *The Judge and His Hangman*, the theme of chance, the possibility of a detective to "calculate exactly and on every occasion the ever-present element of chance" (JHH 63). There are thematic cross-references among Dürrenmatt's prose works, and a detail may grow into a character or into a major theme.[22]

This time Dürrenmatt did not write a separate treatise: he fused his theoretical lines of thought with the story itself. *The Pledge* includes a frame story and a passively listening self-portrait of Dürrenmatt. His alter ego has been lecturing in Chur on the art of writing detective stories; in the hotel he meets the retired chief of the Zurich cantonal police who has his own opinions on that art. The atmosphere of the early scenes is created with Dürrenmatt's customary stylistic wizardry: "Time seemed to be standing still. Outside it had stopped snowing. All movement had stopped; the street lanterns no longer swayed; the wind was still" (P 5–6). Next morning when the police chief and the writer start back to Zurich by car, it is established that this has been a stillness of death:

The city was encircled by mountains, but there was nothing majestic about them. They rather resembled huge dumps of earth, as though an immense grave had been dug here. Chur itself was plainly stony, grey, sown with huge government buildings. . . . It was like a flight. I dozed, feeling leaden and weary. . . . The landscape was rigid with cold. . . . Then we were driving towards a sizeable village, perhaps a small town. We approached cautiously, until suddenly everything lay before us bathed in sunlight, in such dazzling and overwhelming light that the expanses of snow

[22] As Arnold (*F.D.*, p. 59) remarks, there is a corresponding case of connection between a passage in *The Quarry* and the central artistic invention in *A Dangerous Game*: "Imagination, there was the crux of the matter, imagination! Out of sheer lack of imagination a good, upstanding businessman will—between his apéritif and lunch—commit a crime by closing some shrewd deal" (Q 19). "Dürrenmatt is not afraid to introduce similar themes, similar situations, similar points from his view of the world again and again" (Arnold, p. 58).

166

began visibly to thaw. A white ground mist rose, spreading out over the snowfields and once more veiling the valley from my sight. It was like a bad dream, like witchcraft, as though a spell were upon this region, so that I could never come to know it (P 7).

This is the region where the sex murderer moved around; and this is a waste-land region belonging to the world of Dürrenmatt's imagination, with its images of stone, of coldness, of death, of sudden and dramatic changes of light.[23]

We catch only a glimpse of the evil withcraft behind the novel. Next we meet its hero. He is the unwashed and dipsomaniac caretaker of a run-down gasoline station in that valley: Captain Matthäi, previously from the cantonal police. Having shown Dürrenmatt this sample from reality, the police chief is ready with his initial remarks on the art of fiction: "You writers have always sacrificed truth for the sake of your dramatic rules" (P 12). To prove this he tells us the story of Matthäi.

Matthäi was a genius, a detective with a superb mind. "He was always carefully dressed, formal, impersonal, aloof; he neither smoked nor drank, and had a harsh merciless command of his profession." "Matt the Automat" was "his standard name around headquarters" (P 13). Unpopular among his colleagues, single-minded and lacking humor, "he thought about nothing but his work," yet worked without passion— "until the day came when he was involved in a case that suddenly stirred him to passion" (P 14). To give further impetus to that awakening Dürrenmatt arranges a temporary assignment in Jordan for Matthäi, then fifty years old, and probably planning retirement after that assignment. A few days before his departure there is the sex murder in the village of Mägendorf.

The Pledge was originally written as the manuscript for a

---

[23] Oberle has spoken about the appropriate selection of details in these early sequences: they build up a world, "pregnant as reality," yet with firm contours (*Der unbequeme Dürrenmatt*, pp. 21–22).

film planned to inform parents and children about sex maniacs. After the film had been made, Dürrenmatt wrote a counter-sketch to his own manuscript, no longer bound by pedagogic considerations. Yet the character of the original medium can be seen behind the text of the novel: there is quite a lot of movement and action, there are clearly shaped scenes charged with dramatic tension. The peddler Gunten and Matthäi find themselves as major characters in a tense scene between the inhabitants of the village and the representatives of a central authority. There is a Swiss feature in this conflict: from time immemorial people have been used to relying on democracy practiced in small communities.[24] Mägendorf is one of these, Guellen in *The Visit* another.

The villagers are convinced that Gunten is guilty. The *Föhn* is hanging heavily on buildings, fields, and woods. The crowd, wanting "vengeance, justice," all the more threatening because of its silence, throngs close to the emergency squad car, where Gunten is held, "huddling, trembling, between two policemen who sat rigid" (P 26). The local councillor and the magistrate are unable to release the tension; it is up to Mätthai to do so. He gives in to the demands of the crowd and promises to surrender the peddler to them: "You have now decided to make yourselves the Court" (P 30). Yet there is a condition to be met by every court of law: "injustice must be avoided" (P 31). Having thus made sure of the confidence of the crowd Matthäi shows how difficult it is to function as a court, by performing a hearing in public. Justice is better safeguarded by leaving these tasks to the official authorities: a self-evident result, yet a variation of a Dürrenmattian theme, and a principle to be denied by Matthäi later on in the story. The scene, again a social nightmare, does honor to Dürrenmatt's skill as a dramatist, and establishes the stature and cool aloofness of Matthäi. His calculations keep reality under control.

" 'I hope you never give a promise you have to keep' " (P 34), the magistrate says drily to Matthäi after the situa-

[24] Cf. Lüthy, *Die Schweiz als Antithese*, pp. 17–21.

168

tion has cooled down. An ironic line, because Matthäi has just given the parents of the victim a pledge to find the murderer. There is no way out for him; he can no longer hide behind his habitual armor of inhumanity. Gullen's confession and suicide are not sufficient reasons for him to consider the case as closed. On his way to the airport and to Jordan he sees Gritli Moser's funeral procession, and at the airport itself he encounters a group of schoolchildren. He never enters his plane; he decides to stay "to protect the children" (P 61). With Gritli's childish drawing of the murderer as his only clue he goes on with the investigation, now without any official position. He retires and makes himself the Court.

Throughout the novel Dürrenmatt uses silences and chiming church bells as ominous horror effects. The crowd keeps silent; when Matthäi approaches a mental hospital, "there is deathly silence everywhere" (P 67);[25] the church bells are present at every key phase of the action (P 57, 62, 90, 130). Matthäi receives a sketch of the probable mental make-up of the murderer from a psychiatrist: the milieu is an exercise for *The Physicists*, placed entirely behind the walls of an asylum. The next scenes of *The Pledge* are placed at the gasoline station.

Matthäi is a typical Dürrenmattian monomaniac, furnished with the best of motives. No words of forewarning can deter him from following his ingenious plan, aiming at manipulating reality. The murder of Gritli Moser belongs to a series of sex crimes, all repeating a certain pattern: so Matthäi seeks and finds a fatherless girl identical with the previous victims, takes her mother as his housekeeper, hires a gasoline station on the probable route of the murderer and starts angling. After a long and frustrating summer he is about to catch his fish. Somebody gives Annemarie a few truffles, received also by Gritli, and the girl goes to wait for her "wizard" in a clearing in the wood.

This is enough for Matthäi to alert his former chief and a

[25] Brock-Sulzer has paid attention to the "speaking pauses" in this novel (p. 203).

patrol from the Zurich cantonal police to lie in ambush for the murderer:

> It was a brilliant autumn day, hot, dry; bees, wasps and other insects were humming everywhere, birds screeching, and from far away came the echo of axe blows. At two o'clock we heard the bells of the village, and then the girl appeared. . . . The child sat by the brook, almost without stirring, full of anxious, keyed-up expectation, the refuse heap at her back, now in sunlight, now in the shade of one of the tall dark firs. . . . We waited. Nothing existed for us any longer but this autumnally enchanted wood with the little girl in the red skirt in the clearing. We waited for the murderer, resolute,, craving justice, settlement, punishment (P 110–11).

The long wait, splendidly described, takes a day, two days, a week. In the film it ends with a triumph, in the novel with a catastrophe. The police start hating and despising the girl, with her idiotic, repeated song " 'Maria sat upon a stone' " (P 114). Then the magistrate arrives and puts a straightforward question to the girl; when she refuses to betray her "wizard,"[26] everyone loses self-control and starts beating her, "cruelly, furiously, screaming and yelling. . . . 'We're beasts, beasts,' I gasped" (P 116). And the "grotesquely painful," ridiculous scene is completed with the arrival of Annemarie's mother, a former streetwalker: " 'Captain Matthäi, did you take in Annemarie and me solely in order to find this person?' " (P 117). Matthäi can only confess that he did.

That is enough for everyone except Matthäi. He keeps waiting by his bait. Dürrenmatt uses the quiet waters following the above anticlimax to insert his theoretical lines of thought. The former police chief sketches several feasible

[26] In a comparison with *The Turn of the Screw* by Henry James, Heilman speaks about "the possibility of corruption in the pursuit of a meritorious goal" in the case of Matthäi. Annemarie is an example of the unshakeable faith "an agent of evil can evoke" in a child. ("The Lure of the Demonic: James and D.," *Comparative Literature, 13*, 4, Fall 1961, pp. 351, 356).

170

endings for his story, yet calls the real end "so shabby that it simply cannot be put to use in any decent novel or film." Matthäi had been quite right; the murderer had been on his way toward the trap when . . . when chance spoiled everything, and Matthäi lost the game he was playing with his life at stake. "Nothing is grimmer than a genius stumbling over something idiotic." And Matthäi could not accept "the ridiculous thing" that brought about his fall, because "he wanted his calculations to accord with reality. Therefore he had to deny reality and end in a void" (P 126). Having created a long row of idealists trying to manipulate reality, from the prophets of the anabaptists through Romulus, Mississippi, and Nebuchadnezzar to the retired servants of justice in *A Dangerous Game*, Dürrenmatt is now ready to draw a humble and relativistic lesson:

> The worst *does* sometimes happen. As men we have to count on that possibility, have to arm ourselves against it, and above all we have to realize that since absurdities necessarily occur, and nowadays manifest themselves with more and more forcefulness, we can prevent ourselves from being destroyed by them and can make ourselves relatively comfortable upon this earth only if we humbly include these absurdities in our thinking, reckon with the inevitable fractures and distortions of human reason when it attempts honestly to deal with reality (P 126–27).

Dürrenmatt wants to have both, chaos and order. His "reality" is a mixture of these two. Part of his "real" world avoids the grasp of reason, and this part is responsible for the grotesque disturbances, for a senseless justice, for inexplicable fate.

When accepting his grotesque world, when granting the absolute grotesque some space to move within this world, Dürrenmatt rejects two other possibilities. The above passage is a belated answer to Emmensberger, to all of Dürrenmatt's nihilists. Though there is some allowance made for chance, this does not mean that the world is entirely void of justice or meaning. The world is not senseless. And it is an answer to his idealists, to Matthäi, to Mississippi, to all of the rest. The world is not rational. Dürrenmatt's erratic moralists take the absurd as an avoidable error, not as something to be included "in our thinking." On the basis of their illusions "we might find ourselves executing the whole world out of a kind of defiant morality once we undertook to try to establish a flawless rational structure" (P 127). The anabaptists or Mississippi certainly did their best by way of executions; and the "defiant morality" of Matthäi does no good for Annemarie, for her mother, or for Matthäi himself.[27]

The passage quoted above can be read as Dürrenmatt's afterthought on several of his works. It also reveals an underlying connection between *A Dangerous Game* and *The Pledge*. Traps' suicide showed the fatal consequences when an order, a tragic world order, was imposed on a chaotic mind not inclined to cherish any moral ponderings at all. Matthäi has an over-rational mind, he is passionately inclined to impose a sensible world order he has created on a reality including its chaotic elements, too.[28] The results are grotesque in both cases, with the idyllic Swiss countryside serving as an everyday background. Traps' end is a grotesque death, Matthäi's a grotesque death-in-life: a man of unshakable order as a dipsomaniac. The conflict inherent in their fates is that between chaos and order, between two basic elements in Dürrenmatt's world. *A Dangerous Game* and *The Pledge* are focal works because they give shape to that world in such a straightforward manner.

[27] Matthäi, looking for justice, is more and more wrong; his will to avoid compromises leads him to greater and greater compromises; and while trying to maintain order "he only creates disorder" (Hugo Loetscher, "Requiem auf den Kriminalroman?" *Du*, *18*, 12, Dec. 1958, p. 102). His self-sacrifice is ironically unnecessary: chance takes care of justice (Profitlich, *F.D.*, p. 72).

[28] Cf. Holdheim, p. 97: Matthäi is "a consistent man ruined by chance; Traps an everyday man trying to break through into consistence by using chance. They are two antipoles within one and the same field of problems."

How chance nullifies Matthäi's calculations, how chaos breaks his order has still to be described. The police chief gets an invitation to a hospital, to the deathbed of "a little old woman, all delicately wrinkled, hair thin and snow white, enormously gentle, obviously very rich" (P 128). The church bells are chiming and a priest is sitting at the window, patiently exhorting: " 'Tell the story, Frau Schrott' " (P 130).[29] The lady takes her time, her rambling story covers the recent history of an old refined family, including "a filthy torrent of vituperation" aimed at her sister (P 131). It appears that Mrs. Schrott was fifty-five when she married twenty-three-year-old Albert, an orphan boy taken in by her late first husband, and these two lived peacefully in Chur, with Albert working happily in the garden. Until "my dear departed Albert" ("Albertchen selig") one hot summer day comes home covered with blood, and there is a story in the newspaper which the couple read at breakfast:

> "Albert dear, you killed that girl in St Gall canton, didn't you?" Then he stopped eating his eggs and bread and jam and said, "Yes I did, Mummy, it had to be; it was a voice from Heaven," and then he went on eating (P 137).

The lady was, of course, "very worried to think he was so ill," yet decided against calling the doctor: what would her sister say? Instead she was very stern and firm with her dear departed Albert "and told him plainly that this must never, never, never happen again" (P 137). In fact, it only happened a few more times, every time ordered by a voice from Heaven.

In its infuriating combination of breakfast table and total moral blindness the scene certainly surpasses most of Dürrenmatt's grotesque inventions. So does the image of an imbecile sex murderer, "neatly dressed in black, with a black

---

[29] This is "easily one of the most effective scenes in Dürrenmatt's four detective stories" (Pfeiffer, "Windows, Detectives, and Justice," *Revue des Langues Vivantes, 33,* 5, 1967, p. 460). Cf. Brock-Sulzer, *Dürrenmatt in unserer Zeit,* p. 37.

bowler," cycling around in the Chur region, with a basketful of eggs to be delivered to the hated sister of his "wife," "whistling to himself his favourite song: 'I am a Switzer lad and love my country dear' " (P 136). This is the witchcraft pestering the road from Chur to Zurich, this is the "wizard" Annemarie was so patiently waiting for, Matthäi fighting with all his capacity to reason.[30] Almost successfully—for "Albertchen selig" really had a date with Annemarie on that brilliant and hot autumn day. On his way to the gasoline station, he was killed in a car accident.

The Pledge was to be Dürrenmatt's last prose work for fourteen years to come. He gave it the subtitle "A Requiem for the Detective Story." Both the novel and its subtitle hit their mark; the novel is easily one of the three peaks in his prose so far. It can be compared only with *A Dangerous Game* and *The Fall* (1971); all these three are stories with a great density of problems. The prose versions of *The Pledge* and *A Dangerous Game* run more or less parallel with works written for another medium.[31] This may have something to do with their mature style. If *The Pledge* is compared with *The Judge and His Hangman*, Dürrenmatt's starting-point in detective fiction, it becomes obvious that his skill in handling the story has been growing.[32] The narrative sequences do not fall below the level of the central scenes, of the artistic highlights. The scenes of the story interact, building up a continuous whole. The rhythm of the novel is epic, quiet, easy-going—as a contrast to the dramatic, more hectic rhythm of *A Dangerous Game.*

Dürrenmatt's prose is not only a by-product, "not merely

[30] Brock-Sulzer has paid attention to the use of fairy tales in the novel: Annemarie's world is governed by them, they are told to her by Matthäi, and Mrs. Schrott tells her story "as if she were telling a fairy tale to two children" (*F.D.*, p. 203). Cf. Peppard, p. 113.

[31] "Ein Dichter begräbt seinen Film" by Rudolf Stickelberger is a comparison between the film and book versions of *The Pledge*, in favor of the novel (*Reformatio, 7*, 10, Oct. 1958, pp. 592–95).

[32] Cf. Arnold, p. 57.

chips from the workbench" of a dramatist.[33] His special gift to shape grotesque situations, characters, and entire works of art also prevails in his novels. They are an encounter with his most urgent problems, verbalized in highly qualified, artistic, personal prose. If there is a consistent line of development to be drawn between them, this line seems to run through the problems of justice and chance, through the conflict between chaos and order. There is in Dürrenmatt's prose "an intense preoccupation with evil and nihilism gradually giving way to the idea that those forces which appear cruel and meaningless are more inclusively understood as absurd."[34] If Dürrenmatt's intellectual problems had been neatly solvable, they would not have puzzled him over and over again. And if he had solved them once and for all, he would probably have written them down in a theoretical treatise. His fiction exists not for the sake of its answers but for the sake of its questions. It is to be experienced, not solved. As an artist and as a seeker for questions and answers, Dürrenmatt was in those years constantly growing out of his own home-made philosophical garments, and sewing new ones. His prose tells about the immense vitality distinguishing this working process.

[33] Peppard, p. 119. Spycher (pp. 273–77) discusses a chip: "Im Coiffeurladen," published in 1957, is a fragment of a novel.
[34] Gontrum, loc. cit., p. 97.

8 More Than a Reservoir of Themes

RADIO PLAYS

||||||||||||||||||||||||||||||||||||||||||||||||||||||||||||||||||||||||||||||||||||||||||||

The radio play has been a flourishing literary genre in postwar Germany.[1] There have been close to 500 new radio plays broadcast in the Federal Republic each year; out of these, "some 25% can claim a certain artistic quality."[2] The twelve operating networks have created a continuous need for programs: it has been natural that literary débuts have been made on the radio, there have been enterprising young staffs of *Dramaturgs* and producers in action, and the medium itself seemed to fit the general cultural and social atmosphere in the postwar years. A great many writers chose to deal with the sensitive problems of the recent past privately with radio listeners rather than to use the public pulpit of the stage.[3] If Dürrenmatt and Frisch were more or less alone as stage dramatists of international stature writing in German in the late 1950's, as radio dramatists they were in good company. They could always reckon on reaching the German-speaking world immediately.[4]

---

[1] "Flourishing" is the very word used in this connection both by Gunnar Hallingberg (*Radiodramat*, Stockholm, 1967, p. 253) and by Renate Usmiani ("The Invisible Theater," *Modern Drama*, 14, 3, Dec. 1970, p. 259).

[2] Armin P. Frank, *Das Hörspiel*, Heidelberg, 1963, pp. 14, 192, note 8. Frank's figures seem to include translations and adaptations from native and foreign classics. Johann M. Kamps calculates that there is a yearly total of some 180 new original German plays (Koebner, ed., *Tendenzen der deutschen Literatur seit 1945*, 1971, p. 481).

[3] Hallingberg, p. 39; Usmiani, pp. 261–63, 268–69.

[4] The Swiss studios were not able to compete with the German networks for the first rights to broadcast Dürrenmatt or Frisch. The scripts were written in High German; they were artistically demanding; the German networks are financially on a firm ground (Frank, p. 72).

176

Dürrenmatt, living through his most expansive phase of development, probably enjoyed being able to conquer another field of artistic experimentation. Not bound by time limits, by the concrete vision of the stage, or by the whole bureaucracy connected with producing a stage play in a repertory theater, he felt free when writing for this new medium. He once assured an interviewer that he takes a radio play exactly as seriously as a stage play: "It is for me like a short story. You see, thinking all the time about the stage—you are free from it. I find the radio play a splendid new opportunity."[5] On other occasions he has admitted the importance of the financial incentive and of the German market (TS 54–55), and spoken with less enthusiasm about the possibilities and limitations inherent in a radio play. The world is "abstracted onto the single level of hearing, that is the great chance and the great weakness. . . . The theater has a more expressive dimension" (TS 61). He made the last-quoted remark in 1956, the year when he wrote his last two radio plays. He had also arrived at the conclusion that a radio play demanded its own kind of materials, its own "stuff" (TS 62). For ten years, since 1946, he had kept finding this material. Dürrenmatt's *Collected Radio Plays* (Gesammelte Hörspiele, 1961) includes eight scripts.

Germany not only is a leading country in producing radio plays, it also leads the way in studying them. In the inter- and postwar years persistent efforts have been made to define the special qualities that make a script fit for the radio. With the increase of relevant materials these efforts have met greater and greater difficulties. Armin P. Frank is ready to admit that the radio is a platform for varied, even contrasting, materials, yet he builds up a system of nine basic types, to be distinguished by certain structural characteristics—not quite convincingly.[6] Gunnar Hallingberg, writing a few years later,

[5] Sauter, "Gespräch mit F.D.," *Sinn und Form, 18*, 4, 1966, p. 1231.
[6] Frank, pp. 189–90. E.g., "the Panoramic Play," a subdivision of "Radiogenic Plays with Absolute Voices," is quite an artificial category.

is still more cautious and concentrates on concrete examples submitted to a few coordinating factors, such as epic and dramatic elements.[7]

Dürrenmatt's radio plays will be discussed in a similar way, with concrete analyses instead of an over-theoretic approach. Yet the specific features of this medium are not to be forgotten, such as the central role of the spoken word, or the technical possibilities of music, sound effects, fade-in, fade-out, and montage. It may turn out that the acoustic images utilized by Dürrenmatt in his radio plays have something in common with his audio-visual scenic images.

The Double (Der Doppelgänger, 1946), Dürrenmatt's earliest radio play, is clearly parallel with his youthful prose,[8] and with *It Is Written*, his first stage play. It begins with a discussion between a producer and a writer of radio plays. Dürrenmatt's first stage characters tended to be conscious of the theater; his radio characters are conscious of the radio medium. The producer is concerned about a coherent story to tell the listeners, the writer admits that he only knows the barest outlines of his story (GH 11). The play follows these two as they stumble toward a feasible story.

They never find one. The first voice introduced belongs to a man; he is given a name, Pedro, much later. The second voice is his double, Diego, who wakes him up in the middle of the night and tells him that the High Court has condemned him to death for a murder committed by Diego.[9] Pedro insists on his innocence, yet he is arrested and thrown into prison. Diego appears again, and the story also involves Diego's wife Inez, suddenly shot to death by Pedro. This surprise twist is explained by a half-baked paradox: "You have killed, be-

---

[7] Hallingberg, pp. 260–63.

[8] Cf. Peppard, *F.D.*, pp. 90–91.

[9] The man and his double: this is a familiar grotesque theme, used by E.T.A. Hoffmann, Poe, Dostoevsky, Wilde, Stevenson, Hesse, etc. Dürrenmatt himself hinted at it in the short story "The Torturer." Cf. Kayser, *Das Groteske*, pp. 85, 155; Grimm et al., eds., *Sinn oder Unsinn?*, p. 91.

cause you did not want to kill" (GH 29). Then Pedro poisons Diego, and is ready to submit to the unjust judgments of the High Court: "I was a murderer, though I had not killed, I was due to die, though I had not committed a crime." He should only have had faith in the High Court from the very beginning, then he would have been set free (GH 35).[10] The producer interferes once more and wants to appeal to the Court. The concluding minutes follow the writer and producer into a rococo castle, one of Dürrenmatt's poetic constants. In the park surrounding it there are hammering woodpeckers and a cuckoo: other constants.[11] The castle itself is "empty, quite empty. No judge, no defendant, only a window flapping open and shut in the wind, with dusty panes. . . . We all *have* to be content with this" (GH 37).

"It is my principle to tell only irritating stories," the writer quips in *The Double* (GH 33), thus phrasing a kind of motto for Dürrenmatt as a whole. Yet the irritating elements of this early script tend to be fairly conventional, Kafkaesque, expressionistic,[12] and youthfully *weltschmerzlich*. "Who knows himself?" (GH 20). The various ingredients of the play do not meet anywhere: the theme of the doubles is not connected with the religious humility, Inez with anything at all, while the presence of the writer creates a kind of arrogant humor, fun for a closed circle of friends. Several of Dürrenmatt's central concerns can be seen in the script in a fluid state, not yet congealed into art.[13] *The Double* is a confused parable,

---

[10] Several critics have combined the play with the concept of original sin (Waldmann, "Ds paradoxes Theater," *Wirkendes Wort, 14,* 1, 1964, p. 30; Jauslin, *F.D.,* p. 9; Werner Weber, "Ds Hörspiele," *NZZ,* June 19, 1962). Arnold sees the play as an illustration of "the absurdity of a teaching that contradicts every kind of logic, every sensible feeling of justice" (*F.D.,* p. 64).

[11] Brock-Sulzer calls these details Dürrenmatt's "dream constants"; the castle was added to the script in 1952 (*F.D.,* p. 172).

[12] Wilhelm Duwe finds in the play a typical expressionistic theme: we are all both guilty and not guilty (*Die Kunst und ihr Anti von Dada bis heute,* p. 56). Pedro's anxious monologue in the prison sounds like an expressionistic set-piece (GH 18).

[13] Cf. Brock-Sulzer, p. 171.

179

with high intentions, with an abstract and clumsy execution, with a few poetic moments relying on the suggestive power of the language, such as the finale full of horror vacuums, of metaphysical anxiety. *The Double* was produced for the first time in 1961.[14] This was after the 1950's had created a school of intimate, poetic writing for the radio in Germany.[15] In its conscious play with dream-like sequences, in its reliance on the words, in its intimate basic character, Dürrenmatt's earliest radio play seems to foreshadow this tendency. Five years later, in 1951, when writing his second script for the air, Dürrenmatt was after something else, after a panoramic picture of an imaginary society: a "matter-of-fact, analytic" line generally pursued in the 1960's.[16] These two types are clearly distinguishable in his radio plays.[17]

Dürrenmatt's metaphysical and moral analyses of individuals often work with a minimum number of characters or voices. There are three more plays of this type to be discussed. The second half, or four scripts, constitutes Dürrenmatt's world theater for the air: wide social panoramas with a great selection of voices, with satire, puns, spicy colors, and grotesque ingredients. This line of development begins with an adaptation: *Donkey's Shadow* is after Wieland, "but not so much" (GH 39).

Struthion, a dentist in the Thracian city-state of Abdera, hires a donkey. It is a hot day; he wants to rest a while in

14 Bänziger, *Frisch und D.*, p. 254: Dürrenmatt himself read the role of the writer.

15 Kamps in Koebner, p. 484; cf. Usmiani, pp. 262–65, Bänziger, pp. 162–63, and Frank, p. 59.

16 *Die Panne* and *Biedermann* (by Frisch) did not employ a "lyric-magic language," individualizing characterization or dependence on the receptive fantasy of the listeners. In their analytic approach they were different from most German radio plays in the 1950's (Burghard Dedner in Durzak, ed., *Die deutsche Literatur der Gegenwart*, pp. 134–37).

17 A similar division into two basic types is presented by Alexander ("Introduction" to *Die Panne and Der Tunnel*, p. 6).

the shadow of the donkey. This is where *The Case of the Donkey's Shadow* (Der Prozess um des Esels Schatten, 1951) begins: the donkey driver Anthrax refuses to let him do so, because he has not hired the shadow. Following the law of expanding circles, this trivial and unresolvable dispute grows and grows, until the shadow falls on the entire city. The ingenuity of two advocates, greedy for money and sticking to their higher principles, is accompanied by social and political arguments. Two parties are established, one called "the Shadows," the other "the Donkeys." Dürrenmatt draws a picture of the various milieus within the city with enjoyment and satiric touches. His slalom, winding in and out in the harbor, in the streets, in the temples, finishes with a straight downhill run into an abyss. The whole city is burned down, and the donkey, the innocent starting-point of the whole mess, is torn to pieces in the ruins.

Throughout the play Dürrenmatt utilizes the epic possibilities of radio in a clever and effortless way. The major characters among these Thracian hillbillies are granted introductory monologues capturing the imagination of the listeners. They are made temporary reporters on the case, as it were.[18] "This damned case starts with me. It has ruined me completely. Completely, I say. House, practice, marriage, property, everything. Yet I am innocent, perfectly innocent!" (GH 43). Struthion and Anthrax start the story by stating that it will end in a catastrophe: this anticipating feature adds to the tension rather than relieving it. Dürrenmatt is in control of quite a wide range of means of expression, his dialogue is witty and parodic,[19] his scenes are short and scattered all over the city, his usage of fade-ins and fade-outs purposeful.

---

[18] Hallingberg finds a mixture of epic and dramatic elements both in modern stage practice and in radio plays, and analyzes the various possibilities of using storytellers, reporters, or commentators in them (pp. 158–97). Frank (pp. 142–74) follows the same procedure.

[19] *Donkey's Shadow* is "a sustained fantasy, with much low humor, countless puns and punning anachronisms. . . . As an example of the author's ability to show his wit in verbal fireworks it is one of his best, lightest and most hilarious" (Peppard, p. 92).

181

Donkey's Shadow is not an exercise; it is a full-fledged work of art in its own medium.

There are lots of contemporary reflections in the dialogue. "We are living during the most decisive period in the history of the world! Right in the middle of a conflict between Athens and Sparta! Between spirit and materialism!" (GH 79). Humanity, freedom, civilization, homeland were words that had lost their value through the inflated use made of them during World War II. In its satirical attitude toward all kinds of ideals the play is a counterpart to *Mississippi*. Dürrenmatt also abridged and simplified Wieland's story, combined matters in a new way, and made the border lines clearer by sharpening the conflict between the rich and the poor. A summarizing report of two pages in Wieland is extended into a series of scenes covering more than ten pages (GH 55–67). And, as his most significant stroke, Dürrenmatt added Tiphys, a dark angel of revenge, and a predecessor of Claire Zachanassian in *The Visit*.[20]

Like Claire, Captain Tiphys is a comet bringing destruction to a small community. He comes from the sea and he leaves for far-away oceans, having only touched the coast of Abdera. To soften the impression that Tiphys is a sea captain *ex machina*, Dürrenmatt allows him two scenes, one marked by a succulent description of his amorous adventures and his boisterous character, the other drawn in dark colors, like the somber sea ballad written by Brecht that Tiphys keeps growling. Both parties, the Shadows and the Donkeys, hire him to put the temple of their adversaries to fire. Tiphys fulfills this task with such triumphant success that the whole city burns down, to his merriment:

> It's burning! It's burning! . . . There glow your gods, your frogs, your shops, your foolishness! Look, there they run from their beds, your inhabitants, in their shirts, there they

---

[20] Tiphys is compared with Claire, e.g., by Oberle, *Der unbequeme D.*, pp. 16–17.

shout, curse, cry, there they forget their ideals and their trial! The moon shines green due to your glow, Abdera, and the smoke rises vertically into your sky! (GH 85).

These words might be spoken by Bockelson from *It Is Written*, Negro da Ponte, or somebody else from Dürrenmatt's rich gallery of nihilists. Tiphys is a lyrical judge over a whole world; he calls himself "justice that came over this city and will always come" (GH 86). Dürrenmatt needed a strong counterweight to the city of Abdera; he needed an explosive charge powerful enough to destroy the story, thought to its logical end.[21] This time he did not go on after his culmination scene, as he was to do in *Once a Greek . . .*, another story following the law of expanding circles within a community. He found what he sought in Tiphys and in the grotesque acoustic images of the concluding moments of the play.

Dürrenmatt ends his world with a bang, Wieland (1733–1813) with a whimper. "Donkey's Shadow" is "Fourth Book" in *Geschichte der Abderiten* (History of the Abderites), a major work by this representative of German literature of enlightenment. The main emphasis in his more conciliatory version is on quite a subtle description of the political struggle, with moves and counter-moves, with judicial interpretations sharp as surgical knives. Dürrenmatt gave up these refined maneuvers in favor of a more straightforward story. These two versions are both individual works of art using partly the same materials.[22] Dürrenmatt took a story from an enlightened novel, added his own twists and

[21] In the heat of discussion a citizen of Wieland's Abdera says that "he would see the whole city in fire and flames" rather than let the solution go against his own opinion (*Geschichte der Abderiten*, p. 247; cf. similar hints on pp. 273, 283). They may have given Dürrenmatt the idea for the end of his play.

[22] Brock-Sulzer (p. 160) and Arnold (p. 67) emphasize Dürrenmatt's dependence on Wieland, perhaps too strongly. Wieland was a theoretician of the grotesque and of tragicomedy; this may have something to do with Dürrenmatt's interest in him (Kayser, pp. 31–32, 71; Guthke, *Modern Tragicomedy*, pp. 38–39).

jokes, painted the end black and lyrical, thus letting his satire flow into the grotesque. Behind the total pattern of his adaptation there is a social vision, the story of two individuals in the middle of a senseless state.

Dürrenmatt practiced by adapting the material of another writer before turning to his own. His next panoramic radio play *Stranitzky and the National Hero* (Stranitzky und der Nationalheld, 1952) follows the fate of a couple of characters in a heartless society even more closely than *Donkey's Shadow*. In order to compare Dürrenmatt's social panoramas with one another, I have taken them one after the other, even though this means departing sometimes from the correct chronological order.[23] Dürrenmatt's characters are two invalids from World War II, Stranitzky and Anton, a dwarf and a giant. The former is a legless soccer player pushed around in a wheelchair by Anton, a blind deepsea diver. Two Samuel Beckett characters in the middle of a social nightmare.

The distorted, nightmarish features are the result of a clash between two worlds. Stranitzky and Anton live in an apartment house in the slums, with stinking toilets, with a mixture of household noises, with a neighboring streetwalker whose profession is tactfully ignored. Anton dreams of deep dives into the ocean, of corals, cuttle-fish, and treasures of gold hidden at the bottom of the sea, while Stranitzky has "practical dreams" of social reforms and cabinet programs (GH 121). They decide to grasp their chance when the national hero Baldur von Moeve falls ill: he has leprosy in the big toe of his left foot. "He is leprous, and we are invalids. Now he will understand us" (GH 120). Their road to Bethlehem Clinic is lined by Moeve posters, by newsboys crying out the latest headlines, by the public relations hysteria sur-

---

[23] *Nocturnal Conversation with a Despised Person*, also written in 1952, will be discussed together with other intimate analyses of individuals at the end of this chapter.

rounding the "tragic" event.[24] There is a twofold movement as the basic pattern of the play: when approaching the national hero for the first time, Stranitzky falls into a grave in the park of the clinic, among "flowers and grass, locusts and beetles" (GH 130). After he has approached the hero for the second time, he finds his final grave in the sea.

The first combining link between the separate worlds is the radio announcer. Dürrenmatt goes on developing effective variations of these epic possibilities. The play is opened by the announcer, who as an all-powerful storyteller governs the events. He never remembers Stranitzky's name: our nondescript hero keeps correcting him, thus creating a free, nonrealistic form for the play. We are not bound by the acoustic milieus of the play, we are only bound by the medium itself.[25] In this way, Stranitzky is ever-present; his name is used like a leitmotif. The announcer also has a choral function; he takes the general public's view of events, admiring the national hero, belittling the invalids. To make these opposites meet, a miracle is needed, and that miracle is arranged by J. P. Whiteblack, an ex-poet, presently a newspaper reporter.

The national hero has received all kinds of deputations during his days of trial—why not also two little men, two heart-rending invalids? Stranitzky gets his great opportunity and uses it by making a speech for peace, for social reforms, for cooperation between the mighty and the poor. He also proposes Anton and himself as cabinet ministers. Back home in Mozart Street, all the inhabitants of the slum quarter meet to celebrate the great day and to listen to Stranitzky's speech on the radio. What they hear is a neatly edited report on the meeting, with all scandalous elements cut out, with black washed white, with "subdued applause" retained at proper

[24] Dürrenmatt has remarked that his starting-point for the play was "the wave of excessive sympathy released by the death of Eva Peron. I wanted to show that the fate of an individual is of no importance within the whole" (Wyrsch, part five, *Schweizer Illustrierte*, April 15, 1963, p. 37).

[25] Cf. Peppard, pp. 95, 146.

185

intervals. Sitting in his wheel chair Stranitzky directs the blind Anton into their last grave. Next spring the national hero was to meet these two for the second and last time:

> They came from the sea, borne by the tide, two giant-size water corpses, the football player on the shoulders of the blind man, with corals and seaweed on the whitened skulls and starfishes and shellfishes in the eye sockets. They were driven into our city in the sunset glow, with the legless one's defiant fist raised towards the national hero. Then they sank back again with the tide (GH 152).

Anton's dream has come true, not Stranitzky's. The sea is one of the greatest natural backgrounds imaginable; it is used by Dürrenmatt both in *Donkey's Shadow* and here, widening behind the distorted human figures. A grotesque contrast is created between two spheres of life, between man and nature. *Stranitzky and the National Hero* has been called the "most Brechtian of Dürrenmatt's plays."[26] The reference is to its outspoken social commitment, and to the way songs are used to comment on the action and to create a poetic acoustic space. Dürrenmatt's sharpest arrows strike at the way in which the mass communication media are used to manipulate people, so that there are two kinds of pity, one reserved for festive occasions and for national heroes, the other "in everyday clothes" (GH 150).[27] The theme of mass hysterics in the press and radio was to be amalgamated into *The Visit*; here Dürrenmatt already develops a self-ironic or medium-conscious usage, by releasing a scene twice, once as it really happened, for the second time in an embellished version. His biting irony forms a counterweight to the sympathetic portrayal of the nondescript; even the invalids are furnished with "Chaplinesque fun."[28] From the quasi-ancient city of Abdera

---

[26] Peppard, p. 95; cf. Bänziger, p. 164.

[27] Jauslin, *F.D.*, p. 12.

[28] Arnold, p. 68; he sees the play predominantly as a criticism of the mass media. Brock-Sulzer's list of Dürrenmatt's verbal means of creating comedy in *Stranitzky* includes bombastic names, refrain techniques, use of empty words, sudden leaps within a sentence, cultural clichés revealed (p. 170).

Dürrenmatt dropped in to take a look at our own age, did not find things much better here, and returned to antiquity, to a country completely covered with manure.

The name of the country is Elis, pronounced Switzerland. The name of the play is *Hercules and the Augean Stables* (Herkules und der Stall des Augias, 1954). The names of its three radio announcers are Polybios, Hercules' secretary; Xenophon, reporting for the Elis newspaper *Landboten*; and Tantalos, director of the Elis National Circus. As can be seen from this conglomerate of names and cultural spheres, the play has various purposes. It is a satire on Swiss politics, a parody of the hero myth, and an exhortation to patient, stoic work to make the world better. The story: clearing Elis of manure does not take place.[29]

The play starts with Polybios in the role of a radio announcer. Dürrenmatt's attitude is devoid of respect for Hercules, the Greek national hero. He is in debt up to his ears, he employs twenty poets in his propaganda department, he has just refused a special offer from a poet to write his biography: "Homer or Komer, who knows in ten years' time what his name was" (GH 158). Hercules is a man in trouble throughout the play; the only occasion he shows heroic characteristics in action is in beating his secretary. Or for a change Kambyses, the swineherd he hires to play his stand-in to fulfill the demands of the Elis womenfolk. To start with, the Elis politicians are unanimous: Hercules is invited to clear up the mess. Heaps of manure grow up to the level of house gables; a historical oak and an Apollo by Praxiteles, according to tradition placed in the Augias Market Place, are "unfortunately invisible" (GH 171).

We learn this through Xenophon's radio report. Hercules is given a hero's welcome in Elis, with crowds, flags, choral songs, with President Augias sitting on "the traditional silvery milking chair" (GH 172). The choral odes, parodying an-

---

[29] *Donkey's Shadow* shows the growth of a trifle into enormous dimensions, *Hercules* that a plague cannot be driven away; the latter is perhaps a counter-sketch to Camus' novel *The Plague*.

cient Greek tragedy, include a line of refrain later employed in the oath-taking scene of *The Visit*: "Not for the sake of money" (GH 169–70, TV 94). Both communities are doing something ostensibly not for the sake of money, not out of greed, but because of high ideals.[30] In *Hercules* the thing to be done is clearing a country of manure, in *The Visit* it is killing a man. The people of Guellen (Village of Manure) are successful, the people of Elis are not. Hercules' plan to lead two rivers through the country is submitted for the approval of local politicians. They start forming committees, counter-committees, intermediary, sub-, over-, general, and overgeneral committees. The discussion grows more and more heated, until the emotions can be conveyed only by using a kind of montage technique:

> Profoundly convinced of the necessity to be clear of manure
> We cannot yet give up our holiest possessions
> The age-old treasure of our folk songs!
> The spiritual life of our children!
> Our boot industry!
> Our freedom!
> Our manure exports!
> Our army, trained to fight in manure! (GH 187).

Each line has a different speaker; yet the speakers matter less than the coordinated, chorus-like general impression. Dürrenmatt had employed similar techniques in *Donkey's Shadow* to express the conflicting opinions within a community. Now the scene is used to complete three official choruses; they stylize the expression still further.[31]

[30] Placing radio plays on a par with folk theater and ancient and medieval theater festivals, Brock-Sulzer emphasizes that Dürrenmatt keeps speaking in public, not only privately with the listeners. His tone is "very relaxed, at the same time aggressive and trusting" (pp. 155–57).

[31] Hallingberg calls chorus scenes difficult on the radio. A great number of chorus members hampers conveying the sense of the words; on the other hand, the impression may be over-drilled (p. 195). Dürrenmatt's enthusiasm for these scenes may have something to do with the famous speaking chorus (Kammersprechchor) active in Zurich.

"In the politics of Elis, it's never too late, yet always too early" (GH 188). A non-Swiss cannot estimate how far Dürrenmatt's criticism of bureaucracy and inefficiency in the name of democracy is justified, how far it is exaggerated. Dürrenmatt also develops a positive alternative with the help of Dejaneira (Deianira), Hercules' girlfriend. Dejaneira admires her native city of Thebes "because it is created by man. Without man it would have remained a desert of stone, for the earth is blind and cruel without man" (GH 181). Man as a chance, as a hopeful and neglected opportunity for the earth, is a theme Dürrenmatt was to develop further in his next radio play, *Operation Vega*. His play about Hercules closes on a positive note, prepared by the earlier scenes with Dejaneira. Having suffered the final humiliation of appearing as a weight-lifter in the Elis National Circus under Director Tantalos, Hercules is ready to leave Elis.

Augias, not a king, not even a president proper, "to be quite exact, only the richest of the farmers" (GH 162), brings his son Phyleus into his secret garden. Knowing very well that "politics do not perform miracles," he has been doing his best, his own personal deeds, by turning manure into humus. Augias' final speech is written in Dürrenmatt's humble tone, heard previously especially in his novels. "Now take the risk to live and to live here, in the middle of this shapeless desolate country: a heroic deed I now impose on you, my son, the Herculean labor I now put on your shoulders" (GH 202).

Dürrenmatt was to return to this material and write a stage play about Hercules, but the radio version is the more important. The portrayal of the Elis citizens, "a nation of farmers, busy, simple-minded, without culture" (GH 167) certainly has its comic points, appealing to our malicious delight, if not to higher sources of pleasure. In the panoramic plays discussed above Dürrenmatt had thought in German and all-European terms; now he chose to write a satire on his native country.

The artistic principle followed in *Hercules* is that the sudden inventions had to be Greek, Swiss, and satiric, fusible

189

into the general atmosphere of extravaganza. *Donkey's Shadow* and *Stranitzky* were compact, *Hercules* tends toward abundance and looseness.[32] Its subplot, a triangle between Hercules, Dejaneira, and Phyleus, is not concretely or clearly formed. If there is something left of the hero myth, it is a slight sense of sympathy for a national figure pursued by his creditors, by representational duties, by the impossible task of clearing up the whole mess of living.

The time machine of Dürrenmatt's imagination had granted him free movement in the fourth dimension. He had landed in ancient Babylon, Greece, and Rome, as well as in the history of Germany. He could not resist the temptation of jumping forward in time. His jump was impelled by the knowledge that there was a model to be found for his literary space ship, in science fiction. Once more, there was a tension between an artistic formula and the story he wanted to tell, a tension stimulating to his imagination. *Operation Vega* (Das Unternehmen der Wega, 1954) is a science fiction thriller written to drive home a moral point.

The play uses the possibilities of the radio in an interesting way. *Operation Vega* consists of a series of flashbacks played in the correct chronological order and describing the journey of space ship Vega to Venus. The scenes and sounds were secretly taped by Dr. Med. Mannerheim,[33] a Secret Service agent of the Free United States of Europe and America. Three hundred ten years have elapsed since World War II; diplomacy has reached a deadlock, and the leaders of the FUSEA consider a new world war against "Russia and United Asia, Africa and Australia" (GH 211) unavoidable. Sir

[32] "Most of the humor is broad rather than subtle, and an atmosphere of slapstick prevails throughout the play" (Peppard, p. 99). Brock-Sulzer has remarked that Dürrenmatt's early versions are often closer to a cabaret style than the later ones (*Der unbequeme D.*, p. 135); *Hercules* is an early version.

[33] Marshal Mannerheim was Commander-in-Chief of the Finnish army in World War II and President of Finland; he died in retirement in Switzerland.

Horace Wood, Secretary of State for Foreign Affairs, is heading a mission to Venus in order to assure a base for the FUSEA on that planet. Mannerheim is commissioned by the President to spy on Sir Horace. He fulfills his task by taping all discussions of importance; he then plays them to the President, linking them together with his dry comments. The technique fits Dürrenmatt's purposes exactly: the tension of a thriller is immediately created.[34]

First, the take-off from Earth: suspense caused by the technical jargon, by a great adventure not yet successfully undertaken by 1954. Sir Horace is introduced as a cautious conservative, diplomatic and reserved; this is his first space trip in an era of children's flights to the moon, to Mars. He has his misgivings about the presence of Mannerheim, and he is unpleasantly surprised when he finds that the passengers on board include Colonel Roi, who had been responsible for surprise attacks from space against Hanoi and Warsaw. The Vega's cargo includes hydrogen bombs, to be used if necessary against the inhabitants of Venus.

Venus has long served as a penal colony for both of the big powers on Earth. Both have kept sending there "human material of inferior moral quality" (GH 213): the West, criminals and communists; the East, criminals and supporters of Western ideas. The estimated population of Venus has risen to two million. Operation Vega is a difficult one: nothing is known about how these people govern themselves; negotiations are to take place with three criminals reached by a radio message. The conditions on the planet do not make the mission any easier. Heat, moist air, continual earthquakes, strange light under a sunless cloudy sky, hurricanes, thunderstorms, and nightmarish big animals in a jungle: these are some of the ordeals our mission has to face. The group, with three cabinet ministers ("Their Excellencies")

[34] *Krapp's Last Tape* by Beckett uses a tape recorder in an ingenious and poetic way; Hallingberg (p. 174) reports a Swedish play (*Mannen i parken* by Mats Ödeen, 1966) using techniques comparable with Dürrenmatt's invention.

and six high officials, is met by three men in ragged clothes and brought to a primitive U-boat. It appears that there are no cities, no buildings on the uncertain ground, no government. Just people on ships, fighting a desperate battle against the forces of hostile nature.

The negotiators change at every meeting: fishing for whales is more important than the proposals of the FUSEA. The second round takes place in the dirty canteen of a hospital ship, with an ex-streetwalker from Poland as the other party; a deaf-mute is eating soup, and the shouts of a patient being operated on without anesthesia are clearly audible through the wall. The streetwalker simply does not understand Sir Horace's nice diplomatic distinctions about whether she is authorized to represent the planet or not. Sir Horace is the only negotiator from Tellus not to lose his head or health. He insists on offering the people living in those terrible conditions a free ticket to Earth as a compensation for a pact of alliance with the FUSEA. After a time of consideration Sir Horace and Mannerheim return to the hospital ship, where they meet Bonstetten, a starry-eyed friend of Sir Horace's from their student days at Oxford and Heidelberg.

Nobody wants to return to Earth, Bonstetten declares. They prefer to stay in their inhuman surroundings, on a planet where everybody is needed, where they have to make everything themselves, without the help of experience, without medicines, surrounded by gigantic animals, by plants and fruits that are mainly poisonous, threatened by germs, viruses, and radioactive radiation. They have learnt a lesson:

> BONSTETTEN: Man is something valuable and his life a gift of grace.
> WOOD: Ridiculous. On Earth we realized that long ago.
> BONSTETTEN: Indeed? Do you live accordingly? (GH 237).

Everybody on Venus knows that he has to help his neighbor, otherwise all will be endangered. Venus is "a hell that is a paradise" (GH 237); its inhabitants, coming from Earth, know well enough that mankind is interested in them only as a help in killing people. On Venus they have their freedom, different from that prevailing on the Earth:

> The freedom to do right and to do what is necessary. We could not do it on Earth. I could not. Earth is too beautiful. Too rich. Her possibilities are too great. She tempts to inequality. On Earth poverty is a disgrace, and so she is disgraced. Only here is poverty something natural. Our food, our tools are only stained by our sweat, not yet by injustice as on Earth. And then we are afraid of you. Of your abundance, of your false way of living. Afraid of a paradise that is a hell (GH 238).

Sir Horace Wood has nothing to add. His mission has failed. It has been guessed that the Vega carries bombs; to save as many lives as possible, the ships are now scattered all over the planet, though they usually keep together. Sir Horace gives an assurance that he will never drop the bombs: "I am no slaughterer." Bonstetten knows better, he foretells the way his student friend will act. On board the space ship, the suspicion will grow in the back of his mind that the citizens of Venus will after all form an alliance with the Russians, and "because of this tiny little uncertainty in your heart you will let the bombs be released" (GH 240). Bonstetten is right. The laconic lines of discussion, mostly technical jargon, have a powerful emotional impact, when the presence and words of Roi and Mannerheim help Sir Horace overcome his scruples. Ten bombs with hydrogen and cobalt are dropped, all over the planet.

It is an ingenious stroke that Dürrenmatt has made Sir Horace Wood so sympathetic. He is intelligent, humane, sincere, realistic; he reads T. S. Eliot, he has an endearing touch of self-irony. A comment of his on his own high-flown first speech on the planet: "To me Venus sounded reasonable. Every time I mentioned ideals in my speech, there was thunder" (GH 223). He feels tempted to settle down on Venus, yet cannot because of his position on Tellus. This is a sharply critical portrait of a Western intellectual, distorted into a caricature by the final events of the play.[35] Sir Horace is a killer of innocent people, a cruel judge over a whole world; he is what Romulus tried to be. There is a ghastly kind of comedy in his final lines on Venus. Bonstetten, a friend he was to condemn to death, consoles him: "You must not feel sad" (GH 241). A condemned man comforts his executioner.

They have to get back, says the formula of science fiction.[36] The men of the Vega do get back, at the price of a moral defeat. They land on Earth as "human material of inferior moral quality," coming from Venus, from a world Dürrenmatt has turned topsy-turvy. This might be a *maqamat* told by Akki; this is an unconventional story well told. To me, it is Dürrenmatt's best radio play. It shows that his radio plays are something more than just another field of experimentation, or a reservoir of themes to be developed elsewhere. He employs a cool, matter-of-fact tone, letting the horror and the irony grow out of the situation itself, and out of his descriptions of the living conditions on Venus. He uses sound effects more frequently than usual,[37] creating two acoustic worlds, the closed space of sterile technology on board the Vega, the grotesque and wild environment on Venus. He uses to advantage his hobby of amateur astronomy.[38] The stars have led him toward poetry, and toward his best play for the ether.

When at his best, as in *Operation Vega*, Dürrenmatt is a unique and paradoxical combination of a child of nature and a logician. He is a boisterous and sovereign narrator and a precise weigher of words. He can combine logic and whims,

[35] Kurt Marti has connected *Operation Vega* both with the old Swiss humanitarian tradition and with Dürrenmatt's stand against atomic weapons (*Die Schweiz und ihre Schriftsteller*, pp. 48–52).
[36] Frank (p. 56) speaks about German radio plays of adventure and utopia written in the interwar years; this may be a tradition in the background of *Vega*.
[37] Peppard, p. 101.
[38] Cf. Brock-Sulzer in *Der unbequeme D.*, p. 136.

wild outbursts of fantasy and scientific thinking, coherence and abundance, visions of the future and analyses of the present. *Operation Vega* is a display of his scientophobia, of his distrust of the inventions of modern technology. It is comparable with "The Tunnel," although he appears to have traveled several light years since writing the earlier story. And, though shorter and less ambitious, it can be compared with the dystopias of Orwell and Huxley. Dürrenmatt needs a vision of terror to be at his sharpest; and he needs a grotesque element. Perhaps he is a basically grotesque writer because there are these tensions between his various roles and abilities hidden somewhere deep down in his personality as a creative artist.

The remaining three radio plays belong to Dürrenmatt's intimate analyses of individuals or situations. *Nocturnal Conversation with a Despised Person* (Nächtliches Gespräch mit einem verachteten Menschen, 1952) is a kind of crossroad: it can be taken as a point of departure for his panoramic radio plays. A hired executioner enters the room of a writer in the darkness of night, and these two start talking. A thriller situation is turned into a philosophical discussion. Society looms somewhere in the dark, the mighty have sent the executioner; when the writer cries for help, no one appears. There is no clear picture drawn of those who have sent the killer.[39] Perhaps an insinuation was enough in those years shortly after Hitler, perhaps Dürrenmatt aims also at God, and does not want to specify his target. Dürrenmatt takes a close-up view of his two characters; his camera has no panoramic view. This short play is the last clear echo from Kafka in Dürrenmatt—before *Connections*, 1976, with its surprising return to a Kafkaesque story in the fourth and final part of this long essay on Israel.

[39] Arnold (pp. 66–67) sees in the executioner personified death, meeting both the innocent and the guilty. One cannot expect justice from a nonexistent God; it is best to submit to the inevitable and die humbly.

The discussion deals with the best way to die. The writer had been prepared to meet a murderer; he wanted to impart to him some noble words about freedom. The days of death à la tragedy are over, the sympathetic executioner assures him. Nowadays one does not die in public, with noble words on one's lips; one dies alone, by the hand of an executioner.[40] He is so full of praise for the humble death of his innocent victims that the writer succumbs and dies humbly, believing that this is the only victory over his adversaries left to him. *Nocturnal Conversation* is a kind of appendix or footnote to Dürrenmatt's numerous scenes between executioners and their victims; it develops their strange friendship and a partly philosophical, partly mystic gospel of the humble death of the innocent, also preached in practice by Alfred Ill in *The Visit*. In the stage play the humility is an element in a fully concretized work of art, here it remains the core of an abstract discussion.[41]

Both of Dürrenmatt's last two radio plays received international prizes.[42] *Die Panne* (1956) in its prose version called *A Dangerous Game* in English was discussed above (cf. pp. 149–65). In what follows, *Die Panne* refers to the radio play. The radio version plays more with the thriller-like idea of getting Traps into a trap. He is unwilling to play the guilty party; in *A Dangerous Game* he is all too willing. After Traps has at last confessed his guilt and been condemned to death, the hangman Pilet follows him upstairs. There is torturing equipment on the walls and a guillotine in Traps' bedroom. Traps is under the illusion that he will be

---

[40] Allemann has emphasized that Dürrenmatt replaces death à la tragedy with death by hanging, here and elsewhere (Wiese, ed., *Das deutsche Drama*, II, pp. 433–34).

[41] Cf. Peppard, p. 94. Brock-Sulzer reserves quite a prominent place for *Nocturnal Conversation* (pp. 251, 254). Though written for the radio, it was first performed on the stage, in Munich in 1952 (Bänziger, p. 163). There is even an opera based on this script, composed by Jiri Smutny, a Czech (Dieter Schnabel, "Vertonter D.," *Die Welt*, Dec. 12, 1968).

[42] *Die Panne* was given blind German war veterans' prize, *Episode on an Autumn Evening* the Prix d'Italia.

executed, and this impression is confirmed by Pilet's kind but firm exhortations to remove his collar and shoes. Then horror turns into laughter: Pilet's intention was just to get Traps to bed, and next morning our traveler leaves the white-walled villa as a more ruthless businessman than ever. He has gotten over his fit of guilt.

The grotesque final picture of Traps hanging in the window frame is lacking in *Die Panne*. No doubt the end without his death tends to make the radio version more satirical and more harmless.[43] As a prosaist Dürrenmatt could rely on the impact of a visual image and on its aftereffect. As a radio dramatist he had to convey his message to his listeners mainly during the performance. That is why the macabre elements are strongly present during Traps' last climb up the stairs and throughout *Die Panne*. When rewriting his stuff as prose fiction (G 34 confirms this as the order of composition), Dürrenmatt studied its possibilities again, and developed a new variation of its basic theme, that of a grotesque swinging movement between tragic guilt and modern non-guilt.[44] *A Dangerous Game* is a more stratified and a more refined version of this theme than *Die Panne*.

" 'You don't think me capable of murder?' asked the novelist, disappointed" (JHH 72). Dürrenmatt was to play a game based on this innocent line in *Episode on an Autumn Evening* (Abendstunde im Spätherbst, 1956). Questions of tragedy or guilt are not even raised. Maximilian Friedrich Korbes, a Nobel Prize novelist, opens the play with a description of the setting, a room in a luxurious hotel. He is himself a "heavy-set, sun-tanned, unshaven" man "with a huge bald

---

[43] Bänziger (p. 165) and Jauslin (p. 12) give preference to *Die Panne*, while Peppard, having paid attention to the demands of the radio, finds the radio version "much less subtle and satisfying" (p. 103).

[44] Holdheim presents a series of fine distinctions between the versions, finds "tragic definiteness" in neither, and sees in the blurred "guiltless guilt" of modern writers "an inability to realize completely either of the antipodes, being either not guilty or guilty" (*Der Justizirrtum als literarische Problematik*, pp. 99–100). Cf. Ch. 7, note 1 above (p. 149).

197

head" (EAE 26), a favorite of scandal newspapers, a sacred monster in the literary field.[45] His room is entered by Fürchtegott Hofer, a retired bookkeeper and an amateur detective. Mr. Hofer starts from a firmly based critical gospel, that of truthfulness to life: "it seems to me quite impossible to invent something which does not exist somewhere" (EAE 28). Twenty-two bodies exist in Korbes' twenty-two novels, and he is a specialist in describing the psychological pleasure, the "joie de vivre" connected with killing. Ergo: he has killed those twenty-two.

Or, to be quite exact, our detective has proof positive of twenty-one cases. He and Korbes have a tiff on this point, as two brilliant experts sometimes may. In everything else, Korbes admits, Hofer is absolutely right. These two have traveled around from resort to resort, one staying in sumptuous hotels and killing, the other in cheap hostels and investigating. Hofer suggests that Korbes pay him a tiny addition to his pension. After which our modest blackmailer is forced to jump through the window, a suicide of course, and Korbes starts dictating a radio play. Its subject is murder, the twenty-third in order, or is it only the twenty-second?

Dürrenmatt's last radio play is a slickly written bagatelle. Its first point is a comment on critics seeing fiction as derived too directly from the life of a writer.[46] Its second point is a half-serious description of a popular novelist as "a superior creature," as a monster high above bourgeois morality: "We have become the wish fulfillment dream of millions; they regard us as people who may do anything." While trying to "satisfy humanity," writers lead and describe a "life crammed with excitement, with a sense of the moment, with adventure and fulfillment. A life which reality cannot give to the masses

[45] Korbes has been connected with Hemingway (e.g., Horst-Walter Krautkrämer, "Das deutsche Hörspiel 1945–61," Ph.D. diss. Heidelberg, 1962, pp. 75–77). On the other hand, he is a self-portrait of sorts, and a figure foreshadowing Schwitter in Dürrenmatt's later stage play *The Meteor* (e.g., Bänziger, pp. 166, 191).

[46] "The biographical interpretation does not lead far in the case of Dürrenmatt, and D. hates it" (Arnold, p. 71).

in our machine-ridden world, which can only be supplied by art. Literature has become a drug, a substitute for a life that is no longer possible" (EAE 31). Korbes is allowed to murder at will; the police would not pay attention to Hofer's accusations. Yet would not a detective as pedantic as Hofer know this 'secret'? *Autumn Evening* is also a counter-sketch to Dürrenmatt's own *Nocturnal Conversation*. In the earlier and more serious play it was an executioner who entered the room of a writer and killed him. Now it is an amateur detective who enters a similar room, and gets killed.

From a clumsy metaphysical experiment in thought to a fully professional piece on the verge of emptiness: Dürrenmatt's radio plays offer a rapid survey of his total development.[47] They occupy a highly esteemed position in German radio drama after World War II, and they helped him to build up his reputation.[48] The center of artistic gravity is somewhere in the middle and late ones. There is also quite a wide scale of backgrounds, themes, and styles in these eight plays. They range from the quasi-ancient city state of Abdera, built up according to the ground plans of enlightened Wieland, to the planet Venus, inhabited by animals of science fiction and by people of Dürrenmatt's moral cosmos. From a cabaret-like portrayal of his native country to Kafkaesque meetings between executioners and victims. From worldly satire to metaphysics, from parodical lines to grotesque visual images conveyed through the speech of an announcer. From wide visions to profound analyses. There are both intimate portraits of individuals and striking contrasts within social panoramas. These two Dürrenmattian types are in accord-

[47] "In a few years Dürrenmatt progressed from sermons in dialogue form to radio plays of great subtlety and wit" (Peppard, p. 108).

[48] Hallingberg, p. 39, Frank, p. 61. Bänziger remarks that using numerous communication media is "in accordance with Dürrenmatt's expansive disposition"; he might have written radio plays also in order "not to be observed by the critics" (p. 167). Usmiani interprets them as counter-sketches to the conventional formulas of this mass media (Knapp, ed., *F.D.*, pp. 140–44).

199

ance with Hallingberg's vision of the dramatic and epic possibilities open to radio drama in general.[49] Dürrenmatt's radio plays are written by different authors, as it were: by several of the host we set out to find. Dürrenmatt seems to have realized the many tasks of the spoken word on radio from the very beginning. During his career as an ether dramatist he learnt to control without effort certain technical possibilities, such as an epic and ample use of the announcer in several variations, rapid changes of scene, fade-ins and fade-outs, chorus scenes using montage techniques. His experimentation is always connected with the art of telling a story; he did not go as far as free acoustic compositions. As a rule, he did not feel bound by illusionism, by acoustic spaces limited by the walls of rooms or other obstacles. His radio style is a free and spacious one. Radio plays may have given him another impetus toward the epic style employed in *The Visit*: short scenes freely developed on a nearly open stage.[50] They also run parallel with his inclination to write poignant descriptions of nature and of acting surroundings in general: in his novels these are a part of the narrative prose, in his radio plays they are mostly given to the announcers to speak.

Grotesque elements in Dürrenmatt are usually connected with visual imagery:[51] Traps hanging from the window frame, Knipperdollinck and Bockelson on the wheel of torture. Creating grotesque imagery through the ear seems to be no easy task. This is a feature making the variously employed announcers even more important in Dürrenmatt's radio plays. It is their task to paint the image of Stranitzky and Anton rising from the flood, or create the ominous atmosphere prevailing on Venus, complete with sound effects. On other occasions, such as in the farewell words and song

[49] Hallingberg, p. 246. Cf. Brock-Sulzer, pp. 157–58.

[50] It is an overestimation to claim that "most of Dürrenmatt's [stage] plays are more or less successful adaptations of his radio plays" (Krautkrämer, p. 75).

[51] Thomson (*The Grotesque*, p. 57) emphasizes the visual and physical character of most grotesque phenomena.

of Captain Tiphys to Abdera, Dürrenmatt makes one of his characters a painter of the grotesque. The comic and grotesque ingredients, the persistent themes connected with justice, the vitality in creating surprising stories—all these characteristics confirm that Dürrenmatt's radio plays and other works come from one and the same vein of ore. His *Collected Radio Plays*, a volume of nearly three hundred pages, contains some of his funniest, best-written, and most grotesque scenes and sequences.

9 A Judge of His Own Craft

WRITINGS ON THE THEATER

||||||||||||||||||||||||||||||||||||||||||||||||||||||||||||||||||||||||||||||||||||||||||||||||

From *Collected Radio Plays* to *Writings on the Theater*: from one anthology to another. The contents are even more diversified, ranging from memoirs to book reviews, from polemical retorts to statements of theoretical interest. From the point of view of this study, *Theater-Schriften und Reden* (1966) includes both primary and secondary materials. Its contents have been and will be used as secondary materials; its two pieces of memoirs already helped us to create a tentative picture of Dürrenmatt's youth, and the diversity of his opinions was commented upon ("Introduction," pp. 4–9 above). This chapter is devoted to theoretical writings sketching Dürrenmatt's personal view of the theater, his dramaturgy. Some of his *Writings on the Theater* are taken as primary materials. Dürrenmatt as a theorist of the stage: the image is not a constant one, it changes as time passes.

The relevant materials can be divided into a number of groups, roughly in chronological order. (1) Early talks, aphorisms, and exercises from the years 1947–52. (2) Dürrenmatt's work as a critic, his opinions on novels, plays, and performances (1948–59). (3) *Problems of the Theater*, written in 1954–55, his most important theoretical treatise, worth considering separately. (4) Writings from the years 1955–59, culminating in the Mannheim lecture on Schiller. (5) A few scripts from the early 1960's. A time division is fixed by Dürrenmatt's plays after *The Visit*; they will be discussed in the third part of this study, together with their postscripts published in *Writings on the Theater* and other relevant materials. There is a later collection of theoretical writings, called *Dramaturgic and Critical Writings* (Dramaturgisches und Kritisches, 1972), subtitled "Writings and Lectures on the Theater II," discussed in Chapter 18.

Dürrenmatt as a theoretician; there is something paradoxical in the whole concept. A man of wild inspirations as a pedant? Suffering from "systemania," a widespread disease in Germany?[1] The picture is too grotesque to be true; we had better erase it and replace it with a more pertinent one. Dürrenmatt as a public speaker, massive both physically and mentally, aggressive and defensive at the same time, enjoying his exactly calculated polemical fireworks. *Writings on the Theater* is primarily a collection of talks, the spoken word written down.[2] And the man who once made these speeches emphasizes that his words are practical and fragmentary, bound to the fleeting instant rather than to any systematic or generally valid body of thinking. "Dramaturgy" is for Dürrenmatt first and foremost a framework coordinating an artist's individual way of thinking.

One of Dürrenmatt's earliest writings included is entitled "Jottings." The title might also do for two others, all manuscripts from the years 1947–48 published for the first time in the anthology. Two of the three consist of a handful of short notes in the shape of aphorisms; one is a somewhat enlarged note called "Art." There are occasional flashes of black humor, though these are clearly notes written down by a serious-minded young writer disturbed by World War II. The second field touched on is art, especially the theater. These are the spheres of interest from which Dürrenmatt's personal dramaturgy starts growing: he wants to react to the surrounding world, and he begins his long search for an adequate form for his observations, a form fit for the stage. His dramaturgy not only is a technical concept concerned with the stage and with the craft of writing; it is also concerned with Dürrenmatt's experience of the world.

[1] On the other hand, essays on literature, science, etc. form quite a lively tradition in Switzerland (Zbinden, "Zur Situation der Literatur in der Schweiz," *Welt und Wort*, 24, 10, Oct. 1969, p. 311).

[2] Brock-Sulzer remarks on the polemical and oral character of these writings in her preface (TS 9–10). Cf. Peppard, *F.D.*, p. 121: "no unified, coherent system of dramaturgy is presented."

The value of art, young Dürrenmatt writes, lies in "the courage to conquer the world." Art is adventure, it is like navigation, depending on skill in steering, not on the rules of building a galley. To describe is not to copy; art means overcoming distances through fantasy and only through fantasy. A crisis in art begins with the idea that "the world is already discovered or conquered" (TS 42); this might leave art only illustrative or palliative functions. The simile of the ship is in accord with Dürrenmatt's basic attitude emphasizing the creative freedom of the writer. Having caught a breath of sea wind to drive his jotting forward, he gives up specifying his thoughts any further. Yet there are also specific and concrete sayings included; some of them have already been quoted above. "He who has built up a world, need not explain it" (TS 87) advises reticence, not followed by Dürrenmatt in his explanatory and defensive postscripts in the 1960's.

In the next subdivision of writings, dated 1951–52, Dürrenmatt keeps describing his times in negative terms. Europe lives under two shadows, one thrown by the recent war, the other by the atom bomb. "The whole of mankind has grown guilty, everybody tries to save both the ideals and their reverse: freedom and business, justice and violence" (TS 40). One cannot distinguish between the guilty and the innocent: in *Problems of the Theater* Dürrenmatt was to conclude that this makes tragedy impossible. In a few writings he uses quite a pathetic and biblical terminology in denouncing Europe; it is somewhat surprising to hear the word "spirit" (Geist) pronounced by him with that kind of deep and reverent chest resonance an older generation of Germans used to develop for it. In the middle of a world gone bankrupt, facing a Germany "ruined and broken to pieces" (TS 44), Dürrenmatt proclaims with a certain bravado: "I am a Protestant and I protest. . . . I have been spared, but I portray the downfall. . . . I am here to warn you" (TS 45).

This is the background for Dürrenmatt's theory and practice of the grotesque. "I could imagine a terrifying grotesque about World War II, but as yet no tragedy, because we have not gotten a distance from it" (TS 136). The quotation is from "A Note on Comedy" (1952), so clearly an exercise for *Problems of the Theater* that its concluding passus was as such included in the later treatise. Finding the grotesque must have been a kind of "eureka" for Dürrenmatt; he discovered it when practising, then started looking for related phenomena in literature. *It Is Written* is already full of grotesque details, and it is possible to speculate that the destroyed "Comedy," Dürrenmatt's first effort at a play, might have been "a terrifying grotesque about World War II"— and about the atom bomb. At the beginning of Western drama Dürrenmatt found a grotesque playwright: Aristophanes. Greek tragedy is based on myths familiar to its audiences, Dürrenmatt reasons; its stories take place in the distant past brought close to the spectators. Aristophanes invented his stories and placed them in the Athens of his own day.

Dürrenmatt explains this by using two of his central concepts: artistic invention (Einfall) and the grotesque. "Aristophanes lives on invention, is invention" (TS 132); he has the "power to turn the world into a comedy" (TS 133).[3] What artist's alchemy does he use to execute this trick? He resorts to the grotesque, Dürrenmatt answers. The grotesque creates distance, necessary for a comedy; it means "an extreme stylization, a picture drawn all of a sudden"; it makes it possible for a writer to deal with the problems of his own age without falling into "bias or reportage" (TS 136). Aristophanes is not the only alchemist for Dürrenmatt; Shakespeare, Rabelais, Swift, Cervantes, Gogol have also been able to create grotesque worlds based on their artistic inventions. Dürrenmatt's eulogy concludes with the remark that the grotesque presupposes objectivity, sharp intellect, and a moral engagement: "The grotesque is one of the great ways of being precise" (TS 137).

[3] Changing the world into a comedy: Allemann calls this an "ambitious program," and connects it with *Problems of the Theater* and with Dürrenmatt's preface to *The Anabaptists* (Hans Steffen, ed., *Das deutsche Lustspiel*, p. 204).

It has been customary to explain Dürrenmatt's plays with the help of his theory. We might try the opposite for a change, that is, explaining a theoretical work with the help of a play: "A Note on Comedy" was published a month before *Mississippi* had its belated world première in Munich. This "comedy" was Dürrenmatt's first play without a historical setting; it is a consciously grotesque play dealing with contemporary problems and creating a world of its own, based on wild artistic invention. Three years (1949–52) elapsed between two Dürrenmatt world premières, and the playwright used this interval for writing *Angel*, novels, and radio plays, working as a theater critic, and building up his dramaturgy. "A Note" was a way of saying that he believed in the grotesque as a precise way of describing his own age.

This is how a connecting link between Dürrenmatt's practice and theory can be found. "A Note on Comedy" is a temporary judgment declared by theorist Dürrenmatt; it was to serve until *Problems of the Theater* was finished two years later. In two lectures from the year 1951 Dürrenmatt develops his humble working relation with the theater, calling the stage his teacher, the Zurich Theater his favorite field of experimentation, and doubting the value of general dramaturgic rules, as he was to do in his major theoretical opus. His dramaturgy includes a great many aspects; he has a word to say about a playwright's relation to the state, to the classics, to the critics, to the stage, and, most significantly, to tragedy and our age. In the fall of 1954, when Dürrenmatt started traveling around and lecturing in Switzerland and Western Germany with *Problems of the Theater* in his pocket, he had already fought his first rounds with his theoretical materials. His dramaturgy grew like a tree.

One branch of that tree was Dürrenmatt's work as a critic. He wrote quite regularly about the performances at the Zurich Theater during the winter season 1951–52; his book reviews from the years 1951–59 are more occasional pieces. While reading he gathered materials for his later plays, or looked for writers confirming his own opinions. These critical writings cover a third part of the anthology, not its most richly rewarding third. It may be of interest to see how Dürrenmatt analyzes, say, *The Robbers* by Schiller, yet this analysis has not necessarily any relevance to his dramaturgy. However, a few basic attitudes are revealed.

Dürrenmatt admits that he is an admirer of Viennese folk comedy, a colorful, fantastic, and parodical kind of play. He criticizes classical plays for being made harmless—by the productions, by the audiences: "People are not frightened by the classics. They applaud" (TS 304). He suggests that the critic's task is to play a game of chess with his writer and play it according to the opening chosen by the writer;[4] he makes a sincere effort in this direction by playing a game with Frisch, yet leaves his review of the novel *Stiller* unfinished. This is, remarkably enough, the only review revealing Dürrenmatt's interest in novel form; everywhere else he is interested only in dramaturgy. On the other hand, he uses dramaturgic terminology in his novels.[5] He enjoys himself imagining how Shakespeare would have shaped a German comedy from the 1930's, and how Friedrich Dürrenmatt would have written the manuscript for a film dealing with two present-day miracles. He lets playwright Dürrenmatt send an open letter to theater critic Dürrenmatt stating that a play seen by both was impossible. Nothing more emerges; the letter covers four pages. He opens his theater reviews with sentences half a page long. In short, his behavior is just as arbitrary as a creative writer's may be.

Problems of the Theater is not arbitrary. Or, rather, one has to read it carefully to find its questionable points. It is

---

[4] Carlsson connects this suggestion with a dichotomy in criticism: critics tend to take a review as a judgment (Urteil), while writers "from Klopstock to Dürrenmatt and Ionesco wish for . . . a describing characterization (Charakteristik)" (*Die deutsche Buchkritik*, p. 374).

[5] "Certain dramaturgic concepts" have a role in Dürrenmatt's novels, appearing in them "more clearly than in many plays of his (Neumann in *D., Frisch, Weiss*, p. 28).

a lecture built up in a purposeful way. Dürrenmatt supposes that his audiences have no special knowledge of modern drama. He starts from familiar things, he takes up Aristotle as do so many speakers and essayists before and after him, he develops observations and arguments that sound generally acceptable nowadays. They may have been more disputable in the year 1954. Dürrenmatt speaks for moderate stylization of settings, remarks that dramaturgic rules, albeit quite valid, are of no use to a creative writer, while Aristotle's unities are exceptions, not rules. He calls the theater in the German-speaking countries a solemn descendant of the court theaters, and the cinema a democratic court theater, a specialist in simulating reality. The theater is partly a museum exhibiting "the art treasures of former golden ages of the drama" (FP 15), partly an experimental field for modern playwrights. Dürrenmatt puts in a few words for the experiments, several against the German habit of producing the classics as indifferent stage versions; his later adaptations tried to be different. Every play is a new start for a modern playwright, because our age has no uniform style, "only styles" (FP 17), and our audiences do not form a homogeneous community.

To keep the interest of his audience awake, Dürrenmatt intersperses a few personal confessions. "I love a colourful stage setting, a colourful theatre. . . . It happens to be my passion, not always a happy one perhaps, to want to put on the stage the richness, the manifold diversity of the world. As a result my theatre is open to many interpretations and appears to confuse some" (FP 22). These are words uttered by the writer of *Angel* in the middle of the 1950's, by a writer experimenting with a great many colors and literary genres.[6] He also makes the point that the situations in drama have to lead the characters into making major speeches. While speaking his *maqamat* Akki "has become all language"; he is living language, not written word any more. Retaining his modest tone of voice, Dürrenmatt remarks that

[6] The tract seems now "dated in style and attitude and superseded by [Dürrenmatt's] subsequent practice" (Peppard, p. 126).

1. Execution scene in *It Is Written*, with Heinrich Gretler as Knipperdollinck (above). Dürrenmatt's first world première in Zurich on the 19th of April, 1947.

2. Drinking coffee (with poison?) in *The Marriage of Mr. Mississippi*. Eira Soriola and Yrjö Järvinen in the Tampere Theater production of 1964.

3–5. *The Visit.* Sylvi Salonen as Claire Zachanassian (above left). Ill (Hannes Häyrinen) is sitting on the back seat, left, on his last drive with his happy family (above right). Claire (Therese Giehse) making her great speech to the Guelleners (below).

6. The Guelleners are playing trees in the second forest scene (above): Häyrinen and Elsa Turakainen as the "loving" couple.

7. Giehse, a Dürrenmattian actress par excellence, as Ottilie Frank, together with Kurt Horwitz (Frank) and Ernst Schröder (Böckmann).

8–10. *The Physicists.* Three black-clad members of Dr. von Zahnd's private police force (right). Fräulein Doktor and her helpless victim: Ella Eronen and Joel Rinne at the Finnish National Theater (below, left). Hans-Christian Blech as Möbius and Hanne Hiob as the nurse in the world première at Zurich (below, right).

11. Jane Tilden and Gustav Knuth in *Hercules*, directed by Leonard Steckel in Zurich in 1963.

12. *The Meteor*: stage design by Teo Otto, 1966.

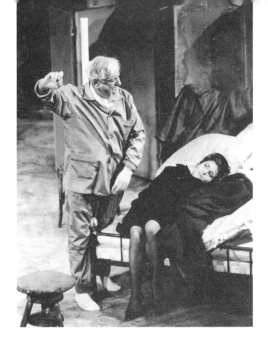

13. Leonard Steckel as
Schwitter in Zurich, with
Kornelia Boje.

14. *Play Strindberg*: Edgar (Erik Lindström) dances, Alice and Kurt accompany him.

15–16. *König Johann* at the Finnish National Theater. Queen Eleonore (Marja Korhonen, top) with torturing equipment: "an old hag, close-cropped and stinking." Cardinal Pandulpho (Risto Mäkelä) and King John (Heikki Nousiainen) under the same cover (bottom).

17. Dürrenmatt in the rehearsals of his *Woyzeck*.

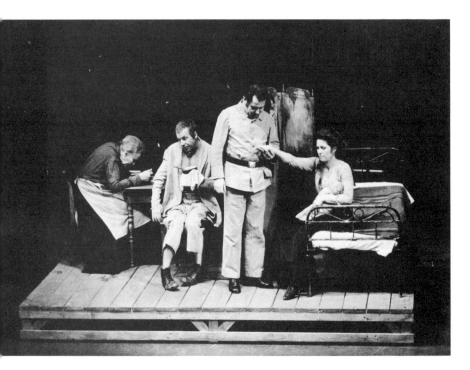

18. Grandmother, idiot, Woyzeck, and Marie: a sample of Dürrenmatt's ascetic staging style.

language may also lead a writer astray. His attitude to his plentiful artistic inventions is ambivalent. He knows he must be on his guard, yet also "have the courage to follow some of them" (FP 27).

Dürrenmatt approaches controversial areas when starting to characterize the protagonists of modern plays. Bourgeois dramas by Lessing and Schiller opened the stage door for middle-class heroes in Germany, Büchner's Woyzeck was a primitive proletarian, Pirandello's characters became "immaterial and transparent." There is a trend toward comedy manifest in the once noble heroes of tragedy, and "analogously the fool becomes more and more a tragic figure." Art is not repeatable, "our own questionable world" (FP 30) cannot be represented by Schiller's characters: "We no longer have any tragic heroes, but only vast tragedies staged by world butchers and produced by slaughtering machines." The state itself "cannot be envisioned, for it is anonymous and bureaucratic. . . . Any small-time crook, petty government official or policeman better represents our world than a senator or president. Today art can only embrace the victims" (FP 31).

What is here expressed is, first of all, Dürrenmatt's Swiss suspicion of modern giant states in general, Hitler's Third Reich in particular. Dürrenmatt turns his experience from the 1940's into a dramaturgic rule, at least for himself. He did not keep the article of "victims only" in force in his later plays. "The atom bomb cannot be reproduced artistically since it is mass-produced" (FP 32)—another absolute position denied later on in *The Physicists*, a play probing the problem of the atom bomb, if not reproducing it. Hochhuth, Weiss, and Kipphardt, three leading figures in the German wave of more or less documentary drama in the 1960's, have succeeded in bringing the mighty onto the stage; whatever the value of their scripts, they have at least turned words spoken or written by our contemporaries into dialogue, envisioned anonymous modern states and other corporations.[7]

---

[7] *The Representative* (1963) by Hochhuth is seen as a turning-point in its attack against a historical person (Koebner in *Tendenzen*

The mighty of this world do not serve as protagonists of plays: this is an observation bound to the sober 1950's, to fictional characters, and to Dürrenmatt's personal qualities, not to all of modern drama.

Dürrenmatt's claim that tragedy and comedy are getting close to one another seems to be of greater general validity. At the same time it leads to some questionable points. "Tragedy, the strictest genre in art, presupposes a formed world" (FP 32).[8] In the next few paragraphs there are several contradictory statements about comedy. "Comedy . . . supposes an unformed world, a world being made and turned upside down, a world about to fold like ours." This is a definition which makes comedy the very opposite of tragedy. Yet in the same paragraph Dürrenmatt gives an example of "how comedy works": "the comical exists in forming what is formless, in creating order out of chaos" (FP 32). Comedy both "supposes an unformed world" and "forms what is formless." At the risk of overinterpreting Dürrenmatt's text, one feels tempted to fill up this gap in the chain of his logic with a reference to his practice. He distinguishes among three categories: 1) the strict order of tragedy, 2) the world as chaos, 3) a precarious and temporary order created by comedy, also including elements of disorder.[9] He takes it as his task

---

der deutschen Literatur, pp. 365–66; Carlsson, pp. 372–73). Carlsson includes a criticism of over-facile judgments: "Now we get plays with contemporary issues, proclaimed dead decades ago, historical plays, morally engaged documentary plays. . . . We heard ten years ago from our augurs that this could not possibly exist on the stage, it was passé. . . . In fact it does exist, in a splendid way" (p. 363: a quotation from Horst Krüger, *Die Welt*, Aug. 19, 1965).

[8] Walter Jens has emphasized the existence of a fixed order within a city-state, a polis, as a starting-point for Greek tragedy [*Statt einer Literaturgeschichte*, 1962 (1957), pp. 87–90]. He also finds connections between ancient and modern plays, e.g., in the fear expressed— mixed, however, with grotesquely comic elements in the twentieth century (pp. 98–100). "In our own time, the 'death of tragedy' has all but become a household phrase. . . . The point is . . . that only the traditional and . . . canonical variety of tragedy has disappeared" (Guthke, *Modern Tragicomedy*, p. 97).

[9] Guthke bases a similar conclusion on Dürrenmatt's "men of courage": there is "a precarious balance, in the tragic comedy of today,

to struggle from 2) to 3), from a chaotic world into a world barely tempered by comedy. He chooses both chaos and order. His world of comedy is in accordance with his experience of the post-war world shared by everybody. Both worlds are "about to fold." In his early notes Dürrenmatt sailed out with the idea of conquering *the* world, our common world. Now he implies that conquering it means steering toward ever new worlds of comedy.[10]

These worlds are to be controlled with the help of artistic invention and the grotesque. The latter is called a perceptible paradox, "the face of the world without face." The functions of these two terms are taken over as such from the earlier "Note on Comedy." In his eagerness to grant general validity to his preference for comedy, Dürrenmatt drifts to his next self-contradiction. "This . . . does not mean that drama today can only be comical. . . . Comedy alone is suitable for us." If we strain our interpretative sympathy again, it is possible to state that the first-quoted sentence formulates Dürrenmatt's liberal, over-all view of modern drama, the second his subjective view supporting his own choice. He is trying to be both fair and strong. "Tragedy and comedy . . . can embrace one and the same thing. Only the conditions under which each is created are different." And those conditions which, after all, speak for comedy and against tragedy, include his often repeated conviction of a collective guilt: "Tragedy presupposes guilt, despair, moderation, lucidity, vision, a sense of responsibility. In the Punch-and-Judy show of our century, in this back-sliding of the white race, there are no more guilty and also, no responsible men. . . . Our world has led to the grotesque as well as to the atom bomb" (FP 33). What

---

of chaos and form, of shapelessness and order. The disastrous chaos of the modern world remains chaotic, order remains lost. But it is countered by the spiritual form and order within the person who courageously faces its meaninglessness and bears it" (p. 134).

[10] Deschner has discovered both of these worlds: "Since the world has lost its perceptible order, there is no way of staging *this* world, *the* world. But comedy can create *a* world by not treating the world as a problem but rather catching it, as it were, on the wing, in one of its many metamorphoses" ("F.D's Experiments with Man," p. 28).

Dürrenmatt is in effect saying is that comedy and tragedy are equal, only comedy is more equal than tragedy.[11] This is a paradox which a reader of *Problems of the Theater* seems to be unable to do without.

Dürrenmatt's curious vacillation can also be explained by his choice of a mixed form, tragicomedy. He rejects the alternative 1) mentioned above, yet wants to retain a tragic dimension in his comedy. In this sense he means that "tragedy and comedy can embrace one and the same thing": "But the tragic is still possible even if pure tragedy is not. We can achieve the tragic out of comedy. We can bring it forth as a frightening moment, as an abyss that opens suddenly" (FP 34). Preserving Dürrenmatt's distinction between "tragedy" and "the tragic" we can conclude, together with Guthke, that the tragic, a still feasible ingredient in drama, means an "experience of human suffering and frustration" not consoled by "that very order and norm to which tragedy has traditionally adhered."[12] Dürrenmattian comedy is not only a precarious combination of chaos and order, it also balances between the comic and the tragic. The conflict between these elements is grotesque and thus unresolvable.[13]

"Comedy alone is suitable for us." When quoted separately, without interpretation, this sentence sounds arbitrary. Even with all of the above explanations it signifies a clearly marked individual choice. One can argue that there are and have been other possibilities open to modern drama, such as absurd farce, poetic drama, documentary play, serious drama, or the theater of cruelty. Dürrenmatt uses the discretion of a creative playwright: "comedy alone." In his next step he rejects the interpretation that comedy can be an expression

[11] "There is . . . a logical leap from the assertion that tragedy is impossible to the statement that comedy alone is suitable for our times" (Peppard, p. 128). Cf. Profitlich, pp. 7–8.

[12] Guthke, p. 133. Allemann has spoken about Dürrenmatt's "detour": through comedy into the tragic (Steffen, *Das deutsche Lustspiel*, II, p. 207).

[13] Tragicomedy and the grotesque have belonged together since "Storm and Stress" (Kayser, *Das Groteske*, p. 56).

only of despair. He does not even consider the possibility that comedy might express happiness or hope: another sign that for him comedy has taken over the dimensions of depth and anxiety traditionally associated with tragedy. And not only for him but also for Ionesco, for Pinter, for other representatives of modern tragicomedy, anxiously looking for sense in the middle of the senselessness of life.[14]

This search motivates the next leap in Dürrenmatt's thoughts. Comedy can be an expression of despair, yet it need not be. There are "men of courage" enduring "this world in which we live like Gulliver among the giants." They are the opposites of Dürrenmatt's despairing nihilists, they are the heroes of his paradoxical, somber, and grotesque tragicomedies (cf. p. 66 above). They are individuals achieving distance, stepping "back a pace or two" and taking measure of their opponents: "The lost world-order is restored within them; the universal escapes my grasp" (FP 34). In making "men of courage" the heroes of his plays, Dürrenmatt is following his own artistic invention, not any universal rule or other necessity.

Dürrenmatt also believes that his inventions are powerful enough to transform modern audiences into a uniformly reacting community. He sees the spectators of comedy as "a mass which can be attacked, deceived, outsmarted into listening to things it would otherwise not so readily listen to. Comedy is a mouse-trap in which the public is easily caught" (FP 35). What limits the moving space of modern writers of comedy, these manufacturers of mouse-traps, is the fact that the world is growing full of the ready-made shapes of earlier artists and scholars. Shakespeare was limited only by storyteller Plutarch when planning his *Julius Caesar*; every modern writer of historical plays has to face "a body of factual information" gathered by an army of scholars. Dürrenmatt's prescription against scholarophobia is that the comedian regains his freedom by parodying his materials: "every parody

[14] Guthke, pp. 122–32, 170–71. Modern tragicomedy even includes a metaphysical aspect (pp. 124–26).

213

presupposes . . . an invention. In laughter man's freedom becomes manifest, in crying his necessity. Our task today is to demonstrate freedom. The tyrants of this planet . . . fear only one thing: a poet's mockery" (FP 37).[15] So Dürrenmatt is about to close the big circle behind his lecture, the circle starting with Hitler and finishing with a declaration for the uncomfortable, dangerous art of comedy.

The most controversial pages in *Problems of the Theater* are followed by a passage emphasizing strongly that Dürrenmatt is only sketching his individual credo. "Art is something personal, and . . . should never be explained with generalities. . . . What logic in matters of art could not be refuted!" (FP 35). Should we perhaps surrender before this polemical plea? Has it been a waste of time to weigh every word in that treatise on the golden scale of pedantry? Hardly; and for reasons Dürrenmatt could not guess when writing that sentence. *Problems of the Theater* has not only a prehistory revealing how it gradually grew out of its writer's earlier theoretical writings. It also has a post-history, and a splendid one.

A Swiss playwright goes lecturing in the fall of 1954. If his lecture had contained only a personal dramaturgy, or if his subsequent plays had been only moderately successful concretizations of this dramaturgy, we probably should not have been worried about every phrase in that treatise. We know that the reverse is true. We know that this lecture grew from the hands of its writer, we know that this personal credo of a dramatist acquired dimensions of general interest. It sometimes happens in the history of art that a particular piece of work becomes the symbol of its age. It sometimes happens in the history of criticism, too: a treatise can become the manifesto of a style. It could not have happened if Dürrenmatt's vision had not been a combination of the personal and the universal. And it probably would not have happened if this treatise had not been launched and put into orbit by

---

[15] Dürrenmatt has a thorough knowledge of the objects of his parody: he is more widely read than he wants to admit (Brock-Sulzer in *Der unbequeme D.*, p. 119).

The Visit. It became a companion piece to Dürrenmatt's grotesque tragicomedy, the most complete embodiment of his theory.

This post-history justifies the above discussion. The reference to Hochhuth & Co. was not quite fair; Dürrenmatt could not possibly have known in 1954 what kind of development German-speaking drama was to experience ten years later, when an old formula was rediscovered: documentary drama. Yet *Problems of the Theater* is a tract of such significance that it has to be tested alongside later developments as well. Whatever its shortcomings, it is the most lucidly reasoned treatise about a whole dramatic genre, about postwar tragicomedy employing grotesque means of expression.[16] It even illuminates the spiritual and intellectual background of plays alien to Dürrenmatt, plays belonging to absurdism. A collection of idiosyncracies could not have done it. It is a generally valid observation that we live in an era of mixed dramatic genres; it is a personal choice to transform the world into grotesque tragicomedies with men of courage as their modest heroes. And, taking *Problems of the Theater* from the point of view of Dürrenmatt's development, it is worth remembering that his career was to go on, through and past this tract. It is characteristic of Dürrenmatt that he is anxious to assure his readers in his most important theoretical writing that he chooses freedom, not formulas. He also prefers practice to theory, inventions to generally accepted myths, the particular to the general, art to scholarly research, parody to solemnity, comedy to tragedy, and tragicomedy to comedy.

The rest is supplementary. *Problems of the Theater*, this general view of Dürrenmatt's dramaturgy, is followed by a few talks dealing with certain particular aspects of it. In

[16] Guthke is critical in his reading of *Problems of the Theater*, yet calls the tract "the most elaborate theory of tragicomedy as the modern dramatic genre par excellence that has appeared to date." It sounds "a note that is widely felt to be representative and exemplary" (p. 129).

September of 1956 Dürrenmatt pondered over the sense of poetry in our time and developed new variations, significant from the point of view of his later practice. The world is becoming full of artistic shapes—and of scientific discoveries. "Our thinking . . . has become mathematically abstract" (TS 56–57); words are replaced by exact formulas, understood only by the initiated; modern philosophy is more and more based on science, it is not so much a branch of humanities any more. "Technology . . . is the thinking of our time made visible" (TS 59). There are fewer and fewer people who understand the new achievements of science, yet we all depend on them. Science and politics, dominated by giant-sized states, are both beyond the reach of the individual; we are only playthings.

These are thoughts from which *The Physicists* was to grow for the stage. Later in his talk, Dürrenmatt found positive features in technology: radio and television have opened up new possibilities for the writer. Yet there must be a word of warning against overestimating his role. The writer cannot make up for philosophy or religion, he senses that present-day reality is "beyond language, not in the direction of mysticism but of science" (TS 62). Instead of chiseling his inexact words the writer should work on his thoughts; this is a negative position toward poets in ivory towers. It is the writer's business "to understand that he has to live in this world. He must not compose for himself another world, he has to realize that, due to human nature, our present time is necessarily as it is" (TS 63). And then, at a key point of his lecture, Dürrenmatt takes a leap forward, developing a thought already formulated in "A Note on Comedy": "A writer's work does not mean copying the world, but creating it anew, setting up new worlds of his own (Eigenwelten) that in themselves give a picture of the world, because their building materials are taken from present times. . . . A logical particular world cannot depart from our world at all" (TS 63).

Can it not? Is there such a great difference between an

Eigenwelt and "another world" not to be composed by a writer? Dürrenmatt cites as an example *Gulliver's Travels*: several logical worlds of Swift's own not departing from our world, due to their inherent logic. This is a matter of some importance, because Dürrenmatt shows an increasing tendency to create worlds of his own, even arbitrary ones, as we shall see later on. Swift and Dürrenmatt, when at their best, certainly succeed in creating "logical worlds of their own" that do not depart from our world but are relevant to it. Yet the certainly complicated problem of a writer's relation to so-called reality[17] is not to be solved with the help of a blind belief in "worlds of his own," though this was a current concept in the 1950's. Modern building materials and designs are as such no guarantee. The question left open concerns the relevance of these worlds to our own. The lecture ends with an exhortation to endure the conflict between thinking and seeing, between science and art: "Science demonstrates the unity, art the diversity of the riddle that we call the world" (TS 64).

In his Mannheim lecture on Schiller (1959) Dürrenmatt defines his own relation to—Brecht. And to Schiller; yet there are fewer new elements in this major section of the lecture. Schiller is a representative of that mechanical, socially static dramaturgy Dürrenmatt had previously renounced as obsolete. Yet he takes the classic writer he was supposed to commemorate[18] as his interlocutor and renders his interpretation of Schiller's well-known distinction between "naïve" and "sentimental" poets. According to Schiller's very special terminology, everything a "naïve" poet creates is nature itself, while a "sentimental" poet has to make a conscious effort to reach nature. Dürrenmatt: the poets "would either be nature or look for nature" (TS 220). Ap-

[17] For Durzak, Dürrenmatt's "worlds" or models are "aesthetic fictions": their relation to reality is left undefined (*D., Frisch, Weiss*, p. 36).

[18] Dürrenmatt made the speech when accepting the German Schiller Prize on the 200th birthday of the poet.

217

plying these terms to drama, Dürrenmatt finds a group of natural dramatists sharing the naïvete of theater audiences; they are actors among the dramatists: Shakespeare, Molière, Nestroy. These are "the most legitimate rulers of the stage, Schiller one of its greatest usurpers" (TS 221). Schiller is a thinker; he has to work hard to conquer nature or the stage; he manages to turn abstractions into an immediate style of dialogue.

"Naïve" and "sentimental" dramatists differ in their basic attitudes to their age. This is a link with Dürrenmatt's own dramaturgy, also growing from a reaction to his time. A "sentimental" playwright is a rebel: "for him, reality is not nature but the anti-nature (Unnatur) he has to put right in the name of nature. . . . In Tyrannos. The stage becomes a tribunal" (TS 222). This is where Brecht enters Dürrenmatt's lecture: as "an extreme form of the 'sentimental' poet," as a rebel turned into a revolutionary. A revolutionary does not only describe an unjust world and man as a victim, but also knows how the world should be changed. He describes "a changeable world" (TS 223).

Hans Mayer has been able to reconstruct quite an interesting exchange of notes between Brecht and Dürrenmatt. A key issue is whether the world is changeable or not. In *Mississippi* Dürrenmatt described man as a victim; he also expressed his doubt whether the present-day world could be portrayed in the theater at all. Brecht answered at a meeting of dramaturges in Darmstadt in 1955: it was possible to describe our world, "but only if it was conceived as changeable."[19] In *Problems of the Theater* there were a few passing shots at Brecht, and a sentence of importance in this connection: "Today art can only embrace the victims, if it can reach men at all" (FP 31). Dürrenmatt's more complete answer was delayed until his lecture on Schiller: "The old dogma of the revolutionaries that man could and should

[19] Mayer, *D. und Frisch*, p. 17; cf. pp. 13, 16. Kesting discusses Dürrenmatt as an independent follower of Brecht: Durzak, ed., *Die deutsche Literatur der Gegenwart*, pp. 76–79.

change the world, has become unrealizable for the individual, has been withdrawn from circulation, the sentence is useful only for the crowds, as a slogan, as political dynamite, as an impetus for the masses, as hope for the grey armies of the starving" (TS 228). Mayer connects the above sentence with a passus in *Problems of the Theater* and concludes that Dürrenmatt rejects both Marxism and religion.[20]

This is not the only or the last dispute or point of contact between Brecht and Dürrenmatt. Both have been fascinated by low-brow art, by cabaret theater, and by detective stories; Dürrenmatt used alienation techniques in his first stage play. Brecht's shadow is so long that no postwar dramatist in German can avoid it. The arguments against Brecht summarized above belong to the phase in Dürrenmatt's development when he became conscious of these similarities and began to reject the outside influence.[21] There are, however, still parallels to be drawn in connection with Dürrenmatt's later plays *Frank V* and *The Physicists*. If we consider both the resemblances and points of disagreement, it is interesting to note that Dürrenmatt manages to admire both Schiller and Brecht in his lecture—and to reject both.[22] Quite a feat in polemics. Brecht's works are "one of the few honest answers to our slogans" (TS 224); "we"—i.e., Western intellectuals —should start "a genuine dialogue with Communism" (TS 225), believing in the superior flexibility of the Western way of thinking. Schiller, though not eligible as the creator of a model dramaturgy, comes close to the 1950's in his disappointment, in his feeling of political powerlessness. He lived in petty circumstances in a midget state, as an outsider. The postwar individuals are also powerless in the middle of a mankind grown into thousands of millions. "In Schiller one can feel the great soberness of mind that we need today when facing a state tending to lean toward totalitarianism. Man is

[20] Mayer, pp. 15–16.　　　[21] Ibid., pp. 13–14.
[22] Dürrenmatt's "ambivalent attitude toward both Schiller and Brecht, compounded of respect and distance . . . reveals shifting emphasis" in TS (Peppard, p. 125).

only partially a political creature, his fate will not come true
through his politics, but through what lies beyond politics,
what comes after politics. This is where he lives or fails"
(TS 232).

In short, Dürrenmatt accepts Schiller as a rebel fighting
for spiritual freedom, rejects him as a model dramatist. Dürrenmatt's attitude to Brecht's dramaturgy is more favorable
(TS 224), yet he rejects Brecht as a social revolutionary.
What does this reveal of Dürrenmatt's own position or dramaturgy? Does he consider himself as a "naïve" or "sentimental" playwright? Where would he locate himself in a
pattern drawn with the help of Schiller, a great German
classic, and Brecht, a great modern dramatist? He does not
say. He chooses his own road somewhere outside the terrain
of both. In a note on *The Visit* he says that the stage directors
"come nearest the mark" when treating him "as a kind of
conscious Nestroy" (TV 106). This note was written in
1957, two years before Dürrenmatt's lecture on Schiller; in
Mannheim Dürrenmatt mentioned Nestroy as a "naïve"
playwright. "A conscious Nestroy": a naïvist tempted by
rebellion? Or by the thinker within himself?[23] Dürrenmatt
can be taken as a natural dramatist, an actor or story-teller
by inclination, yet relying not only on the naïvete of the
audiences but also on their ability to think. He is not convinced that this changes the world for the better.[24] Dürrenmatt in Mannheim: "The art of a dramatist consists in making the audience reflect, but only afterwards" (TS 221).

[23] Both Galilei in Brecht's play and Brecht himself regard thinking
as "a pleasure, vice and temptation." So does Dürrenmatt: "Thinking
as a temptation, yet also a responsibility in an age marked by its
trend toward general irresponsibility" (Mayer, pp. 20–21). "He
obviously wants to present himself as the naïve dramatist . . . and
Brecht as the thinker. But he ends up speaking for both sides"
(Deschner, p. 21).

[24] Dürrenmatt has remarked that the effect of a play on the audience is "very indefinite," depending also on the spectators themselves (Sauter, "Gespräch mit F.D.," *Sinn und Form*, 18, 4, 1966,
p. 1221).

Dürrenmatt prefers practice to theory: let us follow his example. His practice as a playwright in the 1960's is to be described first, his theory in the same years simultaneously or afterward. Yet there are a few lines to be followed, just to complete the picture drawn above.[25] After *Problems of the Theater* Dürrenmatt tends to take comedy as an axiom, as the only opportunity for a present-day writer. He does not even consider other possibilities. Death on the stage is for him nothing terrible, just a "dramaturgic trick" (TS 73). He goes on defining his position against Brecht: "Every literary subject possesses its own inherent life, its own stubborn laws. . . . A subject is never unequivocal, but a message wants to be. . . . Art never proves anything at all" (TS 152). Or he tackles the same dichotomy by stating that he wants to start from a conflict, not from a solvable problem (TS 208–09).[26] And he finds a social or even geographical justification for his enthusiasm to create entire worlds on the stage. A playwright belonging to a big nation, an American for example, can write in a realistic style, because everyone is interested in the American way of living. For a playwright of a small country, the world as such becomes problematic, so he creates "forever new models of the world" (TS 162–63).

In most of his lectures Dürrenmatt makes certain of putting both himself and his audiences at ease by self-ironical or otherwise humorous twists. In the 1960's a tone of impatience occasionally creeps into his voice. All in all, *Writings on the Theater* makes an excellent collection of lectures: personal, matter-of-fact, growing out of a creative writer's practice. Returning to its intellectual core, to the arguments

[25] Brock-Sulzer's list of lines running through all of TS includes Dürrenmatt's interest in comedy, in artistic inventions, in men of courage enduring the world, not changing it, in distance and exaggeration, in inconspicuous morality; he is against solemnity in art (TS 23–24).

[26] Dürrenmatt's starting-point is story, not thesis; conflict, not problem; a model of the world, not the world itself (Diether Krywalski, "Säkularisiertes Mysterienspiel?" *Stimmen der Zeit, 92*, 5, May 1967, pp. 348–49).

on dramaturgy most fully developed in *Problems of the Theater*, one might try to define Dürrenmatt's relation to absurdism. His preference for tragicomedy is shared by a great many absurdists; his tone or pitch of voice follows the tune of the 1950's (cf. pp. 16–20 above). He also shares the current experience of the senselessness of life. Yet his men of courage, as victims, as substitute sufferers, help him to turn an experience of absurdity into a grotesque tragicomedy. This is where we meet him in *The Visit*. The absurdity is faced, accepted, and thus made endurable; an infection is limited before it has time to spread all over the organism. There had to be elements of general validity in both halves of Dürrenmatt's theory, or his treatises would not have been read and discussed so widely. And these elements were there: in the experience of a senseless world, in the form of tragicomedy given to this experience. Dürrenmatt's place is between Ionesco and Brecht.

10 All Roads Lead to Guellen

THE VISIT

||||||||||||||||||||||||||||||||||||||||||||||||||||||||||||||||||||||||||||||||||||||||||

The Visit (Der Besuch der alten Dame) is Dürren-matt's sixth stage play. With it we are back at the center of his creative work. This grotesque tragicomedy not only is his best play thus far, but it also signifies a synthesis between the various aspirations of his career. Like an apex, it gathers together the lines of development followed in the preceding chapters. All roads lead to Guellen, to Dürrenmatt's small-town Swiss community. Guellen is a logical "Eigenwelt" not departing from our common world.[1] It is still in Central Europe, it is still in the middle of mankind.

The play opens at the railroad station. Guellen (in English perhaps "Dungtown") is "a tumbledown wreck," its station-buildings are "equally ramshackle." Four townsmen are sitting on the station bench and watching express trains rushing by. Once the trains stopped in Guellen; they do not stop any more. The opening atmosphere of poverty and disillusionment is confirmed through a few melancholy, elliptical sayings: "Living? . . . Vegetating. . . . And rotting to death" (TV 11–12). These lines are given to unnamed and unindividualized townsmen:[2] Dürrenmatt is opening his mass play. The play will reach a climax in three chorus scenes.

There is a ray of hope for the Guelleners. Claire Zacha-nassian, née Wascher, the richest woman in the world, is returning into her native town. Rumors of her donations else-

---

[1] Dürrenmatt may have had Guellen in his mind when formulating his maxim about "worlds of his own" (TS 63; cf. p. 216 above). The phrase occurred in a lecture given in September, 1956, eight months after the world première of *The Visit*.

[2] Peppard, *F.D.*, p. 55: "their nearly choral way of speaking, the interchangeability of their roles, and their uniform opinions and attitudes introduce the spectator to the city as a cohesive social organization."

where have been circulating, and Guellen is doing its very best to give her a hearty welcome. The Mayor with his two granddaughters will be present, and so will the other town dignitaries: Schoolmaster, Minister,[3] Doctor. The mixed choir and the Youth Club will perform, and a key role is entrusted to Alfred Ill, Claire's beloved of forty-five years earlier. It is a regular feature in the tactics of a playwright to arouse expectations in his audience. Our first expectations as spectators of *The Visit* are great: there is to follow a happy reunion of the lovers, bringing prosperity to the entire town. Having sympathized with the four townsmen in their melancholy mood we are ready to share the budding enthusiasm. We are Guelleners.[4]

Then Claire arrives, and everything goes amiss. It is beneath the dignity of this multimillionairess to travel by a commuter train; she pulls the emergency brake of an express train and arrives in Guellen right in the middle of the festive preparations. The name of her express is "Racing Roland." No detail in this rich text is without at least passing significance, and the tone of a great many names and phrases is both sinister and parodical. To take just one example: "Racing Roland" can be associated with the Renaissance, perhaps even with blood revenge à la Borgia. Claire is a woman of Renaissance dimensions, and she is after vendetta.

Claire's first achievement in Guellen is the comedy of a pompous welcome turned into a fiasco. Next she arouses perplexity as her grotesque retinue is introduced item by item: Husband VII, a butler, a sedan-chair, two gangsters from Sing Sing to carry it, two eunuchs, a coffin, and a black panther. What makes the biped members of her retinue grotesquely distorted is that they are all deficient as human beings: Claire has two artificial limbs, her Husbands VII–IX

---

[3] Because of Dürrenmatt's Protestant background it sounds natural to call Guellen's clergyman a "minister," not a "priest."

[4] Throughout Act I we are made to join the camp of the Guelleners—until it is no easy matter to break with them, even if we are proved to be accomplices in a crime (Jenny, *F.D.*, pp. 59–60).

are there only for display purposes, the butler is senile, the gangsters have no moral sense, the eunuchs, an unreal pair of twins, are also blind. Even if one could put all these characters together, they would not add up to a complete human being. The Guellener least disturbed by these antics is Ill: "Clara has such a golden sense of humor! I could die laughing at one of her jokes!" (TV 33). The Guellener most disturbed is the Schoolmaster: "That old lady in black robes getting off the train was a gruesome vision. Like one of the Fates; she made me think of an avenging Greek goddess" (TV 26). Both are right; Claire is an avenging goddess with a sense of humor.[5] As such she is the full-blooded heroine of a tragicomedy.

Mrs. Zachanassian is also an archetypal figure in Swiss literature: a refugee from "Swiss malaise," from the narrow circumstances of her birthplace—a fugitive bound to return. "A young man leaves his native district full of anger and revolt, grows up into a man far away and comes back, in order to adjust himself to the community and take part in shaping its future."[6] The first half of the definition fits perfectly; yet Claire is an exceptional case and Dürrenmatt's play a counter-sketch to many an edifying novel.[7] Claire has no intention of conforming to the demands of Guellen. Instead, it is her firm decision to adapt the community to her wishes, to her moral demands. Once the morals prevailing in

[5] "The old lady—she can afford it—is given to drastic and macabre jokes" (Jenny, p. 63).

[6] Otto Oberholzer in Durzak, ed., *Die deutsche Literatur der Gegenwart*, p. 411; cf. Wehrli in Kayser, ed., *Deutsche Literatur in unserer Zeit*, pp. 120–22, and Schmid, *Unbehagen im Kleinstaat*, passim, e.g. pp. 174–75, 178, 192–93.

[7] Originally, Dürrenmatt reports in Bienek, *Werkstattgespräche*, pp. 107–08, the topic was to become a short story with a male hero. Then the stations the writer passed by on his frequent train trips captured his imagination, the story started to grow toward the stage, the hero changed into a heroine, and pulling the Emergency Brake was chosen as the most pompous entrée. The station became the setting in three focal scenes, and Claire was furnished with artificial limbs to explain her refusal to travel by car. The stage shapes and reshapes Dürrenmatt's "stuff" and characters. Cf. Wyrsch, part five, April 15, p. 38.

Guellen led to her going into exile; now it is to be her final revenge to twist those morals until they fit into the mold of her own fabrication. She is in complete control of the town; it is up to her to shape its future. The end of Act I in *The Visit* is devoted to revealing Claire's plan.

Claire's target is Alfred Ill. The first encounter between these two protagonists of *The Visit* took place at the station. Ill, "a broken-down shopkeeper" (TV 29), seems to thrive in his role as a mediator between the community and the richest woman in the world, especially in Konrad's Village Wood, their trysting place forty-five years earlier. Claire is playing cat and mouse with him, while evoking tender memories; a basic irony throughout Act I is based on Ill's credulity. He believes in being "psychologically acute" (TV 16), while being acutely studied and trapped by Claire. Dürrenmatt chose to frame his two forest scenes with Guelleners playing trees, does, and cuckoos, not for the sake of surrealism, but to make bearable "a somewhat distressing love-story, . . . an old man's attempt to approach an old woman" (TV 105). He also wanted to avoid traditional German forest romanticism (TS 173). This kind of theatricality, sketched with a light hand, is in keeping with the style chosen for the settings throughout the play.[8] The milieus are suggested or hinted at, not built up solidly and realistically. A Guellener playing woodpecker by tapping his pipe: a stage illusion is punctured, a style is broken—as it is through many a parodical twist.[9] See Fig. 6. Ill kisses Claire's right hand:

[8] Jenny is afraid that the townsmen playing trees makes the dialogue harmless (p. 64), while E. S. Dick overinterprets the symbolic overtones in the forest scenes ("Ds 'Besuch,'" *Zeitschrift für deutsche Philologie*, *87*, 4, Oct. 1968, pp. 503–07). There is an earlier forest scene in Dürrenmatt with a grotesque fairy-tale atmosphere: in *The Pledge* (cf. pp. 169–70 above).

[9] "Dramatic irony of great intensity has been combined with the balancing force of comic relief in such a way that we both experience the pathos of the scene and, at the same time, are prevented from sharing emphatically in it" (Peppard, p. 58).

... The same, cool white hand.

C. Z.: No, you're wrong. It's artificial too. Ivory.

(Ill, horrified, releases her hand.)

ILL: Clara, are you all artificial? (TV 31).

This is an example from a long string of preparatory horror effects. The Minister is told that the death sentence may be reintroduced (TV 23), the Doctor is asked to diagnose heart attack "next time" (TV 32). The full meaning of these and other hints is revealed in the concluding scene of Act I, placed in the Hotel Golden Apostle, with all the Guelleners present at a dinner party. The Mayor, doing his very best to milk money from the distinguished guest of honor, makes a deceitful speech interrupted by Ill's whispered corrections and outbursts of applause. Enjoying her prerogative of complete honesty,[10] Claire rejects the embellishments of the previous speech and lets her first bomb explode: "I'm ready to give Guellen one million."[11] While everyone is sitting dumbstruck, before an indescribable outburst of jubilation, she adds: "On one condition" (TV 37). See Fig. 5.

That condition is bound up with Claire's demand for justice in return for her million. The character of the scene changes: there follows the re-enactment of a trial that took place in Guellen forty-five years earlier. The accused is Ill, the plaintiff Claire; her butler sits as the judge, as he once did, and the eunuchs are two witnesses guilty of perjury. Reason for trial: a paternity claim. Ill denied the claim, bribed the witnesses, and won the case. He married money— that is, Matilda and her shop—not Claire. The child died

---

[10] "She is outside or beyond the deceptions and rationalizations of the townspeople and is able to survey them with a serene kind of cynical detachment. . . . She enjoys a prerogative shared by kings and fools, the privilege of honesty" (Hans P. Guth, "D's *Visit*," *Symposium*, *16*, 2, Summer 1962, p. 100).

[11] The German original has "eine Milliarde" (1,000,000,000). The American word for this figure is "one billion." The translator into English, probably with English pounds in mind, changes the figure into "one million." What Dürrenmatt means is a sum big enough to corrupt a whole town.

227

a year later, and Claire became a prostitute. These rapid trial proceedings lead to a second bomb explosion, to a scenic image carefully prepared: "A million for Guellen if someone kills Alfred Ill" (TV 38).[12]

Act I has brought surprise after surprise to the Guelleners and to the spectators, until the themes of the play are gathered into this super-surprise. The scenic image is built up with the help of suspense and an active crowd present on the stage. The townspeople applaud, dance with joy, change positions, listen intently—and are dead silent. Through the formal positions of characters the case of Claire versus Ill is put before all Guelleners—and before an ancient court, before the theater audience. Every Guellener and every spectator is made a member of a grand jury. Like Matthäi in *The Pledge*, Dürrenmatt is saying to the crowd: you are to judge. Even if this age-old theatrical device is present in every trial play (or, indeed, in any play), it has seldom been put to such a clear and effective use. Once again, Dürrenmatt is moving outside the official judicial machinery of society, yet without losing an ounce of the moral and legal weight of his arguments and counter-arguments.[13] From now on, the trial is a matter between Ill and Guellen; and the various threads of this case are interwoven into a story that is free to move to any locality within the town. As in *Donkey's Shadow*, a case is to grow until it covers an entire town; as in that radio play, the red thread of trial is seen running through each

[12] This is "a typical Dürrenmatt scene. Its structure may be compared to the piling on of straws until the camel's back breaks. Casually the evidence starts building up, dropping negligently, . . . on the imperceptibly, yet very really, increasing pile, until suddenly the whole innocent-and-insignificant-seeming mass is brought into focus by Claire's self-assured, deeply venomous remark" (Wellworth, *The Theater of Protest and Paradox*, p. 140).

[13] Claire does not need any "human law-court in order to reach her goal." Yet this and other points of connection between the Bible and *The Visit* hardly make it a regular passion play as claimed by Jenny C. Hortenbach ("Biblical Echoes in D's 'Besuch,' " *Monatshefte für deutschen Unterricht, 57*, 4, April–May, 1965, pp. 145–61).

scene. The problem of justice is kept unwaveringly before Dürrenmatt's eyes—and before those of every spectator. Dürrenmatt and Claire have a point in common. Both have returned to the milieu of their childhood; both know Guellen by heart. On his flights into history Dürrenmatt had often stopped at stations bearing the signs of German, Greek, or Babylonian city-states; Guellen is a Swiss -*polis* made manageable on the stage.[14] With schoolmasters or slaughterers as its representative citizens, Guellen is a typical Swiss town, a middle-class community. *The Marriage of Mr. Mississippi* is Dürrenmatt's first stage play throwing aside historical decorations; it did not fulfill his ambition to create a modern world theater.[15] *The Visit* does, for two reasons. The idea of using a small Swiss town as his setting activated Dürrenmatt's childhood memories.[16] He was able to concretize his vision, to construct a world employed as a background in his detective stories and thus thoroughly studied. Second, he did not pour out his memories as such; he filtered them through his grotesque creative fantasy and connected them with one of his basic concerns, the problem of human justice. Guellen is a model of the world: of our world—and of a writer's moral world.[17] *Romulus the Great* showed us the center of ancient Rome turned into an idyllic back yard; now

[14] The ancient polis furnished the writers with a solid frame of reference lacking in our age, Walter Jens complains (*Statt einer Literaturgeschichte*, pp. 87–90). Yet has not Dürrenmatt created a modern polis, solid enough to do as a frame, fluid enough to serve as a model of our affluent society?

[15] *The Visit* joins, "with a partly parodical aim," the tradition of "world theater" shaped, e.g., by Calderon and Hofmannsthal (Dick, loc. cit., p. 501).

[16] In his memoir of his childhood Dürrenmatt calls himself "a villager" (TS 30). Brock-Sulzer connects this passage with *The Visit* (*D. in unserer Zeit*, p. 9).

[17] Cf. Dürrenmatt's lecture in New York in 1960: a writer living in Liechtenstein cannot write realistically; he has to turn his tiny native country into "a model of the world, forever new." This makes the world as a whole his problem (TS 162–63).

an idyllic back yard is made the center of the modern world. The similes work, both ways.

The Guelleners, our representatives on the stage, react to Claire's offer with spontaneous consternation. Justice cannot be bought. The Mayor, the voice of the community, as always, rejects the offer in the name of all citizens, "in the name of humanity." Claire knows better, and so she utters her curtain line: "I'll wait" (TV 39).

It is not to be a long wait. Having set "the whole play in motion" Claire remains passive,[18] just following the reactions of the Guelleners from her upstage lookout on the balcony of the Golden Apostle. Downstage, under her eyes, are Ill's shop and the bureaus of the various town officials. Everybody is buying on credit: more expensive cigarettes, milk, chocolate, cognac. And pairs of yellow shoes: completing the above list of purchases these shoes of guilt turn bad omens into a certainty for Ill. Guellen is speculating on his impending death. Quite innocently, in a way; the prevailing thought is that Claire will cancel her condition, not her donation.[19] The town is, of course, on Ill's side; "it's dead certain" that Ill will be elected Mayor next spring (TV 44), his customers assure him—while buying on credit in his shop. This diminuendo sequence of scenes based on everyday business dealings is written in Dürrenmatt's best tongue-in-cheek vein.

Ill cannot afford to remain passive. The yellow shoes start him on a tour of various town authorities. The policeman or the law, the Mayor or political power, and the Minister or the church, all turn him down. "The post of Mayor," the incumbent head of the town lectures Ill, "requires certain guarantees of good moral character which you can no longer

---

[18] Peppard, p. 58.

[19] "What is detestable is not the over-sized, cruel and terrible weirdness of the Zachanassian but the worthy, human and apparently harmless mediocrity of the Guelleners" (Syberberg, "Zum Drama F.Ds," p. 9).

furnish. You must realize that" (TV 54).[20] The Minister's words sound insincere in their scenic context, yet they point the way Ill was to follow later on: "Examine your conscience. Go the way of repentance, or the world will relight the fires of your terror again and again. It is the only way." At that moment a new church-bell starts sounding: "You too, Minister! You too!" (TV 57–58). Ambiguities of this kind abound in Act II, where Ill's growing fear and anxiety cut across the comedy of the Guelleners.

All the while Claire is sitting behind and above on her balcony. She is in control of the informal trial proceedings taking place between Ill and the townspeople; she has been counting on the gradual deterioration of the morals of the town. There is an inner, thematic connection between her small-talk and Ill's desperate activities.[21] Dürrenmatt is using a kind of montage technique, with short poignant scenes on Claire's balcony interrupting the main action of the play—a technique demonstrating his experience as a film writer. Claire's lines to her butler or to her would-be Husband VIII include samples of gallows humor ("Boby, pass me my left leg," TV 41), descriptions of nature, comments on her mail from Eisenhower, Nehru, or the Russians, and reminiscences of her seven earlier marriages. Her retinue also furnishes Act II with guitar music played by one of the gangsters, and with a parallel action. The black panther, a symbol for Ill, has escaped, and the Guelleners are ordered to hunt it down with rifles at the ready.[22] When the animal is shot to death

[20] Marianne Kesting sees sharply the motives of the Guelleners: "they will not—understandably enough—sacrifice their prosperity to save a man who is doubtless the biggest villain among them" (*Panorama des zeitgenössischen Theaters*, p. 226).

[21] Jauslin emphasizes this connection and the significance of anticipating minor details for the compactness of the play (*F.D.*, pp. 92–94).

[22] Dürrenmatt develops his story rationally, yet employs irrational effects to stratify the stage events, such as the panther episode: "scenic analogies, symmetries, inversions" form the structure of his plays (Jenny, pp. 65–66).

231

in front of Ill's shop, our accused knows that there is no hope left for him in Guellen. Act II closes with a nightmarish scene at the station.[23]

Ill comes to the station determined to leave Guellen for good. "As if by chance, citizens of Guellen come gradually closing in on him from all sides" (TV 59). The dialogue consists of lines spoken by Ill, by individual townspeople, and by all of them in a chorus. Paradoxically enough, the scene is soft-spoken: there is not a hint of cruelty or violence on the part of the Guelleners. They assure Ill that they will not prevent him from entering the train, yet they prevent his flight by their very presence: "An enjoyable trip, an enjoyable trip! . . . Long life and prosperity! . . . Get on the train! Get on the train!" (TV 61–62). It is the benevolence of these lines, somehow not entirely ironical,[24] it is the soft movement of the chorus back and forth, closer and away again, that gives the scene its nightmarish terror. Do the voices of the Guelleners sound only within Ill's head? Has not Dürrenmatt succeeded in externalizing Ill's innermost guilt and fear? The conflict between guilt, or a compulsion to stay in Guellen and pay for his crime, and fear, or a desperate effort to escape, nearly tears his mind apart. This unresolvable tension is present between Ill and the crowd, between the accused and a jury to profit from his death. With the help of his stage imagination Dürrenmatt has been able to shape these contradictory impulses into a grotesque, strangely poetic and powerful scenic image.

[23] "There is something of a bad dream about all this," Jan Kott writes in a highly acclamatory review of *The Visit*, "also something of folk imagery, of sensational low-level journalism, and something of the atmosphere of Kafka. Dürrenmatt builds his theatre from a blend of all these styles and elements; a surprising, disturbing, odd mixture. Above all, he blends the grotesque and terror in a new way." Kott calls the end of Act II "a great scene from Kafka" (*Theatre Notebook 1947–1967*, pp. 88, 90).

[24] Bänziger interprets this impression quite subtly. The Guelleners are drifting toward a murder against their will, and this station scene is a point of intersection: an individual reaches an insight and a crowd loses it. "Therefore the request of the Guelleners that Ill should go away is not meant to be absolutely insincere" (*Frisch und D.*, p. 169). Cf. TV 107.

A CREATIVE OUTBURST

Then the train leaves, and Ill collapses in the middle of the Guelleners. He knows that he is lost, and so do we.[25] The station scene at the end of Act II is a dress rehearsal for the ritual killing of Ill at the end of the play.

Act III opens with a suggestive scene in Petersens' Barn, another old trysting place of Ill and Claire. The setting is an example of Dürrenmattian abundance: there is a ladder, a hay-cart, an old hansome-cab, straw, rags, moldering sacks and "enormous outspun spiders' webs" (TV 63). In the midst of these props portraying the distant past, Claire sits in a white wedding-gown: she married her Husband VIII in Guellen Cathedral on that day. Her dress is in grotesque contrast with her surroundings. See Fig. 3.

Bride VIII, so to speak, receives the self-elected deputation of the townspeople. The role of the Schoolmaster starts growing in importance in this scene. The Mayor is the conventional voice of the community, the Schoolmaster its intellectual leader; in two scenes it is hinted that he is the head of the town opposition (TV 15–16, 93). Together with the Doctor he has now come to beg for mercy. As a schooled orator he refers to the personal sacrifices every Guellener has made in the poverty-stricken town, hoping for the best for its future. "We need credit, confidence, contracts. . . . Guellen has much to offer" (TV 65).

Claire's answer to this plea is short and poignant. She cannot buy the factories or other real estate, because she already owns the whole town: Guellen's poverty is solely her creation.[26] "It was winter, long ago, when I left this little town, . . . pregnant with only a short while to go, and the townsfolk sniggering at me. . . . I swore a vow to myself,

[25] Ill avoids an active effort to escape, yet the choice is "made for him." Everett M. Ellestad connects the scene with Kierkegaard's "either-or" ("F.D's *Mausefalle*," *The German Quarterly*, 43, 4, Nov. 1970, pp. 776, 779).
[26] This disclosure makes the hopes and sacrifices of the Guelleners ridiculous: it "pulls the rug from beneath the feet of us all, revealing our order to be chaos" (Eugene E. Reed, "D's 'Besuch,'" *Monatschrift für deutschen Unterricht*, 53, 1, Jan. 1961, p. 12).

233

I would come back again, one day. I've come back now"
(TV 66). This is how far Dürrenmatt goes by way of motivating Claire's revenge not only on Ill but on Guellen, too.[27]

Claire Wascher's vow is probably one of the starting-points
for Dürrenmatt's experiment in thought. I shall show you, I
shall take revenge on all of you; a childish outburst of resent-
ment following social humiliation, is it not? What if it were
to come true? If the girl swearing this vow should become
the richest woman in the world? We have been following
Ill's social nightmare in the middle of a crowd, a nightmare
so typical of Dürrenmatt. On Claire's side there is another
dream, a dream of wish-fulfillment. The figures in her retinue
are grotesquely distorted because they have roles to play in
two dreams: in Ill's nightmare of guilt, in Claire's dream of
revenge. This may have something to do with the fact that
we experience the retinue, or, indeed, the entire play, as
weird and exaggerated, yet strangely compelling. Ill and
Claire are our fellow human beings. We can share their
dreams.

In the reality of Guellen forty-five years after that vow
Claire can impose the conditions. With financial resources
like hers she can afford a new world order. "The world turned
me into a whore. I shall turn the world into a brothel" (TV
67). So much for humanity, so much for a plea for mercy.
Claire is "The Woman that Corrupts Guellen."[28] The Schoolmaster, the more sensitive of the two delegates, will carry
this vision of a new world order in his mind forever after the
meeting in Petersens' Barn, this one-time nest of love.

In the next scene he brings his apprehension into Ill's shop.

[27] "Her plan is ingenious: she punishes Ill through the inhabitants
and the inhabitants through Ill"—by making them murderers (Arnold, *F.D.*, p. 44). Cf. Durzak, D., *Frisch, Weiss*, pp. 92–95.

[28] Charles R. Lefcourt has compared *The Visit* with "The Man that
Corrupted Hadleyburg" by Mark Twain. The themes are similar,
Dürrenmatt's version is more pessimistic and bitter ("D's *Güllen*
and Twain's *Hadleyburg*," *Revue des Langues Vivantes, 33*, 3, Summer 1967, pp. 303–08). Cf. Kilchenmann, *Die Kurzgeschichte*, pp.
44–45.

Since his effort to escape, Ill has lived in seclusion upstairs. Public opinion has now turned against him—and against the Schoolmaster when the latter tries to reveal Claire's plan to reporters drawn to Guellen by her wedding. Ill enters the stage in the middle of a row and quiets the Schoolmaster down. Ill does not fight any more; he even accepts his role as Claire's first love and humors the reporters by letting himself be photographed while selling an axe to Man One, a slaughterer. A scenic image brimful of gallows humor: Herr Hofbauer weighing "that homicidal weapon" in his hand, with Ill following the directions of a reporter and doing his best to look "radiant with happiness, . . . radiant and contented deep down inside" (TV 74).[29]

Ill has conquered his fear in solitude.[30] In his tête-à-tête scene with the Schoolmaster he confesses his guilt. "I made Clara what she is, and I made myself what I am. . . . It's all my own work, the Eunuchs, the Butler, the coffin, the million" (TV 76). Ill admits that his nightmare of guilt is reality, and he is ready to play his role in Claire's dream of revenge. In a similar way the Schoolmaster knows that he is about to turn into a murderer, and his "faith in humanity is powerless to stop it" (TV 77). His only escape is a bottle of Steinhäger: the escape of Bodo von Übelohe in *Mr. Mississippi*. This feature belongs to Dürrenmatt's critical picture of German or Swiss intellectuals, rather of the old school, admirers of Greek classics, weak in their humanism. Our conception of this character will, however, be determined by his ambiguous speech in the murder scene.

With the town conscience silent the Mayor can go on promoting the public good. In a scene between him and Ill there

[29] The scenic image reveals the decision of the Guelleners to murder Ill and Ill's readiness to die (Syberberg, pp. 14, 113). The same scholar has paid attention to the rich and varied usage made of props, quotations, auditive and visual elements throughout *The Visit* (pp. 38–45).

[30] Ill's "breakthrough into greatness" takes place offstage; it is a lonely victory not to be won in a monologue or while conversing with another character (Jenny, p. 67). Cf. Guth, pp. 97–98.

235

is a stream of subtext charged with hidden meanings below
the lapidary lines:

MAYOR: Brought you a gun.
ILL: Thanks.
MAYOR: It's loaded.
ILL: I don't need it.
(Mayor leans gun against counter.)
MAYOR: There's a public meeting this evening. . . . The
motion will be rejected.
ILL: Possibly.
MAYOR: People make mistakes, of course.
ILL: Of course.
(Silence.)
MAYOR *(cautiously)*: In such a case, Ill, would you then
submit to the judgment? Since the Press will be present.
(TV 78–79).

Ill is ready to submit. Yet the suggestion of suicide provokes
him to an answer. His descent into hell resulted in a fear of
death slowly conquered: "If you had spared me that anguish,
that gruesome terror, . . . I might have taken the gun. . . .
There is no turning back. You *must* judge me, now. I shall
accept your judgment, whatever it may be. For me, it will be
justice; what it will be for you, I do not know" (TV 81).
These words are spoken by a man who has found his own
order of things. No matter what Ill's death means for Guellen,
for Ill it signifies a courageous deed satisfying his inner sense
of justice.[31]

Ill has half-departed from this world of ours. His inner
calmness is not disturbed by the fact that his wife and children are grasping their share of Guellen's wealth.[32] They follow him on his last drive in a car (Fig. 4), a ritual compar-

[31] "Ill has become a judge over Guellen. Through his death that
only expiates his betrayal of Claire, not the Guelleners' betrayal of
him, he condemns his fellow citizens" (Jenny, p. 68).
[32] "We begin to appreciate the dignity and self-control of Ill, who
does not rebuke his family, but accepts calmly what amounts to a
tacit betrayal" (Peppard, p. 58).

able with Dürrenmatt's customary last meals. There is a meal turned into a trial in Act I; it is proper that this satiric description of the postwar boom employs the car, a focal status symbol, for a ritualistic purpose. In his farewell to life Ill sees his surroundings as if for the first time: "Look at the plain, and the light on the hills beyond, all golden, today. Impressive, when you go into the shadows and then out again into light. . . . Monster-like clouds[33] in the sky, banks of them, real summer-time castles. It's a beautiful country in a soft twilight" (TV 82–83). In its Swiss lighting effects, in its sharp contrasts between shadows and sunshine, this passage reminds one of the landscapes in Dürrenmatt's novels. Ill is on his way to a fateful meeting, as Chanz once was in *The Judge and His Hangman*. Instead of indulging in wildly poetic outbursts, as in *It Is Written*, Dürrenmatt now writes in the vein of a quiet and concrete poetry of nature.

Ill has his last farewell scene with Claire. Again, these two meet in the forest. The dialogue is barren; it touches ordinary subjects of discussion, then the most delicate point of all, the fate of their child. Ill knows that he is to die that same evening and thanks Claire for the wreaths and flowers waiting on his coffin: a macabre twist. He will be buried in Capri, in a mausoleum with a view over the Mediterranean, Claire consoles him.[34] And she explains her love for Ill, the motive behind her monomaniacal demand for justice, in terms of grotesque imagery of nature: "Your love died many years ago. But my love could not die. Neither could it live. It grew into an evil thing, like me, like the pallid mushrooms in this wood, and the blind, twisted features of the roots, all overgrown by my golden millions" (TV 88). The guitar music is over: "Goodbye, Alfred."

There is a sharp cut from this intimate scene to the mass

[33] With Dürrenmattian grotesque in mind, I prefer translating "Wolkenungetüme" as "monster-like," not "colossal" clouds.

[34] Peppard (p. 58) calls this scene "a masterpiece of the bittersweet grotesque," "calm and composed, quite routine in tone and gesture." The mausoleum makes Claire almost sympathetic: her plan is fulfilled, her life is over, too.

meeting of the Guelleners in the auditorium of the Golden Apostle. A radio reporter opens the scene with a noisy and sentimentalizing commentary: the celebrated Mrs. Zachanassian is visiting her home town. The Mayor announces her endowment; the condition bound to it is, of course, concealed from the news media. Everything in the ensuing scene has false bottoms: the Guelleners know that the single item on their agenda is murder, the outsiders see only a sensational donation. The speech of the Schoolmaster can even be read in three ways. The radio reporter takes it as social criticism along general lines, the Guelleners as a condemnation of Ill's crime.[35] Yet there is still a third layer, a desperate effort of the town conscience to make the people of Guellen realize what they are about to do:

> For what would be the sense of wealth, which created not a wealth of grace? Yet grace can only be accorded those who hunger after grace. People of Guellen, do you have that hunger? Or is all your hunger common hunger, physical and profane? That is the question. As Head of your College, I put it to you all. Only if you refuse to abide any evil, refuse to live any longer under any circumstances in a world which connives at injustice, can you accept a million from Madam Zachanassian, and thereby fulfill the conditions attaching to her endowment (TV 92).

The Schoolmaster is offering the Guelleners a third possibility. Not a return to the good old days, to the stinking double morals that forced Claire into exile; not a world order based on avarice, not the world as a brothel. A world in which there would be a place for grace. Having given up his fight to save Ill's life the Schoolmaster still keeps reminding the townspeople that they are about to expiate Ill's crime with another crime, a murder inspired by greed, a murder masked as an act of justice. Only if there were a complete change in

---

[35] The critics have mostly taken the speech as empty verbiage masking Guellen's crime with high ideals (e.g. Jenny, p. 69; Brock-Sulzer, p. 86; Heilman, *The Iceman* . . . , p. 223, note 1).

their lives, would the Guelleners be justified in accepting Ill's self-sacrifice.[36]

He speaks in vain. The applause and catcalls of the Guelleners turn his speech into an affirmation of their own silent decision. The Schoolmaster is in a situation in which everything he says is corrupted in double-talk. His situation is not far from that of all intellectuals under Hitler's rule.

The Mayor is ready to put the question to a general vote. Nobody has anything to ask Alfred Ill. Not the church, not the medical profession, not the police, not the opposition party. The Schoolmaster is silent; this is his moment of betrayal. The endowment is unanimously accepted. Justice has been bought. The trial of Guellen versus Ill is closed with a death sentence.

There has to be a ritual killing so that no one can back out of the common decision later on.[37] All are guilty together; all are made to repeat in chorus a solemn oath so false that the result is irony almost intolerable. The endowment is accepted, "Not for the sake of money,/But for justice/And for conscience' sake" (TV 93–94).[38] The only one silent is Ill, until at the end of the oath he screams "My God!"—an exclamation not repeated when the oath is taken once more for the newsreel camera, which was out of order on the first occasion. One feels tempted to state that only Dürrenmatt's bizarre fantasy could invent this detail, a repetition making it painfully clear that Ill is the only one with truth in his

---

[36] "The spectator knows that these people have purchased security at too great a price—at the cost of the life of the one man who has found within him the strength to accept moral responsibility— thus with the sacrifice of the universal moral order of which this community was once part" (Reed, p. 14).

[37] Melvin W. Askew has written an enthusiastic study on the myths and rituals in the play ("D's *The Visit*," *TDR*, 5, 4, June 1961, pp. 89–105). Yet it is not necessary to motivate the murder scene with the help of castration complexes, parallels to the Sphinx, etc. The scene is a ritual because of its scenic context and form.

[38] Starting from the chorus scenes, Eli Pfefferkorn probably makes too much out of the uniform way of speaking, seeing the Guelleners as "a human automaton" (*Modern Drama*, 12, 1, May 1969, pp. 30–37).

words.[39] Then the representatives of the news media are ushered out, the stage is darkened, the Guelleners form a line, and after a moment of hesitation Ill steps into it.[40] At the end of it he meets the Gymnast, chosen for the role of an unofficial executioner. The Doctor confirms Ill's heart attack.

A wildly ironic finale closes this wild play. The Guelleners are gathered, "clad in evening gowns and dress-suits," at the renovated station. The world has grown "rich and dazzling new" (TV 98)—a dazzling, graceless brothel. In solos and in a Sophoclean chorus they sing in praise of prosperity, praying for a lasting peace, bidding farewell to their benefactress Claire Zachanassian, who is leaving Guellen with the coffin, now no longer empty. The visit of the old lady is over.

There is not only one Dürrenmatt, there is a host of them. That whole host is present in Guellen. How does it come about that a writer suddenly achieves his aims, realizes all his rich talents? An artistic miracle? We also have to ask: why is *The Visit* a great play, even a classic of our times? Trying to use the first question as an answer to the second, we might state that *The Visit* is a great play because it takes advantage of Dürrenmatt's multipurpose experiments, because almost any detail in its rich texture can be connected to his earlier efforts. The miracle consists in an artist's gaining control over his materials. Some of the connections between *The Visit* and the rest of Dürrenmatt have been shown; others still have to be demonstrated.

The Visit has been a stage success all over the world. The first, very tentative explanation of this phenomenon: there are two demanding main roles and a few interesting supporting roles in it. Claire Zachanassian is a dominant role and rewarding as such, though not without its problems. Claire is a monster, a comedienne, a woman, and a demigoddess.

[39] Cf. Brock-Sulzer, p. 86 and Joachim Müller, "Max Frisch und F.D.," *Universitas*, *17*, 7, July 1962, p. 736.

[40] The oath and the scenic arrangement of the murder have been seen as parodies of famous scenes in Swiss history (Jauslin, p. 98, Jenny, p. 69, and Grimm in *Der unbequeme D.*, p. 88).

There is something fixed and immobile in this role; it moves partly outside the human.[41] Claire's function and character grow, on the one hand, from Dürrenmatt's earlier portraits of tempters and nihilists (Negro da Ponte in *The Blind Man*, the criminals in the detective stories), and on the other hand from his abundant gallery of monomaniacs. Like Mr. Mississippi, she insists on a kind of Old Testament justice; like Romulus, she has no scruples in the pursuit of her aims. And like the Angel or Sea Captain Tiphys she is a meteor bringing destruction to a community.[42]

A central concept in Dürrenmatt's dramaturgy—chance— is included in Claire's role, though kept offstage. She happened to meet Mr. Zachanassian, "that old tycoon" (TV 42), in a brothel in Hamburg, and this chance meeting was the incalculable element not included in Ill's plan of evasion. If we accept the role of chance in Claire's history and her monomania, then we also have to accept her as the catalyst of the play. Her role includes the saving grace of humor and charm, a balancing factor often discernible in grotesque phenomena.[43] There might even be a trace of emotion behind her death-mask of emotionlessness in the second forest scene and in her words of farewell to the dead body of her black panther (TV 97–98).

Claire is a grotesque emissary of alien powers; Ill and the Guelleners are everyday people. It is their task to build up a world to be shattered by a grotesque series of events, and to convince us that our world may also be shattered. The Guelleners are like the passengers in the train rushing into nothingness in Dürrenmatt's early story "The Tunnel." Their

[41] Jenny (p. 65) finds only one tone for Claire, that of "petrified monumentality," while Brock-Sulzer calls her "the catalyst of the play," not to be acted in too human a way (pp. 80–81).

[42] C. H. Drese mentions Negro, the Angel, and Mr. Mississippi as forerunners of Claire ("F.D.," *Eckart*, 28, 4, 1959, p. 388).

[43] Jauslin (p. 101) remarks on this; for Peppard, Claire's humor and frankness make her, "for all her deadly monomania, a convincing stage character with a special kind of diabolic charm" (p. 59). Cf. Dürrenmatt's analyses of Claire and Ill (TV 106–07).

reactions are recorded with expertise and with a malevolent sense of humor. With the exception of the self-contradictory role of the Schoolmaster, the roles do not change, do not develop: they are just marks on Dürrenmatt's chart of a community. They are there so that we recognize ourselves and our neighbors.

Ill's role as a modern Everyman starts on the level of insignificance. It is human, all too human, that he has quite forgotten his betrayal of Claire. Yet this nondescript man, a kinsman to Arnolph Archilochos in *Once a Greek. . . ,* grows into one of Dürrenmatt's men of courage. Ill passes through a phase of utter loneliness, also experienced by the alienated heroes of Dürrenmatt's youthful prose. After his purgatory he does not reach the heights of religious ecstasy experienced by Knipperdollinck in *It Is Written,* yet he is granted a feeling of "belonging," of being one with his surroundings, during the last calm moments of his life.[44] "The lost world order is restored within them; the universal escapes my grasp," Dürrenmatt writes about his men of courage in *Problems of the Theater* (FP 34). Ill's guilt exists "as a personal achievement, as a religious deed" (FP 33); the full implications of this deed for Guellen will have to be studied later on. The role of this commonplace shopkeeper makes its impact on the stage; it has the elements of growth, humor, and tragicomedy in it.[45]

Almost any moment of stage action in *The Visit* is apt to arouse mixed feelings.[46] The principle of tragicomedy gov-

---

[44] Dürrenmatt's heroes become victims by confessing their personal guilt. The grace they meet becomes more and more worldly: Ill and Traps experience it "as a harmony of their last minutes and hours" (Oberle in *Der unbequeme D.*, pp. 19, 23).

[45] Ian C. Loram criticizes the American adaptation of *The Visit* by Maurice Valency for making Claire softer, Ill closer to a traditional tragic hero, and for eliminating "the grotesque humor of the original" (" 'Der Besuch' and 'The Visit,' " *Monatshefte für deutschen Unterricht, 53,* 1, Jan. 1961, pp. 15–21).

[46] Syberberg has described the tragicomic ambivalence and complexity of these moments (pp. 53–57), remarking that comedy and tragedy heighten, not cancel, one another (p. 60).

erns the play, not only the long lines of characterization, not only the total structure, but also the microcosm of each scene, of each scenic image. Man One weighing the axe in his hand, with the ignorant merry-go-round of news media hysteria surrounding him and Ill, the intended victim: a stratified scenic image capturing the essence of the play. The sharp edge of a tragic figure cutting against the comedy of his surroundings is made visible again and again.[47] Ill's fear and apprehensions are present from the very beginning of Act II; they are preceded by preparatory, unspecified horror effects. These feelings are expressed through a mixture of discursive comedy, silent action, and pure, cabaret-like clownery. The strong story line of the play keeps these details together.[48] *The Visit* is Dürrenmatt's best synthesis of numerous artistic inventions and a dominating total idea, between abundance and coherence. *Romulus the Great* is the only earlier play comparable to it in this respect.

Taking a closer look at Dürrenmatt's stage solutions in *The Visit*, we discern a great many familiar scenic units. There are grotesquely abundant settings: Petersens' Barn, the setting of Act II combining Claire's balcony with other milieus. What is new in the total plan for the setting is Dürrenmatt's reliance on quick changes of scenery. He had used stylized, anti-realistic settings before—not, however, with an eye on their changeability, not in this easily manageable, theatricalistic manner. In *It Is Written* he left the problems for the stage designer to solve. He is after a total picture of Guellen, of the world in miniature he has created for the stage, and relies on contrasts and parallels between the var-

[47] Guthke emphasizes the continuous interaction between comedy and tragedy in *The Visit*. There are tragicomic elements also in the corruptibility of the Guelleners: indeed, the play is a mixture between two tragicomedies (*Geschichte und Poetik der deutschen Tragikomödie*, pp. 382–89).

[48] Henno Helbling's simile for the total structure of TV is a "pendulum of mood that moves between jokes and terror, first slowly and with a wide range, then more and more short-winded, back and forth, and finally stands still with a last quiver" (Bänziger, p. 207: from the *NZZ*, March 31, 1959).

243

ious scenes. There are two scenes in the forest, three at the station, two formed as mock-trials.[49] Dürrenmatt's recent experiences as a radio dramatist might have given him an impetus toward an epic line on the stage also, toward a rapid movement from one milieu to another.

Dürrenmatt is in love with "the manifold diversity of the world" (FP 22). He expresses this love with the help of scenes ranging from intimate discussions between two protagonists to mass meetings of the Guelleners. His dialogue is full of parodic and ironic twists. He increases the abundance of his stage action by employing the doubled figures of the eunuchs, parallel action when the townspeople are hunting for the black panther, or a surprising entrance of his heroine. His grotesque, self-contradictory scenic imagery includes Ill's last drive in a car, replacing the customary last meal of a man condemned to death. Man is seen against the sky on that drive; the lines are poetry of valediction. The victim is delivered into the hands of an executioner. There are music and sound effects, posters and an inscription; there are three scenes with a formal chorus and group scenes with pantomime and with dialogue. There are disharmonies and contradictions both within and between the various scenic images. The total impression can only be that of richness.

Four group scenes have a decisive effect on our lasting impression. Claire declaring the condition attached to her donation; Ill's nightmarish attempt to escape; the wildly ironic oath of the Guelleners; the finale with its quasi-Greek chorus. All of these scenic images have a stratified structure. All combine a powerful emotional impact with an ironical or coolly disillusioned intellectual element. All reach a balance between the word and the picture, between dialogue, setting, and stage action. *The Visit* is a play in which every idea is concretized. How to make his vision concrete in terms of the stage is certainly a problem for any playwright. It has been a focal problem for Dürrenmatt, with his visions ranging from heaven to hell. This problem is solved in *The Visit*.

[49] Jenny, p. 67.

Dürrenmatt's works for the stage and for radio consist of two basic types. One is a social panorama, the other an individual case study concentrating on a man facing life and death. *The Visit* is a synthesis of these types. It presents an individual struggling with the problem of his existence in the middle of a community, within a wide social panorama. *The Blind Man* and *Mississippi* are Dürrenmatt's earlier case studies, while *It Is Written* and *Angel* are plays showing a community in action. Remarkably enough, *Romulus*, up to this time Dürrenmatt's major opus, is also his best synthesis of these two aspirations prior to *The Visit*. He was able to concretize his story because he had earlier practice in writing for his world theater, in treating his radical moral and religious problems, and in combining these two modes. It is significant that the most memorable scenic images in *The Visit* depict an individual in the middle of a hostile crowd.

That crowd is guilty of a ritual murder. The Guelleners are a show-piece of Dürrenmatt's dramaturgy. "We are all collectively guilty, collectively bogged down in the sins of our fathers and forefathers," Dürrenmatt writes in *Problems of the Theater* (FP 33). Because of this collective guilt, tragedy is impossible in our days: it presupposes guilt and a sense of responsibility. Dürrenmatt has peopled his model of the world with a crowd incapable of carrying that responsibility. He has given his Ill the dimensions of a tragic hero, yet placed this hero in surroundings that make tragedy impossible.[50] He has written a counter-sketch to tragedy: a tragicomedy.

Up to the middle 1950's Dürrenmatt had tried his hand at various literary genres. He had created tensions between all kinds of artistic formulas and his own thoughts. In *The Visit* he took the formula of tragedy, one of his major satirical targets ever since *It Is Written*, and twisted it to fit his mold of tragicomedy. He did this more consciously than

[50] Dürrenmatt reaches "something highly noteworthy" by elevating a grotesque event to a level close to Greek tragedy (Durzak, p. 96). He attacks not a literary genre but the phenomena in our age that make tragedy impossible (Profitlich, *F.D.*, p. 66).

before, and with greater success. He had just before formulated his theory of modern tragicomedy: *Problems of The Theater* and *The Visit* are intimately related.

Ill's self-sacrificing deed both saves Guellen and condemns it to utter moral depravity. The vicious circle of crime and punishment is not broken by grace; on the contrary, a new circle is formed. Both Ill and Guellen commit crimes.[51] This is the basic ambiguity in Ill's self-sacrifice.[52] It leads to the tragicomic and grotesque uncertainty of the play. A tragic deed would purge us of feelings of pity and fear: a sense of responsibility would be re-established at the end of an unmixed tragedy. A comic solution would turn the play into laughter and harmlessness. Dürrenmatt allows us neither of these relieving final twists. He rejects the strict order of tragedy; he experiences the world as chaos, and lets his protagonist struggle from his personal chaos into a world barely tempered by the order of comedy. He chooses both chaos and order.[53]

At the beginning of the play there exists in Guellen an established order of things. The townspeople have remained true to their native town even in poverty. Claire brings with her a threat against the traditional values of the community. She reveals that Guellen's order has been guilty of killing Claire's child and of turning her into a prostitute. The first reaction of the Guelleners is to reassert their belief in human-

[51] Ill has expiated his crime with his miserable life, Arnold reflects; Claire's insistence on justice is another act of the cruel and revengeful God met in Dürrenmatt's early works (p. 47).

[52] "The tragic comedy that results, is therefore curiously ambivalent and ambiguous: it is a comedy of despair with regard to the greater scheme of things; yet it is a tragedy of confidence with regard to man who courageously takes this despair upon himself" (Guthke, *Modern Tragicomedy*, p. 134).

[53] Neumann speaks of a "boundary position between order and anarchy" represented in Dürrenmatt, e.g., by Claire or by the executioner who "play-acts fulfilling justice without himself possessing justice." By exaggerating the order prevailing in low-brow literature Dürrenmatt achieves the freedom of "as if," of play-acting fate (*D., Frisch, Weiss*, p. 54).

ity; Claire's offer is nominally rejected. Chaos follows, a phase of restless search for values. Instead of acknowledging their collective guilt in expelling Claire and in sniggering at her pregnancy, the townspeople accept Ill's guilt, not their own. Guilt can exist only "as a personal achievement, as a religious deed" (FP 33). Ill's guilt is the only one confessed in Guellen.

Guellen changes from bad to worse. Dürrenmatt does not believe in his own ability to reform his audiences through direct means, through an exemplary action. *The Visit* is one of his answers to Brecht's maxim about the changeability of the world.

And so Guellen slowly drifts toward Claire's order of things. An eye for an eye, corruption for corruption. Ill's betrayal made Claire lose her faith in a moral world order; her revenge is to establish a new one. Guellen exchanges the old corrupt system for Claire's world order, equally corrupt, yet prosperous. Dürrenmatt sees this process very clearly, with disillusioned eyes. He knows that Claire's order is evil, the order of endless avarice, the order of the postwar boom. It results in a world without moral sensibility, a world governed only by breakdowns. If Ill had won his second case, if Claire's order had been rejected, and with it Guellen's prosperity, or if the town had accepted both Ill's self-sacrifice and its own guilt, then a new order of a third kind would have been established. Its barest outlines are sketched in the speech of the Schoolmaster in the mass meeting: it would be an order based on grace and on a genuine feeling for humanity. Ill and the Schoolmaster lose their case, of course; and all Dürrenmatt can do as an artist, as an individual with the gift of vision, is to show the grotesque and unresolvable conflict between Guellen's anachronistic order, chaos, and Claire's order.[54] In a similar way, Dürrenmatt hesitates be-

[54] "It is true and, in a grotesquely ironic sense, good that the city has become wealthy and prosperous through Ill's death. . . . The ending is, at one and the same time, ironically conciliatory and a severe indictment of man's weakness" (Peppard, p. 56).

tween the order of traditional tragedy and that of comedy—to choose his personal kind of tragicomedy in which a precarious order prevails between chaos and various orders. Once again, Dürrenmatt finds his individualistic path between contrasting formulas of thought, the path of a born polemicist.

In a state of chaos all human deeds are ambiguous, both ridiculous and terrifying, both comic and tragic. There are no absolute values available; the yardsticks of tragedy and comedy have lost their scales. Or, rather, there are two scales to be employed at the same time, both equally right —and wrong. *The Visit* is a tragicomedy both in its total conception and in its details.

It is a profoundly human aspiration to arrange the chaos surrounding us, to create some kind of order. What makes *The Visit* a disturbing play is that it shows how an existing order is destroyed and a basically evil order is built on its ruins. The aspiration to create order is doubly frustrated: an old order is proved to be anachronistic, although we may share its belief in humanity, while acknowledging its weaknesses. The new order established is corrupt. Chaos is not to be averted. Every effort of an individual, even at the expense of his life, is fruitless. *The Visit* certainly grows from the disillusion following World War II and its aftermath. Having endured the war, Europe had to endure peace. The new order of things established during the boom was far from ideal. At the same time the play reaches a high degree of general validity. It does not matter whether Claire represents World War II, the Apocalypse, temptation, or the "coca-colonization of Western Europe."[55] Claire is an agent of chaos, of "another reality," and as such she is a menace to our deceptively safe order of things. Chaos remains among us; what will the next crime of the Guelleners be like?

[55] The phrase is employed by Rivers Carew, who does not agree with it. For him, *The Visit* demonstrates that justice "may readily be induced to shift from position to position under pressure" ("The Plays of F.D.," *The Dublin Magazine*, 4, 1, Spring 1965, p. 62). Jauslin equates Claire with temptation (p. 102).

The Visit has been both admired and condemned because of its moral commitment. It shows us how the power of greed, of "low" motives, is greater than the power of humanistic ideals. What price prosperity? Any price.[56] The play is irresistible in its logic and morality, yet "wicked" from the point of view of the prevailing order of things. It speaks against all kinds of official moralities, it reveals the hidden morality followed by all of us Guelleners when we are in a conflict situation between our greed and the highly humanistic ideals of the West. Again, Dürrenmatt has revealed a conflict, not solved a world-wide problem. Again, he has created absolute grotesque. That grotesque includes the saving grace of honesty, of forewarning.

The only consolation *The Visit* leaves us is connected with the personal deed of Ill.[57] Ill accepts chaos in his thinking. With his behavior he turns an experience of absurdity into a grotesque tragicomedy.[58] As one of Dürrenmatt's "men of courage" he endures the world of Guellen, thus saving his personal integrity, thus restoring the lost world order within himself. Not within Guellen—for Dürrenmatt refuses to find a universal doctrine in Ill's deed:[59] "The universal for me is chaos. The world (hence the stage which represents this world) is for me something monstrous, a riddle of misfortunes which must be accepted but before which one must not

---

[56] "I have no wish to simplify such a brilliant play, or to impose one definite meaning on its metaphors. . . . In *The Visit* there is a deep conviction that one can make people do anything . . . for the price of a pair of shoes" (Kott, p. 93).

[57] Cf. Carew, p. 62, and Züfle, part two, *Schweizer Rundschau*, 2, Feb. 1967, p. 104.

[58] Absurdity is "not the last word for Dürrenmatt. His protagonists pass through a state of despair and reach a state of acceptance that somewhat resembles the recognition which the hero of classical tragedy achieves" (Deschner, p. 191). Cf. Volkmar Sander, "Form und Groteske," *Germanisch-Romanische Monatschrift*, Neue Folge, *14*, 3, 1964, p. 311.

[59] The Guelleners are in a dead end; Ill can break out (Syberberg, pp. 132–33). Yet his decision to accept his fate takes place completely "without a consoling aim," as a "self-fulfillment in disaster" (p. 139).

capitulate" (FP 34). "One must not capitulate": not a lesson for many but a maxim for a few men of courage. Or, rather, a question Dürrenmatt was to go on pondering in his next plays.

Dürrenmatt has reacted strongly against being called a "moralist"—probably out of fear of being taken as a preacher of sermons supporting conventional morality. Yet there is no denying that he is a moralist in another sense of the word: as a writer facing difficult problems of morality and putting these as conflicts before us on the stage. In the form of art, not as sermons. For instance, the speech of the Schoolmaster is protected by a thick armor of irony: by the weak figure of the speaker, by his preceding phrases, by the applauding Guelleners not listening to his words. Some basic problems of morality are, however, brought before the theater audience, employed as a grand jury. They are brought there in the concrete language of the stage, in the form of a whole series of tragicomic events and interacting scenic images.

The Visit is a play in which Dürrenmatt's double role as a moralist and as an artist coincide neatly.[60] So do his other multiple talents: his inventiveness as a comedian and as a child of nature, his seriousness as a religious meditator, his logical abilities as a dramaturge and as a practitioner of the theater, his control of the language, schooled also by his explorations of prose fiction. The play sends its arrow right to the center of the target, a target to be called a sickness of our times. It proves that Dürrenmatt lived in 1955 in an all-European present with every nerve in his body. Quite deservedly the play gave him a world-wide reputation. From now on, every world première of a new Dürrenmatt play was to be publicized as a major event in the German-speaking world.

This development had not only its advantages but also its drawbacks. *The Visit* gave Dürrenmatt's critics a yardstick

[60] Cf. Jenny, p. 70.

to be used in judging every new work of his. The wide success of the play on the European continent led to acclaimed productions in London and New York, and to a breakthrough for Dürrenmatt in the English-speaking world. The West End and Broadway performances shone with a certain artistic splendor, yet the dramatic adaptation employed seems to have removed part of the integrity and merciless humor of the original script.[61] These ingredients were even more harshly treated in the film version of the play.[62] Yet the post-première history of *The Visit* shows that the play has stood, by and large, the test of the stage: it has been interpreted in various ways, from time to time.[63] There is even an opera version of it, composed by Gottfried von Einem.[64]

The basic explanation for the lasting value of *The Visit* is that it is a synthesis of Dürrenmatt's early career as a writer. The ingenious artistic invention of the old lady activated Dürrenmatt's childhood memories, the deepest layer in him as a creative artist. His early prose and first radio plays are present as the Kafkaesque atmosphere of nightmare surrounding Ill, Dürrenmatt's protagonist maturing in

[61] Gordon Rogoff criticizes certain commercial features in the New York production with Lynn Fontanne and Alfred Lunt in the principal roles and Peter Brook as the competent stage director; these three were responsible for the London production, too ("Mr. Duerrenmatt Buys New Shoes," *TDR*, *3*, 1, Oct. 1958, pp. 27–34). Cf. note 45 of this chapter.

[62] The film was produced by Darryl F. Zanuck, directed by Bernhard Wicki, with Ingrid Bergman and Anthony Quinn as stars. Neither Wicki nor Dürrenmatt approved of the final version. Claire is made a middle-aged society lady who finally pardons Ill. Cf., e.g., Werner Wollenberger, "Der Besuch der kalten Dame," *Zürcher Woche*, Nov. 6, 1964.

[63] This is shown, e.g., by the fragments of reviews published in Jenny, pp. 115–20.

[64] The diminuendo sequences in Acts II–III are shortened in the opera version (London, 1970). Ill visits only the minister, TV 47–56 and 67–77 are left out. The final chorus is replaced by a dance of murderers. The libretto (by Dürrenmatt and the composer) and the music shift the emphasis toward Claire's revenge and its psychological motives, away from Ill's and Guellen's tragicomedy—at least they did in the 1976 production at the Royal Opera, Stockholm.

loneliness. There is a panoramic view of a community, as in *It Is Written*; there are scenes full of delightful comedy dialogue, thematic climaxes as fully concretized scenic images, and a plot cleverly woven, as in *Romulus the Great*. There is a profound and passionate concern for contemporary issues, as in *The Marriage of Mr. Mississippi*, there is an experiment with a fateful intruder from the outside world shaking a community, as in *An Angel Comes to Babylon* and *Donkey's Shadow*. The play varies Dürrenmatt's basic theme of human justice, a terrifying phenomenon for him; its story develops into the absolute grotesque, as his best prose works had done. It combines an epic flexibility, reminiscent of his radio plays, with strong thematic concentration. It is a modern tragicomedy, thus corresponding with the artistic program Dürrenmatt had created in *Problems of the Theater*. And *The Visit* is a rich, ironic, and stratified play revealing a distinguished, deeply personal mastery of the stage.

252

PART THREE
VICTORIES AND DEFEATS

There is no craft of the theatre; there is only the mastery of the material through language and the stage or, to be more exact, it is an overpowering of the material, for any creative writing is a kind of warfare with its victories, defeats and indecisive battles (FP 28).

11 Freedom Among the Gangsters

FRANK V

||||||||||||||||||||||||||||||||||||||||||||||||||||||||||||||||||||||||||||||||||||||||||||||

Both books and writers have their fates. Friedrich Dürrenmatt rose like a comet above Swiss, German, European, and world-wide theatrical horizons in the late 1950's. After *The Visit* he had to face something we might call "the curse of the second hit." Expectations are high; the writer may still be somewhat embarrassed by his new position as an augur. Yesterday a nonentity; today interviewed by all the women's magazines. This is a curse Tennessee Williams, Arthur Miller and Edward Albee also had to face: what to write after a masterpiece, after *The Glass Menagerie*, *The Death of a Salesman*, or *Who's Afraid of Virginia Woolf?* Dürrenmatt and Albee chose to write flops; the other two playwrights mentioned had better luck.

Dürrenmatt's original intention was to write just an ode. It was commissioned for the twentieth season of the Zurich Theater, reorganized in the late 1930's. His cooperation with composer Paul Burkhard took, however, an unexpected turn, and these two found themselves cherishing the idea of doing a play with music together. During two periods, both three and a half days long, they completed a series of macabre chansons and agreed that it was Dürrenmatt's job to develop a story around them.[1] The result was *Frank V*, "The Opera of a Private Bank," produced by Zurich Theater during its jubilee season, on March 19 and 20, 1959. This was the first but not the last of Dürrenmatt's "double" or "triple" premières: there were so many theater critics and other interested people flocking to Zurich that the "first" performances were extended to cover two or three consecutive nights.

---

[1] These details are told by Hugo Loetscher in the Zurich playbill of *Frank V*.

DÜRRENMATT

First the songs, then the story. This order of things left its marks on Dürrenmatt's "opera." He has insisted on Shakespeare rather than Brecht as a source of inspiration: as in *Richard III*, as in *Titus Andronicus*, there are conflicts within a power system, or between parents and children, in Dürrenmatt's portrayal of a "royal" banking house.[2] These contradictions lead to betrayals and murders. Dürrenmatt also wrote Shakespeare's name openly (and pretentiously) into his script: the prologue of the play is entitled "As Shakespeare's Heroes" (FV 7, 9). There are thus ambiguities and inner tensions in Dürrenmatt's very starting-point. First between the songs and the story line, then between his ambition to reach Shakespearean or heroic dimensions in violence and dark poetry—and his conviction, formulated in *Problems of the Theater*, that this will not do in modern drama. Or will it, with the help of parody?

The prologue is spoken by Richard Egli, Personnel Manager of the private bank run by the Frank family. He invites the spectators to follow a story of crime and murder in which the criminals are bankers, not kings, popes, generals, or emperors. The story is to be "partly a tragedy, partly a farce" (FV 7). In Dürrenmatt's personal language, metaphors of coldness are associated with death, with an uninhabited universe, with a graceless state of affairs: the fifth line in this prologue includes the word "coldness." The play is to close with a cluster of such metaphors. We are entering a graceless kingdom of death.

Our entrance is facilitated by Päuli and Heini, two unemployed country boys, two Guelleners in a city, as it were. Päuli is a locksmith, Heini has the bright idea of robbing the bank of the Franks. They meet at Chez Guillaume, a café dedicated to Shakespeare; their plan is greatly assisted by Frank V himself, who hires both of them. The facade of decency falls down as early as in Scene 3: a funeral is revealed

[2] Bienek, *Werkstattgespräche*, pp. 103–04; FV 90.

as a hoax, with a solemn procession, with a burial speech by
Ottilie Frank, widow of the "deceased" Frank V.[3] Heini has
been used as the body in Frank's coffin: "You're a bank of
gangsters!" (FV 17). Yet this revelation does not prevent
Päuli from feeling at home: he goes on serving Frank V—
and Dürrenmatt, as the stage character introduced into the
business practices of these gangsters. See Fig. 7.

Egli is the superior of the senior clerk Böckmann, three
tellers, and Frieda Fürst, his fiancée for twenty-two years.
Their marriage is postponed by her job as the prostitute associated with the Frank banking house. In *An Angel* there
was a begging competition: harking back to this successful
series of scenes Dürrenmatt now arranges an exhibition in
swindling, with Egli as the master, Päuli as the dutiful ap-
prentice. As a hint to *Angel*, to the source of this scene, Egli
wears a beard and a sun helmet (FV 42). The efforts of
Egli and Päuli are frustrated by chance: there turns out to be
uranium in a broken-down mine they sell, and an insurance
fraud is prevented, as lightning burns down an unprofitable
castle turned into a hotel. Juggling with one of his central
dramaturgic concepts, chance, Dürrenmatt tries to provoke
the spectators of his picaresque opera to laughter.

The discussions and songs of the gangsters concentrate on
a few themes. They sing with nostalgia about the golden
days of enormous crimes: Franks I–IV had it much easier.
They complain about the difficulties in wholesale swindling
in the austerity of present-day honesty. And they repent their
crimes, planning to liquidate the bank and flee to less troublesome days in retirement.[4] Yet the members of this gang,
drifting perilously close to confessing their misdeeds, are
quickly exterminated. Päuli kills a clerk, Egli his devoted

[3] Jauslin (*F.D.*, p. 109) interprets Dürrenmatt's two scenes in the
graveyard as parodies of *Hamlet*, while the Frank–Ottilie relation reminds him of Macbeth–Lady Macbeth. In a scene deleted from the
printed version a maid mentions *Richard III*.

[4] Demonstrating the business methods and liquidating the bank are
conflicting motives, Jenny points out in his clarifying analysis of
Frank V (*F.D.*, pp. 73–74).

Frieda. The excuse Ottilie and Frank use to defend their crimes is that they have been committed for their innocent children, educated far away from the scene of business and crime. The only surprise moment in the later phases of the plot is that the children, dear Franziska and dear Herbert, turn out to be blackmailers and full-fledged gangsters, more expert at concealing their illegal proceedings behind honesty than are their old-fashioned parents. At the end of the play Herbert, alias Frank VI, takes over the family enterprise. Ottilie's plea to a blind president for punishment, for justice, is turned down.[5] The final chorus sings about glaciers and winter, about "rotten grace" and a world of ice: about death (FV 88).

The merits of *Frank V* lie in its individual scenes, not in its story.[6] Moreover, the tone in the various scenes and scenic images tends to lack variety. *Frank V* is a string of one-way jokes, all aiming at the same target, so to speak; the traffic is busy but monotonous.[7] Dürrenmatt's first play as a world celebrity is a cabaret text, with semi- or wholly independent scenes, with flashes of comedy and of the sharp edge of satire, without any clearly formulated or executed central idea.[8]

The best, as well as most controversial, fragment in *Frank V* is Böckmann's death scene.[9] Frank and Ottilie prevent him

---

[5] According to Grimm, this scene is a parody of *Don Carlos*, V, 9–10, by Schiller (*Der unbequeme D.*, pp. 84–85).

[6] This is stated also in positive or cautious reviews of the Zurich première, e.g., in those by Melchinger (*Stuttgarter Zeitung*, March 21, 1959) and Helbling (*Neue Zürcher Zeitung*, March 20). Walter Boesch speaks of repetitive scenes not kept together by a dramatic tension (*Tages-Anzeiger*, March 21).

[7] Philipp Wolff-Windegg calls *Frank V* downright clumsy, monotonous, and not funny enough: its characters are one-dimensional, like figures in advertisements (*Basler Nachrichten*, March 1, 1961).

[8] Jenny, p. 77.

[9] Opinions of the scene differ widely: Henning Rischbieter calls it "exceptionally tasteless" (*Theater heute*, *1*, 3, Nov. 1960, p. 8), Wilhelm Westecker "the climax of the play" (*Christ und Welt*, April 16, 1959). Dürrenmatt catalogues it among the three scenes he is proud of (Wyrsch, part five, p. 38), while Brock-Sulzer speaks of a "highly

from being operated on for stomach cancer, fearing that he might reveal something under anesthesia. Instead, he is given a fatal injection while waiting for a priest to hear his last confession. Frank, masquerading as a priest, sings a gloomy song while his wife takes care of the injection. In his last moments Böckmann arrives at the conclusion that their crimes have not been necessary: "We could have turned back any time, at any moment of our evil lives. There is no heritage one could not decline, and no crime one must commit" (FV 60). Due to its visual and auditive scenic means of expression, due to its intensity and stratified structure, this scenic image is certainly one of the highlights in *Frank V*. Yet it does not grow out of its surroundings: it is just one death scene among others.[10]

On the farcical side, there is quite a clever sequence toward the end of the play. The remaining four members of the gang meet in front of the bank vault in the middle of the night: they sneak around with suitcases and with plans to rob each other. Instead of the daggers employed in *Romulus* they have submachine guns, a couple each, and provision for their escape. Sitting on their suitcases, eating their food, and keeping an eye on one another, they sing about decent people in north and south, in east and west. Their idyllic vigil, this inventive and Dürrenmattian scenic image, is interrupted by the arrival of the blackmailer, alias would-be Frank VI.

The beginnings of Dürrenmatt's "opera" have been seen in his interest in aria-like speeches. Akki's *maqamat* are an earlier example of stories written within a play.[11] It is difficult to judge an "opera," whether in quotation marks or not, on the basis of its text or libretto alone. One feels tempted to believe the majority of critics who see the function of Burk-

---

explosive combination" between "the truth of a too-late recognition, a pious lie and a murderous reality" ("F.D.," *Der Monat*, *15*, 5, May 1960, p. 60).

[10] The scene "remains an isolated high point in the play without visible influence on the subsequent scenes" (Peppard, *F.D.*, p. 65).

[11] Jauslin, p. 78; Brock-Sulzer, *F.D.*, p. 99.

hard's music mainly as making Dürrenmatt's cruel events bearable on the stage. The melodies soften rather than accentuate the total effect; they create a kind of poetic, purely theatricalistic dimension; they are subservient to the word. Dürrenmatt's songs do not interrupt the stage action or comment on it, as Brecht's songs do.[12] The reviews did not give Burkhard's music a specific value separated from the text; it was taken as a parody of Kurt Weill's melodies, or as a new creation moving close to them.[13]

The name of Brecht brings us to a central controversy around *Frank V*. Is Dürrenmatt's play only a "weak imitation of *Dreigroschenoper*,"[14] a parody of it, or a continuation of its themes? The label "Bertolt was here" has been attached to Dürrenmatt's text, and "Kurt was here" to Burkhard's music. It is indeed impossible to read Dürrenmatt's songs or his picaresque story without associating them with the most celebrated success of the young Brecht. Admitting these similarities, Mayer makes an effort to see in Dürrenmatt's play a reverse version of Brecht's theme. Brecht claims: "also gangsters are in fact citizens." Dürrenmatt: "citizens are in fact gangsters."[15] Brock-Sulzer defends Dürrenmatt by stating that Böckmann's death scene includes an anti-Brechtian attitude in favor of the freedom of will, while Jauslin sees in *Frank V* a parody of *The Threepenny Opera* rather than a copy of it.[16]

Dürrenmatt certainly moves perilously close to a classic of our age. This time he chose, more or less consciously, a specific work of art, not a whole literary genre, as the formula

[12] The description is based on Jenny's summary (p. 71). Cf. Loetscher, Westecker, and Peppard, p. 62. Durzak associates the songs with Nestroy rather than Brecht (*D., Frisch, Weiss*, pp. 113–15).

[13] Melchinger; Karl Korn's review (*Frankfurter Allgemeine*, March 23, 1959).

[14] Kesting, *Panorama des zeitgenössischen Theaters*, p. 226. Bänziger calls a few details, among them Egli's prologue, "purest Brecht" (*Frisch und D.*, p. 181); he quotes Helene Weigel's sharp protest against *Frank V* (pp. 256–57).

[15] *D. und Frisch*, p. 15.

[16] Brock-Sulzer, p. 102; Jauslin, p. 107.

he placed beside his counter-sketch. The closeness of *Frank V* to *Dreigroschenoper* tends to lessen the value of Dürrenmatt's play. Highly successful works of art create an aura of hypersensitivity around themselves: don't touch me. Dürrenmatt did touch—and paid the price in the form of a bad reputation among the critics of *Frank V*.

Accusations of plagiarism are not the only criticisms of *Frank V*. Dürrenmatt has remained faithful to his play: there are three versions of the script, as well as three self-defensive interpretations by the playwright. The first of these is published together with the second or Munich version, used above and below as our basic text. In this "Statement" Dürrenmatt sketches a picture of recent changes in his dramaturgic thinking.

Dürrenmatt's first position is familiar from his earlier theoretical writings (cf. p. 216 above). He creates "possible worlds," he does not try to reproduce our common world. What is now given as a sign of a "possible world" is that it depicts "possible human relations" (FV 89). Yet Dürrenmatt does not get around the central problem of art versus reality quite that easily. He admits that "a possible world" must also include "the real world": "An over-reality must face reality in the theater. 'Myths' must emerge from fictions, otherwise they are senseless" (FV 90). His belief in an artist's ability to create such myths is limitless: "it is impossible for artistic thinking to depart from the world" (FV 91) —from our common world. If the critics had been considerate enough to play the game as opened by Dürrenmatt, they would have found in *Frank V* the following themes: "there can be no democracy of the gangsters," or "one cannot demand that one's unjustified hopes be fulfilled." Later on, the playwright specifies the former of these themes as "the question about freedom within a democracy of criminals" (TS 349).

Taking Dürrenmatt at his word: how are "the possible human relations" developed in *Frank V*? Parents love their

261

children and are disappointed in their efforts to make them grow up into decent citizens; a gang murders its talkative members; a young man develops into a big-time criminal, ready to serve any master. Are these interesting, valid, or fresh revelations? Or, rather, platitudes? Do they build up a myth?[17] Can they be made to concern the modern state, or any power system? Is not the entire action of the play so far exaggerated that Frank's bank does not include our real world? Every spectator recognizes himself as a Guellener; nobody recognizes anybody as a member of Frank's gang.[18] Having read *Frank V*, one does not retain the innocent belief that the results of artistic thinking cannot depart from our common world at all: Frank's narrow world falls at breakneck speed.

"Freedom" is a high-sounding word. If a member of a gang of criminals tries to escape with stolen or fraudulent money, this is, however, just another selfish crime, not an incident speaking for the philosophical concept of free will. Häberlin, one of the tellers, would feel free only in prison, out of Frank's control; one can see Dürrenmatt enjoying such a clever paradox. Yet he hardly develops the theme of freedom clearly enough,[19] except in the Böckmann scene. In *Mississippi* the abstract background pattern was only dimly visible through the mist created by the concrete stage events, and so it is in *Frank V*, too. Dürrenmatt has not concretized his themes; instead, he has concretized his enjoyment of his picaresque comedy.

Moreover, the action and the written word are not in

[17] "What is meant by these myths?" Durzak wonders; Dürrenmatt does not substantiate his arguments (p. 37; cf. pp. 33, 106). For Rischbieter, the play "remains a fiction" (pp. 8–9).

[18] Rudolf Goldschmidt speaks about the "boundlessness and aimlessness of Dürrenmatt's attacks": "everything is laid on in a ham-fisted way, so that nobody needs to feel afflicted in the end" (*Der Tagesspiegel*, Oct. 28, 1960). Cf. Hensel, *Spielplan*, p. 1032.

[19] Dürrenmatt had to mention the theme of freedom "in a speech, the play does not state it," Arnold remarks. He also criticizes the inconsequent characterization and the improbabilities of the play (*F.D.*, pp. 74–77). Cf. TS 351–52.

balance in *Frank V*. The dialogue and the songs create an aura of ghastliness around the past crimes of Frank's forefathers and around the future crimes of Frank VI. We hear again and again that the misdeeds we see are nothing compared with those past and those to come. This is not quite fair; we are fed not with deeds but with words and songs.[20] It is bluntly stated, not explored, that Frank's villainy no longer pays, and that Frank VI will establish a monarchy of crime based on rigid honesty. Yet he comes into power by traditional means, blackmail and betrayal. It may have been Dürrenmatt's intention to show that the present-day business world masks its methods with strict legality. Yet this is exactly what is *not* demonstrated on the stage. *Frank V* states this central theme in a curiously oblique way.

In *The Visit* Dürrenmatt demonstrated with the help of stage action that a tragic hero does not save a modern community. In *Frank V* he tries to prove that real villainy is impossible in our age.[21] He starts by equating kings and generals, popes and emperors with the banking business of today. His next step is to deny the value of his own equation. A scenic simile is first built up, then it is shown that it does not fit. The quasi-heroic characters of *Frank V* are furnished with inferiority complexes, with seeds of weakness. A banker is a king—not, however, a genuine king but a fake; Dürrenmatt surprises us, then nullifies the moment of surprise. We are dealing with a parody of a private and literary kind, with an unnecessary twist of self-parody, with a playwright's delight in showing by words and elegiac arias that Shakespearian dimensions in villainy do not exist any longer. Again, parody is served as a dish, as a primary motive behind

[20] "The main reason for the failure of this play seems to me to be its lack of action" (Bänziger, p. 178).

[21] Diller interprets Frank & Co. as victims of "economic laws that operate under the principle of strict materialistic determinism"; the collective of criminals lessens man's value "as an individual" ("Human Dignity," *Modern Language Quarterly*, 25, 4, Dec. 1964, pp. 451–60). Durzak takes the play as a criticism of Brecht's "economic determinism" (pp. 102–12).

263

an entire work of art, not as a spice. If there had been more calories in Dürrenmatt's dish, it might have been easier for us to accept its Brechtian pepper, too.

The discrepancies between Dürrenmatt's theory and practice put his scholars into an awkward position. His arguments may be sound and enlightening when connected with a successful play of his—and misleading in the case of a failure like *Frank V.* "The value of a play lies in its density of problems, not in its explicitness" (FV 92). Quite true of *The Visit*, far from true of Dürrenmatt's "opera." One of the most explicit shortcomings of *Frank V* is that it is narrow and monotonous, not dense with problems. The parodic basic invention produced mostly shallow secondary ideas and self-evident caricatures. The era of greatest abundance is over for Dürrenmatt, both in the number of his new works and in the inner richness of each work. *Frank V* is scattered but not rich.

The third version of *Frank V* is not as incoherent as the script used in Munich. This Bochum version, though not performed in public, was published in 1964.[22] A comparison shows that Dürrenmatt had worked to make his plot tighter, his action more effective on the stage. The musical numbers were cut down considerably; the subtitle was changed from "opera" to "comedy with music." Some of the epic songs holding up the action were rewritten as ordinary dialogue.[23] Scene 13 revealing Frank's children as villains now appears as Scene 8, thus incorporating the children more closely into the play. Dürrenmatt's careful stage directions describe a set lay-out reminiscent of Act II in *The Visit*: the bank facade

[22] Dürrenmatt was to direct the play together with Erich Holliger. After four weeks the rehearsals were interrupted by the Bochum theater manager Hans Schalla.

[23] A tiny change shows that Dürrenmatt is continuously preoccupied with chaos and world order. The President sighs to Ottilie in FV: "Ich müsste ja die ganze Weltordnung umstürzen" (87). Bochum version, p. 88, has "Weltunordnung": "world disorder" instead of "world order." Peppard finds the play "a parody of order" (p. 63).

upstage, the café and other interior scenes in front of it. The everyday business transactions in the bank are worked out in detail, and one of Dürrenmatt's scenic units, the last meal, is introduced, this time with a variation. After his "resurrection" Frank V takes part in his own funeral banquet. In his postscript Dürrenmatt makes his last or third plea for the play, with hardly greater success than before.[24]

Have we the right to expect only masterpieces from the acknowledged masters of the stage? As critics, spectators, or readers? I do not know; yet we certainly have the right to say when we do not get them. After *The Visit* there was every reason to call Dürrenmatt a ruling prince of the stage. Among his six first stage plays there was also another clear success, perhaps of lasting value (*Romulus the Great*), a clear failure (*The Blind Man*), and three more or less promising and chaotic plays. *Frank V* is chaotic rather than promising; it speaks of routine rather than of a freshness of approach. A fragment from *Problems of the Theater*, placed as the motto of the third part of this study, reveals Dürrenmatt's skeptical attitude to playwriting as a learnable craft to be conquered through experience. This is how his career was to go on: marked by victories and defeats, keeping his audiences on tenterhooks all the while. After a defeat there was always the hope of a rapid recovery.

[24] In his estimate of the Bochum version Jenny says that Dürrenmatt's courageous involvement with Shakespeare, Schiller, and Goethe "creates a style, but no world" (p. 77).

12   Doctoring a Hopeless Patient

THE PHYSICISTS

||||||||||||||||||||||||||||||||||||||||||||||||||||||||||||||||||||||||||||||||||||||||||

The Physicists (Die Physiker), not *Frank V*, was to be Dürrenmatt's second hit. After its world première at the Zurich Theater on February 20, 1962, the play spread like an epidemic throughout the German-speaking world. It was the most frequently performed play of the 1962–63 season, with 1,598 performances at 59 theaters. *Andorra* by Max Frisch, first performed in Zurich in the fall of 1961, had 1,564 presentations during two theater seasons: a rare stellar moment for Swiss drama.[1] Also a moment not to be repeated: the binary star of Dürrenmatt and Frisch was soon to be eclipsed by a period of rapid growth in drama in Germany itself.[2]

The roots of *The Physicists* lie far back in Dürrenmatt's earlier writings. As far back as they could go: his first play, the destroyed "Comedy," dealt with the topic of the atomic bomb. In the short story "The Tunnel" he expressed his "scientophobia," probably emphasized by his studies in modern philosophy and by his interest in science.[3] In two theoretical

[1] The figures are from the official statistics covering the German Federal Republic, Switzerland and Austria, published in *Die deutsche Bühne*, 7 (34), 12, 1963.

[2] German theater repertoires were dominated by "the classics of modern theater" in 1947–57, to make up for the arid Nazi years; a new wave brought in the absurdists after 1957 (Rischbieter, *Theater heute*, eine Auswahl, p. 51: reprinted from *2*, 12, Dec. 1961). Jack D. Zipes sees the season 1961–62 as a turning point toward political and documentary plays; he mentions *The Physicists, Andorra*, and plays by Kipphardt and Lenz as indications of this change (Koebner, ed., *Tendenzen der deutschen Literatur*, 1971, p. 462).

[3] Dürrenmatt has spoken about the interest he has "always had in science. I know a great many physicists. . . . I talk very much with them" (Sauter, "Gespräch mit F.D.," *Sinn und Form, 18*, 4, 1966, pp. 1218–19).

266

works, both from the fall of 1956, he developed ideas later discernible in *The Physicists* or in its background pattern. *Brighter Than a Thousand Suns* by Robert Jungk is a report on the history of the atomic bomb; Dürrenmatt reviewed this book, calling it "a chronicle about the end of the world of pure reason" (TS 272), and characterizing the efforts to keep the bomb secret as "insane" (TS 273). A computer called "Mania" had its (her, his?) role to play in Jungk's documentary story. Dürrenmatt was to choose an asylum as the setting of his play, which finishes with a vision of the end of the world; one of his main themes is that even the purest reason cannot help the physicists to retract their dangerous knowledge. According to Jungk, Einstein and Szilard tried to cancel their proposal to construct the bomb; Einstein was to become a character in Dürrenmatt's play—in a way. Only international cooperation between the physicists could have prevented the bomb, Dürrenmatt reasons; yet the decision drifted from their hands into those of politicians and generals.

These thoughts found their way into Dürrenmatt's play, finished five years later. In a lecture summarized above (p. 216) he touched upon the inability of a present-day individual to understand and influence scientists and/or politicians (TS 58–60). The two writings are, on a conceptual and intellectual level, the starting-points for Dürrenmatt's eighth stage play. On the emotional level there must have been a sense of fear caused by the spiritual atmosphere during World War II, Dürrenmatt's formative years. His method of writing seems to rely on rapid artistic inventions, on a kind of improvisation. Yet, paradoxically enough, this method leads to the best results if the themes he develops with such improvisatory ease have had a long period of incubation within his mind. *The Visit* and *The Physicists* are both plays with intricate interrelations with the rest of Dürrenmatt; they are, in anyone's judgment, better plays than *Frank V*, sketched in seven days. Dürrenmatt's most fertile inventions grasp at situations, conflicts, themes, or characters familiar from his earlier improvisations. A writer needs both an impulse to activate his mind—and a mind containing something to activate. Jungk's book was such an impulse;[4] and the atomic bomb was a nucleus around which Dürrenmatt's thoughts had been circling for years.

This encounter between an outside impulse and a ripening idea was to produce a play of an unconventional kind. In 1961 Dürrenmatt was standing on the threshold of a period of documentary drama in Germany. He did not know it; he turned his documentary materials into a grotesque comitragedy placed in an asylum. It is fascinating to see how Dürrenmatt's powerful imagination was to turn words like "insane" or "pure reason," both dropped from his own pen, into a fully conceived play, into a thoroughly personal analysis of one of the most burning problems of our age. How to survive with the bomb?

On the first pages of *The Physicists* Dürrenmatt indulges in a novel-like description of the surroundings of his asylum.[5] Les Cerisiers is situated in a peaceful Swiss landscape, with "blue mountain-ranges," "a fairly large lake" and "a medium-sized or even smaller town." Nothing dramatic could happen in this quiet little spot, the text implies; yet the stage is turned into the scene of events of world-wide significance, as Guellen was. The first ominous feature is that our unscrupulous age has upset the natural balance of the region: there are "hideous edifices of insurance companies," there is "a house of correction" sending "silent and shadowy bands and little groups of criminals hoeing and digging" (FP 299) into the landscape.[6] This is, of course, for the reader to know,

[4] Dürrenmatt confirms these conclusions: even his most fantastic stories are based on his own experiences (G 57–59). Cf. TS 21.

[5] According to Reich-Ranicki, asylums and neurotics were typical surroundings and characters in German literature around the year 1960. They were favored by writers of the first and second postwar generations; in 1962 there were symptoms of a change toward concreteness, toward "our factual surroundings and tangible thoughts"— again, a wave of "Neue Sachlichkeit" (*Literatur der kleinen Schritte*, pp. 320–25).

[6] Brock-Sulzer calls these surroundings "a fairly ironically seen Neuenburg," where Dürrenmatt has mostly lived since the 1950's,

not for the spectator to see; yet a similar contrast is present also in the only stage picture of the play. The drawing-room of a former summer residence has seen better days, the walls are covered "with hygienic, washable, glossy paint" above which "the original plaster emerges, with some remnants of stucco mouldings." The furniture "belongs to various periods" (FP 301)—as it did in *Mississippi*. The three physicists inhabiting the villa are "harmless, lovable lunatics, amenable, easily handled and unassuming" (FP 300). Yet there is a body of a strangled nurse in the drawing-room.[7]

Violence in the middle of blissful harmony: a Dürrenmattian theme, a grotesque discord. A conflict between past mores of living and a modern madhouse: this is what Dürrenmatt's play is about. Upstage there are three doors leading to the rooms of the patients. "The sound of a violin, with piano accompaniment, comes from Room Number 2 (the middle room). Beethoven. Kreutzer Sonata" (FP 301). The murderer, a physicist who imagines himself to be Einstein, is playing; the doctor in charge, Fräulein Doktor Mathilde von Zahnd, is accompanying him. The music is continued during the hearings conducted by Richard Voss, Inspector of Police, during the early scenes establishing the impression of everyday hospital routine being resumed. With the help of music, with the help of the setting, Dürrenmatt creates a contrast between shabby present-day realities and a more harmonious past. These scenic means of expression are less obtrusive than the songs of *Frank V*.

The Inspector is a representative of the spectators: an intruder into the small community of the asylum. With the normal equipment of justice in his pocket, besides a cigar case and a notebook, he does his best to understand the

and where he and Burkhard used to walk along a road between an asylum and a prison while working on *Frank V* (*F.D.*, pp. 123–24).

[7] "With this ominous tableau Peter Brook escorts us unto his production of *The Physicists*. . . . Dürrenmatt plays on our nerves and through them reaches our brains, using the techniques of detective fiction to convey an apocalyptic message: the effect is that of a Hitchcock turned prophet" (Kenneth Tynan, *The Observer*, Jan. 13, 1963).

strange events surrounding him. A nurse has been strangled for the second time within three months; again, the assailant is a patient, not to be reached by the long arm of law. The Inspector's assistants are "stolid, good-natured fellows" (FP 301); these civil servants are incapable of coping with the problems of nuclear physics. One of Dürrenmatt's points is that the world of the physicists has nothing to do with normal concepts of morality: these have been exploded by the atomic bomb.

The patients, the personnel, and a few visitors are introduced one by one, as the grotesque retinue of Claire Zachanassian was. Sister Boll is certainly very efficient in her profession: everything is in order, the peculiarities of the patients are understood and defended. These include a harmless joke: "Newton" confesses that he isn't really Newton, he only play-acts this role, in order to conceal from "Einstein" that he is in fact Einstein. This is the beginning of Dürrenmatt's fun and games with his "Who's Who" cast. Much later revelations are prepared with the help of similar turns of dialogue: "Is it because I strangled the nurse that you want to arrest me, or because it was I who paved the way for the atomic bomb?" The physicists "elaborate a theory," then the engineers start exploiting it by building machines "independent of the knowledge that led to its invention. So any fool nowadays can switch a light or touch off the atomic bomb" (FP 308). The scientists have no control over the results of their findings.

"The sane commit murders more often than madmen" (FP 311). All through Act I Dürrenmatt keeps smuggling thematically important materials into his innocent and expository discussions between the Inspector and other characters on the stage. These materials are understated by attributing them to madhouse humor.[8] Hunchbacked Fräulein Doktor is the offspring of an old established family; it needs

---

[8] Jenny (*F.D.*, pp. 79–81), presents similar observations. The misleading exposition is "splendidly played"; the prevalent elements are "the horror of a gangster play and the comedy of a madhouse" (p. 80).

an accustomed reader of Dürrenmatt to realize that this is no recommendation. Hospitals as money-making institutions belong to his nightmares of terror, as in *The Pledge*, in *The Quarry*. The weakness of the patients in the hands of their doctors is a symbol of the more profound helplessness of us all.

We are more than halfway through Act I before Johann Wilhelm Möbius makes his entrance. He is "about forty, a rather clumsy man" (FP 319); his delusion is that King Solomon appears to him. In a farcical and embarrassed scene of farewell he receives his former wife, his three sons, and the new husband of his wife as his visitors.[9] Mr. Rose is a missionary: "Truly a divine peace reigns over this house, just as the psalmist says: For the Lord heareth the needy and despiseth not his prisoners" (FP 315). Möbius hardly recognizes his wife; he does not remember the names or ages of his sons. The story of the marriage is told: it is one of endless self-sacrifice on her part.[10] Fifteen years ago there had been hope of a professorship for Möbius, a talented young physicist; he then fell ill. When his three sons start playing recorders, this innocent idyll grows unendurable for Möbius, a man of intellect *and* emotion, and he dismisses his family by reciting a song of King Solomon, now "the pauper king of truth" crouching "naked and stinking" in his room. It is a song "to be sung to the Cosmonauts" (FP 323); at the end of their journey they steer out of our solar system:

> Outcasts we cast out, up into the deep
> Towards a few white stars
> That we never reached anyhow
>
> Long since mummied in our spacecraft
> Caked with filth
>
> In our deathsheads no more memories
> Of breathing earth (FP 324).

[9] "Strange and silent he stands in front of his dependents who wish to make his existence harmless in such a childish way" (Bänziger, *Frisch und D.*, p. 187).

[10] "This dramaturgically extremely clever scene shows the entire prehistory of the play" (Jauslin, *F.D.*, p. 112).

271

Outer space is for Möbius an immense realm of death, uninhabited and uninhabitable. In Dürrenmatt's personal idiom this counter-sketch to the pious phrases of Mr. Rose means that Möbius lives in a graceless state, in a kingdom of death. And in the total atmosphere of Act I it means a courageous and sharp cut from the farce of the family scene to a poetic vision of the end of the world, into a highly charged scenic image. When reciting his mad poem of valediction, Möbius sits between the legs of an overturned table, in a spacecraft, as it were.

This emotional climax is followed by another surprise twist. Möbius is calmed down by Sister Monika, a self-sacrificing nurse who knows that Möbius is perfectly sane, because she is in love with him. She has taken care of everything: these two are free to leave the asylum, to marry and settle down. Yet Möbius is in such an exceptional situation that even the wisest human arrangements are only folly. No order prevails; or the only order is dictated by the firm decision of the physicist to do his best to preserve mankind.[11] Not himself or Monika: mankind. And so, with only the silhouettes of Möbius and Monika visible on the darkening stage, he strangles his nurse, while "Einstein" starts playing Kreisler's "Humoresque," and the curtain falls.[12] See Fig. 10.

It is a commonplace in drama to test a protagonist with love. Is the impulse to avenge his father more powerful than Hamlet's love for Ophelia? Does Peer Gynt love himself more than Solveig? Dürrenmatt goes to the extreme of letting his Möbius kill the woman he loves: rejecting her is not enough. It was not enough for Richard Egli in *Frank V* either —or for God in *It Is Written*, to take an example from a love relation of another kind. This surprise moment just before

[11] "The cause of humanity outweighs all other considerations. To this is sacrificed Möbius' chances of personal happiness" (Michael Morley, "D's Dialogue with Brecht," *Modern Drama*, 15, 2, Sept. 1971, p. 233).

[12] Jenny (p. 83) calls Monika's role and this scene "a little too courageously thought out, hardly actable in its suddenness"; it "demands ecstasy, even if the dialogue remains barren and dry."

the end of Act I certainly leaves the spectators dumbfounded: what is taking place in Les Cerisiers?[13]

Besides, there has been a sense of mystery hovering over the entire opening act. Are the physicists sane or mad? Was the murderer, after all, "Einstein"? Having a Police Inspector brought on stage is bound to lead one's thoughts along these lines, familiar to every reader of detective fiction. No doubt Dürrenmatt is doing all this on purpose; he is writing a counter-sketch to a thriller for the stage. There are confessions after confessions, secrets behind the secrets, truth in ironically innocent lines of dialogue.[14] The action of Act I consists of an elaborate maneuver, planned to lead the spectators both astray—and to the point. Yet one has to ask whether this does not mean stage irony pushed too far. *The Physicists* is a difficult play to produce, and not only because of its precarious balance between farce and tragedy.[15] It is not self-evident that the isolated foreshadowing features pointed out above can be successfully connected on the stage. They should, however, give us clear enough hints about what the playwright is going to do in his Act II.

At the same time one is bound to admit admiration for Dürrenmatt's cleverness. The themes are there, for the stage director to find and develop.[16] The chance is given. Suspense is screwed up in a purposeful way; there is nothing superfluous in the dialogue or action. *The Physicists* is a play in which Dürrenmatt's customary abundance takes the form of

[13] Both Jauslin (p. 113) and Arnold (*F.D.*, p. 78) assume that the spectators are bound to feel confused during the intermission.

[14] "Each bit of information that clears up one situation serves to create a new mystery. Thus the play grows in fascinating complications, confounding its audience, even while it is progressively clarifying itself" (Norman Nadel, *New York World-Telegram and Sun*, Oct. 14, 1964).

[15] Several reviews of the world première reveal divided impressions: the critics accepted either the comedy of Act I or the tragedy of Act II, not both (Wolff-Windegg, *Basler Nachrichten*; Friedrich Luft, *Die Welt*; Irma Voser, *NZZ*; all Feb. 23, 1962).

[16] "Presentiments and forebodings have been scattered through the first act" (Peppard, *F.D.*, p. 71). Dürrenmatt "is now able to utilize the laws of the theater as a virtuoso" (Brock-Sulzer, *F.D.*, p. 113).

a plot intricately woven. Richness here means a great number of surprises within a limited time. The closest precedent in the canon is *Romulus the Great*; another point of connection is that both of these plays are analyses of individuals rather than wide social panoramas. Yet social views of world-wide significance open up behind the characters. *The Physicists* is Dürrenmatt's main work within compressionism.

The term is used in the sense given to it by Laurence Kitchin. "A compressionist play is one in which the characters are insulated from society in such a way as to encourage the maximum conflict of attitudes."[17] As examples Kitchin catalogues *The Dance of Death* by Strindberg (a key work), *The Hairy Ape* by O'Neill, *Journey's End* by Sherriff, *No Exit* by Sartre, *The Chairs* by Ionesco, *Endgame* by Beckett, and several plays by Pinter.[18] Compressionism is an alternative in modern drama to a more open and epic style, as in the plays referred to above as Dürrenmatt's "social panoramas." The walls of the asylum insulate the physicists from the outer world, from the surrounding Swiss idyll; the walls are like Guelleners turned into a setting. The individual or a few individuals are in the middle, enclosed within a claustrophobic circle. In this compressed arena Dürrenmatt can keep all the Aristotelian unities operative, as he says in his first stage direction, adding an ironic twist: "Only classical form can cope with an action taking place among madmen" (Ph 12). "Classical form"—in tension with modern contents, with a grotesque comitragedy.[19] Dürrenmatt's compressionism is full of nightmare and black comedy.

In Act II the playwright goes on developing "the maximum conflict of attitudes." We find the Inspector and his assistants

---

[17] *Drama in the Sixties*, 1966, p. 46. Kitchin connects *The Physicists* with physical cruelty, a stock feature in compressionism (pp. 21–22).

[18] Ibid., pp. 47–52.

[19] The discrepancy between Dürrenmatt's classic form and "non-classic" contents leads to a kind of parody, pointing out "the inner paradox of the entire play, reflecting the paradoxicality of existence" (Uwe Massberg, "Der gespaltene Mensch," *Der Deutschunterricht*, *17*, 6, Dec. 1965, p. 70).

busy at work again: as the murder was repeated, so is its aftermath, too. Inspector Voss is dead tired; he is a character out of focus: the time for writing more or less traditional detective stories is over for Dürrenmatt. Yet he allows Voss to have a couple of whiskies and grow talkative, which helps Voss to make his point. Not being able to arrest three murderers made him first disappointed, then joyous: "For the first time justice is on holiday—and it's a terrific feeling" (FP 338). Les Cerisiers is indeed a place where human justice is on holiday.[20]

The Inspector's visits also mean the only interference from the outside world during the action of the play. Fräulein Doktor has to give in to the demands of the public prosecutor and replace nurses with male attendants. It is, on the surface, a typically Dürrenmattian joke that the replacements are enormous men—and boxing champions. As a consolation our three physicists are served a festive meal: a kind of memorial banquet for Möbius' dead beloved and his lost life.

This is the first time we meet all three physicists by themselves. The moment for the taking-off of masks is imminent. "Newton" is revealed as an intelligence agent from the West, "Einstein" from the East.[21] Both have been spying on Möbius; they know that our "lunatic" is the greatest genius in the history of physics. Each of the agents is eager to get Möbius on his own side: all of a sudden both have pistols in their hands. This conflict ends in a tie, in a demonstration on the stage of the Balance of Terror: as there are two equal parties threatening one another, they can agree to lay down their weapons. And then, in a scenic image consisting mainly of silent action, the male attendants start carrying out certain

[20] Cf. Hildegard Emmel, *Das Gericht* . . . , p. 168: "In his own way, the Inspector re-establishes order in the middle of general confusion." The asylum is the only place where chaos has taken over; elsewhere, "justice is justice" (FP 338). Les Cerisiers is an isolated island governed by the absolute grotesque.

[21] This twist is foreshadowed in Dürrenmatt's book review: he speaks of "an imagined armament race" between the USA and Germany during World War II, turned into a real race between the USA and the Soviet Union (TS 273).

new security measures. They place metal grills over all the windows: "The room now suddenly has the aspect of a prison."[22] The dialogue spoken is barren and functional: the emphasis is on the action, made impressive through interaction with the entire plot of the play. Just before, "Einstein" had called the meal "a real gallows-feast" (FP 343).

The situation has changed: the agents know that their only chance to get out lies in cooperation. Möbius refuses to follow them. He is happy inside. He has completed his life's work, he has both solved the problem of gravitation and found "the Principle of Universal Discovery."[23] He faces his responsibilities: these discoveries make "possible a technical advance that would transcend the wildest flights of fantasy if my findings were to fall into the hands of mankind" (FP 345). There is no real freedom for the physicists in the West, and no real political influence for them in the East. The only safe place for Möbius is the madhouse. Besides, he has burnt his manuscripts.

Once the ideological discussion has started, Dürrenmatt sticks to his point. The spectators know now what the play is about. Reasoning about their situation coolly, "in a scientific manner" (FP 348), Möbius remarks that humanity has not been able to follow on the heels of its physicists: "Our knowledge has become a frightening burden. . . . We have to take back our knowledge and I have taken it back. There is no other way out." And he is able to convince his fellow physicists, trained as spies late in life: "Today it's the duty of a genius to remain unrecognized. Killing is a terrible thing. . . . We are wild beasts. We ought not to be let loose on humanity" (FP 350–51). The scene has been full of unexpected twists in the plot; it closes with a toast to the nurses,[24]

[22] The stage as a prison occurs also in other compressionistic plays, e.g., in *The Brig* by Kenneth Brown (Kitchin, p. 63).

[23] A word-for-word translation would be "the system of all possible discoveries" (Ph 59).

[24] This is "certainly the moment most difficult to act in the play" (Brock-Sulzer, p. 118). It "must be played with genuine solemnity and with no suggestion of irony or mock seriousness, since the action is already dangerously close to the risible" (Peppard, p. 69).

to the sacrificial killings each of the three has committed to preserve his secrecy. The conflicts between the three physicists, developed to the maximum degree of repeated pointing of guns, are solved in a spirit of good international understanding:

NEWTON: Let us be mad, but wise.
EINSTEIN: Prisoners but free.
MÖBIUS: Physicists but innocent (FP 352).

The slalom-like plot of *The Physicists* has reached its last twist.[25] It is to be the worst possible turn. The physicists leave the stage; the attendants, now in black uniforms, clear the table, and the upturned chairs are put on a table, "as if the place were a restaurant closing for the night" (FP 352). The changes in the setting are limited to a minimum: each of them is thus emphatic. This scene of silent action shows who is in control of all events in that asylum, through her attendants dressed in black.[26] They are shown in Fig. 8.

Justice is on holiday: it is replaced by Fräulein Doktor. She overheard the discussion of the physicists; she has known about Möbius' inventions all along and photocopied his secret papers. Her attendants, members of her private police force, confiscate the hidden radio transmitters of the agents; searchlights are put on in the surrounding park, and laughter dies in "Newton's" throat. When the attendants have been sent away, Dr. von Zahnd reveals her secret to the physicists, now to be safely imprisoned for the rest of their lives: King Solomon appears to her.[27] Obeying his commands, Fräulein Doktor is ready to start exploiting the Principle of Universal

[25] The asylum is close to "the surreal and grotesque dimensions of absurdism," yet Dürrenmatt replaces its customary shocks "with the more moderate means of repeated sudden reversals in the action" (Kesting, *Panorama des zeitgenössischen Theaters*, p. 227).

[26] Morley remarks that the ancestors of Dr. von Zahnd (mentioned in dialogue) represent "business, political, or military" power, and associates her with Goering, Goebbels, and Hitler; her black-clad works police with the SS (p. 236).

[27] In von Zahnd's description of the King's first appearance to her, there occurs one of Dürrenmatt's fateful sound effects: "a woodpecker was hammering somewhere in the park" (FP 355).

277

Discovery, conquering the earth and steering her journey out of our solar system, "beyond the great nebula in Andromeda" (FP 357). The song of King Solomon, recited by Möbius, has come true. The physicists protest in vain. They are guilty of murder; the nurses were driven into their arms on purpose. They have taken refuge in a prison they built for themselves.[28] "The world has fallen into the hands of an insane, female psychiatrist. . . . What was once thought can never be unthought" (FP 358). Left alone, the physicists can only resume their old roles, as a final gesture of utter despair.

> MÖBIUS: I am Solomon. I am poor King Solomon. Once I was immeasurably rich, wise and God-fearing. The mighty trembled at my word. I was a Prince of Peace, a Prince of Justice. But my wisdom destroyed the fear of God, and when I no longer feared God my wisdom destroyed my wealth. Now the cities over which I rule are dead, the Kingdom that was given unto my keeping is deserted: only a blue shimmering wilderness. And somewhere round a small, yellow, nameless star there circles, pointlessly, everlastingly, the radioactive earth. I am Solomon. I am Solomon. I am Solomon. I am poor King Solomon (FP 359).[29]

This is Dürrenmatt's version of the Fall of Man, combined with his vision of the end of the world. The last we hear is "Einstein" playing his fiddle.

[28] The complete victory of Dr. Zahnd is, of course, a theater coup. As such it has been severely criticized, e.g., by J. Chiari, *Landmarks of Contemporary Drama*, p. 188. Yet it should be judged in the light of the total structure of the play and of Dürrenmatt's dramaturgy of chance, discussed below.

[29] There are two images of King Solomon in the play: the poor or naked king, the powerful master of knowledge. Möbius had no intention to "*misuse* knowledge"; yet both he and Solomon were destroyed by it. "It is ironic that Dr. von Zahnd, who lacks Möbius' concern for humanity and Solomon's wisdom, . . . will not be destroyed by the forces she intends to unleash" (Morley, p. 238). Cf. Bänziger, p. 189.

It is as if the solutions of Dürrenmatt's "men of courage" were growing more and more futile, more and more desperate.[30] Ill was able to save his own integrity, if not Guellen's morals; the self-sacrifice of Möbius and his colleagues saves nothing, nor does Monika's feminine plan. They can help neither themselves nor mankind.[31] The powers of order, especially of a sensible, human kind of order, are diminishing on Dürrenmatt's stage. The atmosphere has been darkening, even if the plays are, when taken moment by moment, full of comedy and delightful surprises. *The Physicists* does not conclude with a stalemate between chaos and order. There is an out-and-out victory for the powers of chaos, one leading to the end of the world. Möbius is helpless (Fig. 9).

The only consolation we receive from *The Physicists* is a hardening vision of our present-day reality. We have to survive with the bomb—somehow. The absurd possibility of World War III with atomic weapons is a part of the reality everyone has to accept, has to include in his or her thinking. True to his basic quality as a man of wild fantasy, Dürrenmatt has stylized and emphasized this predicament still further. He imagines new findings of the physicists, leading to the world's being conquered by a power maniac. There are three dimensions of time meeting on his stage. *The Physicists* is a historical play in the sense that the atomic bomb had already been constructed. It is a contemporary play in the sense that the question of having atomic weapons or not was put to a national referendum in Switzerland during the very months *The Physicists* was playing in Zurich.[32] And it is a utopian (or dystopian) play in its vision of the future.

[30] Brock-Sulzer finds in the play "a certain cancellation of 'the man of courage'" (p. 114). For Mayer, Möbius shows still more clearly than Ill that Dürrenmatt has passed "sacrificial idealism" (*Zur deutschen Literatur der Zeit*, p. 329).

[31] The common frontier found by the physicists was not meant to be Dürrenmatt's "positive message." It just brings them to "a position of maximum height of fall" (Jenny, p. 85).

[32] Marti, *Die Schweiz und ihre Schriftsteller*, pp. 53–54. Dürrenmatt took an active stand against atomic weapons.

Starting from his documentary materials Dürrenmatt was able to make these materials grow from history through the present day toward the future. This is the basic advantage in his treatment of his topic: he was able to bring more than a stageful of events onto the stage, as it were. His vision of terror, his nightmare of the atomic age, reverberates in our recent past, in the present day, and in the days to come. If there is any "message" included in the play, if there is anything pointing toward the future in this description of an unresolvable conflict between science and humanity, this is expressed in two of Dürrenmatt's "Twenty-one Points" to *The Physicists*. He calls these points afterthoughts, written down after the play had been completed.[33] The results of physics concern all people, and "what concerns all people, can only be solved by all" (TS 194).

Möbius made the mistake of trying to solve his problem alone. Trying to save mankind means doctoring a hopeless patient. In this character Dürrenmatt is, in fact, criticizing his own concept of a "man of courage." His characterization is growing cooler, more disillusioned. He speaks through situations rather than through characters.[34] There is something mechanical, puppet-like, in the way all the figures are marshalled in *The Physicists*.[35] Möbius, the most fully realized character in the play, claims that it is necessary to "surrender to reality" (FP 350). Yet while saying so he is in fact trying to reform reality, by taking back his revolutionary findings. He is not a master of his reality, not even of his own thoughts. They cannot be taken back. The reality Dürrenmatt wants him to surrender to includes Fräulein

---

[33] Sauter, p. 1219.

[34] Ernst Wendt, having seen six productions of *The Physicists*, discerns in the play "something of clockwork—Swiss work, so to speak": the parts fit together, the mechanism functions faultlessly, inhumanly (*Theater heute*, 3, 12, Dec. 1962, p. 12). Peppard (p. 69) remarks that one has to sympathize with Möbius, otherwise "the emotional impact of the play is slight."

[35] Dürrenmatt is "concerned with summing up the overwhelming problem of our time into the simplest and clearest allegory he can devise"—rather than with characterization (Howard Taubman, *New York Times*, Oct. 14, 1964).

Doktor, includes the possibility of a blind, evil chance. "Chance" is a central concept in Dürrenmatt's "Twenty-one Points."

"The Points" are written crisply, with aphoristic accents and elliptical statements; yet they make a logical and inevitable total impression. Dürrenmatt starts from a story, not from a thesis; he develops his story to its end, to "its worst possible turn." This turn is unpredictable and takes place through chance. "The art of a playwright consists in inserting chance into an action as effectively as possible." Chance hits systematic people most severely of all, and these most heavily when it brings them to the opposite of their acknowledged aim. "A story of this kind is grotesque" and paradoxical, not absurd.[36] Dramatists, physicists, or logicians cannot avoid paradoxes: a play dealing with physics "must be paradoxical" and deal with the results of physics. These concern all people and must be solved by all. "Drama can outwit the spectator into facing reality, but it cannot compel him to withstand it, let alone master it" (TS 193–94).

This summary is applicable to *The Physicists*. Dürrenmatt's postscript has more validity than any of his self-defenses in the case of *Frank V*. Dr. von Zahnd makes the story take "its worst possible turn"; she is chance personified, she replaces human justice, or a sensible world order. Möbius, one of Dürrenmatt's systematic, rational characters, and a sympathetic monomaniac, is hard hit by this incalculable chance which brings him directly to the opposite of his aim. His story is grotesque and paradoxical;[37] Dürrenmatt's modest wish is that it would make his audiences face reality, not master or change it.

[36] Waldmann interprets: the object of Dürrenmatt's comedy is "the absurd," the form he uses is extraordinary and grotesque, not absurd in the meaning of senseless or unreasonable. "The absurd is not, so to say, the last word" ("Ds paradoxes Theater," *Wirkendes Wort, 14*, 1, 1964, p. 31).

[37] Chance as a factor in the action is a grotesque phenomenon (Kayser, *Das Groteske*, p. 45). Kayser's study also touches other characteristics of *The Physicists*: "the world as a madhouse" (p. 63), "the motif of the mask" (64), or disproportion between crime and punishment (79).

We can, of course, argue that it might be possible to write a "non-paradoxical" play about physics. Dürrenmatt is motivating a specific case, his play, with generalized arguments. His key positions are made valid by his own practice: is there any better way for a playwright to prove his theoretical points? There is a fair enough chance that the most devastating weapons man's ingenuity can develop might fall into the hands of a power maniac, depicted on the stage as an insane female psychiatrist. There appeared on the stage of world politics a man called Hitler not so long ago. Dürrenmatt succeeded in inserting chance into his action in the case of *The Physicists* in a manner both effective and indisputable. This does not, however, say anything about his success in similar undertakings earlier or later. Life is wild and chaotic, the stage is a realm of iron rules, of inevitable consequences. Ever since Ibsen, this has been a major problem in the modern theater; witness a great many reform movements and, as extreme phenomena, the experiments with "happenings," or several avant-garde groups trying to erase the border line between life and the theater.[38] How far does chance introduced on the stage remain chance?

Only when connected with a specific theme, is one bound to conjecture. Paradoxically enough, as soon as chance is introduced as a key factor, we are inclined to stop accepting it as chance. Instead, we start taking it as a vehicle of manipulation utilized by the playwright. If the play is 'plotty,' if it depends for its effect on a twisted plot line, our suspicions are apt to grow stronger.[39] We have been following various modifications in Dürrenmatt's dramaturgy of chance; the earliest formulations occur in his prose stories, e.g., in

[38] Joachim Kaiser has remarked that improvisation or playing with chance is in the theater mostly taken as parody or as a joke ("Grenzen des modernen Dramas," *Theater heute*, 5, 12, Dec. 1964, pp. 14–15).

[39] Dürrenmatt is smuggling the old concept of "tragic necessity" into his thinking with the help of his "worst possible turn." He identifies freedom with comedy, yet freedom can be shown only in a tragicomedy, "in a paradoxical conflict with the necessity of the worst possible turn." His way of writing leaves him at the mercy of "the productive moment and the central artistic invention" (Allemann in Steffen, ed., *Das deutsche Lustspiel*, pp. 212, 216).

282

"Theater Manager," where this power maniac was accused of expelling chance from his stage altogether (S 61). On one hand, chance has guaranteed Dürrenmatt freedom for his artistic inventions. On the other, it has been a part of his view of the world, a factor behind the absurd, uncontrollable phenomena of life.[40]

Romulus and Matthäi precede Möbius in being rational characters destroyed by blind chance. What is new in *The Physicists* and in its "Points" is an effort to motivate inserting chance into a play with a tightly knit action, with a story thought out to a conclusion. Dürrenmatt gives chance a specific function: it is to gear a story to its worst possible turn, it is to take the spectator by surprise. Chance is given a key mission in the structure of the play. This means formulating the dramaturgy behind Dürrenmatt's compressionism, behind plays built around just one basic paradox, not around a host of varied artistic inventions. Dürrenmatt has been fighting and utilizing all kinds of artistic formulas during his twenty years of creative writing; now he is about to find a formula for his own usage. It remains to be seen whether this formula, acceptable in the case of *The Physicists*, will retain its usefulness and flexibility later on. This will be mainly dependent on Dürrenmatt's ability to invent stories and themes open to chance, yet not open to accusations of manipulation.

Without doubt *The Physicists* belongs to Dürrenmatt's major works. Compared with *The Visit* it is a somewhat narrower, more concentrated play, less rich: this is mainly due to its very subject matter and to its character as a compressionist play. As Dürrenmatt puts it himself (Ph 13), it con-

[40] Züfle connects the playwright's view of the world with his dramaturgy. "The world is for Dürrenmatt a priori the worst possible, because the absolute possibility of chance can always cause . . . the worst possible turn to take place" ("F.D.," *Schweizer Rundschau*, 66, 1, Jan. 1967, p. 36). Wendt sees Dürrenmatt's paradox as a purely formal concept, as "chance inserted according to a plan" (p. 12). Analyses of Dürrenmatt's works certainly speak about a paradoxical view of the world.

sists of a satyr play preceding a tragedy;[41] this divided basic structure, combined with the thriller-like elements, has led to unfavorable criticism, some of which has been discussed above. On the other hand, the play has been praised as Dürrenmatt's "most closely knit" achievement.[42] There are fewer and longer scenes in Act II, there is more space for Dürrenmatt to develop his argument. The final twist, the worst possible one, compels us to read Dürrenmatt's characters twice: the second reading is from the end to the beginning.

When Dr. von Zahnd is read this way, it is possible to see in her "an incarnation of evil," a new variation of Claire Zachanassian.[43] The only firmly established, unshakable order in the play is her evil order. The last speeches of the physicists have been interpreted in various ways.[44] "Newton" and "Einstein" accept their false roles, and their last words are short autobiographical statements; Möbius' curtain lines are quoted above. Have these three now turned into real lunatics?[45] Several readings (and stage interpretations) may

[41] "Tragedy presupposes guilt, despair, moderation, lucidity, vision, a sense of responsibility" (FP 33). Brian Murdoch shows point by point how these demands are fulfilled in the story about Möbius. For him the play represents "a final stage in the tragic tradition," because it depicts "the fall of the whole of mankind" ("Duerrenmatt's *Physicists*," *Modern Drama*, 14, 3, Dec. 1970, pp. 270–75). Heilman senses "an intimation of the tragic" in Möbius' curtain speech (*The Iceman* . . . , p. 227; cf. pp. 237–38).

[42] Garten, *Modern German Drama*, p. 260; cf. Arnold, p. 77. Jauslin (p. 115) refers to the figure three as a structural principle: there are three physicists, nurses, murders, forefathers for the doctor. Möbius is tempted to return to the outer world thrice: by his family, by Monika, by his colleagues.

[43] Jauslin, p. 117.

[44] Möbius has even been taken as "a disguised presentation of Christ" (Hartmut Sierig, *Narren und Totentänzer*, p. 146), his last instant on the stage as "a moment of grace" (Kurt J. Fickert, "The Curtain Speech," *Modern Drama*, 14, 1, May 1970, p. 45).

[45] E.g., Jenny (p. 87) and Hermann Pongs (*Romanschaffen im Umbruch der Zeit*, p. 476) take them as genuineley insane. Steiner disagrees: the play presents so-called maniacs as sane, and "comes close to considering us as madmen. Dürrenmatt's comedy makes us dubious by making itself and everything else uncertain" ("Die Komödie Ds," *Der Deutschunterricht*, 15, 6, Dec. 1963, p. 97). Ar-

284

be possible; yet the tone of voice, as I hear it, is that of a lucid, bitterly ironic confession of failure and of the unsolvable dilemma faced by modern physicists. These three are perfectly sane, yet all that is left for them is their old deceitful roles. The nuclei of their personality, their real selves, have been crushed.[46]

The physicists are victims, judges of themselves, and executioners. They are given all of these Dürrenmattian roles to play; their last entrance is decorated with a touch of poetry, in addition to the unreal aura surrounding their last speeches. When Möbius meets Zahnd for the last time, he is exalted: "A night of prayer. Deep blue and holy. The night of the mighty king. His white shadow is loosed from the wall; his eyes are shining" (FP 353). This is the more remarkable in a play with mostly quite barren dialogue: considerable sections are only functional, expository, or otherwise one-dimensional. In this phase of development, Dürrenmatt's creation for the stage aims more or less consciously at a poetry of the theater, not of words alone. Picture and word are in balance, the dramatist plays with quite a large orchestra of scenic means of expression: music, sound effects, action, scenes of pantomime, the setting, dialogue—all these are used with consummate skill. They build up a string of scenic images, all interacting, all alive with their grotesque contrasts. Möbius reciting his song, a lonely figure saying farewell to his family, to an ordinary way of life, to our earth. The murder of Monika on a dimly-lit stage. Changing the asylum into a prison: a scene speaking mainly with its action. The temporary harmony among the three scientists, their toast to

---

nold (p. 80) calls it a "subtle possibility" that von Zahnd is as mad as all people: "only three are normal and these are in a madhouse."

[46] Raymond Williams sees all the roles as shifting between lunacy and normality: "absurdity and violence coexist" on Dürrenmatt's stage. Physics is only a subject of discussion; the play is complex and disturbed beyond its warning about nuclear physics. With the help of the "dramatic image" of physics, it connects "a formal public violence and an inarticulate private violence" (*Drama from Ibsen to Brecht*, pp. 312–15).

their nurses, their feeling of relief: "Physicists but innocent."
And the final speeches by all three, finishing with Dürrenmatt's ultimate vision of the end of the world: a radioactive,
deserted earth circling a nameless star.

The end of a world: this is also how *Operation Vega*, a
radio play, concluded. Science fiction is now just an overtone
in Dürrenmatt's nightmare about nuclear physics. This vision
is turned into plot and action, into a compressionist play
combining surprising twists with a strictly limited area of
action. Chance has a key function in building up a paradoxical story; it is employed in accordance with the reality behind
the play. *The Visit* and *The Physicists* are plays both similar
and dissimilar, as two major works by one playwright often
are: similar in the integrity and nightmarish terror of their
basic vision, similar in their mixture of comedy and tragedy,
dissimilar in their form and scope. The later play hardly
challenges the position of *The Visit* as Dürrenmatt's masterpiece; yet it had a world-wide, hardly undeserved success.[47]
The swell of this success made Dürrenmatt's audiences and
critics forget or forgive the failure of *Frank V*, and his play
was compared with other modern dramas dealing with the
predicament of nuclear physics, among them *Galileo Galilei*
by Brecht, a classic of our age.[48] The comparisons did not
bring discredit upon Dürrenmatt.

[47] The play was quite well received in London and New York,
where it opened in January, 1963, and October, 1964, respectively.

[48] Both Brecht and Dürrenmatt emphasize the responsibility of the
physicist; the latter is more pessimistic in his refusal to point out a
clear answer. Morley calls Dürrenmatt's play "the last word on the
fate of the scientists" (pp. 241–42). Mayer connects *The Physicists*
with a long-lasting encounter between these two playwrights (cf. pp.
217–20 above). When Dürrenmatt puts the solution into the hands of
all people, this brings him into Brecht's vicinity: "What was once
thought can never be unthought. Not Brecht either. Dürrenmatt
knows it" (*D. und Frisch*, pp. 17–21). Sierig, pp. 147–54, compares
The Physicists with Kipphardt's documentary play *In the Matter of
J. Robert Oppenheimer*, 1964, and Karl S. Weimar both with *Galilei*
and with *The Cold Light*, 1955, by Carl Zuckmayer ("The Scientist
and Society," *Modern Language Quarterly*, 27, 4, Dec. 1966, pp.
432–48).

13 The Other Half of the Paradox

HERCULES, THE METEOR

‖‖‖

Hercules: a poetic play? There was once a radio play called *Hercules and the Augean Stables* (Herkules und der Stall des Augias), written by Dürrenmatt in 1954, discussed above on pp. 187–90. After the success of *The Physicists* Dürrenmatt started adapting this script for the stage, and the play was ready to open in Zurich in March, 1963. There was again a lengthy incubation period, this time, however, with a difference. The topic had been given a finished and enclosed form ten years earlier; now, Dürrenmatt was not just working with an idea or nucleus. The opening of the stage version shows that he was over-conscious of what he was doing. The Prologue, spoken by Polybios, the secretary of Hercules, does its best to convince the spectators that they are sitting in the theater, not listening to a radio play.

Polybios refutes the possibilities that *Hercules* was to be a play with a lesson (Lehrstück) or had anything to do with the modish theater of the absurd. Instead, it is "a poetic play" (H 12). The original production may have had its poetic side, especially thanks to Teo Otto's designs, which covered the entire stage with shimmering manure. The text is closer to cabaret than poetry. Dürrenmatt starts by displaying his tricks, not only using them. The full moon, a platform, and a wild sow are introduced during the Prologue. These theatricalistic details are less disturbing than the inclination of the characters to relapse into monologue, addressing the audience directly. There are such epic interludes spoken not only by Polybios, already used as a radio announcer, but also by President Augias, Dejaneira, and mailman Lichas, an added character. These speeches are an alien element in the

287

play;[1] they strengthen the impression of cabaret further by including anachronistic jokes and quite irrelevant materials. Dürrenmatt even lets his characters describe the settings, a bad habit we remember from his earliest stage plays.

A country completely covered by manure: a central artistic invention more at home on the air than on the stage. Hearing about Elis may well give our fantasy wings; these wings are clipped if we are made to look at a stage covered by poetic manure for a whole evening.[2] *Hercules* was not a rewarding starting-point for an adapter for the stage. Things were not helped by Dürrenmatt's additions or deletions. The outline of the story was retained; the discussion can be limited to a few additional points of comparison between the two versions.

Chorus and group scenes, crisp and sharp on the air, have lost their sting rather than gained anything. Certain new inventions are drawn-out and repetitious: Augias rings a cow-bell and calls for quiet six times—without any reason. Dürrenmatt expressly wants the rhythm of this first parliament scene to be slow (H 22). This may well characterize the state of affairs in Elis, a country of gauche farmers, yet it endangers the conciseness of the scene. The death of Hercules and the final fate of Phyleus, the son of Augias, are shown in a kind of "flash forward" in the mailman scene. Phyleus has hardly been introduced to the audience when his grave is shown. These solutions are artificial rather than effective.[3] Fig. 11 shows us Hercules and Dejaneira.

Act I of the world première ended with Scene 9. This is probably the most successful addition: Augias and Kambyses

---

[1] "The elements of the epic theater . . . function as tricks, because they are not of necessity developed from the basic conception" (Bänziger, *Frisch und D.*, p. 184).

[2] A radio play leaves "one's imagination free," the presence of manure on the stage "impedes rather than helps the imagination"; the monologues of Polybios and Litas are "inappropriate to the stage" or "gratuitous" (Peppard, *F.D.*, p. 74).

[3] Cf. Voser, *NZZ*, March 22, 1963.

are milking four imaginary cows while discussing matters of state with Hercules. The imagination of the actors and spectators is allowed to expand by the absence of the cows. It is also a scene in line with the greatest merit of the play: *Hercules* doubtless appealed to its Swiss audiences because of its satire on certain national characteristics.[4] But it also provoked them to resistance.[5]

Early in Act II Dürrenmatt goes on developing the serious rather than the slapstick elements of his play. Hercules' efforts are about to be inhibited by the stubborn bureaucracy of Elis' innumerable committees and commissions. The triangle Hercules-Dejaneira-Phyleus and a new love relation between Hercules and Iole, Augias' daughter, are treated in a melancholy mood, even in a moonlight scene. Whatever Dürrenmatt may be, he is not a great poet of love. It is easy to imagine audiences following the early cabaret scenes with curiosity and full attention, then falling into boredom with the increasingly frequent longueurs and the repetitiveness. Phyleus and Dejaneira keep falling in love, the parliament keeps assembling. Polybios is repeatedly severely beaten by Hercules: hardly a "refined" invention. There is no tension powerful enough in Act II to carry the interest of the spectators.

A basic split in the play is revealed by its most controversial scene, the final one. Dejaneira and Hercules have left Elis. They keep together, and by chance Dejaneira rescues the vial containing the blood of centaur Nessus. Dürrenmatt does not deviate from the ancient myth which says that Hercules died wearing a shirt dipped in Nessus' blood; he

[4] The jacket of the book version gives *Hercules* the subtitle "festival play" (Festspiel). It is thus a parody and a continuation of a type of historical drama popular in Switzerland, "more a series of scenes than a genuine play," performed by amateurs mostly out of doors (Calgari, *Die vier Literaturen der Schweiz*, p. 237). The parody includes the irreverent treatment of heroics.

[5] The inherent Swiss qualities are a major argument in articles defending *Hercules* (A. J. Seiler, *National-Zeitung*, March 26, 1963; Wollenberger, *Zürcher Woche*, March 29). Wollenberger finds the play "light, brilliant and elegant." Arnold supposes that the play was also taken as an insult in patriotic circles (*F.D.*, p. 83).

motivates the myth with chance. President Augias brings Phyleus, the rejected bridegroom, into his secret garden and exhorts him to work patiently turning manure into humus. The age of heroics is over,[6] politics means fulfilling one's minor duties every day. Phyleus does not listen to his father; a change made after the opening night shows him striding to his death.[7] Dürrenmatt's satire closes with a sermon.

A country covered with manure: a satirical artistic invention. In its own negative terms, satire is a sermon; combining it with a straightforward sermon leads to two strong points of view being placed side by side. A twist from one style to another is an artistic weapon of high, even explosive force; it is used as such in a great many works by Dürrenmatt. Yet a tragicomic mixture of satire and sermon makes an impossible cocktail. Moreover, Augias' sermon on proportion, on a theory of relativity, is delivered in the middle of a topsy-turvy, disproportionate world of comedy. An extravaganza is closed with a speech for moderation. A conscious paradox? Probably. Not, however, a paradox that would be artistically fruitful. The end of *Hercules* is unbelievable, yet not true: true in the sense of being artistically consistent and convincing.[8]

The impression of a stylistic incongruity is greater in the stage version of *Hercules* than in the radio play. The stage made the satire more concrete, thus widening the gap between the various elements discernible in other scenes of the

[6] Walter H. Sokel has compared *Hercules* with seven other plays treating the same topic. Dürrenmatt is closest to Euripides in his rejection and parody of the myth and its heroics (Joachim Schondorff, ed., *Herakles*, pp. 9–39).

[7] Heinz Liepman reports this change (*Die Weltwoche*, May 10, 1963). Cf. Wyrsch, part six, *Schweizer Illustrierte*, April 22, 1963.

[8] Luft (*Die Welt*, March 22, 1963) reacts strongly against the end: there are "false bells ringing" in "a paradise of little tracts." Brock-Sulzer calls the end "too surprising" in a spontaneous defense of the play (*Schweizerische Theaterzeitung*, April, 1963), yet withdraws this criticism in her book. The revised finale is judged as "dignified, courageous, wise and adequately formed" (*F.D.*, p. 144).

290

play, too.[9] Most markedly, "the best possible turn"[10] at the
end is placed in alien surroundings. Something similar had
happened in *Frank V*: Böckmann's death scene, with its
serious implications, did not work in its cabaret-like surroundings, in a play in which death was mostly taken as a
joke. Nor does Augias' solution in a play taking the clearing-
away of manure as an enormous, nationwide joke, built up
with the help of action, the setting, all kinds of scenic means
of expression. When a whole world of comedy has once been
thought out, a final speech cannot make it unthought. *Hercules and the Augean Stables* is a play in which Dürrenmatt's
best talent is on holiday.[11]

The murderous criticism directed against *Hercules* incited
Dürrenmatt to furnish the book version of the play with
drawings, in which he murders the critics. This may thus be
as good a place as any to say a word about Dürrenmatt's
drawings and his prefaces to certain collections of graphic art.
Most of the jackets of his books are based on sketches he
drew himself; after his decision to devote his energies to
writing, he continued to draw as a hobby. It certainly has its
effect on the scenic form of his plays that he usually starts
with and from the setting, sketching pictures for each scene.

[9] Gody Suter finds all elements of a typical Dürrenmatt play in
Hercules—yet out of order, "as if somebody had tried to write a
parody of Dürrenmatt with less useful means" (*Die Weltwoche*,
March 29, 1963). "Myth, realistic details (the manure), poetry, parody, digressions, arbitrary sequences of episodes, moralizing scenes
and sermons" might have done "if the play had some clearly central
principle of organization." Hercules has become "a sentimental philosopher of history" (Peppard, pp. 75–76).
[10] Jenny, *F.D.*, p. 92; he also remarks that the end makes the
entire action quite illogical: if Augias knew how to turn manure into
humus, why invite Hercules at all? Cf. Arnold, p. 83.
[11] The reviews of the world première were mostly poor, excelling
in refined mud-slinging (e.g., Wolff-Windegg, *Basler Nachrichten*,
March 21; Luft). Yet there were also feelings of disappointment
expressed: why had the playwright chosen to write so much below
his usual level? (Voser, *NZZ*, Kaiser, *Süddeutsche Zeitung*, Hellmuth
Karasek, *Deutsche Zeitung*, Stuttgart, all March 22).

Brock-Sulzer sees in Dürrenmatt's drawings a development parallel to his various creative phases as a writer: the early works are anxious, sinister, fantastic, apocalyptic; the later ones may rely on narrow, graceful lines combined with large white surfaces.[12] The drawings for *Hercules* belong clearly to the late ones. A memorable cover jacket is that of *The Physicists*: a mouse-like creature hanging from the lower lip of a big mouth. He takes painting seriously (G 15–17, 36).

Homeland in Posters (Die Heimat im Plakat, 1963) is a collection of satiric drawings by Dürrenmatt, originally sketched as posters for the edification of his children. The younger Dürrenmatts certainly grew up without undue respect for their teachers and without Swiss chauvinism. A series of sketches deals with a public scandal in 1963, a typhoid epidemic in the health resort of Zermatt; juxtaposing the traditional symbols of death and those of tourist propaganda: "Look for peace in Zermatt"—a coffin. Others have more general targets, such as wine advertisements. There is an arrow in the forehead of a small boy: "Tell drank Kläfner." The emphasis is on the satirical ideas rather than on their smooth execution, a principle Dürrenmatt expressed in his preface to a collection of drawings by Ronald Searle.

Searle and Paul Flora: two caricaturists in love with the grotesque, two graphic artists honored by Dürrenmatt with prefaces.[13] "Satire is a precise art, just *because* it exaggerates; only an artist seeing the shade and the ordinary at the same time is *capable* of exaggerating" (TS 290). Searle achieves black humor by making schoolgirls commit all kinds of crimes: people of our age go on murdering and torturing, schoolgirls are people, ergo they murder. The scarecrows, ravens, anarchists, or Napoleons drawn by Flora start Dürrenmatt's imagination functioning: without noticing it, he

---

[12] Brock-Sulzer, *F.D.*, pp. 256–58.
[13] Searle, *While the Little Lamp is Still Glowing* (Weil noch das Lämpchen glüht), Zurich, 1955 (1952); Flora, *City Views and Figures* (Veduten und Figuren), Zurich, 1968. There are no page numbers in Flora's and Dürrenmatt's volumes; the preface to Searle is reprinted in TS 289–90.

VICTORIES AND DEFEATS

writes stories or scenes around the pictures. Napoleon on
Saint Helena is "a drawing developed to its conclusion."
Flora is "the thinker and ponderer among the caricaturists";
he creates myths, his jokes grow ominous and poetic.[14] These
definitions are like mirrors to the man who wrote them. They
reveal Dürrenmatt's efforts to reach precision with the help
of the grotesque; or his preference for the discomforting,
dangerous art of comedy; or his ambition, not always fulfilled, to make his stage inventions grow to the dimensions
of myths, of poetry.

Hercules, with its aspiration to reach poetry, was written
by the child of nature within Dürrenmatt. It was a social
panorama; his next play *The Meteor* (1966) was to be a return to his second basic model, to a case study. It was also
a return to his youth, in a way. Writer Wolfgang Schwitter,[15]
a Nobel Prize winner and Dürrenmatt's protagonist, comes
back to the studio where he had worked forty years earlier,
before exchanging his brush for a typewriter. The abstract
painter Passap had a studio on the attic in *Once a Greek
. . .* , the writer Korbes was a Nobel Prize winner and a
monster in *Episode on an Autumn Evening*, a radio play.
The materials of *The Meteor* had thus been touched upon
before—not, however, in connection with the basic idea of
the play: resurrection.

There is just one door leading into the studio: the setting
is a claustrophobic and compressionistic dead end. The room
is inhabited by Hugo Nyffenschwander, an unsuccessful
young painter; there are nudes hanging everywhere, and Au-

[14] Cf. Dürrenmatt's homage to the humor of Varlin, published in
Loetscher, ed., *Varlin*, Zurich, 1969, pp. 54–60, reprinted in DK
47–59.
[15] Peppard (p. 81) associates the name Schwitter with German
words "schwitzen" (to sweat), "Zwitter" (a hybrid) and "Schwyzer"
(a Swiss). A fourth possibility might be artist Kurt Schwitters, a
specialist in making works of art ("Merzbilder") out of rubbish;
Zurich was a center of Dadaism (Herbert Read, *Vuosisatamme
maalaustaiteen historia*, pp. 118–20).

guste, the painter's wife, is modeling, as the first shock to the spectators—with her back, however, decently toward them. An iron stove stands in the middle of the stage, with "a fantastic pipe, divided above the stove," then twisting its way to the right side wall: an unusual, grotesque detail in Dürrenmatt's only stage picture. The only outlet upward is a twisted one. Above the roofs of apartment houses glows the stifling sun of "the longest day of the year" (M 8). See Fig. 12.

The curtain has hardly risen when Schwitter enters. He is wearing "an expensive fur coat in spite of the murderous heat" (M 8), yet he complains of the cold. He brings greetings from the other side: he has risen from the dead. Or has he? All we know for sure is that his 'death' took place in the hospital a few hours earlier; when left alone, he crept from below the wreaths and took a bus to the studio of his youth, where he wants to die without the pomp and publicity surrounding the passing of a Nobel Prize winner. This is his second "last" wish, so to speak. He is rather fond of dying: "The thoughts one gets, the inhibitions one gets rid of, the insights that dawn upon one. Simply great" (M 11). Having hired the atelier for ten minutes, he lies down on the bed and starts waiting for death.

It never comes. We have arrived at the basic situation of the play: Wolfgang Schwitter cannot die. Yet he sows death all around: when the action is over and the losses are counted, there are four bodies lying in various corners, in addition to three people killed professionally. "Resurrection is something terrible," Dürrenmatt has explained.[16] Like a meteor, like this terrifying natural event, Schwitter develops "an immense energy" when approaching the end of his life: he burns everybody in the vicinity.[17] They have been chosen by chance alone.

[16] In an interview with Jenny (*Theater heute*, 7, 2, Feb. 1966, p. 11).

[17] This is how the name of the play is explained by Loetscher in an article based partly on discussions with Dürrenmatt and published in the Zurich playbill (pp. 1–4). The metaphor has been used elsewhere, too: "I shall fall like a shining meteor through your nights"

The first choice is the Reverend Emanuel Lutz. He has "a kind, almost childlike appearance," slim and fair (M 14). Having testified to Schwitter's death in the hospital Lutz is now to bear witness to his resurrection. Dürrenmatt needed a clergyman to suggest the possibility that Schwitter rose from the dead, and there he stands behind the door of the studio, quite by chance, ready to rejoice at the divine miracle. Schwitter takes his case to be one of faulty diagnosis: "Resurrected! I! From the dead! What a joke!" (M 18). Which of these versions are we to believe? Dürrenmatt presents both.

Lutz kindly assists Schwitter to burn his last manuscripts and his whole property, some one and a half million in bank notes, in the stove. After that Lutz is ready to die, a victim of the happy commotion:[18] it would now be so much easier to preach about resurrection. A farcical scene follows in which four characters are needed to carry away Lutz's dead body. This is part of Schwitter's unscrupulous arrangements: never mind anybody else, as long as this monster of a Nobel Prize winner can die "in *his* bed and in *his* manner."[19] Schwitter's sudden outbursts of activity change everything in the studio at regular intervals: the curtains are drawn and opened, pieces of furniture shuffled back and forth, solemn candles lit and put out. Nothing helps. Up he pops again, ready for his next chance encounter.

The choice of Lutz gives the impression of chance being manipulated by the playwright. Dürrenmatt succeeds better with his next character. "Big" Muheim, an eighty-year-old building contractor, happens to own this tenement house. Schwitter tells him quite casually that he used to deceive him with Muheim's dear departed wife forty years earlier. The

(Esg 19), Bockelson exclaims; cf. TS 69. Peppard calls the meteor inappropriate as a symbol of chance, "since Schwitter neither burns luminously nor disappears" (p. 78).

[18] Melchinger remarks that this is the only death directly caused by Schwitter's resurrection ("Ds Salto mortale," *Theater heute*, 7, 3, March 1966, p. 18).

[19] Karl Fehr in his review (*Der Landbote*, Winterthur, Feb. 18, 1966).

wife turns out to be the soft spot in the armor of this hard businessman, and so his world collapses irrevocably. Schwitter's fourth wife is Olga, a nineteen-year-old former call-girl, a lovely and faithful wish-fulfillment. Not, however, for Schwitter any more: he drives her away quite brutally—surprisingly, to commit suicide. Schwitter's monomaniac death wish dictates all his deeds. He can terrorize everybody, because he is about to die. In Fig. 13 he is with Olga.

This is what Schwitter's only son Jochen, a playboy, finds out in his scene with his papa. There is no money to be inherited, there is only ash in the stove. Schwitter pours out his disgust with life in general, his own in particular, not only by deeds but also through venomous remarks. Success, prizes, and publicity have spoiled his life: "A writer who embraces our modern society is corrupted for all times" (M 33). The only creature he still endures is Mrs. Nyffenschwander. Act I of *The Meteor* ends with Auguste's obediently taking off her clothes, while Schwitter is waiting on his would-be deathbed. The curtain fell on a murder in Act I of *The Physicists*, now it falls on another kind of act.

The next twist in Schwitter's upward journey shows him lying on the bed covered by wreaths. When the curtain rises on Act II, the studio is full of gentlemen in black; photographs are taken, and Friedrich Georgen, a star critic, makes a quasi-acclamatory speech in honor of the deceased. Toying with certain key concepts in Dürrenmatt's dramaturgy, such as despair, reality, justice, senselessness, belief, moralist, nihilism, and grotesque, the speech creates a strong impression of self-parody. "His theater, not reality, is grotesque" (M 41). Dürrenmatt has been ready to confess certain similarities between Schwitter and himself, yet has denied a complete identification.[20]

[20] The numerous parallels between Schwitter's and Dürrenmatt's biographies are summarized by Usmiani ("F.D. as Wolfgang Schwitter," *Modern Drama*, *11*, 2, Sept. 1968, pp. 143–50). Dürrenmatt has explained that he did not want to leave himself outside his play,

Carl Koppe, Schwitter's publisher, thanks the critic for his speech: "splendidly defined and malevolently phrased" (M 41). The public figures of the literary establishment, seen by Dürrenmatt in a satirical light, make their exits, and the Nyffenschwander family starts clearing the air. It only grows thicker: Auguste is proud of her adultery with Schwitter, and leaves her untalented husband on the spot, taking her twin babies with her. The stage is set for Schwitter's next resurrection: up he gets, and starts instructing Nyffenschwander how to rearrange the furniture. He could not die, because the bed was not in its usual place.

Dürrenmatt's enthusiasm for his own surprising inventions now leads him to frequent repetitions. The stage effect of Schwitter's constant dyings and awakenings is no easy matter to assess: repetitions may be either funny or silly. Brock-Sulzer gives special praise to the scenic image of this awakening: the boastful speech means that Schwitter's efforts to escape from "literature" have been in vain, and his simple statement about the bed leads to a phase of absurdly comic action.[21] His egoism is endless and irresistible: Nyffenschwander, with his marriage just broken by Schwitter, can only follow his orders, quite involuntarily. When this phase of stage business is over, the painter returns to his major concern and threatens his unwelcome guest with a poker. Schwitter has nothing against being killed, yet the scene is interrupted by Muheim, by another manipulated surprise entrance. Muheim, though deadly jealous of Schwitter, cannot stand a dying man's being assaulted. His interference leads to unexpected results: he throws the painter down the stairs, with fatal consequences.

Muheim never finds out the truth about his late wife. Perhaps Schwitter slept with her, perhaps the entire story

as a "not engaged moralizing spectator" (interview with Rainer Litten, *Heim & Leben*, Feb. 5, 1966). Melchinger (p. 16) remarks that Dürrenmatt uses himself as his materials, exposing "himself to his own powers of invention."

[21] *Schweizerische Theaterzeitung, 21*, 2 (Feb. 1966), p. 30.

was just a fabrication. Muheim is taken away by the police, accused of having killed Nyffenschwander: both are destroyed by their chance meetings with Schwitter, our fateful meteor. This pattern is to be repeated three times before the final curtain.[22] Professor Schlatter, a surgeon of worldwide reputation: killed professionally by his repeated false diagnoses. Publisher Koppe: thoroughly ruined as a part-owner of the million and a half francs. Mrs. Nomsen, a lavatory attendant from the Hotel Bellevue and Schwitter's mother-in-law: suddenly dead in her armchair.

Mrs. Nomsen is the last secondary character to enter the studio, tell the story of her life, and die. The artificiality of this arrangement is somewhat reduced by the fact that Schwitter establishes contact with her, thus allowing Dürrenmatt to develop one of his themes fully. Mrs. Nomsen, in a grey dress, with pinks in her hand, meets her son-in-law for the first time. She brings greetings from an underworld of crime and prostitution, a contrast to the high-brow death ceremonies with wreaths from UNESCO or the Nobel committee. She mourns for Olga: it was a fatal error for a high-class call-girl, carefully trained by her mother, to get married. "You, as a writer, did you ever afford yourself feelings in your profession? One must not have feelings, one has to make them. If the customer demands" (M 67).

Following this philosophy of life had made Madame Nomsen, who is as hard as nails, the owner of two villas and an office building in the city center.[23] Captured by the disillusioned parallels between their careers, Schwitter falls into a self-confession, into an anti-sermon. He speaks like a criminal from Dürrenmatt's detective stories. Never mind guilt, expiation, justice, grace, love; life is "cruel, blind and transi-

[22] These repetitions have been criticized, e.g., by Karasek. A wicked theme is treated on the level of trite contemporary jokes, and Act II just repeats the amusement (*Stuttgarter Zeitung*, Jan. 24, 1966). Cf. Kaiser, *Süddeutsche Zeitung*, Jan. 22–23.
[23] Schwitter and Nomsen are Dürrenmattian monsters, comic in their sincerity, terrifying in their immorality (Profitlich, *F.D.*, pp. 86–88).

tory. It depends upon chance." He has been surrounding himself with the over-logical creations of his imagination, he has not been reaching reality, which appears only in her "blue-tiled underworld." "Death is the only reality. . . . I'm not afraid of it any more" (M 68). Madame Nomsen does not listen to Schwitter's moment of truth: she is dead.[24]

There is not much to add: a judgment on Schwitter's life's work is declared by his disinherited son Jochen: "You're out of fashion, old man. . . . The world wants to have hard facts, not invented stories. Documents, not legends. Knowledge, not entertainment" (M 69). And, as a final ironic twist, the stage is filled by a chorus of Salvation Army officers, by a group honestly believing in Schwitter's resurrection.[25] Their pious psalm is no answer to his last exclamation: "When shall I finally perish!" (M 71).

It is possible to read in Jochen's words a joking and self-depreciatory reflection of Dürrenmatt's own situation in 1966. He had to make his return to his home theater in a changed situation: 1963–66, the years since *Hercules*, saw the beginning of a new phase in the history of German drama.[26] *The Deputy* by Rolf Hochhuth, *In the Matter of J. Robert Oppenheimer* by Heinar Kipphardt, *Marat/Sade*

[24] Luft calls the end downright "painful" in its effort to be profound (*Die Welt*, Jan. 22, 1966), Hugo Leber suspects that the Nomsen scene comes too late and deviates too sharply from its surroundings (*Tages-Anzeiger*, Jan. 22). The scene "fell into a vacuum": the spectators were acclimatized to shock effects, yet now they were supposed to listen and reflect (Voser, *NZZ*, Jan. 21). "Compared with the whole, the words have too little weight" (Arnold, p. 86).

[25] Brock-Sulzer says that it was not Dürrenmatt's purpose to ridicule the Salvation Army; she rejects the gross interpretation of this scene in Zurich (*Die Tat*, Jan. 23). Albert Schulze Vellinghausen accepts the treatment of the scene (*Theater heute*, 7, 3, March 1966, p. 17).

[26] "A renaissance of German drama has now begun," Henry Beissel writes in 1965. A national trauma had been healed, *Marat/Sade* was a proof of "the growing maturity of the German theatre" ("Between Two Nightmares," *Seminar*, *1*, 2, Fall 1965, p. 67, footnote).

DÜRRENMATT

and *The Investigation* by Peter Weiss, and *The Plebeians Rehearse the Uprising* by Günther Grass, all more or less documentary plays, were produced during these years.[27] Was Dürrenmatt's grotesque comedy style becoming out-dated? These were not fruitful years for him; he was also disturbed by the death of several close friends. This might account for part of the bitterness and introverted self-examination prevalent in *The Meteor*. Apart from this, the play is more open to contradictory critical and stage interpretations than any other of Dürrenmatt's plays since his first two efforts.[28]

First of all, the possible social relevance of the play. It has been suggested that *The Meteor* describes a society in which "man cannot die in peace any more," and a society that downgrades the work of its artists to the level of comic enterprise.[29] If so, if the only or main raison d'être of the play is criticism against our present-day death rites or of literary hero-worship, then Dürrenmatt marshals quite an assembly of characters and events to make a fairly slight point. Social comments are definitely a side issue in *The Meteor*.

More conspicuously, *The Meteor* is a play for actors. Or for one star actor and a company of supporting players. The acting qualities inherent in the play and in its central role have been universally acknowledged and praised.[30] It is no exaggeration to speak of a "star role," or of moments comic in such an irresistible way that they could be invented only

[27] Ernst Schumacher, accusing *The Meteor* of a lack of social commitment, compares it with still another contemporary play: *More Than Life-Size, Mr. Krott* by Martin Walser ("Der Dichter als sein Henker," *Sinn und Form, 18*, 1966, Sonderheft I, p. 776).

[28] "This play gives the interpretation hard nuts to crack. Is it a metaphysical joke? A blasphemy? Does it play old Harry with the mystery of death? Or is it indeed a Christian play?" (Kurt Weibel, "Der gläubige D.," *TV-Radio-Zeitung*, Feb. 12–18, 1966, p. 37). Cf. Wehrli, "Gut christlich," *Theater heute, 7*, 3, March 1966, p. 17.

[29] Ernst Kux, "Der Meteor schlägt ein," *Epoca*, April 1966, p. 18. Cf. Krywalski, "Säkularisiertes Mysterienspiel?" *Stimmen der Zeit, 92*, 5, May 1967, p. 356.

[30] Hans Rudolf Hilty has characterized the play both as "a gaily iridescent bubble" void of social commitment and as "splendid theater for the actors" (*Volksrecht*, Zurich, Jan. 22, 1966).

300

by Dürrenmatt.[31] This time he also plays quite a lot with props: paintings are turned toward the walls and back, pieces of furniture are afloat, and the family idyll of the painter is expressed by napkins hanging in the studio. Contrasting lighting effects are built up with the help of candles and curtains. "Picture-like situations drive the action forward."[32]

On the other hand: do we not get rather an overdose of both elements? Of the actor's art and of clever scenic situations? When played with vitality and imagination, Schwitter is bound to be a tragicomic star role, dominating other characters—to the point of scant motivation. Has he not been, due to his resurrection, such a force of nature for Dürrenmatt, that we are supposed merely to follow his reactions with awe and amusement, without further question? The play just registers Schwitter's caprices, not caring to make them consistent or probable. In a way, everything is to be accepted without specified motives: Schwitter's rejection of his fourth wife, his disgust with his son, his sudden passion for Auguste, his outbursts of activity. All the time this star role is spoonfed by the playwright: the secondary characters are brought in only to reveal some additional facet in Schwitter's life.[33] They are supposed to be propelled by blind chance; they are propelled by Schwitter. The play manipulates more openly than *The Physicists*, Dürrenmatt's preceding compressionist play. A meteor crushing a puppet theater: this is the event described in the play. Dürrenmatt sentimentalizes Schwitter with the help of his subordinate characters; this is in contrast to the mercilessness of his tone of voice. A stageful of figures

---

[31] Bänziger, *Frisch und D.*, p. 193; Kaiser, loc. cit.

[32] Manuel Gassner, *Weltwoche*, Jan. 28, 1966; cf. Peppard, p. 81.

[33] Mayer has found a possible model for the structure of *The Meteor*: the expressionistic "play of positions" (Stationenstück). Schwitter is made to "face all positions and constellations of his life": the atelier, the son, the fourth wife, his modest beginnings, and world reputation. The scenes are not, however, scattered throughout society but brought together into the atelier ("Komödie, Trauerspiel," *Theater heute*, 7, 3, March 1966, pp. 23–24).

301

is used to build up a portrait of the artist as a middle-aged Nobel Prize winner wanting desperately to die. It is as if Schwitter existed most intensely on the level of the theater, as a star role.

The merits of *The Meteor* are in its individual scenes, not in its total structure.[34] Some of its striking, personal, and amusing details have been described above; let us add one more sample of gallows humor. Muheim, revengeful yet firmly determined not to touch the dying writer, is waiting for death to come. It takes its time, and our businessman grows impatient:

> MUHEIM: Go ahead and die!
> SCHWITTER: Doesn't work.
> MUHEIM: I'm waiting.
> SCHWITTER: Feeling in fact quite OK.
> MUHEIM *(frightened)*: Damn it (M 50).

The passage is not an emotional climax; it just uses the basic paradoxical situation of the play in a funny and effective way.[35] It speaks more loudly with its visual ingredients than with its commonplace dialogue, and so it is throughout *The Meteor*. There is nothing wrong with Dürrenmatt's stage imagination; there are unevennesses in his ability to put his pieces together. What does the play add up to? What is the sense of the above and other similar details? Of Schwitter's resurrection?

When preparing for a public discussion on *The Meteor* Dürrenmatt made an effort to justify the idea behind the

---

[34] Wollenberger declares the play a masterpiece, not quite knowing why. Possibly because it made "splendid theater out of its splendid theatrical invention"; the deeper significance of the play was a side issue (*Zürcher Woche*, Jan. 28, 1966). Leber states that there are questions left open, Voser that the theme is sacrificed to theatrical effects. Georges Schlocker calls *The Meteor* "leaves from a scenic sketchbook" (*Handelsblatt*, Düsseldorf, Jan. 26).

[35] This passage is chosen for special praise by Mayer.

play.[36] Early in his "Twenty Points" he states the demand that everything in a play must stem logically from the idea behind it. The idea of *The Meteor* is "the story of a man who is resurrected and who does not believe his resurrection." Resurrection is a miracle, Schwitter "a double scandal": for some because resurrected, for others "as a person who does not believe." At the same time he is a paradoxical, tragicomic "figure of the Christian Western world." "Christianity believes in the promised resurrection of man at the Last Judgment—the question is only to what degree Christians today believe it." Because Schwitter cannot trust other people, he isolates himself. "Dying is the last possible isolation. In dying, man becomes a total individual. Schwitter isolates himself twice: by not believing and by believing that he is dying." *The Meteor* can be "criticized, that is to say, scrutinized," only on the basis of these points. It is also to be remembered that "a play is the transformation of an idea into something absolutely spontaneous."

Let us go ahead with our scrutiny. It is an old rule (and valid, even if both old and a rule) that the very first moments are decisive for the impression we get from a stage character. Schwitter, this "figure who symbolizes modern Christianity," uses his first minutes to tell who he is, to admire the naked breasts and other merits of Mrs. Nyffenschwander (their going to bed together proves Schwitter's isolation beyond reasonable doubt), to hire the studio for ten minutes in order to die there, and to recite a speech on the great feeling one gets at the moment of death. Sitting in a dark corner of the auditorium Dürrenmatt sighs to his spectators: don't you see? He is a resurrected man who does not believe his resurrection.

Schwitter's disbelief in his resurrection is quite a marginal phenomenon in *The Meteor*. It is touched upon in two scenes,

---

[36] These "Twenty Points" were originally published in the *NZZ*, Feb. 28, 1966, reprinted in DK 156–61. My quotations are from a translation into English published by Peppard, pp. 142–44.

those with Lutz and Schlatter; yet the play as a whole and those very scenes are too full of other ideas to allow this decisive piece of information to leave a mark on one's mind. The discussion with Lutz is furnished with the additional action of burning the money. Even if the stage were an aquarium, it could not be fuller of red herrings. In his "Points," however, Dürrenmatt bases quite fine distinctions on Schwitter's disbelief.

Moreover, Dürrenmatt has made it next to impossible for his spectators to believe that Schwitter was genuinely resurrected.[37] If the first occurrence in the hospital is counted, Schwitter is supposed to die six times; four times under the very eyes of the spectators. Six cases of resurrection? Or two cases of it, officially certified by medicine, and four mistakes? Why should the resurrection be repeated at all? Dürrenmatt attaches specific hopes to Schwitter's awakening early in Act II: this is a moment of genuine resurrection,[38] preceded by a medical examination, decorated with the wreaths and the speech. Yet the spectators, acclimatized by the earlier awakenings, are bound to take it as another repetition, another mistake. Because of this, *The Meteor* loses its serious Christian overtones. If the basic invention of a play includes a miracle, the playwright should take great care in making this miracle plausible. Instead, Dürrenmatt jokes at the expense of his own invention. My source materials include no review of the Zurich première interpreting Schwitter's resurrection as genuine.[39] The play is ambiguous, the "Points" are unequivocal.

[37] Schwitter's reactions include "no sense at all of the miraculous or religious" (Peppard, p. 85).

[38] In an interview with Mayer, the Zurich playbill, p. 6. Having done his best to accept the play, Spycher retains some doubt at this point (Knapp, ed., *F.D.*, p. 181).

[39] According to unanimous reports, Schweikart gave his production a fresh expression in Munich by taking Schwitter's resurrection in earnest. This was shown both in the acting of Paul Verhoeven and in the reactions of the secondary characters, also greatly developed in other respects, e.g., through silent acting (Kaiser, *Süddeutsche Zeitung*, Feb. 14, 1966; Johannes Jacobi, *Die Zeit*, Feb. 18; Jenny,

The resurrected man needs, of course, individuality, character, profession, sex life, relatives, etc. Could not Dürrenmatt have made these a little closer to an ordinary "figure of the Christian Western world," even if less colorful, less shocking? Instead he went to extremes in every respect. Schwitter is "a total individual" sowing destruction and death all around, he is a brute, a Nobel Prize winner, and a he-man for whom the wife of a man falls on his very deathbed. His fourth wife is a call-girl, his mother-in-law a lavatory attendant and his only son a caricature. Such a man represents only himself; his sound and fury signifies nothing outside his thunderous stage personality.[40] Going to extremes at every point must leave the middle empty. The only suggestion that Schwitter "symbolizes modern Christianity" is included in the "Points," not in the text of the play.

It is as if Dürrenmatt had been interested only or mainly in the characters' various reactions to Schwitter's resurrection. They range from disbelief (Schwitter himself) to pious belief (Lutz and the Salvation Army), from cynical amusement (Koppe) to scientific curiosity (Schlatter). Dürrenmatt probably hoped that his artistic invention would be taken by the spectators as Claire was taken in *The Visit*: as a starting-point for an experiment in thought. The contents of that experiment: "to what degree" do "Christians today" believe in resurrection? In executing his experiment Dürrenmatt was guilty of several miscalculations. Resurrection is such a sensational stage event that it is difficult for the spectators to concentrate only on its consequences. They have the right to ask whether the miracle is intended to be genuine or not. Moreover, too much attention is stolen by the genuine and

---

Theater heute, 7, 3, March 1966). Jacobi's headline is "The Theater Helps the Playwright."

[40] Peppard, p. 83, finds an "emphasis on a strictly personal fate and an individual death. Schwitter does not suggest anything more in his person than what he is. . . . A comedy about death requires some representative individual to express it and experience it." Schumacher (p. 777) speaks about "the quasi-problems of resurrection . . . lacking every possible generalizing feature."

farcical death scenes of almost all the other characters and by the colorful events of Schwitter's biography, taken, as it were, directly from the popular press.

Dürrenmatt's plays are full of monomaniacs, most of them with strong inclinations to cause the death of other characters. When the playwright took up the theme of a modern Lazarus it was somehow self-evident to him that Schwitter was to be a monomaniac falling into raptures at the mere thought of death. It was equally clear that everybody in Schwitter's vicinity was to be in mortal danger. This is, however, a non sequitur. A man is resurrected; it does not follow that he would persistently want to die, even less that he would be a meteor burning everyone around him to death. The first half of Dürrenmatt's paradox was that a man resurrected wants to die;[41] to furnish this paradox with another half, he imagined a group of characters not wanting to die, yet killed by the resurrected man. This is unbelievable; is it also true? How great a portion of our common human reality is included in Dürrenmatt's paradox?

In his interview with Jenny, Dürrenmatt stated that the value of a good invention "depends on how much reality is caught through it."[42] By this very criterion the invention of *The Meteor* is not a good one. We know nothing at all about how one of us might experience resurrection or death; Schwitter's situation is bound to remain remote from us. It does not capture our reality. Things are not helped by the extreme circumstances of his life. He is in every respect an exceptional man, "a total individual." As such he is as far from our reality as the murdering bankers of *Frank V.* Supposing a man like Schwitter were resurrected: would it be an idea enlightening our reality that a group of other characters, by chance, or by the manipulating hand of a playwright, die all

---

[41] Point 15 is quite vaguely reasoned. Schwitter's "despair is the fact that he must die." Schwitter disagrees: he despairs because his death "never works all right" (M 45). Throughout the play he tries to die, not to survive, with a singular determination.

[42] *Theater heute*, Feb. 1966, p. 11.

of a sudden? This throws light on nothing; it only means that the improbabilities are lifted to their third degree.

The thought behind *The Meteor* is full of holes.[43] When transforming his idea "into something absolutely spontaneous" Dürrenmatt was misled by his aspiration to reach the absolute, and by his spontaneity.[44] He has never lacked ambition: death and resurrection are themes worthy of his courage, his world-wide imagination. When treating these themes he achieved a series of wild, extreme, and shocking scenes, spontaneous in the sense that his ability to replace the pity and fear of tragedy with the laughter and fear of tragicomedy is always present on his stage. His background and his foreground, his idea and its concretization on the stage, are not in balance.[45] Something similar had happened in *Mississippi*, a play reminiscent of *The Meteor* also in its arbitrariness and in its awesome, darkly grotesque atmosphere. Both are black cabaret plays; *Hercules* is light-hearted.

What there is to admire in *The Meteor* are its many striking details, its powerful roles, its mastery of the stage, and its paradoxical final impression.[46] There is a vital imagination

[43] George Salmony sees the play as a "thought construction weakly riveted together. . . . *The Meteor* exaggerates provocation up to a conscious scandal" (*Epoca*, April 1966, pp. 24, 26).

[44] *NZZ* (Feb. 28, 1966) includes a report by Wilfried Spinner on the public discussion where Dürrenmatt read his "Twenty Points" and made a difference between the idea of his play and its execution. There is indeed a difference, according to Jenny wider than anywhere else in Dürrenmatt: chance is employed in a mechanical way to connect situations chosen quite arbitrarily (*Die Zeit*, Jan. 28).

[45] "The provocation of resurrection, however, where did it remain? . . . What was played on the foreground was modern man's lacking or false relation to death, not his nonexistent relation to resurrection" (Manuel Isler, "Nicht sterben können," *National-Zeitung*, Jan. 24). Dürrenmatt made it easy for the majority of his spectators "to take delight in a drastic foreground" (Iso Keller, *Neue Zürcher Nachrichten*, Jan. 22).

[46] *The Meteor* was received in London less enthusiastically than *The Visit* or *The Physicists*, according to summaries of reviews published in *Süddeutsche Zeitung*, Aug. 3, 1966, and *Weltwoche*, Aug. 26.

present, an imagination impressive through its sheer ability to overpower—running amok, yet irrefutably an artist's imagination. The use of the stage, of various scenic means of expression, is not problematic for Dürrenmatt;[47] it is his story material that makes his works in the 1960's problematic for him and his audiences. Are they no longer appropriate as demonstrations of his ideas and themes? Has something gone wrong, is Dürrenmatt's theater growing out of and losing contact with his literature? Is he just play-acting, lifting sets up and down, because he is unable to find a framework for his seriousness? The next thing he undertook was to put one of his old stage stories to the test of his present craftsmanship as a writer for the stage.

[47] "The scenic constellations are by far superior to the words. . . . The characters of Dürrenmatt, a mediocre rhetorician, never catch up with what Dürrenmatt, by no means a mediocre artist, has already been able to make clear in a splendid way during the first moments of their stage appearance" (Kaiser).

14 His Own Dramaturge

THE ANABAPTISTS

‖‖

Every second play a social panorama: this was Dürrenmatt's formula in the middle 1960's.[1] *Die Wiedertäufer* (The Anabaptists, first performed in March 1967) is a thoroughly rewritten version of the panoramic *It Is Written*, discussed on pp. 44–60. Wolfgang Schwitter returns to the studio of his youth, Dürrenmatt to his very first play. Both feel at home and start making changes, shuffling things back and forth, rearranging the lighting. Dürrenmatt does not try to die; on the contrary, he even permits his guilty protagonist Johann Bockelson to survive the blood-bath following the siege and conquest of the city of Münster. The reason for his survival: he is such a superb actor.

The Anabaptists also marks the beginning of a new and productive phase in Dürrenmatt's work. During the previous seven years, 1960–66, he had let his theoretical writings be collected in an anthology and published three plays; of these, one (*Hercules*) was an adaptation of his earlier radio play. In the seven years to come (1967–73) he was to publish two new original plays, a novel, a travel book, a long essay, a further volume of theoretical treatises, and no fewer than six stage adaptations, of which only *The Anabaptists* is based on an earlier text of his own. After seven meager years Dürrenmatt entered a new period of plenty, almost comparable, quantitatively speaking, with his great decade of 1948–57. The number of adaptations is greater than that of new plays:

---

[1] In his 1966 interview with Sauter Dürrenmatt characterized his two basic types of play. *The Meteor* and *The Physicists* are "strictly composed works" written "entirely from a certain idea"; the other possibility is to take "the theater as a great narrative form," playing with it, writing "with a great many characters, scenes, various colors" (*Sinn und Form, 18,* 4, p. 1226).

this was to become Dürrenmatt's dramaturgic phase. The story of *The Meteor* had not concretized his ideas; now he was to mold stories by others to fit his ideas.

The change from Dürrenmatt's earlier practice is one of degree, not of principle. He had rewritten some of his plays for major revivals; *Mississippi, Hercules, Die Panne,* and *The Pledge* were revised for various purposes. *Donkey's Shadow* was his first adaptation of a classic; elsewhere, he had preferred writing counter-sketches or parodies of entire literary genres, not of particular works of art. *Frank V*, with its problematic relations to *The Threepenny Opera*, is an exception. Dürrenmatt's dramatic adaptations of classics were to become counter-sketches openly acknowledged; his polemical inclinations were to flourish in tensions between the sources and his own ideas. He was not to develop into a Stanislavskian adapter, so to speak—it was not his method to enter the skin of another writer so completely that he could be regarded as a reincarnation. Rather, he was to adopt the position of a Brechtian actor, demonstrating his criticism of his roles, of his sources. First of all, the Dürrenmatt of 1966–67 was to look back at the Dürrenmatt of 1946–47. *The Anabaptists* is an encounter between these two writers.

Dürrenmatt twenty years older is twenty years wiser in his use of the stage. *The Anabaptists* is a technically much more advanced play than *It Is Written*. There is no surplus of monologues: direct addresses to the public are mostly eliminated, epic elements are dramatized into scenes, and excessive verbiage is replaced by a direct and functional dialogue.[2] *It Is Written* opened with three unnamed anabaptists delivering a Brueghelian apocalyptic prologue consisting of poetry-reading rather than of dialogue. The introduction of the adaptation describes the arrival of seven named leaders of the anabaptists at Münster: their speeches are short, and the role

[2] "Reports were turned into stage action," lyrical outbursts replaced by reflection (Martin Schaub, *Handelsblatt*, Düsseldorf, March 22, 1967).

of the fraudulent Bockelson is started right away by giving him all the pious phrases. Of the 62 lines of this sequence, 17 are taken from *It Is Written*, either as such or in a changed form. This is how Dürrenmatt proceeded in his dramaturgic work: the amorphous scenes of his source, often continued beyond their actual contents, were replaced by shorter glimpses including both old and new materials. The scenes are numbered from 1 to 20, and given headings. The story is orchestrated around the leading figures of Bockelson, Matthison, Knipperdollinck, and the Bishop. Somewhat surprisingly, there is only one short scene (Sc. 10) not derived from the original text.

Technical changes are bound to affect the contents, too. *It Is Written* is a religious play, dealing with the various wrong ways and dead ends people choose when trying to fulfill God's orders as written in the Bible. The dictatorship of the anabaptists led to terrorism and the sufferings of the innocent in the Germany of the 1530's; this framework is retained. Yet there are new colors on Dürrenmatt's palette: he now takes the rebellion more in social than in religious terms. Social causes are mentioned from the fifth line of *The Anabaptists* onward. There is a short report on the farmers' rebellion, caused by the avarice of "the Pope, the Kaiser, the Prince, the Lutheran, the merchant, the judge and the mercenary" (W 11). "Épater le bourgeois" had always been Dürrenmatt's motto; now he is more willing than before to irritate his middle-class audiences with social causes, with the contrast between the rich and the poor; the mighty and the powerless; the Catholic, Lutheran, or political superstructures of the society and the commoners of Münster. The princes gathered around Karl V take no interest whatsoever in the dilemma of the Bishop, until he mentions that the anabaptists have introduced communal ownership of property. This hits the gathering like a bomb, and the Bishop gets what he wants.

Dürrenmatt's special interest lies, however, in the position of the artist, of the intellectual. *The Anabaptists* is partly his reaction to the atmosphere of the late 1960's, with its wave

311

of documentary theater, its heated discussion on political issues among intellectuals, and its restlessness that was to lead to the chaotic year of 1968 in France. Dürrenmatt's references to class contrasts are vignettes rather than a main issue; his masses are without a fixed purpose.[3] The paradox of the rebellion of the anabaptists, its hysterical mixture of the consciousness of sin and gross intolerance, are expressed in a couple of lines uttered first by Bockelson, then by a chorus. "Repent! Repent! Be converted!" In the same breath these prophets curse their enemies, whether Catholics or Lutherans: "May they be damned! Damned!" (W 12).

Bockelson, now turned into a professional actor, uses his talent in rhetoric to stir up the masses. An individual faces a crowd: a classic situation in Dürrenmatt. When the curtain rises, the anabaptists have not yet established their power in Münster; this helps Dürrenmatt to make the early scenes more dynamic. The city fathers arrive at a Council meeting in procession, carrying crosses; during the meeting they reassemble as a procession, this time with burning candles in their hands. Their leader is Matthison, a monomaniac "enlightened by God" (W 33). The city is proclaimed New Jerusalem at the meeting, and Bockelson pushes through Matthison's irrational decree that the city was not to be defended against the enemy, thus assuring Matthison's death and his own accession to power. Hans Zicklein, a former monk and an avowed humanist, is a counterpart to Bockelson. Sentenced to death, he barely escapes the masses in an expansively conceived execution scene on the market place, and joins the besieging enemy, believing in human reason as the winning force in life. Ironically enough, this intellectual is executed by his new masters for a trifle: reason does not prevail. Cf. Fig. 1: the marketplace scene in *It Is Written*.

In the new character constellation of the play the Bishop becomes a theater lover. He made a fatal mistake in not en-

---

[3] Hilty remarks that the crowd scenes of *The Anabaptists* never show "people acting and reacting as a group in a sociological sense" (*Volksrecht*, March 23, 1967).

gaging Bockelson for his episcopal group. Zealously grasping at spectacular roles, if not on the stage then in reality, Bockelson places himself to the throne of New Jerusalem, fully enjoying the privileges of his royal position. Polygamy (he keeps sixteen wives) is for him "a problem in stage directing" (W 71). As a power maniac he is preceded in Dürrenmatt's works by Negro da Ponte, by Doctor von Zahnd, by the theater manager of the early story who also employed theatrical means to advance a political career. The Bishop is used to following theater performances at a distance, with "a pleasant thrill" (W 19); now he has to take measures against the anabaptists. Dürrenmatt's Act I is closed with his monologue, addressed to Matthison's head severed from his dead body. The Bishop is full of reluctant admiration for his adversary: "A rude fellow, perhaps . . ./Full of plans to overthrow things, surely,/Yet possessed by justice, driven by hope." For himself, the Bishop has mainly contempt; he calls himself a clown, a supporter of a rotten order, wanting "to remain reasonable amidst unreason." "What a farce!" (W 52–53).

Karl V is another guardian of order. In the monologue opening Act II he dreams about his future in a monastery: tired of governing he would walk around a statue of justice erected in an inner yard. The conference of the princes, not far from a present-day cocktail party, ends with the victory of the obstinate Bishop—and with one of the points connecting *The Anabaptists* with Hitler.[4] The Kaiser decides to nominate a nonentity as a member of the Viennese Academy of Painting so that he would be able to harm only art. Bockelson and Hitler were more harmful in the political arena.[5]

[4] Evaluating the war years once more was a general feature in the German literature of the 1960's: "All of a sudden everything is again questionable" (Mayer, *Zur deutschen Literatur der Zeit*, p. 332). Dürrenmatt had created his Hitler figure in "Theater Manager"; now he found this figure questionable again.

[5] Bockelson and Arturo Ui are "archetypes of an irresponsible tempter" in politics (Brock-Sulzer, *Die Tat*, March 20, 1967).

313

The fate of Münster has in fact been sealed. There follows a series of scenes (13–17) describing the hardships to be endured in the besieged city—not a very exciting series.[6] There are no new elements introduced: Knipperdollinck just strolls around in search of more painful poverty, Bockelson goes on with his 'dolce vita,' the commoners with their bitter lot; the all-European mercenaries and the vegetable woman, three unscrupulous war profiteers, practice their cynical professions. Judith Knipperdollinck makes an effort to kill her Holofernes, alias the Bishop: this subplot is retained, with no advantage to the play. Hymns are employed to give life to the mass scenes, and so is a collage technique reminiscent of *The Visit*, intermingling shouts, stanzas of songs, and short scenes.

The Anabaptists concludes with four final scenic images. Two are derived from *It Is Written*: the moon-dance scene of Bockelson and Knipperdollinck, the last words of the merchant on the wheel of torture. The dance, if taken seriously, may have seemed too theatrical for the Dürrenmatt of 1966; he solved the problem by theatricalizing it for good. The King and his fool meet on the stage of the episcopal theater, and Knipperdollinck challenges God: "Thunder, Almighty, thunder, break me for my sins!" Bockelson, an expert in acting: "Great. Sounded genuinely despairing. Congratulations" (W 88). And they dance, on the empty stage.

The adapter and the writer of the original are different men; this is shown beyond doubt by the above sample. The words of the only genuine God-seeker among the anabaptists are deflated by mere play-acting and become a metaphysical joke. All through the play, Knipperdollinck has been a lonely figure,[7] out of touch with the events surrounding him, even

[6] The middle section of the play is characterized as overlong or boring by Leber (*Tages-Anzeiger*, March 18) and Felix Thurner (*Luzerner Neueste Nachrichten*, March 22).

[7] Jenny calls Knipperdollinck "sadly isolated, literally a figure from another play" ("Das kleinste Risiko," *Theater heute*, 8, 4, April 1967, p. 15). Karasek finds this character quite senseless in a total

though he was given, somewhat surprisingly, the role of an agitator against the established church in Scene 3. In *It Is Written* Knipperdollinck and Bockelson were two halves of Dürrenmatt's paradox: penitent or sinner, man was struck to death by God. This paradox was hardly handled in the best possible way by the inexperienced playwright. Yet when the sinner is made merely an actor by the experienced one, that paradox dissolves altogether; there are hints of another paradox. On Dürrenmatt's stage the artist, whether a writer like Schwitter or an actor, often has a double role as a charlatan and as a despairing seeker of truth. Yet it is difficult suddenly to take Knipperdollinck as an artist, as one half in a double figure. Should he not have been entirely deleted? In the ingenious play of power politics staged by Bockelson he has no role to act; one cannot help suspecting that the moondance scene is retained mainly because of its stage effect.

Making Bockelson an actor also lessens the impact of Knipperdollinck's lines on the wheel of torture about the grace of God. This scenic image, definitely a coordinating factor in Dürrenmatt's loosely composed first play, is now preceded by Bockelson's star moment, by an amazing theatrical coup. The King of New Jerusalem opens the city gate for the enemy and delivers his last great speech. He has only been acting the role of a king, for the delight of the Princes: "The play is over . . ./I wore your mask only, I was not like you" (W 92–93). As a reward for his creative efforts he expects a laurel wreath, not the wheel of torture. And he is rewarded: declared a great artist, embraced and engaged by the cardinal.[8] Münster, his kingdom, is delivered to the plundering soldiers, their sins forgiven in advance.

These final developments are the last straw for the Bishop.

---

rejection of the play (*Stuttgarter Zeitung*, March 18), while Voser evaluates the scene as such as great, yet wonders why Knipperdollinck should fall a slave to Bockelson, and start reciting poetry "in unison with him" (*NZZ*, March 18).

[8] Leber names it Dürrenmatt's "most malicious invention" that Bockelson survives and "stays among us." Cf. Schaub, loc. cit.

Everything has gone wrong. "The blessed on the wheel, the tempter pardoned,/The tempted slaughtered, the winners disgraced by their victory" (W 94) : all this accuses the Bishop. And so our hundred-year-old Bishop pushed around in a wheelchair, an impeccable pillar of order, can only rebel; he stands up on his paralyzed legs, throws away his cross, and stamps his foot on it:

> This inhuman world must become more human
> But how? But how? (W 95).[9]

The curtain lines of *The Anabaptists* are most emphatic. The entire mad story told on the stage is crystallized in the repeated question, in this scenic image, preceded by three climaxes of stage action, by three equally important scenic images. Dürrenmatt sees the story of the anabaptists as an introduction to uncertainty, to an uncomfortable feeling that something is amiss in the world and there is no prescription available for healing it.[10] The character brought to this recognition tramples on the symbol of everything he has fought for in order to voice this crucial question.

The worldly-wise and human Bishop is doubtless the most complex character in the play.[11] Dürrenmatt sees him as "a despairing spectator, acting without conviction," yet "releas-

[9] Deschner sees the Bishop as a "man of courage" transformed by chance "into an impotent and infuriated onlooker." The play does not deal "with the man-God relation" but with man's encounter with chance and reality ("D's *Die Wiedertäufer*," *The German Quarterly*, *44*, 2, March 1971, pp. 227–34). It is questionable whether the Bishop with his despair endures his reality at all and remains "a man of courage." In late Dürrenmatt, the ends of the plays tend to grow unequivocally sinister (Profitlich, *F.D.*, pp. 96–97).

[10] The play discusses "the eternal blind absurdity of history," Jenny states, even if Dürrenmatt's postscript avoids the word "absurd," immediately associated with "absurdism" in those years (*Süddeutsche Zeitung*, Nov. 25, 1967). Hans Heinrich Brunner sees the entire play as a question to the audience ("Aber wie?" *Kirchenbote*, *53*, 4, April 1967).

[11] The Bishop is called by Brock-Sulzer "one of the richest roles Dürrenmatt has ever written" (*Die Tat*, March 21).

ing events" that make him a helpless, though rebelling, spectator (W 108). The role of the Bishop as an outsider is stressed by placing him in a wheelchair; on the other hand, he shows quite peculiar obstinacy in fighting the Münster rebellion. He is a theater-lover; his main opponent, Bockelson, is an actor. For Dürrenmatt, the history of the world, or a bloody and cruel phase representing it on his stage, is a magnificent drama. This is, of course, a possible vision written clearly enough into Dürrenmatt's adaptation. *The Anabaptists* is not muddled or obscure as *The Meteor* was. The fate of Münster staged by an actor; is this not, however, rather a cheap way, a short cut, to Dürrenmatt's vision?

Once again, Dürrenmatt goes to an extreme. He does not leave it for the audience to conclude that the history of the world is to be identified with a theatrical performance. Nor is he satisfied with letting one of his characters (the Bishop) recognize his equation. He turns his protagonist into a self-conscious actor, fully aware of the histrionic qualities in all his undertakings.[12] Bockelson shows no trace of belief in his own words or deeds, and this is a factor that tends to narrow the play down. However one interprets *The Anabaptists* or Dürrenmatt's postscript to it, the play certainly tries to build up a model of "possible human relations." Should not the relationship between an aspiring dictator and his followers be based on a mixture of sincerity and calculation, of belief in his own words and false hysteria? False in the opinion of critical onlookers, not in that of the speaker and politician himself. The Hitlers of this world as frustrated artists; a valid observation? Rather, an observation of some validity in the case of Hitler—and less interesting when generalized, when cut loose from the factual circumstances of Hitler's character or of his emergence into power. *The Anabaptists* is a broad play with a small target.

---

[12] Hitler believed in his message, Bockelson did not; Dürrenmatt draws parallels between these two. Bockelson could also have staged some other play; this makes his story lose part of its necessity (Jenny, "Das kleinste Risiko," pp. 14–15).

Dürrenmatt does not describe the rise and fall of the Reich of the anabaptists, he tells a story about an actor as their king.[13] Giving Bockelson a new function is the most questionable point in the adaptation, a new idea incompatible with the old play. Furthermore, his wildly poetic, self-possessed outbursts, a rough yet charming feature in the earlier version, were deleted and replaced by parodical quotations from roles our actor had played.[14] With his lunacy Bockelson lost a major part of his immense gusto in living, his bravado as the fullest portrayal of a nihilist, a character young Dürrenmatt felt tempted to depict over and over again. It was essential to adapt *It Is Written* before reviving it, in order to tone it down, to turn its monologues into scenes, to integrate its structure etc.; yet one cannot help feeling disappointed at the loss of poetry.[15] The hope not fulfilled by *The Anabaptists* was that the adapter might recognize the genuinely poetic values inherent in Knipperdollinck and Bockelson and turn them into dramatic poetry, through some artistic alchemy not to be envisaged by the critics. Of all possible dramaturges, the Dürrenmatt of 1967–68 was to fail.

Bockelson is also the protagonist in the postscript to the play (W 101–09, DK 162–78). Dürrenmatt tries to make his fictional world independent of our common reality, yet has to retain an umbilical cord to it: a play is "a comparison, to be thought out again and again, with the tendencies of reality" (W108). He pleads for a pure "comedy of action" (W 106), not for a mixed genre, for tragicomedy: "The

[13] "What do we care about an actor?" Heinz Beckmann asks a downright question; Bockelson bungles the entire adaptation (*Merkur*, Köln, March 26). With him, an historical vision shrinks into an aesthetic one (Durzak, *D., Frisch, Weiss*, p. 57).

[14] Kaiser regrets the loss of poetry (*Süddeutsche Zeitung*, March 18), and Luft calls Bockelson's double role too clearly transparent: the figure is "overwritten" (*Die Welt*, March 18).

[15] "As to stage techniques, *The Anabaptists* is definitely a better piece of work," speaking in "a more conventional, amusing, refined way, yet perhaps less impressively" (Arnold, *F.D.*, pp. 27, 29).

318

worst possible turn for a story to take is the turn into comedy" (W 102).[16] Yet the very word "paradox" seems to include a sinister aspect for him. It is as if he equated tragedy with illusionism, it is as if there were for him only one type of tragedy demanding from us a continuous identification with the hero. What is overlooked here is a general trend in modern drama: there are all kinds of mature hybrids of realism and theatricalism, there are tragic heroes allowing spectators both empathy and criticism.[17] One of these is Alfred Ill.

More narrowly than in *Problems of the Theater*, Dürrenmatt pleads for his own personal kind of comedy. Yet "comedy of action" is not the only possibility open to a modern playwright, as shown by Brecht, Beckett, Hochhuth, and Weiss, all remembered by Dürrenmatt in his argument. There may well be a wider margin for a writer's creative imagination or for a conscious theatricalistic stylization in comedy than in tragedy; it does not, however, follow that we should stop testing comedies with our own conception of reality. Dürrenmatt also denies that *The Anabaptists* is a parable about Hitler; yet this interpretation is supported by many a reference in the script itself.[18]

[16] Mayer accepts Dürrenmatt's definition of his intention: the serious original was turned into its own counter-sketch, into a comedy. Its end is both painful and comic, "because thoroughly mean"; the play closes with a question "according to good expressionistic manner." "One has to laugh at this story"—a joyless laughter ("F.D.," *Zeitschrift für deutsche Philologie*, 87, 4, Fall 1968, pp. 493–94, 496–97).

[17] There is a wide-ranging discussion of the combined forms of theatricalism and realism in John Gassner, *Form and Idea in the Modern Theatre*, pp. 133–224. Behind this phenomenon there is the duality of experience "for both the performer and his audience: action in the theatre is both make-believe and actual for them." "We can focus on 'real life' . . . at one point of the performance, and soon thereafter respond to a thoroughly theatrical effect which we know to be 'theatre' rather than 'real life' " (pp. 210–11).

[18] According to Voser there are so many hints to Hitler that "this special case threatens to exceed the general character of a parable" (loc. cit.).

The Anabaptists as an adaptation: there was not much shuffling of furniture or scenes from one place to another, although there was quite a lot of remodeling of them, and of giving them a modern polish in the hands of an experienced craftsman. There was a sharp change in the lighting plan for the entire play, caused by a difference of twenty years in the individual qualities of adapter and adapted. Religious problems stepped upstage, social causes toward stage center. What was a scream of horror uttered by a young idealist reared during the holocaust of World War II was turned into a skeptical and weary statement by a middle-aged practitioner of the theater with grotesque effects as his most characteristic mannerism, with no belief left in a reasonable world order.[19] What was an untroubled play of games with the beguiling possibilities of the stage, with direct addresses to the public, with many a parodical trick, was made into the self-conscious play-acting of a professional actor. The language of poetry was flattened into the jargon of the stage.

The result was a string of scenic images unanimously praised for their stage qualities.[20] The result was a somewhat shattered constellation of roles, with an actor play-acting a king, a star role whose impact cannot easily be read from the written page alone. The result in the setting of the original production was a post-Brechtian style typical of the late 1960's in Germany, with two back-drops across the stage, with wooden platforms, with iron and leather as other materials (W 99). And the result was a chronicle play not quite in focus, a play in which Dürrenmatt's customary statement about the absurdity of the world is not only a consequence of the qualities inherent in a world of comedy fully concretized, created for the stage and on the stage. It is also an

[19] Arnold arrives at a similar conclusion (p. 27).

[20] The praise was partly followed by reservations. Dürrenmatt's "unprecedented power to create images" makes him include excessive elements (Hans Elsner, *Kurier*, Wien, March 22), or gags not bound together by a total conception (Hansjürg Briggen, *Zolliker Bote*, March 23).

320

outcome of Dürrenmatt's theatrical invention, of his coup de théâtre,[21] of his "splendid" idea to make Bockelson an actor. After *The Anabaptists*, after this initial effort with a script of his own, Dürrenmatt was to continue his work as an adapter of plays by others.

[21] According to Jenny, Dürrenmatt now equates the world and the stage so that both live under the "law of maximal effect": "The worst possible turn is always also the last possible coup de théâtre that catapults the play from the area of tragedy into a despairing farce" ("Das kleinste Risiko," pp. 11, 14).

15 "Strindmatt or Dürrenberg?"

||||||||||||||||||||||||||||||||||||||||||||||||||||||||||||||||||||||||||||||||||||||||||||||||||

First his own dramaturge, then theirs. "They" include Strindberg, Shakespeare, Goethe, Büchner, and Werner Düggelin. Of them, Düggelin belongs to rather a different category. He directed the world première of *The Anabaptists* in Zurich, and the cooperation thus begun was to be continued. For Dürrenmatt, Düggelin was a new acquaintaince: a talented representative of a younger generation of stage directors, a man favoring strong colors, movement, gags, and crowd scenes. Shortly afterward he was appointed artistic director of the newly organized Basle City Theater, and at his invitation Dürrenmatt accepted a job as a resident dramaturge in Basle at the beginning of the theater season 1968–69. The alliance, nicknamed Dü-Dü, resulted in an adaptation of Shakespeare's *King John*, then in *Play Strindberg*.

Play Strindberg is thus opus number two in the sequence of Dürrenmatt's adaptations. Yet there are reasons for discussing it first of all, as a specific case. *The Dance of Death* (1900) by Strindberg is the only modern classic Dürrenmatt has chosen to adapt. It is a compressionist play in two parts based on the problem of marriage; Dürrenmatt's other adaptations of classics continue, more or less clearly, along the line of his world theater. As to the total number of productions, *Play Strindberg* has proved to be Dürrenmatt's most popular dramaturgic work, helped as it is by the small number of actors needed. There were even several productions in Sweden, Strindberg's native country, shortly after the world première in Basle in February, 1969.

The name of the adaptation is parallel to a jazz adaptation of Bach called *Play Bach*. In a similar way, *Play Strindberg* means playing with *The Dance of Death*, adding a modern swing.[1] The adaptation is decidedly a piece of work for the theater and in the theater: the cast took an active part in revising the script, and a major portion of the work was done during rehearsals. Dürrenmatt was also a co-director of the production, sharing this function with Erich Holliger. Having just completed *King John*, Düggelin did not choose to direct this time. Rightly or wrongly, the group worked under the illusion that they were doing something unique. Dürrenmatt was using a working method further developed toward the practical theater than his earlier habits. He felt that he was turning an old dream of his into reality: he had placed his desk on the stage itself.[2]

A comparison between *The Dance of Death* and *Play Strindberg* is made necessary by Dürrenmatt's professed aim. He is after "a comedy about bourgeois tragedies of marriage" (PS 67). On the first pages of the adaptation, he orders a simple non-realistic arrangement of the setting, further clarified by a ground plan. He omits creating the atmosphere of the old fortress where Edgar and Alice, a captain of artillery and his wife, have kept tormenting one another for the twenty-five years of their married life.[3] All he wants to have on the stage are a few pieces of furniture and properties: a desk with the telegraphic instrument, a piano, a hatstand for Edgar's military equipment, a few chairs, a round table, a couch. There is no gateway in the back wall opening toward the battery and the sea, there is no sentry passing back and

[1] Werner Ross, "Zimmerschlachten," *Merkur*, 23, 10 (Oct. 1969), p. 969. DoD is short for Norman Ginsbury's translation into English, published in J. C. Trewin (ed.), *Plays of the Year*, 1966.

[2] "Mit Strindberg in den Boxring," an interview with Fritz Rumler, *Der Spiegel*, 23, 6, Feb. 3, 1969, p. 120.

[3] For Kitchin, *The Dance of Death* is a key work on compressionism, "because it spares us from discussing 'impact,' 'intensity' and other qualities difficult to present as evidence. The setting and the characters do the job for us" (*Drama in the Sixties*, p. 47).

forth on the battery. Dürrenmatt cuts away a dimension of depth from his setting—and from his adaptation as a whole.[4] All that matters is the relations between three actors.

Between their scenes the actors sit on either side of the stage in full view of the audience. These solutions have been employed before, of course, in productions of our age. The actors bring the necessary extra props with them to the stage and announce the beginning of the twelve scenes or rounds, as they are called here. Above the stage there is a circle of lighting equipment: this is a setting for a boxing match. The focal image present in this setting is a ring.

Second, Dürrenmatt makes his dialogue sharp, crisp, and poignant by drastic cutting of the sentences themselves. He continues his work on the lines found in *The Anabaptists*. A typical example can be taken from an early scene describing a quiet phase in the tempestuous married life of Alice and Edgar. Strindberg:

ALICE: . . . Don't you want your whisky yet?
EDGAR: I'll wait a little . . . (DoD 18).

And Dürrenmatt:

ALICE: Whisky?
EDGAR: Later (PS 8).

The dialogue of *Play Strindberg* consists mainly of short sentences without any subordinate clauses. The lines are grouped by marking pauses of two lengths. Especially in Round One, in which the relation between Alice and Edgar is established, there is a repeated pattern within each group. Almost every sequence of a few lines is finished with a bald negative statement denying the value of something: "Then I know of no happy marriage." "Nobody has ever known you." "Nobody knows you any more" (PS 12–13). These

---

[4] "Should one really demand reverence for Strindberg?" is a question raised by Hilde Rubinstein. Her answer: "What is open to criticism is the result compared with the intention" ("Der Schaukampf des F.D.," *Frankfurter Hefte*, 25, 3, March 1970, p. 202).

finishing remarks sound like the famous refrain in the poem "The Raven" by Edgar Allan Poe: "Nevermore." With their help Dürrenmatt creates circular structures within his dialogue.[5] These matters have been discussed over and over again, as parts of a marital game, as repeated punches in an endless boxing match. *Play Strindberg* is constructed on an intricate system of repetitions, partly verbal, partly expressed through repeated actions and situations. The ring is present in the action of the play, too.

Repetition is a normal structural element in compressionism. If there are no major changes in the setting, other means must be employed to organize the stage action in the dimension of time. A possibility is offered by repetitions, used either as final points in consecutive sequences, or as points zero, as starting-points for new developments. These strategies are resorted to by both O'Neill and Albee in their compressionist chamber plays, in *Long Day's Journey Into Night* and in *Who's Afraid of Virginia Woolf*. In *Play Strindberg*, "Let us not speak about it," is a sentence uttered five times within a little over two pages (PS 19–21). It is said by Edgar after Alice's cousin Kurt has entered the stage, to listen patiently to the main characters and to complete the triangle of the play. This repeated phrase creates an atmosphere of secrecy: there are lots of unpleasant subjects to be avoided rather than explored. At the same time the repetitions turn the line into a joke.

A repeated focal situation is Edgar's fainting fit. Believing that he is unconscious, Alice and Kurt say things not to be heard by him. A major event in the plot of *The Dance of Death* is that Edgar goes to town and tells a pack of lies on his return to the island. Dürrenmatt stylizes this deceitful feature in Edgar's character further by making him feign an attack of illness. He is present on the stage and overhears the

---

[5] Ross (p. 970) mentions these refrain-like repetitions and Dürrenmatt's parodies of pathetics including, e.g., conjugation schemes: "You are timid, you have always been timid, and you will always be timid" (PS 15).

love-making scene between Alice and Kurt. Strindberg's Captain only guesses the existence of this liaison; Dürrenmatt's Edgar knows it. By a shift in motivation Dürrenmatt makes it clear that Alice commits adultery only out of a lust for revenge, not out of any childhood attachment to Kurt.

Alice and Kurt do no longer take Edgar seriously when he gets a real attack and begs for help. In this scene, one of the grotesque highlights of *Play Strindberg*, Alice and Kurt just go on playing cards: "Why don't you die, then we'll take you in earnest" (PS 55). A serious moment is here made grotesque and tragicomic. This brings us to Dürrenmatt's definition of *The Dance of Death* as a "bourgeois tragedy of marriage" and to his announced aim to give it the "worst possible turn," the turn into comedy. Is *The Dance of Death* a bourgeois tragedy of marriage?

Hardly. Strindberg's chamber play is already a grotesque tragicomedy. Or, rather, a comitragedy. We all know about Strindberg's seriousness, about his ability to turn his private anxieties, obsessions, ambivalent feelings of love-hate, or insults, suffered or imagined, into a poetry for the stage. We think about him mostly as August the Terrible. We are less intensely aware of his sense of the comic, of the sharp edge of observation to be glimpsed in his dialogue.[6] Strindberg's sense of comedy is one of his characteristics not seen or appreciated widely enough outside Scandinavia. He made his real breakthrough in Germany in the 1910's, during the growing period of expressionism; the world première of *The Dance of Death* was in Germany in September, 1905.[7] These details of stage history may have something to do with his reputation ever since. There is reason to raise a mild Scandinavian protest against some one-sided Anglo-American and German attitudes toward Strindberg—and toward Ibsen, for that matter. Both wrote comedies, too. The prevalent image

[6] "Strindberg had no humor at all, as far as I can see in any play of his" (Melchinger, "Was hat der bitterböse Friedrich," *Theater heute, 10*, 3, March 1969, p. 38).

[7] Gunnar Ollén, *Strindbergs dramatik*, p. 179.

of these authors may well be that they are profound and unsmiling bores, brooding at their desks in the middle of a dark Arctic winter night, with the wind blowing, snow falling, and with their thoughts circling around the consoling notion of happy and peaceful suicide. Perhaps this has a connection with an image of Scandinavia generally. Critics sometimes treat Strindberg in the way they might face their first journey to Scandinavia: aghast, yet bravely determined to confront the coldness and somberness of the atmosphere and other hazards.[8]

Dürrenmatt seems to have been blind to the light shed by Strindberg's sense of the comic. It is preferable to speak about his sense of the comic, or of comedy, not about his sense of humor. There is nothing mellow in Strindberg's sharp comic observations; there are certainly grotesque and tragicomic features in *The Dance of Death*. If one were to choose just one memorable scene from *Dödsdansen*, Part I, the chances would be that most of us would prefer Edgar's dance, with Alice and Kurt playing "Entry of the Boyars" on the piano. The dance is interrupted by Edgar's falling down, as a victim of a serious attack: a shock turning a comic scene into a grotesque one. At the same time this moment of Edgar's fall is an example of a scenic image in which action, movement, background music, the dialogue and tension between the actors are interwoven into a climax full of thematic significance. Edgar's dance is shown in Fig. 14.

The dance scene is a great moment of the theater, not only of literature. The central elements of the play, and of Edgar's marriage, are present in this scenic image: Edgar's mad

---

[8] When Adolf Hitler was giving dinner in his headquarters on June 5, 1942, he entertained his dinner party with this topic. The specific observation was the abnormally high number of insane people in Finland, due to feelings of loneliness in farmhouses 30 to 60 miles from one another and to the resulting religious needs satisfied only by "the Jewish demagogy of the Bible" (*Hitlers Tischgespräche*, ed. by Henry Picker, pp. 365–66). Hitler's vision of Finland as a somber and Biblical madhouse is a grotesque distortion of a prejudice not unknown among non-Scandinavians.

327

clinging to life and his fight to the last breath, Alice's out-dated dreams of an artist's career, Kurt's role as an accom-panist. *The Dance of Death*: this is the scene in which Edgar dances.

Dürrenmatt has, of course, retained the dance scene. He has even emphasized it further by mentioning the "Entry" and "Solveig's Song," the two musical leitmotifs of his adap-tation, right in the first lines of the script. He ends his play by letting Alice sing once again "Solveig's Song," hitting exactly the right grotesque mood of his adaptation.[9] He adds a clever visualization of the past by making Alice and Kurt run through an album of photographs. These are examples of a harmony between the original script and the adaptation. Strindberg and Dürrenmatt play the same melody.

There are also discords. In spite of his general aim to turn Strindberg's "tragedy" into a comedy, Dürrenmatt cut away part of Strindberg's lines of comedy. When Edgar has described in glowing words the pleasures of a grilled mack-erel, Alice quips drily: "You're getting quite eloquent" (DoD 18). This line is dropped by Dürrenmatt, the come-dian, and so is Edgar's self-ironical and certainly comic state-ment about the constant repetitions in the matrimonial dis-cussions at the fortress: "When you lashed out just now with your good old standby . . . , my counter should have been. . . . But as I've already hit back a good five hundred times with that one, I yawned instead" (DoD 27). The circular patterns occur already in Strindberg's dialogue; they were further stylized by the adapter. Dürrenmatt may have struck out that line because he got his idea of circular repetitions exactly from this speech. Having it stated in the dialogue would have left too programmatic an impression.

The Dance of Death can be called a black comedy or a comitragedy.[10] "Comitragedy" in the sense that the somber

---

[9] The end is praised, e.g., by Günther Rühle, *Frankfurter Allge-meine*, Feb. 11, 1969.

[10] Rubinstein calls *The Dance of Death* "a black comedy"; the dance scene is "exorbitantly funny." Dürrenmatt follows numerous

tones of voice prevail, yet there are also tones of comedy. Strindberg's script is not a tragedy proceeding in only one tone of voice; Dürrenmatt needed this misinterpretation in order to get his work started with his usual polemical gusto. As early as in *Mississippi* he had parodied Strindberg. *Play Strindberg* is an openly acknowledged counter-sketch in which the mold to be filled with Dürrenmatt's own metal is present in the name of the play, in its characters, in its total idea. Using his familiar dramaturgic terminology Dürrenmatt speaks about the basic idea behind Strindberg's play as an "artistic invention."

For Dürrenmatt, Strindberg's "invention" is "interesting" (PS 67). How did the adapter express his interest? A comparative reading of the plays amazes one at the great number of parallels, rather than at the deviations.[11] Dürrenmatt has made statements to the contrary effect, emphasizing his own work. Every idea on the first three pages also occurs in Strindberg, even in the same order. Dürrenmatt renders them in an abridged form. Then, as the play proceeds, the deviations take the upper hand. Alice's great outburst of feelings during Edgar's unconsciousness is a conglomerate from Parts I and II (DoD 39–40, 139–40); it is delivered twice. Strindberg opens his Scene 4 with a pantomime of Edgar's: our Captain wipes his slate clean by throwing things out of the window, among them the key of the piano; by wrapping Alice's laurel wreaths into a bundle; by tearing a portrait of his wife to shreds. Instead of this pantomime scene we have a typical Dürrenmatt scene in *Play Strindberg*: the Captain eats an enormous and grotesque meal. Quite literally, we see Edgar happily consuming "the good things of this world"

---

inventive details of Strindberg; the dialogue of the adaptation is not only abridged but also diluted and schematized (pp. 202–03).

[11] "Surprisingly many original sentences by Strindberg were retained," yet Dürrenmatt changed the total atmosphere of the play (Johannes Jacobi, *Die Zeit*, Feb. 14). In a pre-première interview with Aurel Schmidt, Dürrenmatt calls *The Dance of Death* "absolutely third class" and "theater of the past," its Part II "hopeless." He has given up Strindberg's form, he claims (*National-Zeitung*, Basel, Feb. 6).

(JHH 105); the next moment he may be dying. Edgar's meal also hints at an off-stage action, the sexual meal just offered by Alice to Kurt.

Strindberg's Kurt is one of the long dull roles in world drama: a mirror to Alice and Edgar, little else. Dürrenmatt's Kurt is a big-time criminal, so powerful that he is above and outside the law. This twist is served as a surprise moment in the last scenes of *Play Strindberg*. Otherwise the end is a compromise between Strindberg's Parts I and II. In Part I the couple totters to a kind of relieving, reconciling end: let us celebrate our silver wedding, after all. The tone is reconciling only in comparison with the other possible endings: divorce, Edgar's death, Alice's elopement with Kurt. Part II finishes with the Captain's death, to the joy and relief of Alice—after which she is made to speak admiring words about her late husband. The theme of love-hate is continued beyond Edgar's death. Dürrenmatt's Edgar sits paralyzed on the stage in the last scenes, with his back turned toward the audience and uttering unintelligible noises interpreted by Alice. He is treated like a helpless child.

Dürrenmatt's additions are typical of him. Last meals and big-time gangsters belong to his mannerisms. Kurt is a new variation of Claire Zachanassian in *The Visit*, or of the gangsters in *Frank V; The Physicists* leaves its mentally healthy characters as helpless patients behind the walls of the asylum. Whether his desk is on the stage or in his study, these are figures and situations occupying Dürrenmatt's mind.

The total effect of Dürrenmatt's deletions is something more than a stylistic brush-up making the dialogue sharper and quicker. When reading *The Dance of Death*, Dürrenmatt was disturbed by its "literature," by its literary quality. In his telegraphic style he defines this "literature" as "plush multiplied by infinity" (PS 67). Let us interpret: "plush" means local color and a sense of the period, centering on the furniture and the dresses, around the mental attitudes.[12] "Infinity"

---

[12] "Plush means the good living room of private life, infinity means multiplying the private with transcendence." Having torn down the walls of the Ibsenesque living room, Strindberg showed that there

means Strindberg's metaphysical aspect, parodied by Dürren-matt in two scenes of self-conscious philosophizing. When wiping his slate clean of these elements Dürrenmatt wanted to create a kind of "anti-Strindberg dialogue." "An actors' play" was to become "a play for the actors." What Dürren-matt wanted to preserve was the story and the basic theatri-cal invention. "The actor was not any more to practice de-monic studies of soul, but to make an extremely condensed and abridged text possible on the stage" (PS 67).

What happened, in effect, was that Dürrenmatt cut away the texture of life from his script. *The Dance of Death* is hardly such an incomparable masterpiece that it would not need any abridging and adapting at all. Its Parts I and II have many times been given in a combined, heavily abridged version, in recent years, e.g., at the English National Theatre. The crucial question is how this is done. Away with "demonic studies of soul": all right, exit characterization.[13] "A play for the actors": yet the result is that a star vehicle with a dimen-sion of depth is transformed into a star vehicle without that dimension. Away with "infinity": yet there is no overdose of metaphysics in this particular play of Strindberg's.

When grouping his dialogue into short sequences Dürren-matt kept hunting for points, as a boxer might. Not for human beings, as an artist may or perhaps even should do.[14]

---

were problems not to be solved by practising social criticism: death, evil, "the connection between sadism and masochism" (Melchinger, pp. 36, 38).

[13] In an interesting report on the rehearsals in Basel, Hans J. Am-mann emphasizes that a conscious effort was made to "avoid fixing and differentiating the figures psychologically" (*NZZ*, June 15, 1969). "Dürrenmatt's figures are no longer bearers of an individuality, but of arguments. . . . Because the play does not grant a vision into the depth anywhere at all, the fight presented grows uninteresting" (Schmidt, *National-Zeitung*, Feb. 10).

[14] Dürrenmatt's scenes tend to grow independently from a total conception, his dialogue aims at picking up points, and these verbal effects disturb his contents. These observations, based on *The Meteor* and *The Anabaptists*, have validity elsewhere, too (Max Peter, *Schaffhauser Nachrichten*, April 14, 1967). Cf. Jenny, *Süddeutsche Zeitung*, Feb. 10, 1969.

The points Dürrenmatt achieves through repetitions, through the circular structures immersed in the dialogue, are always alike. In *The Dance of Death*, the everyday discussion between Alice and Edgar keeps wavering from one subject to another, thus offering possibilities to characterize the figures.[15] There is air between the lines: air for the actors to breath in and out. In Dürrenmatt all wanderings of thought are cut away or made to serve only one purpose, that of a desperate boxing match between the actors.[16] The fight is so violent that nothing else comes out except the fight itself. Concentrating on one theme means that other themes are left aside. Dürrenmatt was not interested in love-hate, a very Strindbergian theme. It was "plush" for him.

Actors may certainly help a dramaturge or a director to abridge a play. Yet their professional mannerisms tend to emphasize features bound to each individual moment of acting, not to themes to be developed throughout a play or a performance. Actors want to employ words as swords, as weapons to fight their fellow actors with. As a result Dürrenmatt was driven to "exhaust the various theatrical situations" in the play, as he puts it himself (PS 67).

How important are the "theatrical situations" in Strindberg? Do we remember his stories? Strindberg is one of the most subjective dramatists in world literature,[17] Dürrenmatt an objective story-teller hiding himself and his view of life behind his grotesque tales. The really important and characteristic elements in Strindberg can be groped for with the help of concepts like "atmosphere," "ambivalence," "exter-

[15] The adaptation is "exceptionally unequivocal. The floating in Strindberg's play, the continuous changes in illuminating the characters, are sacrificed . . . to a straight-line development, up to the K.O. of Edgar" (Peter Rüedi, *Zürcher Woche*, Feb. 14, 1969).

[16] Dürrenmatt created literature of a new kind in his dialogue: a simplified, manneristic style not expressing anything beyond the unmotivated fight between the actors (Leber, *Die Weltwoche*, Feb. 14).

[17] "Strindberg is hardly surpassed in subjectivity by any other dramatist of this century" (Irmeli Niemi, *Nykydraaman ihmiskuva*, p. 13).

332

nalizing a state of mind," or "characterization," and perhaps even "demonic study of soul."[18] Strindberg was shocked when looking at "the little hell" he had created; Dürrenmatt is expertly amused as a sports reporter might be.[19] It is as if Dürrenmatt had added to the inessential elements in *The Dance of Death*, that is to the story and the theatrical situations, while deleting part of the really essential elements in characterization.

Ever since *The Physicists*, Dürrenmatt's characterization has been growing cooler, more and more disillusioned. There was a time when his relation to some of his characters was colored by sympathy and/or pity. Count Übelohe, Akki, Ill, or Möbius were still described with a certain amount of warmth. The Bishop in *The Anabaptists* has a great many sympathetic features, yet his deeds lead to miserable results, and his recognition of his own folly is the final twist of the play. Is it a sign of modernity to describe man as a cipher? Hardly of the only kind of modernity, and hardly that since the late 1960's. It might have been, back in the 1950's, when Dürrenmatt implied that an average consciousness does not contain such refined feelings as guilt or responsibility for the state of affairs in the world. Dürrenmatt is offering objects for criticism, not for identification; in the postscript of *The Anabaptists* he pleaded for reflection, for alienation, for the spectator's ability to step back from the events and problems of the stage and have an objective look at them from a distance. Objectifying Strindberg? Enter an adapter into the ring with this aim; exeunt Alice and Edgar, two "total individuals" on their island. And the play with them.

---

[18] Strindberg's *Ghost Sonata* is "not really an action, rather an atmosphere," Dürrenmatt states in an extremely laudatory theater review from 1952. It is also one of those plays in which Strindberg creates poetry through the stage, not only on the stage (TS 340–41). Yet *The Dance of Death* left Dürrenmatt only a memory of the actors in 1948, none of the play (PS 67).

[19] Sister Corona Sharp has emphasized that there are all kinds of games played in Dürrenmatt's version: card games, music, dance, sex as "a game of revenge" ("D's *Play Strindberg*," *Modern Drama, 14*, 3, Dec. 1970, p. 277).

In the final balance one readily admits that the working method employed in Basle was advanced. Intimate cooperation among the director, playwright/adapter and the cast is right in the direction of some compelling and fruitful experiments in the modern theater. The success of *Play Strindberg* in the theater was considerable. Yet Dürrenmatt's script hardly stands comparison with the original. Under the influence of an unsmiling, post-expressionistic stage tradition of producing Strindberg, he failed to bring out the essential elements in the Swedish master of the stage. A powerful creative dramatist, of the stature of Dürrenmatt, is not necessarily one of the very best adapters of plays. Not at least when the source is a masterpiece alien to his own quality. Dürrenmatt translated Strindberg's original idiom to fit his own poignant language of the stage.

Play Strindberg is not a script replacing *The Dance of Death* for all future time. Instead, it is a "Play Dürrenmatt."[20] A boxing match between two actors, with Kurt as a pale referee. A play repeating its focal image of the ring in its setting, in its dialogue and action. A tract concluding that marriage is an endless fight; the story of the play does not carry any more complicated theme. A theater experience intellectually stimulating, emotionally trite. An exercise in a dialogue not only sharp, crisp, and demanding for the actors but also rhythmically monotonous, verbally poor.[21] A script moving somewhere between a full-fledged parody and a straightforward adaptation.[22]

[20] Reinhardt Stumm does not find any justification for the adaptation, yet gives high praise to the performance (a general feature in the reviews of the world première). Stumm's question "Strindmatt or Dürrenberg?" is quoted as the title of this chapter; his answer is that the play is a Dürrenmatt (*Basler Nachrichten*, Feb. 10). Cf. Arnold, *F.D.*, pp. 89–90, and Schmidt.

[21] Dürrenmatt's dialogue is "full of stereotyped phrases and clichés" (Jürgen Buschkiel, *Die Welt*, Feb. 11). Cf. Günther Grack, *Der Tagesspiegel*, Jan. 18, 1970).

[22] *Play Strindberg* was further adapted into a wholesale parody at the Stockholm City Theater: the actors changed roles in the middle of the performance etc. There were positive reviews, e.g., by Mario

Dürrenmatt's "anti-Strindberg dialogue" is sometimes "anti-Strindberg," sometimes "pro-Strindberg," because there are already self-ironical and self-parodical elements in Strindberg's own text. The grotesque elements are partly transferred as such from Dürrenmatt's source, partly stylized toward greater sharpness,[23] partly transplanted from Dürrenmatt's own imagination, not quite without a border line between them and the rest of the play. The grotesque presupposes a conflict between opposite impulses; in this phase of his development Dürrenmatt is losing contact with the emotionally positive or warm elements in the grotesque and directing his journey toward the pure macabre. Also toward monotony, away from an abundance of contradictory tones of voice. A theme of great significance in *The Dance of Death* is a paradoxical tension between love and hate; there is no love left in *Play Strindberg*. It is rather as if Edmund and Goneril had left King Lear and were living together as a married couple at a fortress on the coast of Sweden. By giving his play the framework of a boxing match Dürrenmatt tempted many of his critics to use boxing terminology. According to my score card the old champion wins on points.

Grut (*Aftonbladet*) and Hans Axel Holm (*Dagens Nyheter*), both on Sept. 26, 1969.

[23] According to Ammann, loc. cit., Dürrenmatt took special care in clarifying the grotesque elements extant in Strindberg.

16 Shake-Scening the Bards

FOUR ADAPTATIONS

||||||||||||||||||||||||||||||||||||||||||||||||||||||||||||||||||||||||||||||||||||||

An artist of our late age facing an immense amount of ready-made artistic shapes: one of Dürrenmatt's dilemmas. In *Problems of the Theater* and in his early practice he found his way out through parody. Parody presupposes a fresh artistic invention; it makes the artist free to deal with those shapes. In the late 1960's Dürrenmatt discovered another possibility: he started adapting classics. In so doing he felt free to reshape his sources according to his new and personal artistic inventions. Parody means a direct confrontation between a model and its ridiculing distortion: these are, so to say, on opposite sides of a circle, 180 degrees from one another. Dürrenmatt's first counter-sketches to classic plays are closer to their models. He arrives at them by giving his source a twist of 90 degrees.

In the case of *King John* (König Johann) that twist is to the left. It was originally one of Düggelin's favorite ideas to produce this play of Shakespeare's; after a few efforts with various translators the script was turned over to Dürrenmatt. Instead of a new translation Dürrenmatt produced an adaptation; his work as an adapter of classics, not only of his own scripts, was started by chance rather than conscious choice. An additional motivation found during the work itself ran parallel with the prevalent German fashion in drama favoring documentary materials and political themes. *King John* is a political play; Dürrenmatt used it as his documentary material, as it were, reshaping it somewhat, to prove warfare to be senseless. The play opened in September, 1968, heralding the beginning of Düggelin's and Dü-Dü's era in Basle. Once again, a Dürrenmatt première was a major publicity event. The playbill did its best to clarify the political parallels of

336

König Johann: there were photographs published of historical peace conferences, including those of Versailles 1919, Yalta 1945, Paris and Bratislava 1968.[1] This was the beginning; there were four more adaptations to come within a few years. Dürrenmatt faced new problems each time, and solved them with varying degrees of success. His wide range as an adapter does not make the role of his critic enviable; one should be competent both in Shakespeareonomy and Büchnerology, both in Strindbergism (an occult science) and Goethenomics. These branches of study will be less heavily emphasized than Dürrenmatt's creative efforts in the ensuing discussion. What does our modern playwright do with his source? Having parodied *Julius Caesar* in *Romulus the Great*, having received an impetus for his *Frank V* from *Titus Andronicus*, Dürrenmatt was now to twist *King John* and *Titus* into new positions.

The traditional *trois coups* open Dürrenmatt's *König Johann* while the curtain is still down. Then the curtain rises and the *trois coups* turn out to have been three beheadings (KJ 96).[2] The first deeds are done by an executioner, while King John and the leading members of the English court are present. "Kings are murderers" (KJ 58); this claim is proved

[1] The crisis in Czechoslovakia made the première "acutely topical" (H. Moser, *Schweizer Heim*, Oct. 9, 1968). Ten days in advance the Basle City Theater arranged a matinee in which well-known intellectuals, among them Grass, Frisch, and Dürrenmatt, made speeches published later as a pamphlet (*Tschechoslowakei 1968*, Zurich: Arche). Dürrenmatt's contribution is reprinted in DK.

[2] KJ is short for *König Johann* by Dürrenmatt; Shakespeare's lines are marked in the traditional way (e.g., IV.iii.140). TR is *The Troublesome Raigne of John King of England*, an anonymous Elizabethan play in two parts. It is "generally agreed" that Shakespeare's script is an adaptation of TR (Lily B. Campbell, *Shakespeare's Histories*, p. 132), though E.A.J. Honigmann takes *King John* to be earlier (New Arden edition, pp. xliii–lviii). Cf. Geoffrey Bullough's introduction to TR, *Narrative and Dramatic Sources of Shakespeare*, IV, pp. 5,15,17. Dürrenmatt knew TR (KJ 99); he received a few impulses from it, yet developed them independently, as shown in the notes below.

337

true before a word is uttered. And so it is throughout the adaptation: the courts of England and France are two gangs of criminals, given to murder, destruction, and warfare as soon as they see some possible gain. When peace is the most advantageous alternative, King John and King Philipp are bosom friends again, taking their royal business merely as business.[3] What never occurs to them is their responsibility to the living bodies of their citizens.

Shakespeare's heroics are replaced by satire; Shakespeare's English patriotism, a marked feature in *King John*,[4] is replaced by internationalism, by a protest against the senselessness of war, then and now. These are essential elements in Dürrenmatt's twist. So is his refashioning of the role of Philipp Faulconbridge, the bastard son of King Richard Cœur-de-Lion. In both plays, the Bastard is quite a prominent figure. Leaving the landed gentry, he acquires a position in the court, yet remains an outsider. The nature of his birth makes it impossible for him to compete for power. For Shakespeare, he is the patriotic voice of loyalty to the crown of England; for Dürrenmatt, the voice of reason and of the common people.

King Philipp of France lays claim to the English crown in behalf of Prince Arthur, son of King John's elder brother Richard. These family relationships between the Plantagenets bring in Arthur's mother Konstanze and his grandmother, Queen Eleonore of England.[5] The family reunion in II,1 opens in an atmosphere of affectionate quasi-heartiness parodying the chivalrous manners of these royal villains: "Konstanzchen! Arthurchen!" (KJ 21). Two pages later grandmother and daughter-in-law lapse into an abusive language bringing them down to a level closer to modern audiences.

[3] What matters is business, not personal feelings, Rühle remarks when analyzing the themes of violence and arrogance in KJ (*Frankfurter Allgemeine*, Sept. 20, 1968).

[4] Campbell (pp. 144–67) sees *King John* as a reflection of the major political events and problems of Elizabeth's reign. Cf. New Arden, p. xxix, and Bullough, pp. 22–23.

[5] The spelling of the names is according to Dürrenmatt.

338

The topical allusions include a paraphrase of Brecht ("Courage, Mutter" KJ 17), and references to the Swiss and Austrian troops in the French army. Dürrenmatt's hints at the national mores are not always on a high level of sophistication: his courtiers are made to play croquet and drink tea (KJ 96). The aim is a stratified theater style full of anachronisms, grotesque disharmonies, and twists from one stylistic level to another. Details may be parodic, the totality is not.

The Bastard uses every chance to mediate for peace and reason. The inhabitants of the French city of Angers are asked which of the two aspirants to the English throne they are ready to acknowledge as their ruler. Wisely enough, they refuse to choose. Right on the verge of peace, the Archduke of Austria, a brutish warmonger, decides the issue by breaking the armistice. The English loose 6,000 men on the battlefield, the French close to 7,000—only to accept the second proposal for peace put forth by the Bastard. Angers has insured itself against the victory of both parties; it could not guess that the result might be a draw. The kings join forces in destroying the city as a punishment for its reasonable impartiality, and 'an eternal peace' is celebrated in front of the demolished cathedral of Angers with a double marriage between the royal houses.

"And of heroes there are none. Only victims" (KJ 33). This could be a bitter motto for the festive nuptial meal before the ruins, for a grotesque scene with telling inner contrasts.[6] A high price in human lives has been paid for nothing; there are the happily sighing reminiscences of Queen Eleonore and the bloodthirsty curses of Konstanze, betrayed by King Philipp in his peacemaking mood. Before the meal is over,

[6] Rudolf Stamm has spoken about "a disharmony between word and gesture or word and picture" as a "Dürrenmatt effect." There is a "continuous absurd tension" between the events at the table and the speeches of the noblemen. The action reveals their "average, everyday humanity," the speeches show the responsibilities they do not cope with: they can either preserve or destroy human lives (*"King John–König Johann," Deutsche Shakespeare-Gesellschaft West*, Jahrbuch 1970, p. 48).

339

the carrousel starts its next round: Cardinal Pandulpho, a papal legate, enters and excommunicates King John for violations of the privilege of the church. King Philipp cannot afford excommunication; he has sworn "in the name of God against God" (KJ 48). Peace was not, after all, eternal. What is eternal is Dürrenmatt's ability to develop new variations of last meals. All through III,1, Austria keeps eating avidly; III,2 opens with the Bastard carrying Austria's head and concealing it in a soup-tureen.[7] An invention bearing the signature of Friedrich Dürrenmatt.

The results of the resumed fighting are shown in both camps. Arthur is taken prisoner by the English, Eleonore by the French. Both Konstanze and Eleonore know that the game is over for them. A hangman, a monstrous old queen, and a despairing mother meet in a grotesque scenic image, in Eleonore's farewell to her daughter-in-law and to life:

> We loved
> Power and men, vowed oaths, betrayed,
> Deceiving were deceived. All that
> Is over. Power, ambition, riches, fame,
> As well as passion. Here I am, facing you,
> An old hag, close-cropped and stinking,
> Prepared for the hangman, cold and ugly.
> My end is yours. Had I some feeling left,
> I should deplore your fate, my child.
> I'm eager to die, yet you must live on
> In this empty world, a womb that bore
> Merely to bring forth flesh for butchers,
> A victim of your deeds, as I am of mine (KJ 61).[8]

[7] The critic of *The Times* finds an "element of unbridled gruesomeness" in this detail (Nov. 15, 1968). It was not easily solved, Dürrenmatt reports, because the spectators experience a dummy on the stage as a dummy. When the head was placed into the tureen, they laughed, and this reaction "produced, in a paradoxical way, the necessary cruelty of the scene" (DK 148).

[8] The situation is absurd: translating Schlegel's German translation from 1799, as adapted by Dürrenmatt in 1968, back to blank verse in English. The above passage does not occur in Shakespeare; the

What emerges from Dürrenmatt's handling of the rhythm and diction is a kind of laconic and abstract tautness, built up with the help of phrases charged with harsh, ironic meaning.[9] Through the frequent use of enjambement Dürrenmatt creates tensions between the two units of his diction, between line and sentence structure: his blank verse is rhythmically alive. It certainly lacks the exuberance of Shakespeare's metaphors, yet it achieves strong effects by using contrasts, puns, anachronisms, twists from one stylistic layer to another, and cool yet dynamic metaphors, caught, as it were, on the verge of a jump forward.[10] There is a surprising link to be drawn back to the imagery of Dürrenmatt's youthful prose.

"Three acts of Shakespeare and two acts of Dürrenmatt."[11] The authorship of *König Johann* cannot be divided quite so rectilinearly as that, yet there is no denying that Dürrenmatt's deviations from his source grow in importance in the last two acts. The Bastard saves Prince Arthur from the hands of murderers sent by King John; the effect of this human and sensible deed is spoiled by chance, as the prince dies accidentally. The plot forms a pattern similar to that of the source text, although it passes through almost or totally rewritten scenes. There is an echo from *Romulus the Great*

---

rendering is tentative; the early lines read in the original: "Wir liebten/Gewalt und Männer, schworen, brachen Treue,/Betrügend wurden wir betrogen. Alles/Ist nun vorbei. Macht, Ehrgeiz, Reichtum, Ruhm/Und Liebe auch." Fig. 15 shows us this scenic image.

[9] Konstanze commits suicide during the speech. Hansres Jacobi has remarked that Dürrenmatt extended especially the scenes with the ladies; they and the later abdication scene with Pandulpho reveal Dürrenmatt's "rich fantasy and his power to create images" (*NZZ*, Sept. 19, 1968). TR has a scene between Konstanze and captive Eleonore (I.1057–88); the tone is quarrelsome.

[10] Stamm's careful discussion of Dürrenmatt's diction reveals the constant "discrepancies between the matters, the characters and their language." The two playwrights meet one another in puns and in drastic expressions. Dürrenmatt uses thin contemporary clichés and cuts away Shakespeare's references to patriotism and the "characteristic ambiguity and unpredictability" of his figures (pp. 42–47).

[11] Paul Hübner, *Rheinische Post*, Dec. 23, 1968.

in the comic abdication scene between King John and Pandulpho. Both crawl around the stage shivering from cold and mortal terror, eager to surrender to one another; when they finally meet, and King John gives away his crown, these new-found allies spend, literally, a few moments under the same cover.[12] See Fig. 16. Another invention puts King Philipp and Dauphin Louis in washtubs for a scene of negotiation. The Bastard is punished for his reasonable actions by Blanka, a royal heiress whom he loved yet sacrificed to political expediency. Whipped like a dog he is present at King John's death scene, in which Magna Charta is announced, then returns to his starting-point among the common people. Both the play and his guest performance among the princes are over.

"Mad world! mad kings! mad composition!" (II.i.561). This exclamation of the Bastard's may well have aroused Dürrenmatt's interest in *King John*, even though he left it out of his composition. The line opens a monologue; monologues and other longer speeches are revised by Dürrenmatt most drastically of all, due to his efforts to give a new function to the characters. A protagonist facing a mad world: a vision placing the Bastard into line with a great many Dürrenmattian characters ever since Romulus: Count Übelohe, Nebuchadnezzar, Matthäi, Möbius. Shakespeare's Renaissance Bastard follows the motto "blows, blood, and death!" (II.i.360); he is a character resembling Hotspur, "a man of deeds rather than words."[13] Dürrenmatt's Bastard is an outsider from our time, a prominent man of sound reason, in the right in all his undertakings, yet beaten by life, by its

---

[12] This scene, praised by *The Times* as "a brilliant piece of egregious fooling," is called a "blemish" by Hans R. Linder because so typical of Dürrenmatt (*National-Zeitung*, Basel, Sept. 19, 1968). TR (but not Shakespeare) makes the King kneel before Pandulpho (II.290); the tone of the scene is not comic, as in Dürrenmatt.

[13] Stamm, p. 38; Dürrenmatt's Bastard is "an envoy from the twentieth century in the medieval world," with "a fragrance of a figure carrying a thesis" (p. 41). The other characters are only "functions of their social position" (p. 34).

irrational, incalculable elements. "This inhuman world must become more human: but how?" the Bishop sighs in seventeenth-century Germany—and the echo answers through the Bastard from medieval England: not now. Changing the relation between King John and the Bastard "shifted the switch" that sent the plays, like two trains, toward their various end stations. "By changing a little at the beginning," Dürrenmatt writes, "I had to change everything in the end" (KJ 99–100). By choosing the Bastard as his private eye looking into the Middle Ages, Dürrenmatt insured a consistent point of view. His wheel or carrousel of power politics had found its pivot. Yet this solution deprived the other parts of their freedom to move: they exist only in their relations to the pivot. The Bastard is a human being in a world of satirical caricatures, or a stain of blood on a sociological chart depicting power relations under feudalism.

On that chart the characters lost their Shakespearean roundness and were developed into symbols of social forces, in accordance with the tradition of the epic theater.[14] The world of medieval England and France was turned into a power system in which regents, noblemen, the church, and the common people collided or joined in temporary alliances. King John tried to find a balance by cooperating with the forces available to him, one at a time. Blanka, an ingenue, had no anchoring place in this system; her role was rewritten, although Dürrenmatt regretted the loss of her "moving lament" (KJ 97).[15] All drama is based on certain assumptions; it was a general belief in the late 1960's that revealing the mechanics of a particular power system meant that *all* power

[14] For Rühle, *König Johann* is a simplifying play sacrificing the vigor and probability of its characters to a structural analysis. Kaiser admires Dürrenmatt's dramaturgic skill, yet remarks that his "small-time profiteers" cannot provoke fear (*Süddeutsche Zeitung*, Sept. 20, 1968).

[15] The love relation between Blanka and the Bastard is based on TR (I.700–17, 790–99). TR's Bastard refers to Queen Eleonore's "halfe a promise" that Blanka would marry him; this grows in Dürrenmatt into a scene with a full promise (KJ 13). Cf. Stamm, p. 32.

systems were revealed. Sharing this belief helped Dürrenmatt to insure the contemporary impact of his adaptation. By describing the feudal fights in medieval England and France one made points about Vietnam or Czechoslovakia.

There was a corresponding current of thought behind absurdism, reducing man to a helpless marionette of alien forces. The Bastard is a victim of the alien force of chance. In this respect he is related to the figures prevalent in absurdism and in Dürrenmatt's tragicomic practice. Yet the Bastard is employed as the pivot in a chronicle play belonging to the epic theater. The destination of Dürrenmatt's train is the kingdom of Tragicocomoedia, west of Epicalia, east of Absurditas. It is a Central European kingdom, if not an unknown canton in Switzerland.

Moreover, the Bastard is an experiment for Dürrenmatt. In *Hercules*, in *The Meteor*, in *The Anabaptists*, he had tried to shape serious moral conflicts on the stage by using hero-like clowns as his protagonists. When the spectators took Schwitter as a hero, when they identified with him, the playwright disagreed, and rightly so. The play was, after all, a comedy, a travesty of the hero myth. When our Nobelist was taken as a clown, the playwright disagreed, and rightly so. The play was not, after all, a harmless comedy. The only public reaction Dürrenmatt accepts is a total vision of the moral conflict discussed, to be achieved not through identification with a character, but through an intellectual insight leading the spectator to face his own reality. Fear through criticism. Too great a demand? A hero-like clown: a character so ambiguous as to be hopelessly open to misunderstandings? Probably; this is a partial explanation of the unsatisfactory reactions to those plays. In *König Johann* Dürrenmatt chose to move closer to the traditional hero myth. The Bastard is a hero-like outsider from our own age in a country of clowns.[16]

---

[16] Old tragedies are difficult for us, Dürrenmatt reasons, because they are not comedies. "Yet the mighty are the clowns among people, albeit the terrible clowns: their power makes them detached, separated

As Dürrenmatt's mouthpiece, the Bastard has to be constantly in the right: an annoying feature in a stage character.[17] Even if beaten by chance, even if despised and crushed by his feudal superiors, the Bastard remains an exemplary figure. The superior knowledge of our late age makes up for the wrongs done to him. This over-conspicuous pedagogic feature in the pivotal role of *König Johann* also reflects on its surroundings.[18] King John is made a conscious, analytic ruler, ready to review the changing political situations; Pandulpho is given a personal background and a vision that reaches our age (KJ 89–90). *King John* is a rhetorical play; *König Johann* a discursive one. Dürrenmatt's decision to keep the commoners offstage lessened the impact of the action. Yet eliminating the battle scenes was made up for. Elements of the Elizabethan theater of cruelty were retained or reformulated: the head of Austria, the executioners, the princes appearing in blood-stained butchers' aprons, a scene to be staged as if in "an ecstasy of blood" (KJ 97).

König Johann was a victory for Dürrenmatt, and a deserved one. He solved the problems of diction and meter, urgent for any adapter of Shakespeare, with honors.[19] He created a new stylistic whole, with its telling grotesque disharmonies and anachronisms, occasionally disturbed by con-

---

from people and thus from their victims, inhuman" (DK 130). This is one of Dürrenmatt's justifications for turning tragedies into comedies.

[17] Hans Heinz Holz sees the Bastard as "half beatnik, half Dutschke, a concentrate of undigested conclusions based on Marcuse" (*Frankfurter Rundschau*, Sept. 21, 1968), while C. R. Stange puts him into an ironic light (*Basler Nachrichten*, Sept. 19).

[18] Several critics found symptoms of over-obviousness in the play (e.g., Buschkiel, *Die Welt*, Sept. 20, 1968; Hans Schwab-Felisch, *Frankfurter Allgemeine*, Dec. 24, 1968). The King has an inclination to political analyses in TR (II.222–52, 258–84). His dying monologue in Dürrenmatt (KJ 91) was possibly influenced by two monologues in TR: "Disturbed thoughts . . ." (II.110–32) and "How have I livd, but by anothers losse?" (II.1046–71).

[19] Melchinger praises Dürrenmatt's blank verse as the work of a poet coming closer to Shakespeare than Schlegel did ("Grimmiger D.," *Theater heute*, 9, 10, Oct. 1968, pp. 15, 17).

temporary platitudes.[20] He repeated Shakespeare's situations and numerous peripeteias, charged with strong emotions and political impact; he gave them a turn toward harshness, grotesquerie, and irony, often by changing the settings, or by putting scenes or passages into new contexts. He twisted the story ninety degrees to the left: instead of a parody of nationalism he wrote a play pleading for internationalism; instead of making the speeches ridiculous he made them grotesquely stratified and tragicomic. Whenever he was in need of a passage of poetry of lamentation, he moved close to Shakespeare. He realized an old dream of his, by making a classic dangerous, by giving it coherence and a contemporary significance. The closest precedent in Dürrenmatt's canon is *The Anabaptists*, another chronicle play with direct and functional language, with a similar contrast between the commoners and the princes, with a plot touching the fate of a city demolished by war. Submitting the Elizabethan story to Dürrenmatt's moral vision led to certain limitations in the portrayal of the characters; these drawbacks are less conspicuous than in the case of *Play Strindberg*. Shakespeare is a closer relative to Dürrenmatt than is the Strindberg of the chamber plays: both are playwrights creating for a world theater.

The Dü-Dü era in Basle began with *König Johann*; it concluded with *Play Strindberg*. Both Dürrenmatt and Düggelin gave enthusiastic and optimistic interviews during the autumn season of 1968, confirming their enjoyment of the cooperation;[21] ironically enough, it was all over with Dürrenmatt's resignation in October, 1969. In a case like this, newspaper and other reports do not necessarily contain the whole truth; the gravest differences of opinion between these two seem to have concerned Dürrenmatt's adaptation of *Minna von Barn-*

---

[20] Stylistic criteria valid for Shakespeare are not applicable to Dürrenmatt's grotesque stage language and his rough dialogue (Jacobi).

[21] E.g. *Abend-Zeitung*, Basel, Sept. 18 (Moser); *Tages-Anzeiger*, Zurich, Sept. 14 (Litten); *Femina*, Zurich, Oct. 4, 1968.

346

helm by Lessing.[22] Contrary to a pre-première announce-
ment, the play was produced without being attributed to
Dürrenmatt; it is not included in the source materials of this
study. After his year in Basle, Dürrenmatt resumed his working relations with the Zurich Theater. There were no fewer
than three Dürrenmatt world premières in October–December, 1970, one in Zurich (adaptation of Goethe's *Urfaust*),
two in Düsseldorf. The last of these was *Titus Andronicus*,
Dürrenmatt's second adaptation of Shakespeare.[23]

King John is a political play; in Dürrenmatt's adaptation
it remained within this genre. *Titus Andronicus* (1589–90)[24]
is an early Elizabethan revenge tragedy and a melodramatic
horror play; reshaping it turned out to be more than problematic. The action is crammed full of all kinds of events, and
Dürrenmatt is not an adapter to moderate anything. He adds
explosives. When young Shakespeare's Senecan melodramat-
ics were combined with Dürrenmatt's extremism, the result
was a Molotov cocktail. Unfortunately enough, this charge
was aimed so carelessly by the playwright that it did not hit
any social institution at all. It misfired, having splashed a few
drops of its explosive contents at the door of a courthouse.

Dürrenmatt's Scene 1 achieves a new world record in total
and surprising reversals of plot within a scene. Titus Andronicus, commander-in-chief of the Roman army, arrives
home after having won a victory over the Goths. The events
of this miraculous scene include a combined funeral and
triumphal procession, the election of a new Caesar, three

[22] Melchinger, "Ein Kommentar," *Theater heute*, *10*, 12, Dec. 1969.
Cf. *Basler Nachrichten*, Oct. 6, 1969, and Hans Daiber, *Deutsches
Theater seit 1945*, pp. 208–09: Dürrenmatt found the required number of premières too high (DK 31–32) and did not want to go on
compromising.
[23] *Porträt eines Planeten* (Portrait of a Planet), Dürrenmatt's first
new original play since 1966, opened in November, 1970, also in
Düsseldorf. It is discussed in Chapter 17 of this study.
[24] "There does not seem to be anything that flatly contradicts a date
of about 1589–90" (J. C. Maxwell, New Arden, p. xxv). TA is short
for Dürrenmatt's version. The translation into German is by Ludwig
Tieck and Count Wolf von Baudissin (cf. Schlegel-Tieck, I, pp. 66–71).

engagements, two with Caesar Saturninus as the bridegroom, two with Titus' daughter Lavinia as the bride, two killings, one on the stage, the other off-stage, five death sentences, their cancellation, three burial speeches, the dismissal of Titus, and so on. Tamora, Queen of the Goths, makes a meteoric progress from prisoner of war to Empress of Rome. Most of this is taken from Shakespeare's Act I. Yet Dürrenmatt could not resist the temptation to sharpen the animosity between the Andronicus family and the new Caesar to the point of the death sentences. The surviving three sons of Titus are among those condemned; they are Tamora's archenemies, having tortured one of her sons to death during that very scene, yet she saves them by pleading for mercy. There is merely a dramaturgic reason for this behavior: the five are to die in later scenes. As in *Play Strindberg*, Dürrenmatt is aiming at "exhausting the various theatrical situations in the play." He sacrifices consistency of characterization to one more twist in the twisted plot.

The real flood of horrors begins in Scene 2. The imperial hunt is stripped of young Shakespeare's Stratfordian nature poetry; a few remnants are given to Saturninus. Dürrenmatt fashions the Caesar into an amateur poet, thus awakening associations to Nero, Bockelson, and Hitler. On the other hand, his dialogue is partly so laconic that it approaches self-parody; there are six consecutive speeches consisting, all in all, of eleven words (TA 29–30). In *König Johann* there were passages of poetry written by Dürrenmatt; in *Titus* his achievements move on the lower level of modern slang, conceptual discussions, and a few quasi-Brechtian songs, undistinguished in their diction.[25] When Shakespeare's wild poetry

[25] The diction is "spare, sometimes nearly sloppy"; it leads to a neglect of "psychological nuances" (H. Jacobi, *NZZ*, Dec. 15, 1970). Urs Mehlin speaks about Dürrenmatt's "stichomythic dialogue, falling apart into separate exclamations" in Scene 4, entirely an addition ("Claus Bremer. . . ," *Deutsche Shakespeare-Gesellschaft West*, Jahrbuch 1972, p. 81).

is mostly deleted, together with his excessive rhetoric,[26] what is left is the naked horror of Lavinia's rape and mutilation, or of Titus' sacrificing his left hand to no purpose; in addition, there is the entire mad revenge of baking Tamora's beastly sons into a paste.

No doubt Dürrenmatt tried to revise the story toward contemporary relevance and political implications. Tamora's lover Aaron is made a representative of Black Power; he escapes punishment and settles down in Africa together with his blackamoor baby, looking trustingly forward to the bright days of cannibalism (TA 54). Marcus Andronicus, tribune of the people, in Shakespeare a loyal friend to his brother and a voice of moderation, is reshaped into a weathercock dutifully executing Saturninus' cruellest and most unjust orders.[27] Titus is made a lonely figure, rejected both by his brother and the other relatives and supporters surrounding him in Shakespeare and electing his only surviving son as the Caesar. He is supported only by a few war invalids representing the common people. This group gives grotesque theatrical performances with Titus as their stage director.[28] A party leader is turned into the director of a group theater. After the horrors of Scenes 1–3 Dürrenmatt gives us a caba-

[26] Eugene M. Waith has connected Shakespeare's *Titus* and its rhetorics with Ovid's *Metamorphoses*: both describe unbearable, extraordinary pitches of emotion. Images of nature symbolizing horror constitute "a narrative rather than a dramatic device" ("The Metamorphoses of Violence," *Shakespeare Survey*, *10*, p. 47). R. F. Hill's analysis of the rhetorical figures and their deficiencies supports an early date for the play ("The Composition of *Titus Andronicus*," ibid., pp. 64–69).

[27] Marcus is a "surprisingly versatile opportunist, always faithful to the state and government." For Mehlin, this is an indication that the ideal of the middle road is devaluated today (p. 84). This agrees with Dürrenmatt's extremism.

[28] Schwab-Felisch calls Dürrenmatt's "interlude from *Threepenny Opera*" a thin addition, showing how little he had succeeded in putting Shakespeare into a new light; the adaptation is called a "Grusical" (*Frankfurter Allgemeine*, Dec. 14, 1970). Fault was found also with the work of Karl Heinz Stroux as the stage director of the world première: the deeds of violence were located somewhere between "a naive realism and the commercial fun of cabaret" (Jacobi).

349

ret in Scene 6, still expecting us to be shocked by the pile of freshly killed bodies waiting for us in his concluding scene.[29]

There is quite a lot of talk and singing about justice in *Titus Andronicus*. Justice is a basic concern for Dürrenmatt; its problems are not treated in a clear or coherent way in this play. Titus is an innocent victim of injustice from Scene 3 onward. Yet he is guilty of murdering his own son Mutius in Scene 1.[30] The young are furnished with Dürrenmatt's sympathy (plus hippie clothes and rock music in the production). His criticism of his protagonist, partly dating back to Shakespeare, jeopardizes the later portrayal of Titus as an innocent victim;[31] he is both pure and guilty. Why is he entitled to sing and speak so many pompous words about justice?[32] Dürrenmatt's right hand cuts off his left to no purpose. Or is the intention to make Titus carry a very Dürrenmattian theme of injustice: mankind cannot administer justice? The concluding lines speak about the vicious circle of justice and revenge and about the senselessness of dying. This theme is, however, incompatible with the entire idea of a revenge play. If the world is senseless, why take the trouble of executing this monstrous and bloody revenge?

One has an annoying impression of intellectual rape. A powerful creative mind tries to twist an action to fit *his* ideas, *his* vision of the world, yet does not quite succeed. The resistance of the material is too tough. The result is a caricature

[29] After mutilated Lavinia has entered the stage, "there is no point any more in little amusing details of comedy-acting" (Alfons Neukirchen, *Düsseldorfer Nachrichten*, Dec. 14).

[30] Hill's discussion reveals "uncertainty of moral direction and characterization" in Shakespeare's *Titus* (p. 64). Instead of healing these artistic bruises Dürrenmatt created his own uncertainties.

[31] Maxwell sees Titus as a figure foreshadowing Lear, Othello and Hamlet. Titus' "anger and inflexibility" remind one of Lear, the motif of madness of Hamlet (New Arden, pp. xxxix–xl). Dürrenmatt plays down the madness: modern audiences are apt to start pondering whether a madman is a schizophrenic, a traumatic neurotic, or a victim of his parents.

[32] Dürrenmatt's "great lamentation about the decay of justice" has "no persuasive power in connection with this unconscious comedy" (Neukirchen).

of the work of all adapters. Dürrenmatt's *Titus Andronicus* does not make sense, not because of the senselessness or cruelty of the world, but because it was a senseless effort by this adapter to try to overpower the story by mainly verbal means. To judge from the results, there was a coherent total plan behind *König Johann*, a plan brought to completion without anything left over. If there was such a plan in the case of *Titus Andronicus*, it was not brought anywhere near completion.

Adapting a horror melodrama presupposes an iron grip on the part of the dramaturge. In Dürrenmatt's version of *Titus Andronicus*, there are fifteen members of the cast killed —of these, ten on the stage; the ten surviving characters include four badly mutilated war invalids. Violence is not a background feature in this play. The playwright is moving on sensitive areas within the minds of the spectators, tightroping on some utter extremes of their receptivity. However cruel the political reality of our age, however powerful the current of the theater of cruelty during the reign of Elizabeth II, we are not totally insensitive to violence on the stage. The shocks become understandable and tolerable only if they are bound to a significant theme with inviolable links, only if they send a vibration to our intellect, too. These links, developed in Dürrenmatt's dialogue, are not strong enough in *Titus*; there is little to stimulate our intellect. Words do not weigh much against action, and neither do songs against murder. The atrocities are an end in themselves.[33]

Relieving *Titus Andronicus*, leaving a single drop of blood unspilled, was against Dürrenmatt's extremism. Yet those fifteen killings and one rape were not twisted into a new position at all. Dürrenmatt also failed in his effort to turn this

[33] The reviews of the première were almost unanimously condemnatory. A considerable part of the audience left the theater during the performance, leaving the critics in a dilemma: they could neither agree with this protest, nor deny the "total failure of the première," as Gerd Vielhaber puts it (*National-Zeitung*, Basel, Dec. 16). Dürrenmatt was convalescing from a heart infarct during the première; the text was printed beforehand.

melodrama of horror into a "comedy," whatever meaning one might give to that term. All imaginable combinations of farce and tragedy do not work on the stage. There were two kinds of laughter provoked by *Titus*: the hysterical laughter of fear, normally occurring when a terrible stage event exceeds a spectator's tolerance and must be rejected, and laughter at the expense of the playwright.[34] In his striving to reach a grotesque balance between the macabre and the comic, the Dürrenmatt of the so-called mature years is in danger of falling head over heels into the one-sidedly and monotonously dreadful, rather than into a harmless comicality. In the case of *Titus Andronicus*, his efforts to furnish his adaptation with contemporary relevance were more scattered and less successful than in *König Johann*. It is easy to imagine a more convincing exponent of racial liberalism than Aaron, after Iago the blackest of Shakespeare's villains.

Imagine Goethe's Faust hanging up the washing together with his Gretchen, imagine him as an M.D. about to dissect a cadaver who suddenly jumps up: Mephisto. Dürrenmatt was not satisfied with imagining; he realized these inventions on the stage in his scenic version of *Urfaust*. Man's Faustian striving to enlarge the sphere of knowledge; Goethe's best-known play, a synthesis of his life's work; Marlowe's wild tragedy: these, rather than washing, are one's first associations when hearing the name of Faust. The name is focal, comparable with Hamlet's.[35] If Dürrenmatt was after a ready-made literary figure to be reshaped by his vision, he could not have made a better choice from German drama. *King John* and *Titus Andronicus* are lesser-known Shakespeare plays, remote for German-speaking audiences. *Faust* is close at hand. How did he reshape it?

[34] "The play itself destroys its moral alibi. At the end slaughtering people is not even comic or dreadful-grotesque any more, but ridiculous and boring" (Plunien, *Die Welt*, Dec. 14).

[35] Henry Hatfield lists Faust together with Hamlet, Don Giovanni, and Don Quixote among those rare literary figures "who have become genuinely mythical" (*Goethe*, p. 6).

Dürrenmatt's *Urfaust* deviates from his previous adaptations. It has not been published as a book; there is a manuscript in the archives of the Zurich Theater, called a "scenic version," not a play "according to Goethe."[36] The ideas of Dürrenmatt the dramaturge are intimately bound together with their execution by Dürrenmatt the stage director: he had this double role to play in the world première. Faust hanging up washing, Mephisto rising from the dead: directorial rather than literary inventions. We are thus, more than usual, dependent on the reviews of the production; the manuscript is not a complete "producer's book," with a careful staging plan written down during the rehearsals. Rather, it shows Dürrenmatt's literary starting-point.

This includes the idea of using *Urfaust*, young Goethe's first sketch, not *Faust I*, the script published by the fifty-nine-year-old Weimar classicist in 1808. *Urfaust*, written before Goethe was twenty-seven, is incomplete;[37] Dürrenmatt completed it with passages of prose taken from "the so-called Spies *Faustbook*" from 1587,[38] and with "Wild Rose," Goethe's adaptation of a folk song. Contrary to his practice in the Shakespearen adaptations, Dürrenmatt did not write any lines of his own. His twin brother the stage director was responsible for developing additional action, surprising situations, a stage-on-the-stage setting, and unconventional interpretations of roles. The changes made in *Titus* were literary, ineffectual in reshaping its series of events. The adapter, present at every rehearsal of *Urfaust*, took an active role in refashioning its action.

There are two holes in *Urfaust* every adapter has to fill up. The script lacks Mephisto's entrance scene, and the fa-

[36] The MS. consists of 29 typewritten sheets interspersed with printed pages taken from the Reclam edition of *Urfaust*. MS. is the abbreviation for the typewritten pages, Re for the printed ones.

[37] *Urfaust* is preserved only as a copy written down by Luise von Göchhausen, a lady-in-waiting, shortly after Goethe's arrival at Weimar in 1775 (Hermann Reske, *Faust—Eine Einführung*, pp. 56–57; Re 6). It was found and printed in 1887.

[38] Hatfield, p. 136.

mous pact between Faust and his devil is not introduced. Having solved Mephisto's first appearance with his cadaver trick, Dürrenmatt went on by letting Mephisto speak a few key fragments from *Faustbook*, the most important document of the Faust legend before Marlowe. The text of the pact is read aloud by Faust; he sells his soul to Mephisto without any possibility of retraction (MS 4).[39] Faust M.D. appears in the white apron of a butcher; behind his back Mephisto writes occult symbols on a blackboard, among them the Einsteinian formula mc^2. After his first speech Mephisto lies down again, and Faust goes on with his dissecting business drawing a long piece of intestine from Mephisto's abdomen, while speaking Goethe's line about the exhilaration of finding earthworms (Re 16).[40]

The detail is typical of Dürrenmatt's treatment of the play. Away from an over-festive and respectful attitude to the Olympian Goethe, toward a non-pathetic rendering of the verse, toward concrete stage events, toward *Faustbook*. Passages from this source amount to some three pages; they form a layer of barren documentary prose in the texture of the play. An everyday and physical rather than metaphysical Faust, a balladesque form including epic elements (DK 204–05).[41] A stage was built on the stage: a combining link to

[39] Faust is saved by God at the end of Part II; the pact has been quite a problem for scholars. According to Hatfield's sensible discussion Faust does not sell his soul, "he 'bets his life' . . . that he will remain dynamically unsatisfied. . . . While the wager is extremely important as a dramatic device, it is not in itself decisive" (p. 151).

[40] The description is based mainly on Rühle's review; he approves of Mephisto's entrance, this "wild invention," disapproves the bowels business: "such a demonstration, such an introduction of a gag, puts a play quickly out of joint" (*Frankfurter Allgemeine*, Oct. 26, 1970). Voser agrees; when Mephisto is made to repeat the parody of research by ripping open a straw cadaver, this "harasses the idea to death" (*NZZ*, Oct. 24).

[41] Richard Newald has spoken about "the balladesque style of *Urfaust*": the emphasis is on inner, mental events (Helmut de Boor, and Newald, eds., *Geschichte der deutschen Literatur*, VI: 1, p. 254). Dürrenmatt had the outer and scenic form in mind; he made the chorus of extras repeat a few starkly expressive lines as a refrain (Re 65, lines 1436–41).

the pre-Goethean theater performances in market places, given by touring live and puppet theater companies. The stage also served as a scaffold for the final execution scene, concretized further than in Goethe's text. It was surrounded by extras playing students, churchgoers or theater spectators, or acting as stage hands. *Faust* for popular theater.

So far so good. Most critics agreed with Dürrenmatt's aim; disagreements began with his choice of the means.[42] "Earthworm" was not the only word pictorialized with the help of stage action; Dürrenmatt's ideals of a popular theater style enticed him to use over-obvious and heavy means of expression.[43] *Faust I-II* is Goethe's great synthesis; Dürrenmatt analyzed it into one of its constituents. Even if *Urfaust* lacks many a poetic highlight written later, it has an unpolished, fresh charm, its verse a rough power; it is clearly written by the youthful leader of the "storm-and-stress" movement.[44] Dürrenmatt acknowledged this by casting quite a young actress for the tragic role of Gretchen, first Faust's innocent beloved, then an infanticide. Another, quite incompatible invention led the adapter-director to engage Attila Hörbiger, a fine character actor from Vienna, as his Faust; Hörbiger was eighty-one, and was made to look and sound his age. Gretchen looked fourteen; their love scenes were bound to be comic in an unintentional and distracting way. Instead of

[42] "A legitimate basic conception falls apart into gags," Peter Meier writes, agreeing with Dürrenmatt's aims, praising the setting by Raffaëlli, calling the extras "strangely passive," and disagreeing with a great many gags, especially with those repeated (*Tages-Anzeiger*, Oct. 24). Rühle compares Dürrenmatt with a wood-carver interested in medieval subjects: his imagination produces "particles for a vision of a play."

[43] Buschkiel entitled his review *"Urfaust* for Beginners" (*Die Welt*, Oct. 27), Paul Schorno spoke about "exaggerated clarity," and about "a picture book for people" not wanting to take trouble (*Basler Volksblatt*, Nov. 23).

[44] "Storm-and-stress" had two sacraments, emotion and nature Ernst Beutler, *Faust und Urfaust*, Schönemann, p. X). For passages influenced by these sacraments see, e.g., Re 10–11, lines 57–65, 79–80; Re 32–33, lines 539–46, 563–73. Cf. Reske, pp. 52–53; Otto Mann, *Geschichte des deutschen Dramas*, p. 192.

some of the most delicate love scenes in German literature, Dürrenmatt's *Urfaust* included discussions between a grandpa and granddaughter.[45] A grotesque contrast misplaced.

In *Faust I* Goethe rejuvenated his protagonist. Dürrenmatt disagrees: for him, it is a modern idea that an old man seduces a young girl (DK 203–04). On the other hand, it has been argued that making Faust younger shortens the gap between the disparate parts of the play, between Faust's search for knowledge and Gretchen's tragedy.[46] In Dürrenmatt they remain apart. The result was an uneven production, with its merits in Gretchen's unadorned tragedy, especially in the cathedral and prison scenes, in the stark simplicity of the visual elements, and in those courageous inventions not repeated to death. This *Urfaust* was not very Faustian; rather than an explorer of the unknown coasts of knowledge, Faust is another figure in Dürrenmatt's spacious wax cabinet of antiheroes, a resigned seeker of truth, and a lascivious old man guilty of Gretchen's death without any extenuating circumstances, without being actively tempted by Mephisto, who is shown as a nice chap and a comedian rather than as a devil.[47] If we are not disturbed by Grandpa Faust, this is how we were supposed to take him. Faust M.D. sells his soul and is condemned. Dürrenmatt, the writer of *The Physicists*, is a post-Einsteinian critic of science; he has no sympathy left for man's eternal striving. Goethe's youthful sketch was turned into a new position, not without a jarring sound.[48]

[45] The mental picture of a grandfather disturbed several critics; director Dürrenmatt refused to see his Faust "as the spectators must see him" (François Bondy, *Süddeutsche Zeitung*, Oct. 26). Cf. Voser.

[46] Reske, p. 59.

[47] Brock-Sulzer accepts Dürrenmatt's old and guilty Faust as such: "one might even state that Faust also seduces Mephisto to a certain degree" (*Die Tat*, Oct. 26). Faust's guilt is totally accepted also by Kurt Weibel (*TV-Radio-Zeitung*, Nov. 1–7, 1970).

[48] Carl Holenstein has spoken about "a fight between the language and its scenic presentation"; Goethe's text could have done without "these emphatically wilful scenic additions" (*Neue Zürcher Nachrichten*, Oct. 24).

Dürrenmatt the adapter is obviously interested in first sketches, in scripts not yet mastered by their youthful creators. Using a parallel to *Urfaust*, he called *Titus Andronicus* Shakespeare's "Urstück," a draft containing the kernel of later masterpieces. The implication is that an adapter is needed to thresh away the chaff. *Woyzeck*, Dürrenmatt's next dramaturgic work, does not need such an excuse. All that Georg Büchner left us of his magnum opus at his untimely death is a cluster of scenes, some clearly sketches, others worked toward completion. Without an active effort by an adapter, there is no actable play at all; with his help we have a masterpiece.

Büchnerology means an effort to foretell the future from tiny fragments of a play. It can be divided into two branches, pure and applied. The purely scholarly approach tries to establish what Büchner really wrote; the applied has the practical aim of constructing a reading and/or stage version from these fragments.[49] Dürrenmatt is an applied Büchnerologist. His *Woyzeck* is the last part of a trilogy of plays dealing with the problems of science. The other members of the trilogy are *Urfaust* and *Portrait of a Planet*.

The first connecting link between Büchner and Dürrenmatt is their interest in science. Goethe, an amateur scientist, died in 1832; Büchner, a professional, in 1837. Yet these two belong to layers far from one another in the history of German literature. Büchner, dead before his twenty-fourth birthday, precedes naturalism and Gerhart Hauptmann by half a

[49] Most editions of *Woyzeck* are derived from Fritz Bergemann, *Georg Büchners Werke und Briefe*, 1922; taken as an authority in the field of pure Büchnerology it reached its ninth edition in 1962. Two recent readings of the original papers show, however, that Bergemann constructed a reading version from the various sketches, published as they are by Egon Krause (*Woyzeck*, Insel Verlag: 1969) and Werner H. Lehmann (*G.B.: Sämtliche Werke und Briefe*, I, Christian Werner Verlag: 1967). See Krause, pp. 15–20. Dürrenmatt quotes Krause in the playbill of his *Woyzeck*: as there is no final version authorized by Büchner, he felt free to practice applied Büchnerology, constructing his own collage.

357

century, expressionism and the epic theater by nearly a hundred years. He is a lonely predecessor of all these movements, a rebellious yet scientifically cool observer of life. His second point of connection with Dürrenmatt is his sympathy for the down-and-out.[50] *Woyzeck*, based partly on documentary materials, tells the story of a rank-and-file soldier: the first member of his class to enter the German stage as a protagonist.

Dürrenmatt's *Woyzeck* is not a counter-sketch. The adapter neither twists Büchner's play into a new position, nor criticizes it; he just completes it using his best judgment. Dürrenmatt shares Büchner's aims to the extent of bridling polemical inclinations for once. Of all of Dürrenmatt's adaptations, this is the closest to its source, both in spirit and the letter. As in the case of *Urfaust*, Dürrenmatt played the role of the stage director, too. The ensuing discussion is based on an unpublished manuscript in the archives of the Zurich Theater; the copy includes additions, deletions, changes, and stage directions, presumably written down during the rehearsals. It is worked further toward a prompt-book than the script of *Urfaust* discussed above. See Figures 17 and 18.

The story of *Woyzeck* is straightforward. A research doctor exploits Woyzeck as his guinea pig, letting him eat only peas; while shaving his captain, Woyzeck has to listen to lectures on morality. He has a child by Marie, to whom he is not married; he hears strange voices, and when Marie commits adultery with the Drum Major, an imposing military figure, his voices order him to kill Marie with a knife. Harassed by his superiors, the loser in the love triangle, Woyzeck follows these orders. None of the four manuscript versions includes an end that could be called definite. The end usually employed is a free interpretation and continuation of several short glimpses: Woyzeck drowns while trying to hide the murder weapon. Yet there is a scene in which he appears, wet through, before his child.

[50] Hans Mayer speaks about Büchner's "double optics" combining a satirical distortion of the upper class with a "powerless pity" for Woyzeck and his like (*G.B.: Woyzeck*, p. 64).

Though he retains this general outline of action, Dürrenmatt has his own solutions to offer. First of all, he not only connects scenes and sequences from the various versions, but also has speeches made up from several sources. The number of such mixed speeches is 20 or close to 8 percent. Everything Büchner wrote is material for dramaturge Dürrenmatt; contrary to his methods with Shakespeare and Strindberg, he refrains from writing new lines.[51] Goethe and Büchner, two German classics, are rearranged, not rewritten. Dürrenmatt starts from the last and most fully developed manuscript version H4, as all adapters of *Woyzeck* do; he completes it with both of the scenes from the partial version h3, and with scenes, speeches, and sentences from the early sketches h1 and h2.[52] He creates continuity by repeating songs or stanzas in several scenes. His most remarkable construction is a second barber scene, in which Woyzeck shaves the Drum Major. Without twisting the story Dürrenmatt creates inner connections and new emphases within the script through these inconspicuous means, and by arranging the scenes in a different order.

A comparison of four reading versions of *Woyzeck*, between four results of applied Büchnerology, reveals Dürrenmatt's aims and achievements. Werner H. Lehmann moves closest to H4; Fritz Bergemann and Carl Richard Mueller, an American editor and translator, take greater liberties.[53]

[51] The only passage I have been unable to trace back to the various versions of *Woyzeck* is a handwritten addition to a song: "und schoss das Wild daher, gleich wie's ihm gefällt" (Wk 26). The addition is possibly taken from some version of the folk song employed by Büchner.

[52] Dürrenmatt's *Woyzeck* includes 129 speeches from H4, 62 from h1, 31 from h2, and 14 from h3; with the 20 mixed speeches added this makes a total of 256. The murder sequence occurs only in h1; there are twice as many speeches from it than from the somewhat fuller h2 (62—31). The manuscripts are numbered according to Krause.

[53] Lehmann has three versions to offer: a reprinting in the supposed chronological order (pp. 145–81), an arrangement of the parallel scenes side by side (pp. 337–406), and a reading version (pp. 407–31). Mayer includes an impression of Bergemann's ninth edition (pp. 5–26) and other materials (pp. 27–50). Mueller's edition is pub-

DÜRRENMATT

Dürrenmatt opens his version with Woyzeck's hallucinations in the open field, as Lehmann and H4 do, not with the first barber scene (H4,5), like Bergemann and Mueller. He places both Woyzeck's scenes with the Doctor early in the play (Scenes 3 and 8). Because of this order, the emphasis is on Woyzeck as a victim of scientific experiments rather than of military chicanery. Both themes exist in the play, also in Dürrenmatt's version; yet he gives preference to Büchner's and his own criticism of science, of its inhuman methods. The impression was confirmed by Dürrenmatt's choice of actors. His Captain was big, fleshy, and indolent, his Doctor small and agile. Woyzeck has two evil spirits, one soft and sentimentally egocentric, the other hard and exploiting.[54]

Another unconventional arrangement concerns the growth of jealous suspicions in Woyzeck's mind. Dürrenmatt gives time to his Woyzeck and his audiences to formulate them. The Drum Major gives earrings to Marie; in all the other versions she wears them immediately after these two have met in a fair booth. Woyzeck's jealousy is aroused right away. Dürrenmatt interposes three scenes, among them H4,6, a love meeting between Marie and the Drum Major, and places them in bed. When the Captain has cruelly revealed the liaison to Woyzeck, Marie and the betrayed husband meet in front of the house, while the Drum Major is hiding in her bed. Dürrenmatt takes pains to make the love triangle develop gradually and concretely in terms of the stage, with dramaturgic advantage. All kinds of intentions have been read from and into Büchner's various versions; it seems to be safe enough to say that the action evolved toward greater complexity. Dürrenmatt's retarding treatment of the theme of jealousy is in this direction.

---

lished in *G.B.: Complete Plays and Prose*, New York: Hill and Wang, 1963, pp. 107–38; his aim was to enlarge earlier translations into English (p. xxxi).

[54] For Günther Penzoldt, the Captain represents "the commonplace joviality of German garrison officers," the Doctor both a certain professor at Giessen and the learned at large (*G.B.*, pp. 45–46). Mayer emphasizes that the morals of these two are "socially determined" (p. 65).

Dürrenmatt's second barber scene adds both to the theme of science and to the love triangle. The first half of it is a somewhat shortened version of h1,10, a scene usually left out: a discussion between an unnamed barber and an equally unnamed sergeant. Dürrenmatt gives it to Woyzeck and to the Drum Major and uses it as an introduction to the fight scene between these two, usually included (H4,14). As it is, the scene adds a facet to Woyzeck's crude philosophy of life: "What is Man? Bones! Dust, sand, dung" (Wk 29–30). It also gives Woyzeck the upper hand of the Drum Major, for a passing moment. The razor is on the throat of his rival: one slash, and . . . The moment passes: Woyzeck is not a man to grasp at it. He is too servile, too weak—and too inescapably under the influence of his Captain: "You're a virtuous man, a good man, a good man" (Wk 13).[55] And so our good man is beaten by the Drum Major, then made to drink some shaving water, as a touch of the theater of cruelty; two soldiers passing by complete his social humiliation.[56] Ironically enough, Woyzeck directs the revenging act of murder toward Marie, the weaker, more innocent, and repenting partner in the adultery. The scene closes with Woyzeck's seeing the knife with the eyes of his lively mind.

The new barber scene, certainly an interesting addition, uses speeches from three sources. Dürrenmatt goes still further in his Scene 13, a crowd scene with a complicated action at the inn. His collage consists of materials from eight scenes.[57] Woyzeck sees Marie and the Drum Major dancing

---

[55] Translations by Mueller, pp. 129, 110; h1,10 is included as a separate scene.

[56] Brock-Sulzer calls this a scene of "wild, dreadful power" (*Die Tat*, Feb. 21, 1972), while Rühle and Meier feel that it interferes with other motivations for the murder (*Frankfurter Allgemeine*, Feb. 22; *Tages-Anzeiger*, Feb. 19). There were perhaps exaggerated hopes attached to this new discovery, both by Dürrenmatt and his critics; the scene can also be taken as a part of his total dramaturgic conception.

[57] There is some confusion in Dürrenmatt's scene division. The revised script includes scenes numbered as 13, 13a, 14, and 14; what is above called Scene 13 is a combination of scenes 13, 13a, and the first Scene 14. If the last of these is taken as a separate scene, there are 'only' seven sources for Scene 13.

together, and Marie's words "Don't stop! Don't stop!" (Immer zu!) start going around in his head. His emotionally highly charged speech (Wk 28) is made up of extracts from three scenes. Details in the dialogue also show that Dürrenmatt has used Bergemann as his source, and not only Egon Krause's 'pure' edition. In the last sequence of the play, Dürrenmatt leaves out the dramatic and thriller-like moment of Woyzeck's exposure at the inn: there are stains of blood on his hands. Having shown Woyzeck's development into a murderer Dürrenmatt is no longer interested in his reactions. He brings Woyzeck back from the pond, ready for the trial prophesied in the ironical curtain line given by Dürrenmatt to the Doctor: "A good, genuine, beautiful murder" (Wk 41).[58] A final result of his experiments, too.

Some of Dürrenmatt's solutions are both dramaturgic and directorial. In the sketch showing Woyzeck wet through, an idiot appears; in Dürrenmatt's stage interpretation this figure was present in all family scenes with Marie and also spoke a few lines given to "the Clown" and to unnamed children in the manuscripts. His spastic movements and painful efforts to handle a spoon made him a parallel to Woyzeck's equally futile strivings to gain control over life. Büchner's scientifically cool insights were responsible for another parallel, in the figures of the circus ape and horse: two thinking animals surrounded by beastly men. The grandmother, the fourth member in Dürrenmatt's family group, kept sorting peas throughout the play, and the noise of peas falling into a bucket was an audible punctuation at many a moment.

Against a grey backdrop and side curtains, against an

---

[58] Penzoldt remarks that "the inner action of the play" is over with the murder, and this explains the success of *Woyzeck* even without a definite ending (pp. 39–40). Krause starts from the fact that the murder sequence exists only in h1, and arrives at the speculative conclusion that Büchner intended to leave the murder out altogether (pp. 168–72, 204–33). The Biblical echoes and other pieces of evidence remain scanty and ambiguous, however; there is no way of knowing Büchner's final intention, had he lived. Translations by Mueller, pp. 124, 137–38.

ascetic visual conception, Dürrenmatt staged a play for the actors. The performance was under- rather than overplayed,[59] though invigorated with a few cabaret tricks. The Captain's lecture on morality was accompanied by an empty bottle being found in his boot. Seriousness with satiric ingredients: Dürrenmatt's *Woyzeck*. The anxiety of his protagonist hardly did justice to the wildness and universality inherent in this role. In the fairy tale, told by Dürrenmatt's Grandmother in a sharp and loud, quite monotonous tone of voice, the anxiety moves into space, reaching for the stars.[60]

Dürrenmatt as a stage director: an object for a specific study, to be completed with the help of interviews with actors, stage designers, and other collaborators. A premature first impression suggests that our playwright feels at home in designing the visual totality of his interpretations rather than in instructing the actors.[61] Dürrenmatt as the adapter of *Woyzeck*: discreet, sympathetic in his treatment of the protagonist and the message, skillful in his sentence-by-sentence puzzle play, a legitimate game. His efforts to concretize and create continuity, his new invention in constructing the barber scene, give his version certain advantages over other results of applied Büchnerology. For stage directors sharing Dürrenmatt's basic theatrical vision in 1972, and his belief in grotesque contrasts within an ascetic style of staging,[62] this

---

[59] This is especially true of Hans-Helmut Dickow in the title role: a controlled, skillful performance, declining toward the end. "One never senses his anxiety," Rühle says.

[60] Büchner was an early acquaintance for Dürrenmatt: there is an echo from this fairy tale in his exercise "Christmas," placed as the opening piece in *The City*, as Spycher remarks (*F.D.*, p. 40). There is a barber scene in KJ: the Bastard as Woyzeck.

[61] Meier, Benjamin Henrichs (*Süddeutsche Zeitung*, Feb. 22, 1972) and Thomas Terry (*Tagesspiegel*, Feb. 23) esteem Dürrenmatt's achievement as a dramaturge more highly than his work in instructing the actors.

[62] Gerhart Baumann emphasizes the collision of contrasting elements as a focal element in *Woyzeck* in his descriptive study on Büchner (*G.B.*, e.g., pp. 149–50, 158, 172–73).

certainly actable *Woyzeck* must be a reliable starting-point for a stage interpretation. In his search for a laconic, fast-moving, and matter-of-fact poetry for the stage, in his search for new formulations of the problems of science, Dürrenmatt found a kindred spirit in Büchner. The Bastard in *König Johann*, the protagonist of Dürrenmatt's first adaptation of a classic play, is a marionette of the alien force of chance. His Woyzeck, a less energetic and humbler representative of the common people, is a victim of the inhuman forces in science and in society, on the stage and within his mind.[63]

Dürrenmatt as a dramaturge: the balance is temporary. Six of his adaptations were produced between 1967 and 1972; only one of these was based on an original text of his own. Of these, one has been immensely popular throughout Europe (*Play Strindberg*), two had a wide circulation (*The Anabaptists, König Johann*), one was a downright flop (*Titus Andronicus*), two were local Swiss events rather than products for a larger market (*Urfaust, Woyzeck*).[64] Popularity, of course, is no absolute yardstick; in spite of its wide acclaim, *Play Strindberg* is hardly an artistic success, while *Woyzeck*, competent as a piece of dramaturgy, has had to stand some tough competition.

Is Dürrenmatt a remarkable dramaturge? Yes, he is, by any standards; yet one cannot help voicing a feeling of slight disappointment. Dürrenmatt's dramaturgic phase has meant that the interest in him has lessened in London, in New York, in the Anglo-American world as a whole. One of the greatest creative dramatists of our age as a dramaturge, more

[63] "The terrible fatalism of history," a formulation from one of Büchner's letters, is taken as a key concept to his work (Ernst Johann, *G.B.*, p. 86; cf. Mayer, p. 61, Penzoldt, pp. 19–20). One might speak of a fatalism of chance in Dürrenmatt.

[64] According to statistics published by Patterson, *German Theatre Today*, pp. 114–17, Dürrenmatt was clearly the most popular living German-language playwright during the ten-year period 1964–74. He had 213 productions in West Germany, Austria, and Switzerland; he was followed by Peter Hacks and Peter Handke (111 and 91 productions). PS was the most popular play with 62 productions; KJ was tenth in order with 27.

or less competent, more or less controversial: with all due respect to this profession, has it not demanded rather too much of Dürrenmatt's time and energy? Resorting to stories invented by others: a sign of diminishing powers of creation in this inventive playwright? *The Visit* is a contemporary classic; *König Johann* and *Woyzeck*, Dürrenmatt's most successful adaptations, are classics made contemporary. All right, one does not fabricate classics of our age on a conveyor belt, they just happen, but not without creative efforts by talented playwrights. The early 1970's were to see two efforts by Dürrenmatt—probably not, however, signalling the end of his work as a dramaturge.[65] A reconciling point is that Dürrenmatt is clearly the same man as a dramatist and as a dramaturge, both creative and critical, both skilled and whimsical, both ingenious and a victim of his own idiosyncracies, not always for the good of his work, in either of these fields.

[65] During his year in Basle Dürrenmatt planned adapting *Troilus and Cressida* by Shakespeare and *The Acharnians* (Acharnes) by Aristophanes. Several remarks in his theoretical writings make one speculate that he might adapt *The Robbers* by Schiller one day—turning it into a comedy. He directed *Emilia Galotti* by Lessing at the Zurich Theater in 1974: the original text, not his adaptation. To his disappointment, the production ran only for four weeks (G 47–48); in 1975 he stated that he needed distance from the practical theater work (G 20).

17 Cosmic and Underground Visions

PORTRAIT OF A PLANET,
THE PARTAKER

||||||||||||||||||||||||||||||||||||||||||||||||||||||||||||||||||||||||||||||||||||||

"If one could but stand outside the world, it would no longer be threatening. But I have neither the right nor the ability to be an outsider to this world" (FP 34). These words were written by Dürrenmatt in 1955, published in *Problems of the Theater.* His *Portrait of a Planet* (Porträt eines Planeten, 1970-71)[1] begins with a scene among four outsiders to Earth. They are gods, distant and indifferent. Is Dürrenmatt now asserting his right to be an outsider sharing their cool cosmic vision of Earth as a nameless and unknown planet, just about to be destroyed as its sun explodes, "pegs out"? He is not; the gods appear only in the first and last scenes of the play. The nineteen scenes in between are menacing earthly visions, written by a 'partaker' for the benefit of other inhabitants of Earth.

The planet Dürrenmatt portrays is seen from two contrasting viewpoints, from the remote outer space and from amidst human life as it was lived about the year 1970. Cosmic photographs are mixed in with close-ups. Dürrenmatt starts with the idea of the sudden end of the world: our sun, even if a stable star, may turn into a supernova and explode, thus destroying us all. He takes advantage of his hobby as an amateur astronomer and as a critic of science, not, however,

[1] *Portrait* opened in Düsseldorf in November 1970, as the middle item in Dürrenmatt's trinary offerings that dark autumn; his other world premières were *Urfaust* and *Titus.* There were two productions of *Portrait* in 1971, one in Zurich, directed by the playwright himself, the other in Berlin. The Zurich version was authorized for publication as a book including detailed stage directions concerning the movements and positions of the actors. The spelling "Portrait" is used in the Düsseldorf and Zurich playbills, "Porträt" in Berlin and in the book version.

simply to prove himself knowledgeable about the stars. He has harassing questions to put to his audiences: are we prepared for the end of the world? Can we survive the prospect of an imminent world catastrophe? Have we used the chances offered by Earth?

Very Dürrenmattian questions, no doubt. Just as Dürrenmattian as the answers he implies: no, we are not prepared, we shall not be able to survive, we have not made use of the chances offered. These questions and answers are reminiscent of *Operation Vega*, of *The Physicists*, of Dürrenmatt's entire position as a hidden moralist who stepped openly into the limelights during the 1960's, both in his plays and adaptations. *The Meteor* left us wondering whether Dürrenmatt had been able to find a framework for his seriousness; now he presents us a cosmic framework. *Portrait of a Planet* is written with a collage technique new to Dürrenmatt. Behind this freshness of approach there are clear enough connections with his moral world.

A collage for the stage: the body of the play consists of short glimpses of life on Earth, with all the misery caused by man, his self-interests, cruelty, political and other stupidity, intolerance, bestiality. Dürrenmatt has eight characters with Biblical names in his cast; the actors have to jump from one role to another throughout the play. Adam, for example, is the Swiss-born Secretary General of a world-wide humanitarian organization, a G.I. shot to death in Vietnam, a colored man in love with a white woman, a disillusioned working-class ex-politician, and the first god. All actors take part in group scenes. The sketches fade into one another, so that Adam's dead body from Vietnam remains on the stage during the next two scenes dealing with war widows and with Vietnam peace negotiations. The setting of the Zurich production consisted of a slightly oblique platform with slopes all around; there was a round horizon with the Milky Way to be lit from behind (PeP 12). The props needed in the scenes were brought in and out by the actors.

367

There is nothing extraordinary in these arrangements. Dürrenmatt avoids the more conspicuous technical appliances frequently employed in documentary theater, such as projected pictures, film sequences, a plentiful usage of loudspeakers or sound tape. Loudspeakers have a role only as necessary props in his moon-landing scene; there is a musician sitting at the side of the platform. The style chosen by Dürrenmatt for his portrait is that of a "living newspaper" played by eight actors. His preface emphasizes his reliance on their work: "I do not write my plays for the actors any more, I compose my plays with them" (PeP 10).

After the gods the stage is entered by primitive people. The female members of the cast use sex and the superiority granted by modern technology to induce a distant tribe to give up cannibalism. Getting rid of barbarity on an island leads to hunger on the continent; Dürrenmatt's sardonic comment on humanitarianism includes a dig at Switzerland in the figure of the Secretary General and in the symbol of the Red Cross. The points are fairly slight, considering that the scene occupies nearly a sixth of the whole play. As in *Play Strindberg*, as in *Urfaust* and *Woyzeck*, Dürrenmatt's concept of rhythm includes a process of acceleration toward the end. The scenes can grow shorter, as the spectators are acclimatized to the continued role changes. Hints in the costumes and props are enough to mark the beginning of a new role and a new scene.

The scenes touch upon a whole batch of contemporary phenomena with breathtaking speed. At first sight there does not seem to be any connection between the sketches; yet a closer look reveals that they are carefully juxtaposed.[2] The worry of a Western couple about their son corresponds with the anxiety of an oriental one; both pairs of parents re-enter the stage toward the end of the play. There is a connection

[2] Hansres Jacobi and Voser are among the few critics paying attention to the contrapuntal arrangement of the sketches. The former connects the three love scenes and the two monologue scenes, the latter also the family scenes (*NZZ*, Nov. 12, 1970; March 27, 1971).

to a fifth scene, portraying the encounter between a father and his rebellious daughters living in a commune of hippies. Four old ladies in a ward assess their lives in monologues, and so do four men in an asylum. Three love stories end in separation or death caused by racial hatred or space catastrophes. Dürrenmatt's first loving couple on the moon never comes back: the bride dies with the nightingale speech from *Romeo and Juliet* on her lips, the man saves the Mars program with a patriotic last word.

Secret agents and political prisoners face torture, death, or oblivion. A central position in the play is occupied by a drug-addict scene: a senseless phrase variously uttered by all members of the cast. Toward the end of the play, the cosmic catastrophe approaches; the politicians are just as ineffectual in dealing with the increasing number of hurricanes as they were in stopping the war. The themes of the play are gathered together in Scene 20: a surprising jump into a psalm-like, powerfully Biblical diction, a song of praise to God for His gifts and tribulations.[3] After that, only a return to the four indifferent gods: our sun has "pegged out" (PeP 83).

A collage should have a value independent of the materials used to construct it. No matter how trite and commonplace the newspaper clippings painted over or connected with other materials, we should be impressed by the total effect thus created by the artist.[4] In a similar way Dürrenmatt believes that *Portrait*, his scenic collage, has a value

---

[3] The reactions to this controversial stylistic twist range from unreserved acceptance (Voser; Brock-Sulzer, *Die Tat*, March 29, 1971) to rejection. Rühle suspects that Dürrenmatt is enforcing the emotional tone from *It Is Written* through his later dramaturgy (*Frankfurter Allgemeine*, March 29, 1971). The prayer to God was taken ironically in Düsseldorf. Cf. Durzak, *D., Frisch, Weiss*, pp. 137, 143.

[4] The Düsseldorf production probably tried to visualize the collage-like quality of the play: there were newspapers lying all around. The effect was misleading; the actors were like clochards or hobos creeping forth from below the papers in the early scenes. Dürrenmatt praises Erwin Axer, the director, in his preface, yet presents the afterthought that an arena stage was not the best possible choice for the play (PeP 11).

369

beyond that of the contents of its materials, beyond these scenes covering topics treated almost daily in the newspapers. That is why he gives his seemingly arbitrary series of scenes a structure based on contrasts and parallels; that is why there are thematic cross references between his sketches. Writing sketches for a cabaret is the business of a sprinter, so to speak: a contemporary topic, a short distance, is to be covered quickly and without over-laborious preparations. A full-length cabaret program may include faster and slower dashes, more or less successful sketches. Dürrenmatt is trying to combine the virtues of a cabaret program with those of a full-length play: a six-mile sprint.[5]

This is a risky procedure, for various reasons. First of all, Dürrenmatt is making matters both easy and difficult for his spectators. Easy in the sense that his scenes as such are low-brow, based on newspaper materials; the playwright uses his best skills in giving them a striking foreground. Difficult in the sense that one should be able to construct a total picture of the life on this planet out of these snapshots. There is little interaction between the scenic images. One doubts whether the thematic parallels and the opening and concluding scenes with their four gods are means powerful enough to guarantee that a total vision is communicated.[6] A spectator sensing the totality should resist the temptation to compare the scenes with one another: the scenic images are not to be taken as independent items, as cabaret numbers, more or less relevant, more or less trite. Yet can we help ourselves?[7] Most critics

[5] According to Walther Karsch, Helmut Käutner succeeded well as the director of *Portrait* at the Berlin Volksbühne. On one hand, he took the play as a cabaret and achieved stunning visual effects with the help of a mirror; on the other, the actors retained a constant feature in the middle of variety: Eva reacted as Eva throughout the play (*Tagesspiegel*, Nov. 30). Cf. Luft, *Die Welt*, Nov. 29, 1971.

[6] A senseless world destroyed by a senseless cosmic event: this is Hans Rudolf Haller's definition of Dürrenmatt's basic idea. "Yet does it find a form on the stage? . . . It does not touch us" (*TV-Radio-Zeitung*, Apr. 4–10, 1971).

[7] Voser sees *Portrait* as a totality; she calls "certain images" thin and devoid of substance, but voices a question: "is one permitted to

370

yielded to the temptation; they compared the sketches not only with each other but with the treatment of similar topics by other playwrights and by Dürrenmatt in his earlier plays. Points of comparison, most of them unfavorable for *Portrait*, range from *The Skin of Our Teeth* by Wilder to *Vietnam Discourse* by Weiss, from *The Physicists* to *Operation Vega*. Again, Dürrenmatt shows a nuclear physicist in an asylum; again, he imagines a cosmic catastrophe. He cherishes quotations—not from Chairman Mao, but from his own plays: "advertisements of myself."

Furthermore, the materials chosen for the various scenes seem unnecessarily banal. When a playwright sits down to ponder the situation of the world in 1970, are there any topics he must not omit? Vietnam, the generation gap, the moon landing. *Portrait* consists of scenes Dürrenmatt could not possibly leave out, rather than of scenes he had to get in. In other words, one has a strong impression that the playwright proceeded deductively, starting from a total vision and demonstrating it with a number of examples, with snapshots.[8] The story of *The Visit* grew, quite by itself, into a kind of myth of the 1950's; in *Portrait* Dürrenmatt took it as his task to create a series of mythical events embracing all significant aspects of our life in the year 1970. The result might have been more inspired and significant if he had started inductively, from sketches personal and striking enough to demand a place within the whole.

Dürrenmatt was conscious of the risks inherent in his approach. He says in his preface that Earth portrayed at the moment of its destruction includes "a disorder of moments of action, an enormous quantity of banal, terrible, ordinary,

---

look at them in isolation?" Her final conclusion is that Dürrenmatt's experiment deserves serious consideration from the spectator.

[8] Brock-Sulzer calls the figures types, *Portrait* "a paradigmatic play" written for a world theater. Dürrenmatt, once "an embodiment of sensuous abundance," now lets the structures appear naked on the surface: a return to abundance may possibly follow his present ascetic usage of language (*Die Tat*, March 27, 1971).

extraordinary, absurd, monotonous, grotesque, unhappy, but also happy scenes." Facing the difficulty of choosing between these scenes, Dürrenmatt found a paradoxical way out: "If there are innumerably many scenes possible within a stuff, it can also be presented with a few scenes; these few scenes become more and more important, even if they look banal as such" (PeP 9). A valid paradox? Can a scene be both important and banal? How to treat a banal subject so that the treatment is not banal? Dürrenmatt believed in the elevating force of his total vision, of his collage techniques, of his actors. A spectator bombarded with "banal, terrible," etc. scenes for ninety-five minutes was to leave the theater having experienced something important. One is inclined to be skeptical about the ability of the theater to succeed this far in treating topics made banal also by the news media.

The style or formula of collage techniques induced the critics to expect clearly formulated points of view, a black-and-white vision of the world. Dürrenmatt's scenes certainly include their sharp edges and satirical passing shots. Yet his main interest lies in opening up conflicts, not in solving problems.[9] For him, the stage is an "immense field of human conflicts" (PeP 8). His snapshots in *Portrait* reveal a series of such conflicts. Parents and children confront one another; Dürrenmatt gives arguments for both—and achieves a kind of triple offense. Some parents are annoyed by the words written for the hippies, some youthful or liberal spectators by those given to the father, and a few critics by the absence of any clear viewpoint pro or con, such as documentary dramatics usually present.

Showing a whole batch of conflicts within a full-length play creates an over-all impression of facility, no matter how carefully the conflicts are subjugated to a cosmic vision. In

[9] Holenstein closes his interesting analysis by remarking that Dürrenmatt is "almost oppressively undecided"; the spectators are led into continued discussion of the topics treated (*Neue Zürcher Nachrichten*, March 30, 1971). "Agnosticism as a dogma" is Durzak's summary of Dürrenmatt's latest phase (pp. 143–44).

The Physicists Dürrenmatt took the trouble to imagine a full-length action around the atomic bomb. The play ended in resignation: the controversy between the scientists and other people included a basic conflict of visions, not a neatly solvable problem. A full-length play allowed the writer to enlighten the conflict from various points of view. It is too facile to reveal an unresolvable conflict within a scene, as the total length of the treatment does not allow of any effort to solve the "human conflict." Before the various scenic images of *Portrait* have time to gather thematic significance, they are replaced by new images.

The conclusions reached above are somewhat ambiguous. *Portrait of a Planet* is not merely a motley anthology of black humor and newspaper clippings, nor is it a play too sloppy to have any coordinating point of view at all. Yet Dürrenmatt fails in communicating his cosmic vision in a number of ways and for various reasons, mostly because of the banality of the materials employed.[10] One cannot resist the temptation to pick out certain scenes, either because the materials are less banal than in the surrounding scenes (reciting the psalm-like prayer), or because the treatment elevates them (the monologues helped by the stage presence of the actors). The impression of unevenness is inescapable.

Portrait of a Planet is a play in which an established play-wright leaves his accustomed field and tries to conquer new territory by adopting a new kind of technique. Dürrenmatt took this risk when returning to his own original plays after a series of adaptations. A teller of grotesque stories tries to be

[10] The Düsseldorf production was almost unanimously discarded by the critics (e.g., Schwab-Felisch, *Frankfurter Allgemeine*, Nov. 12; Volker Canaris, *Die Zeit*, Nov. 20, 1970). The opinions of the Zurich and Berlin productions were more varied; the banality of Dürrenmatt's scenes was objected to, e.g., by Heinz Thiel and Meier (*Abend-Zeitung*, Zurich, March 30; *Tages-Anzeiger*, March 27, 1971), and by Anton Krättli, who praises *Portrait* as a script for the actors ("Nackter Hamlet und Welttheater," *Schweizer Monatshefte, 51,* 2, May 1971, pp. 89–90).

373

up-to-date, cultivating his inclination to separate artistic inventions within a dispersed yet thematically coherent whole. He adapts newspaper materials. Dürrenmatt is ambitious enough to say "memento mori" to all mankind; what he achieves is a series of drab and flat, clearly derivative scenic images within a grand framework, within a world theater based on a disillusioned portrayal of our present-day situation. His effort to combine two extreme visions, a cosmic and an earthly one, has not been considered a success by anyone; the best one can state is that the effort was not unworthy of Dürrenmatt.

From earthly to underground visions: the descent into the hell of *The Partaker* (Der Mitmacher, 1973). The play takes place five floors below the earth, in the living and working quarter surroundings of Doc, a corrupt scientist. There are bulky pillars of concrete, a door to a cold-storage room on the left, a lift as the only exit upwards on the right, and, in between, a cubicle in which Doc lives. The sound of dripping water is heard every now and then. The invisible ceiling "vanishes in the background into darkness, into apparent infinity"; there are perhaps a few electric bulbs hanging from a cable. The background is full of heaps of empty coffins (Mit 8–10).

Doc is a "necrodialyzist." It is his invention and job to make dead bodies dissolve into nothing; the bodies are the product of Murder Inc. led by Boss. Dürrenmatt fills his hell with a criminal melodrama intended to make critical points against intellectuals and their participation in the business of life (to be read: business of death). He serves up a thriller minus tension. Or a thriller turned upside down, told from the end to the beginning. The terrible secret behind the workings of the undertaking is revealed right away. Dürrenmatt does not trouble to excite our curiosity, but jumps right into the conclusions of his extreme situation. The sensational artistic invention of dissolving bodies wears thin during the

374

first half-hour of stage action.[11] When the treatment of the fourth body begins in the cold-storage room, a red light starts burning and, after a while, water starts dripping, there is little curiosity left in us. We know Dürrenmatt's—once Agatha Christie's—system by heart: ten little Indians.

Chance plays a prominent role in Dürrenmatt's melodrama. Boss and Doc meet by chance in the taxi driven by our scientist. He had given up his university career and accepted a job in industry, lured by money—only to be ousted from his factory during an economic crisis. This drove him to participate in mass murder. When Doc leaves his underground hell for the first time in over a year and goes into a bar—bang! there she sits, the incomparable Ann, a photomodel and a gangster bride. May I sleep with you? she whispers to Doc, chosen quite by chance, and down they go together to Doc's place. Bill, the richest man in the country and the most tempting customer for Murder Inc. happens to be both an extremely radical anarchist and Doc's son.

Boss is a big-time gangster whose "Rolls Royce is full of bullet holes" (Mit 16). During his drive with Doc there are rival agents in ambush; they are killed in passing. Yet Boss melts like wax when expecting a dangerous visitor; there are no safety measures. He is hunted and finally killed by a corrupt police officer he had met when they were young;[12] this

[11] Polish film and stage director Andrzej Wajda was engaged by the Zurich Theater for the world première of *The Partaker*. His inventions included a conveyor belt transporting the bodies, hooked and in sacks, into the cold-storage room. On the day of the opening night Wajda published a statement in a Zurich newspaper denying responsibility for the production because of interference from Dürrenmatt.

[12] Cop continues Dürrenmatt's modifications of Jekyll–Hyde: Mississippi and Saint-Claude had a shared youth, Gastmann and Bärlach met early in life. Doc refuses to inherit Bill and thus become a Cinderellus; he goes on living in his underworld, among rats, as Knipperdollinck and several characters in Dürrenmatt's youthful prose did. These details connect *The Partaker* with the 1940's rather than with the 1970's.

375

Cop, furnished with an artificial leg and arm, develops an idée fixe about catching Boss. It is a mild surprise toward the end of the play that Cop was not, after all, totally corrupt, but wanted to realize a little bit of justice by committing two murders gratis. He is quickly executed for this decent deed. Ann happens to be both Boss's and Doc's mistress; Boss knows it, Doc does not. Knells for Ann—sorry: red light. The result of the Indian episodes is that Murder Inc. is taken over by the Governor, Chief Justice, Public Prosecutor, and Lord Mayor in harmonious cooperation.[13] The end of the play shows Doc, the miserable partaker, assaulted by Sam and Jim, two new agents of injustice, who are still harder than Boss.

The possible merits of *The Partaker* are not hidden in its story. In *Portrait of a Planet* Dürrenmatt adapted newspaper materials: leading articles, reports from various parts of the world. Now he adapts comic strips.[14] The result is a hodge-podge just as improbable as the Arabian story he criticizes in his essay *Justice and Human Rights*.

Leaving the verisimilitude of the plot aside: what about the characters? Moral probing? Verbal jokes? Stage situations? The figures are oversized, as if inflated with air; in the case of Doc, that air is thick with suffering; in the case of others, mostly with wickedness. Samples of moral probing: "Everything is indecent today." "We are all involved in everything." Trite sayings like these hardly make Doc a model representative of modern intellectuals. Cop: "Yet I stopped the fatal rattle of business for a short world second" (Mit 87, 88, 194). It is not fair to quote isolated phrases from separate scenes; yet this is the level on which these walking platitudes converse.

---

[13] Luft calls *The Partaker* an out-and-out "childish play of horror" that misses the intended shock: Dürrenmatt will not let anyone exceed his "coquettish pessimism." Brock-Sulzer finds fault mainly with the performance (*Die Welt, Die Tat,* both March 12, 1973).

[14] Paul Schorno remarks that Dürrenmatt's cliché-like figures include nothing new. One can sneak away from his world as from "a super-comic-strip-story" that leaves "our insides cold": "It does not concern us any more" (*Neue Zürcher Nachrichten,* March 10, 1973).

There are occasional happy turns of phrase: "One hand washes the other dirty." Leaving dead bodies lying around means "environmental pollution" (Mit 57, 23). These are, however, exceptions; as a rule, the dialogue is barren, monotonous, and full of clichés.[15] Eliminating unnecessary elements is a valuable artistic principle, if there is something to leave out; in *The Partaker* there was not. The impact of stage situations is lessened by interspersed monologues sketching backgrounds and even announcing key twists of the plot: a procedure slackening the little tension that might have been left. Yet there is one stage situation, one scenic image, charged with a powerful, even if calculated, irony. Boss eats a meal while Doc enters the cold-storage room in order to start treating the body of Boss's mistress. He sees Ann, yet does not say a word. Then he comes back on stage—and does not say a word about his love for Ann.[16]

The Partaker is based on a sketch for a short story written down by Dürrenmatt in 1959.[17] It is an aftermath of *Mississippi* and *Frank V* in its description of a gangster empire, of *The Visit* in its offers to buy murders for amounts ranging up to ten million francs. Still more clearly it is a play demonstrating one of Dürrenmatt's basic difficulties. Where and how to find a context for the results of his macabre creative imagination? The grotesque, Dürrenmatt's forte, presupposes some kind of balancing factor, a minimum amount of everyday probability, to be effective. Ill's ritual murder, the only killing shown in *The Visit*, is in its commonplace inevitability a more shattering experience than Dürrenmatt's later orgies of murder. His innate inclination to go to extremes and his

[15] Hansres Jacobi finds Dürrenmatt's "improbable grotesque of crime" "highly undramatic"; its efforts at aphorism are "mere platitudes" (*Tagesspiegel*, Berlin, March 10, 1973). Dieter Bachmann sees the basic fault in Dürrenmatt's formalism; the dialogue is without substance, "a rattling skeleton of a dramatic construction" (*Die Weltwoche*, March 14). Cf. Voser, *NZZ*, and Leber, *National-Zeitung* Basel, both March 10.

[16] Both Schorno and Weibel (*TV-Radio-Zeitung*, March 18–24, 1973) choose this scene for special praise.

[17] Interview with Bachmann, *Die Weltwoche*, March 7, 1973.

increasing impatience, both in his craft of writing and in his social attitudes, shake all kinds of balance. Resurrection, the explosion of our sun, the state running Murder Inc.: more and more artificial contexts for Dürrenmatt's grotesqueries, less relevant, more arbitrary stage worlds. Scraping the barrel filled up with sketches during the glorious 1950's is hardly the best possible method to find a way out. For the discouraged critic of these two original plays there is consolation offered only by the fact that Dürrenmatt also kept writing in other genres during the same years.[18]

[18] Late in 1976 Dürrenmatt published a book version of *The Partaker*. Its subtitle is "A Complex: Text of Comedy, Dramaturgic Notes, Experiences, Reports, Stories." The "comedy" covers 78 pages; its postscript, 208. Dürrenmatt directed the second production of the play at Mannheim in 1973; he gives exact descriptions of silent action, lighting, the setting, etc., thus helping us to concretize our impressions, e.g., of Doc's development in the opening scenes. The dialogue has undergone only minor changes; the longest addition is a *maqamat* told by Cop, describing the corruption among the servants of the state (pp. 70–71). There is a rambling monologue written after Mannheim and published separately in the postscript.

The volume suffers from elephantiasis: its last part is called "Postscript to the Postscript" and runs for 96 pages as one giant-size paragraph. There are a few interesting lines of thought—a childhood memory about God's "inexorability" (pp. 112–15) supports certain conclusions presented in this study (pp. 10, 40, 53–55 above), yet has nothing to do with Ann; once again, Dürrenmatt emphasizes his individualism (pp. 178, 183, 287). His polemical inventions are partly far-fetched: to me, Doc, Faust and Socrates are totally incommensurable, and so are *Hamlet* and *The Partaker*. Justifying Bill's anarchism by telling a history of life on Earth (pp. 123–48) does not help, as little of this is written into the play itself. Toward the end of the volume, Dürrenmatt tells two stories: "Smithy," his starting-point for *The Partaker* originally sketched in New York in 1959, and *Oedipus Tyrannus* à la Dürrenmatt (pp. 202–26, 238–74). They are well-written, worth publishing by themselves—yet trying to connect them with the play, or, indeed, writing the entire postscript, has been mostly a waste of time. *The Partaker*, with its clumsy criminal melodrama, does not grow into a metaphor of the modern scientist.

18 Models of the State

FIVE PROSE WORKS

||||||||||||||||||||||||||||||||||||||||||||||||||||||||||||||||||||||||||||||||||||||||||

At first sight this last chapter seems to discuss a miscellaneous pile of books. A long essay, a travel book, a novel, a rhapsodical lecture about Israel, a collection of journalistic writings: can these various genres be brought together? During and after his year at Basle and parallel with his continued efforts as a dramaturge Dürrenmatt felt free and tempted to try his hand at various literary forms, mostly along journalistic lines. Four of the books appeared between 1969 and 1972: a volume a year. They are thus bound together by the time of their birth—and by a continuous interest in Dürrenmatt's mind. These five books constitute a kind of political pentalogy.

Gerechtigkeit und Recht (Justice and Human Rights)[1] is a long lecture delivered by Dürrenmatt to a student audience in 1968, published the following year. *Sätze aus Amerika* (Sentences from America, 1970) contains his travel impressions; *Der Sturz* (The Fall, 1971) is his first novel since 1957; and *Dramaturgisches und Kritisches* (1972) makes up a second volume of "Writings and Lectures on the Theater," as its subtitle shows. *Connections* (Zusammenhänge, 1976) is "an essay on Israel" and "a sketch"; there were two other works published in 1976. These books include several portraits or close-ups of the state, of the organization we have built up in order to live together on this planet. The portraits are drawn with the help of Dürren-

---

[1] *Monstervortrag über Gerechtigkeit und Recht nebst einem helvetischen Zwischenspiel (Eine kleine Dramaturgie der Politik)* is a title long enough to remind one of *Marat/Sade*. Possible translations into English might also be "Righteousness and Right," with Dürrenmatt's pun retained, or "Justice and Freedom"; it is, above all, the human right of freedom Dürrenmatt emphasizes.

matt's "dramaturgic thinking," a concept as focal in his work of the 1960's as "artistic invention" has been in his theory and practice since the 1950's.

"Dramaturgic thinking" in five books of prose? How does Dürrenmatt, an experienced playwright and adapter of classics, apply his customary way of thinking when writing a lecture, a travel story, a novel, an essay? We shall see below. As a starting-point it is enough to know that Dürrenmatt's "dramaturgic thinking" means that the various possibilities inherent in a story are tried out and developed. Dürrenmatt is a storyteller; this group of five books invites us to have a closer look at his way of proceeding during the very act of telling stories. Stories about the modern state.

Justice and Human Rights opens with a story from the *Thousand and One Nights*. Mohammed sees a horseman lose his purse at a distant fountain, a second horseman find it and sneak away, a third arrive and be killed by the first, who has come back looking for his purse. The prophet protests loudly against the obvious injustice of the entire series of events, only to be corrected by the voice of Allah. Divine justice, concealed from our mortal eyes, has taken its course. The first horseman had stolen the money from the father of the second, the third had raped the wife of the first. What happened at the fountain restored the just world order.

Not entirely happy with this story, Dürrenmatt starts adapting it and develops a thousand and one variations. Some of his versions come from his enjoyment of the act of story-telling, or are part of his tactics for keeping his audience amused. Why did the prophet not interfere? Dürrenmatt's first major objection to the story is that chance, a central concept in his dramaturgy, plays quite a prominent role in the events. The life stories of the three horsemen are interwoven, quite by chance; Allah speaks, a rare event. The story does not prove anything, it only conjectures. If the prophet were replaced by a scientist or scholar of our age, this observer would accept the improbable events as statistically possible, yet demand that any generalizations be based on a greater sample chosen from three billion potential subjects. The story is too specific to say anything generally valid about life in modern giant states.

Dürrenmatt goes on to delineate two models of the modern state. A citizen of a bourgeois country would characterize the behavior of the horsemen as understandable yet illegal. He is a realist recognizing that man is a wolf to his neighbor. The task of the bourgeois state is to guarantee that certain rules and laws are observed. Everyone has the right to play with the tokens he possesses: the rules of the Wolf Game determine his profit. The tokens mean money or capital; they may be furnished with other people's work, much as chessmen are furnished with certain possibilities to move (GuR 22). The state is a judge or a referee with the power to tax every player and to fine or imprison players breaking the rules of the game.

Instead of the Wolf Game the socialist countries play a Good Shepherd Game. The basic assumption is that man is a lamb to his neighbor. All tokens won by the individual players go to a common fund: profit belongs to all. Yet this idealistic arrangement does not work. Some of the lambs dream of becoming wolves, and the state is threatened by wolves from outside its borders. Some of the agents of justice have to put on wolves' fur to keep an eye on the players: they become Good Shepherds. They are only "temporary wolves, humanistic wolves" (GuR 30)—though tempted by the possibility to establish themselves as powerful wolves for good. The players of the Good Shepherd Game are divided into two groups, the guards and the guarded.

If leading players of these two games were to meet at that fountain and under Mohammed's eyes, what would happen? Nothing. Industrialists or politicians from the West, members of the Politburo or field marshals from the East, would hardly start stealing portfolios from one another. Yet Mohammed's outburst of joy at the just state of affairs would be over-hasty. Allah would thunder: "These horsemen need

381

not steal or murder, because they have control over human powers that allow them to commit unpunished unjust deeds much more shameful than you can suspect in your simplicity of mind" (GuR 36). Dürrenmatt's models of the state are anything but rosy.

The Wolf and Good Shepherd Games constitute a frame of reference for Dürrenmatt's later thoughts and stories. His following move connects these models with his two title concepts, with justice and the rights of the individual. Man is a double concept, meaning both something unique and something general. Everyone experiences his own individuality: this is the existential concept of man. Man among his fellow men: this is the general and logical concept of man, not to be experienced immediately but to be conceived of intellectually. Every individual has the right to be himself: "we call this right freedom." Society has the right to guarantee the freedom of every individual, a task it can fulfill, paradoxically enough, only by limiting each individual's freedom: "we call this right justice" (GuR 41). It is possible to imagine a world of absolute freedom and another of absolute justice; both would be hells, the former "a jungle in which man is hunted like a game animal, the world of absolute justice a prison in which man is tortured to death. The impossible art of politics consists in reconciling the emotional idea of freedom with the conceived idea of justice: this is possible only on the level of morals, not on the level of logic" (GuR 42). Again, Dürrenmatt is balancing chaos and order.

If an effort to reconcile freedom and justice starts from the individual, it leads to the Wolf Game—if from society, to the Good Shepherd Game. The rules of the Wolf Game guarantee the freedom of those who possess a great quantity of tokens or hope to one day; the poor are free yet unable to utilize their freedom. The game can develop in various ways, the judge can tax the rich players more heavily than the poor, or take care that the decisions follow the opinion of a majority. If the judge grows too powerful, the rulings approach those of a hidden Good Shepherd Game. The players of the latter are apt to lose their interest in the game as they are made to give up the tokens they have won to the common fund. Both games are complicated by the high degree of cooperation and organization demanded by modern technology and industry: individual players are exceptions. These and other crises may prevent the agreed-upon order of things from balancing the ideals of freedom and justice. According to Dürrenmatt's disillusioned view, this is the phase when ideologies make their entrance. "A social order uses an ideology when it is not in order any more. . . . Ideologies are excuses to remain in power or pretexts for rising to power" (GuR 45, 51).

Ideologies speak to the emotions in us. Dürrenmatt's models of the state are based on economics; now he completes them with an emotional dimension. We have an inclination to enlarge the sphere of the existential ego, while narrowing down the logical, general concept of man. There exist emotional categories like "the intimate *We*, the more general *Our Likes*, the intimate *Enemy* and the more general *Others*" (GuR 56). When this inclination is utilized by politics and politicians, the emotionally neutral "state" is turned into a native country, or foreigners into a hostile race. Being ruled by a Superwolf gives an illusion of safety and freedom to an ordinary wolf, through identification. Dürrenmatt dislikes emotional and ideological overtones in words like "native country" or "our football team." Equipped with these concepts and dislikes he approaches a concrete example in his "Swiss Interlude."

The official ideology in Switzerland is based on passivity. "Switzerland is a Superwolf that declares herself a Superlamb by calling herself neutral" (GuR 62). The Swiss are wolves protected by a Superlamb: a self-contradictory situation, also manifest behind the attitudes of "mental self-defense," prevalent since World War II. Like several other intellectuals, Dürrenmatt is a rebel against this ideology.[2] He has little sympathy for the instinctive self-preservation of each state,

[2] E.g. Peter Bichsel, *Des Schweizers Schweiz*, 1969, pp. 12–13; cf. also Bichsel's preference for "a sensible Switzerland" (p. 19), or his concern for and anger with the Swiss (pp. 22–23).

including Switzerland. The economy of the country might be joined with southern Germany's, her hotels with Tyrol's, he remarks. Dangerous thoughts like these are fought by mental self-defense: Switzerland is declared "a God-given Super-wolf" of "metaphysic dimensions." The Swiss are expected to be exceptionally noble Noblewolves, "free, obedient, capi-talistic, social, democratic, federalistic, believing, anti-intel-lectual, and prepared to fight" (GuR 65).

Dürrenmatt devotes a few pages to a closer description of these expectations. It is not for a non-Swiss to decide how far his national self-criticism and satire are justified. It is for us to notice that his opposition to atomic weapons dates back to a public stand in the early 1960's, during the days of *The Physicists*. It is for us to listen to Dürrenmatt's "incidental remark" that he is fond of living in Switzerland and "likes to have a fight with the Swiss" (GuR 74). And it is for us to connect this "Swiss Interlude" with the general line of thought in Dürrenmatt's lecture and to conclude that he uses the country he knows best of all to reveal the dangerous or harmful effects of emotional ideologies on our image of the state. Dürrenmatt wants a matter-of-fact, critical attitude to-ward the state and its shortcomings. The state is there for the benefit of its citizens; the citizens are not there for the benefit of the state.[3]

Having assured himself and his listeners that he does not wish to spare his home country, Dürrenmatt goes on to criti-cize the untoward influence of political ideologies in Switzer-land and elsewhere. Fascism is based on emotions: "Only emotional realities make fascism possible. . . . *We* becomes an absolute native country, *Our Likes* a master race" (GuR 78). Dürrenmatt finds "(pre)fascistic features" in various phenomena: behind mental self-defense, in cultic, emotion-ally hot art, in communism. His definition of fascism as the

---

[3] Marti refers to a similar statement of Dürrenmatt's from 1961 and connects it both with a Swiss tradition emphasizing the rights of the individual and with Dürrenmatt's proclamation against the atomic bomb (*Die Schweiz und ihre Schriftsteller*, pp. 50–55).

Wolf Game carried to a logical conclusion is historically reasonable, if we think of the Weimar Republic; yet he also characterizes present-day communism in many respects as "a logically disguised fascism, a fascistic state with a socialistic structure" (GuR 86). Starting from the logical, general concept of man the Good Shepherd Game had to construct an existential reality for the lambs to identify with. The genius Marx found the classes and, more specifically, the exploited class to function as *Our Likes* (GuR 82).

Dürrenmatt is not the first to use religious terminology to describe communism. He speaks of "dogmas," "theology," "cultic forms," "communistic church," and remarks that emotional realities have been reintroduced: "native country," "nation," "race" (GuR 84–85). Requirements are put on Noblelambs similar to those imposed on Swiss Noblewolves. The ideas Dürrenmatt finds behind his two games are thus mere ideologies: freedom and justice are words used as lip-service. Through these steps he arrives at a temporary balance: "Social orders are unjust and unfree orders that we must establish to have orders at all, because we are incapable of practicing purely rational politics due to the self-contradictions in human nature. Still worse: there is no just social order, because a man looking for justice is justified in finding every social order to be unjust, and a man looking for freedom is justified in finding every order to be unfree" (GuR 88).

After this matter-of-fact analysis of the present-day situation Dürrenmatt jumps into discussion of the future and into science fiction. As the existential concept of man defies every effort to rule, it is wisest to distinguish the two concepts altogether and let the computers rule over the definable part of man: "man can be governed objectively only through machines" (GuR 89). It is not quite clear how seriously Dürrenmatt wrote this sequence:[4] he probably gave in to the lure of a comic invention, sudden and delightful—after hav-

[4] Spycher calls the sequence "a somewhat mysterious speculation" (*F.D.*, p. 335).

ing kept his fantasy in check for quite a while. Freed by automation from all material worries, man would perhaps indulge in receiving and practicing the arts to an unprecedented degree; a darker vision shows mankind governed by a handful of computer technicians. As in *Portrait of a Planet*, Dürrenmatt sees something basically new in the hippies, in motorcycling nomads who use and abuse the incomprehensible results of modern technology as if they were natural phenomena.

Allah is silent. Dürrenmatt's mock-serious glimpse of the future is followed by a return to the initial story. And to the cruel and indifferent god of his early stories: perhaps this is an off-stage character ruling over his entire canon. The unjust state of the world depends only on man's injustice: "The world is as man makes it." Dürrenmatt's world is as his dramaturgic thinking makes it. According to his own definition, the Wolf and Good Shepherd Games are "comical repetitions of political structures in which we and others live" (GuR 94–95). They are results of an enjoyment of play-acting; they consist of analyzed parts of reality put before the spectators; they include paradoxes and inner contradictions. Dramaturgic thinking, when applied to politics, aims at revealing its emotional factors and its "rules, not its contents." Thus—and now we come to Dürrenmatt's idealism—dramaturgic thinking might act as a corrective to politics, by bringing it into "the glaring light of satire," by inviting us to think over reality playfully, critically, "unideologically and with phantasy" (GuR 97–98). Dürrenmatt's lecture concludes with an exhortation to students, the still free intellectuals, to think critically about the establishments they are to join, to scrutinize them, to take them literally, demanding democracy from democracy, socialism from socialism, and Christianity from the Christians (GuR 110).

Justice and Human Rights grows out of Dürrenmatt's interests and working habits developed ever since the 1940's. Its central concepts of freedom and justice are new formulations of chaos and order, two ideas contrasted and reconciled in his earlier practice and theory. It tackles justice as a metaphysical problem, it states the impossibility of a rational world order, it portrays the modern state as an unreliable giant organization to be carefully watched by the individual. It combines the traditional Swiss idea of the state as the servant of its citizens with national self-criticism and with Central European neutrality: the weaknesses of the Western and Eastern systems of government are revealed with equal acumen. Encircled by wolves and lambs, Dürrenmatt writes himself into the role of an intellectual wasp buzzing in their fur.[5] The lecture was given in a university milieu: Dürrenmatt, a mixture of fantast and logician, sees himself surrounded by scholars and scientists, student leaders and hippies, happily satisfied middle-class theater audiences and toughly professional politicians and technocrats, all with their justified or unjustified suspicions of free intellectuals.

Dürrenmatt believes in his stories. In an era of hard-core facts, of documentary drama, facing the young generation of the late 1960's that doubted rather than admired everything that was fictional, Dürrenmatt tried to amalgamate politics into the world of his creative imagination. He defended his right to reveal conflicts, not to solve problems. He did these things—and this is a new feature in *Justice and Human Rights*—by inviting his listeners and readers to enter his study or his mind in order to experience how his dramaturgic thinking operates. His guests were not only to get acquainted with the results of that thinking; they were to live through the thinking process itself. The various possibilities inherent in the Arabian story were developed under their very eyes— as the possible endings of *The Pledge* were by the police chief. The story was not carried to its worst possible end; every facet developed during the lecture has its own value in illuminating the subject of discussion, the modern state.

[5] Dürrenmatt diagnoses the state of the world with his radical test of "freedom—justice," "finds it ill and makes only quite general therapeutic suggestions" (Spycher, p. 336).

Justice and Human Rights is thus an introduction to Dürren-matt's matter and manner about the year 1970, and, to a lesser degree, as a whole. We are reminded that Dürrenmatt needs a story to get his imagination functioning, that he is a storyteller interested in pondering whether a story is feasi-ble and relevant to our age or not.

"Model" is another key to Dürrenmatt's dramaturgic thinking. In an interview in 1968, the year *Justice and Hu-man Rights* was written, he speaks about dramaturgic think-ing as an equal alternative to philosophical, sociological, or psychological thinking. All of these methods have to simplify, to choose a partial view of the complex world.[6] Dürrenmatt's partial view on the state results in two models, the Wolf and Good Shepherd Games. They are, albeit embedded in a lecture, dramaturgic models in their concreteness; Dürren-matt applies the total grasp of a dramatist, an ability to con-dense wide perspectives into a limited area.[7] The stage is a small place in comparison with the world. With his bitter and happy experiences as a dramatist Dürrenmatt the lecturer knew that he had to practice dramaturgic selection when filling the small space of a lecture with something that would cast a shadow on the surrounding world. He built up two models.

Dürrenmatt hardly created all of his building materials. Similar lines of thought have doubtless occurred before in recent political journalism or literature. Yet showing these parallels would not only be beyond my competence but also beside the point. *Justice and Human Rights* is to be primarily judged on the basis of its dramaturgic qualities. It has con-

6 Melchinger, "Wie schreibt man böse, wenn man gut lebt?" *Theater heute*, 9, 9 (Sept. 1968), shortened in the *NZZ*, Sept. 1, 1968. Leng-born (*Schriftsteller . . .* , pp. 228, 253) finds in Dürrenmatt's middle position a bias against Western democracy.

7 Spycher remarks that Dürrenmatt's "political 'dramaturgic think-ing' takes three kinds of shapes": 1. the "particular worlds" of his fiction; 2. allegories; 3. immediate statements concerning politics. As examples of the allegories Spycher mentions the Wolf and Good Shepherd Games (p. 332).

siderable merits. It is concrete, clear, funny, logical; it sticks mostly to its points, and hits the nail on the head in many respects. Dürrenmatt's soberness of mind, a paradoxical contrast to his whimsicality, is attached to his prose more strongly than to his plays or adaptations. There are a few details open to criticism, in addition to Dürrenmatt's surprising jump into science fiction in his vision of the world governed by computers. Dramaturgic models may be selectively and satirically exaggerated, in order to be effectively contrasted with one another; yet Dürrenmatt is over-eager in defending the streamlined beauty of his thought constructions against all compromises. Both the Wolf Game and the Good Shepherd Game have their weaknesses; would not there be something to be achieved by making them approach one another? Dürrenmatt finds symptoms of this; he disfavors rather than supports them. Are all lambs in the Wolf Game fakes? Dürrenmatt hints at this question in his Swiss interlude (GuR 67–68); his selective pessimism also makes him blind to the developments towards detente and a feeling of mutual responsibility between the superpowers. This development was less conspicuous, it is to be admitted, in 1968 than it was later on.

There are centrifugal and centripetal forces in action in Dürrenmatt all the time. His adaptations were the result of an effort to widen the sphere of his literary activity. His returns to playwriting in *Portrait of a Planet* and in *The Partaker* signified an effort to concentrate his powers on a main line of activity. Yet there was a centrifugal trend driving him forward at the same time: toward journalism, toward prose fiction. *Justice and Human Rights*, an ambitious sample of his dramaturgic thinking, occupies a central position in this trend, comparable to the focal significance of *Problems of the Theater* in the 1950's. It is typical of the late 1960's that this major essay deals with politics, not with Dürrenmatt's individual approach to his art. What he called "A Small Dramaturgy of Politics" is in fact "A Short Catechism for Political Dissenters." The average tribulations and frustrations of the individual within the powerful political systems of our age is probably a subject more appropriate to the lecture room than to the stage.

The USSR and the USA, two superpowers, are compared with one another in Dürrematt's travel book *Sentences from America*. He is interested in them as parts of reality, as objects of his visits, not only as dramaturgic models. Having visited the Soviet Union for a month in 1964,[8] he went to the United States to receive an honorary Ph.D. from Temple University, Philadelphia, and to spend a few weeks in Miami and in the West Indies around the New Year, 1970. Dürrenmatt as a traveler is not quite in character; he bears closer resemblance to a hard-thinking and serious-minded Swiss self-made man from the Berne region than to a man of the world. *Sentences from America*, with its pointless reports on hotel life, with its belief in all kinds of gossip, with its lack of background information, is clearly the least important and most journalistic of these five books; it is written with a light left hand. Its only interest lies in its comparisons between Russia and America, crystallized in a few metaphors, in scenic images, as it were.

The USSR thinks in terms of power politics, the USA in terms of economics. In the former everything takes place against the background of a "subjugated society," in the latter "within a chaotic one" (SaA 59). Traditions, of the holy state, or of holy freedom, are important in both; Dürrenmatt sees Ivan the Terrible and Rockefeller, a powerful ruler and a business tycoon, as their personifications. With an eye on his past and future models of hierarchies of power, Dürrenmatt compares the inflexible political system of the Soviet Union with a series of concentric pyramids built up by the Mayas. If we proceed from the outside toward the inner

[8] Dürrenmatt's impressions of the Soviet Union were expressed in a series of interviews in the *Zürcher Woche* right after his return home. According to Spycher the image sketched in *Sentences from America* is "colder and more pessimistic" (p. 341).

polygons, the pyramid would consist of the Communist Party, with the Politburo as the top plane of the truncated pyramid, then the state bureaucracy, the army, the scientists, and the intellectuals as the next thin layers, all surrounding the bulkiest, innermost and least influential pyramid of all, consisting of the common people (SaA 51). Diagnosing the United States, Dürrenmatt finds a harder task; he registers an image of an unstable landscape disrupted by outbreaks and streams of lava (SaA 53). As a critic of the state Dürrenmatt joyfully greets elements of American self-criticism. He crystallizes his own criticism in a vision of a killer whale in too small a pool, an image charged with potential danger.

After the United States, Dürrenmatt turned to the Soviet Union. *The Fall*, his novel or long story from 1971, is a tragicomic description of the top level in the outermost and most powerful pyramid of power in a post-revolutionary country. The highest governing organ, here called the Political Secretariat, meets in an ascetically furnished room. There is a long table, with A, the chairman, sitting at its end, with the others, named from B to P in the order of their rank, facing one another across the table. "Think about a secret session at the Kremlin, about Stalin's fall," Dürrenmatt had described the starting-point of his novel in an interview in 1966.[9] Later he developed his script toward a dramaturgic model, toward general validity: the characters were made exchangeable by marking them with letters, not with names, and the plot was marshalled without connecting links to any definite time or political issue. The characters are powerful guards over their fellow citizens, Good Shepherds that have established themselves as Wolves for good. They are carefully guarded by A, a dictatorial Superwolf playing Superlamb: a Stalin figure. The story lies somewhere between a key novel and a model.

---

[9] Jenny, "Lazarus der Fürchterliche," *Theater heute*, 7, 2 (Feb. 1966). Dürrenmatt's summarizing sentence about his planned work is an adequate description of *The Fall*, completed five years later.

The events of *The Fall* are seen through the eyes of N, Minister of Postal Communications, a colorless functionary. N feels safe only within the walls of the Secretariat meeting room. His apprehensions start creating the atmosphere of fear, secrecy, and terrorism dominating the entire novel: its characters or events never leave that room. The members of the Secretariat are introduced one by one, in the order in which they enter the room. Before that they have eaten a cold buffet: for one of them, it was to be his last meal. A feeling of nervous tension grows due to the absence of O, Minister of Atomic Energy.[10] Arrested or liquidated? No one knows; all feel uncertain. Neither N nor any of the others can help calculating what this turn of events might mean to him or to the two competing power groups within the Secretariat.

One of these is led by D, Secretary of the Party, bon vivant, "thick, huge and intelligent," "a technician of power." A has nicknamed him "Wild Sow." G, Theoretician of the Party, leads the competing section: nicknamed "Saint Tea," he is an ascetic teetotaller with a white mane, spectacles and a "professor-like head" (Sz 13, 19). Other key figures for the plot are L, a former blacksmith and an honest revolutionary, now on the decline, so that he is called "the Memorial," and F, Minister of Heavy Industry, an ambitious and unscrupulous climber and informer. And of course A, the powerful and violent dictator with a macabre sense of humor, a nomad in origin, a friend of ancient art and popular music, living in a bunker-like house outside the capital.[11] No one knows whether his fourth wife is alive or dead.

[10] O and P are not fully authorized members of the Secretariat. As O is absent, there are, in all, fourteen people but thirteen members in the room. Having a Minister of Atomic Energy alienates the novel from the 1920's, the era from which a few models for the characters are taken. For some reason, the letter J is not utilized.

[11] Spycher mentions a long list of partly alienated details that make us "inevitably think about Stalin's Russia," and publishes a summary of an expert opinion by Professor Adam B. Ulan, Harvard University. According to it Stalin, Beria, Malenkow, Mikojan, Chruschtschow,

The reader is made to share a degree of uncertainty. This is due not only to the sinister atmosphere felt and communicated by N but also to the technique of writing. How to distinguish one letter from another? Or, rather, how to keep in mind three frames of reference: the letters, the nicknames, the various party and government positions? There are fourteen descriptions of appearances and thumbnail life stories told during the expository first third of the novel: it needs an exceptionally assiduous reader to keep all these apart without the help of a memo pad. On the surface, each character has a similar function in the early part of the plot: they all enter the room, reveal their fear through their reactions, and start waiting for A to open the session. They are distinguishable neither by their names nor by their individual functions within the plot, as characters would be in almost any other novel. This is either the price Dürrenmatt has to pay for such abstraction, for the exchangeability of his characters, or part of his conscious strategy in creating an impression of "total uncertainty," as Weber suggests in his review.[12] Everything in the novel is lucid and controlled, yet not effortlessly comprehensible.

The members of the Secretariat are bound together by a common fear. "There was no way back. A wrong move, an incautious statement could mean the end, being arrested, interrogated, condemned to death. . . . They were forced to do a great many things that were degrading and ridiculous" (Sz 24). Yet they are powerful Good Shepherds, making decisions concerning their flock of lambs—decisions affected

---

Suslow, Bulganin, Woroshilow, and Furzewa are close or distant models for, respectively, A, C, D, E, F, G, H, K, and M; some characters are crosses between several possible models. Yet Spycher and Ulan also emphasize Dürrenmatt's creative work: it must have been one of his main pleasures to "caricature historical figures in a manner grotesque-fantastic and yet serious"; the characters are "in essentials inventions rather than copies" (pp. 345–48).

[12] Weber also remarks that the narrator N does not offer any fixed-point: as a member of the Secretariat he moves and is moved, thus creating "the paradox of a floating perspective" (NZZ, May 2, 1971).

by their fear, by their mutual sympathies and antipathies, not only by political matter-of-fact considerations: "Reason did not matter" (Sz 25). Thus, there are intrigues woven around the changing sleeping partners of A's daughter; a lawyer and a balletomane nicknamed "Ballerina" is the Minister of Agriculture; or corruption takes the ridiculous form of smuggling Bordeaux wines into the country, to be used as gifts among the Good Shepherds. These are samples of comic or grotesque consequences of the entire power game. O's absence is an entirely serious matter. That is why N tries so anxiously to find at least some kind of answer in the behavior of his colleagues. A certain greeting is hearty, another only friendly; yet one can interpret any gesture in precisely opposite ways.

Then A opens the session and the second part of the novel begins. Anchoring his long speech in a summarizing history of the entire revolution, A suggests the annulment of the Secretariat in the name of democracy. It was needed during the fighting period, but now it is an impediment in making the revolution the concern of the masses. This surprising proposition aims at assuring A's dictatorship; it endangers the position of all members of the Secretariat, as they are quick to see. Yet the danger is not absolute, if the annulment is not connected with a general purge; even without the Secretariat, its individual members might keep their offices. A ends his speech by knocking out his pipe: a sign that he wants no discussion of the matter. Under normal circumstances, nobody would have ventured to oppose A, out of fear for his own position; now, alarmed by O's absence, acting from despair and drunkenness, L, or "the Memorial," opposes him by denying the authority of the session, as O is absent. While the matter is under dispute, the meeting is interrupted by the temporary security officer on duty: L's wife is in the hospital about to die.

This is the first time Dürrenmatt introduces chance into the plot of *The Fall*. L is bound to conclude that the interruption is staged by A: if he leaves the room he will imme-

394

diately be arrested. The situation releases his mortal fear and under its influence he breaks a code of behavior. He tells his entire life story, he returns to the role of an old and fearless revolutionary: "Power has seduced me, comrades, . . . what friends have I not already betrayed and given up to the secret police? Shall I still be silent?" (Sz 59). N's interim thoughts reveal that A, a skilled tactician and a sovereign judge of human nature, is no longer used to being openly opposed. His habit has been to lie in ambush and strike from the shadow. Before A has time to act, there is another nervous reaction. F, the despised climber used for all the dirty jobs, sees his lifelong efforts coming to nothing due to L's foolhardy opposition, and starts striking out in all directions— only to be interrupted by another chance message: he is urgently needed at his ministry.

A adjourns the meeting for five minutes, and gives absolute orders not to be disturbed again by the colonel. His quasi-benevolent jokes come too late to save the situation: warned by the cases of L and F, no one dares to leave the room. The hidden anxiety has now taken the concrete form of a fear of crossing the threshold. Before, they were not only united but also isolated by fear: there was always the possibility that a functionary confessing his fear might be informed on to the police by a colleague, by anyone. From now on, they are only united. F says openly what everyone thinks: "We are all in a blue funk" (Sz 80). To the surprise of his colleagues, F shows moral strength: he quotes a long list of old revolutionaries executed as traitors, he protests their innocence. Misled by his disgust with human nature, A underestimates F as an opponent; when reopening the session, he insults G quite unnecessarily. The Party Theoretician is not slow to get his own back: he gathers the isolated opponents irrevocably into a common front against A—by agreeing with A's proposal to annul the Secretariat. The common fear of a purge has proved that this organ has outlived its time. By this clever move G establishes an identity between the old purges and the present-day situation,

395

and reminds the Secretariat that the decision is in its own hands. A's next step is a further mistake. He attacks C, head of the Secret Police, and places him under arrest for having detained O without A's knowledge. A tries to call in the colonel—against his own express orders not to interrupt the meeting. The colonel does not appear. For greater safety, C disconnects the house phone, and the doors of the session room are locked. All of a sudden, it is "endgame" for A: "You have checkmated yourself" (Sz 94). C produces A's list of the names of those to be executed if the Secretariat should oppose its own annulment, as it has now done. Circulating the list round the table means that A's death sentence is confirmed. D, a man of action, takes the decisive initiative, and asks for a volunteer. Everybody looks at "the Memorial." A takes it all quite calmly, goes to the other end of the room, puffs away three times at his pipe, and is strangled to death by the old honest revolutionary with the belt of the President of the State at the only window in the room. The body is removed, the seats are rearranged, with D now in A's place, and the Secretariat welcomes O. He had mistaken the date of the meeting.

In the final account, A's fall is caused by pure chance. Had O not been mistaken, the members of the Secretariat would not have been alarmed, or ventured to build up a common front against A. A's fatal mistake was to attack C, the only person he could imagine as being responsible for O's absence: C, in possession of that list . . . A's way to the worst possible turn of the story is also paved by two other chance occurrences, those ill-timed appearances of the colonel.[13] A is an exactly calculating character lured into a trap by chance: a typically Dürrenmattian figure. Or, like Gastmann

[13] Spycher sees A's fall as being caused by a major interference of chance and a series of subsidiary ones (the colonel), by his own mistakes and "finally also by the machinery of the collective of power" (pp. 357–58; cf. pp. 361–62).

in *The Judge and His Hangman,* he is a supercriminal executed for a crime he did not commit. This is the final irony of fate in *The Fall.*

Up to this point, we may be quite in agreement with Dürrenmatt's handling of the story. It is also possible to accept A's arrogance: he is a master tactician out of practice.[14] Yet A's sudden surrender still takes us by surprise: could he not have gone on fighting? There is something not quite consistent in this figure: we never experience all of his might in action, we merely have to accept his dictatorial powers as hearsay evidence, mostly through stories remembered by N. His unexpected withdrawal from life may arouse our slight disappointment: was he ever as mighty a figure as the stories claimed? This doubt is a result of Dürrenmatt's projecting techniques, of his dramaturgic thinking. Again, he goes to an extreme. The furthest fall imaginable is that of a dictator, here presented as a precipitate tumble within the time limits of a meeting. On the other hand, the detail of A's body being carried away, as if it were trash, is an improbable phase of action, yet somehow accords with the grotesque artistic whole Dürrenmatt has created.

Otherwise, I have only praise to offer. *The Fall* is a clever study in the dynamics of a political body: the action is carried forward by its various members, one at a time. Whoever senses the feeling shared by all, or by a majority, speaks for or executes the will of that majority. A, a leading individual, does not face a uniformly reacting mass of people, as in so many of Dürrenmatt's previous works; all members of the Secretariat have their own functions within the streamlined structure of the story. The atmosphere is well achieved and precisely described; the action has its grotesque moments, such as when Marshal K suddenly urinates because of old age, drunkenness, and nervous tension. The characters are types brought to life by the vivid description of their reactions during the action of the novel. *The Fall* has both

---

[14] There is an additional interpretation presented by Spycher: A had always taken life as a game, and was prepared to die (p. 364).

flesh and bones, both an underlying thought construction and a taste of life. Its style is both laconic and expressive.[15] Thirteen angry men and one woman enclosed within the walls of a room: a natural subject for a play, is it not? Yet Dürrenmatt the playwright chose to turn this subject into a novel, into a compressionistic thriller. The decisive factor in his choice may well have been the opportunity to use a narrator, and thus intersperse the concentrated action of the novel with epic flashbacks. These possibilities are skillfully utilized, especially toward the end of the novel. From the viewpoint of action these inner stories or interim thoughts are retarding moments, yet they are necessary and stratifying. A's order to make a naked female octet play Schubert to an audience of deaf-mutes: a story characteristic of Dürrenmatt's and A's macabre sense of humor. When N senses the truth behind A's role as a Superlamb, his thoughts represent a short history of the revolution.

The old revolutionaries, admired by N, were individualists: "deserted priests, dipsomaniac theorists of economics, fanatical vegetarians, dismissed students, underground lawyers, out-of-work journalists" (Sz 97). Anarchism was their forte. After the revolution they had to face a new race of opponents, this time within the party: a younger generation of functionaries and technocrats. Over them was A's ruling father figure, playing these groups against one another, using emotional and ideological factors to build up his own image and power, canalizing feelings of disappointment and depression through public trials of traitors. The fault was not in the system, it was in individuals guilty of high treason. Revolution may well turn out to be a focal theme in the literature and reality of the late 1960's and/or early 1970's. When the literary history of that period comes to be written, there will

---

[15] Weber speaks about "a typology of functionaries" and about verbal clichés—yet the novel is vivified by F's confession of fear and by Dürrenmatt's juicy and black humor. Bondy praises the terseness of *The Fall* (*Die Weltwoche*, Aug. 27, 1971).

be a place reserved in it for Dürrenmatt's cool analysis of post-revolutionary development in *The Fall*.

Paradoxically enough, there are elements of ritual in A's execution scene. He is killed by an old revolutionary, with the belt of the President; he is granted a last puff on his pipe; his body remains sitting, with its face turned upward, in front of the window frame.[16] Heaven is present, as in the death scenes of Traps or Gastmann. Moreover, the execution sequence is interrupted within N's mind by a reminiscence of the funeral of "the Untouchable," a disgraced leader of the revolution. His coffin was carried to the grave by the members of the Secretariat: it was snowing. These two rituals, one of killing, the other of burying, create an intensified, coordinated impression. In *Justice and Human Rights* Dürrenmatt described communism in religious terms; now he uses overtones of rituals in the climax of his novel, in its 'scenic image.' And A meets his death calmly, accepting his role as a sacrificial lamb, as Ill did in *The Visit*. *The Fall* describes a collective body ruling over an entire country; Guellen is a nondescript village. Yet there are curious parallels between these stories. The existence of both communities is threatened; both are 'saved' by a ritual killing. Yet 'saving' does not signify any fundamental change of direction. The atmosphere in the concluding pages of *The Fall* is desolate. N is appointed the seventh man in rank, and the last sentence paints a landscape symbolizing death in Dürrenmatt's private art gallery: "Outside it began to snow" (Sz 118).

The Fall is closely related to *Justice and Human Rights*. In *A Dangerous Game* Dürrenmatt wrote a theoretical treatise preceding a story; *Justice* is such a treatise preceding

---

[16] A is "executed ceremonially": by an old revolutionary, with the President's belt, in front of "the church-like window." Spycher (p. 365) also connects this "religious dimension" with death scenes from *Nocturnal Conversation*, DG, TV, and JHH.

The Fall. The novel selects a part of the materials of the essay for closer inspection and builds up a dramaturgic model of the top level in the Good Shepherd Game. At the same time it aims at revealing the rules, not the contents, of politics. It is a matter of conjecture how far we as readers are ready to generalize on the basis of the story, how far we are willing to see its concluding ritual murder as a sample of how a leader, any leader, is killed professionally, its Secretariat as a prototype of all kinds of collectives of power, whether political or economic, whether yesterday's or today's. Dürrenmatt has at least consciously avoided associating his novel with any precise time or political phase of development.[17] He concentrates on the game itself, on its shifting frontiers and psychological moments, thus concretizing his idea of the undesirable influences of emotions and ideologies on political decision-making.[18]

With the help of a play-like model Dürrenmatt condenses wide social views into a compressionistic thriller. This time he shows the results of his "dramaturgic thinking," not the thinking process itself. *The Fall* is a synthesis of Dürrenmatt's social panoramas, difficult to build up on the stage or in a novel, and his penetrating studies of a collective of individuals. It is also a synthesis of richness and coherence. Chance, one of Dürrenmatt's key concepts, both artistically and philosophically, has a heightened explosive power within the closed form and logical structure of this story. *The Fall,* a return to prose fiction, is a peak performance, perhaps the highest, in Dürrenmatt's work about the year 1970, bearing

[17] In an interview about *The Fall* Dürrenmatt calls himself "more a constructor than an observer": "I do not copy." There are impressions about Eastern and Western collectives of power behind his model; he also emphasizes their role throughout history. Alexander the Great and Napoleon were perhaps only names for collectives (DK 267–69).

[18] Peter Lauterburg finds *The Fall* over-psychologizing: it simplifies "the complexity of the problem of power" by excluding factual political causalities (*Tages-Anzeiger,* May 18, 1971). The marked role of emotions in politics is, however, one of Dürrenmatt's objects of criticism.

comparison with any other achievement, including *König Johann* and *Justice and Human Rights.*

Before and during his year in Basle Dürrenmatt planned writing "a greater basic dramaturgy."[19] The plan has not yet been carried out; if one looks for such a coherent theoretic treatise in *Dramaturgic and Critical Writings*, one is bound to be disappointed. There is no sequel to *Problems of the Theater* included, no revised judgment on the entire craft of playwriting placing Dürrenmatt's familiar concepts, such as "chance," "artistic invention," or "comedy" within a logically constructed and motivated whole. There are a few fragments pondering the possibilities of "dramaturgic thinking" or applying this method of thinking to a subject, as was done with greater consistency and ambition in *Justice and Human Rights.* The anthology, consisting of twenty-six items and a postscript, is a collection of materials assorted and condensed in *Justice*, as if this essay had been a lens focusing rays of light from a wider area.

Dramaturgic and Critical Writings also includes pieces of biographical rather than critical interest, of Swiss rather than universal impact. Dürrenmatt, one of the publishers of the weekly *Sonntags Journal/Zürcher Woche*, has written partly for the moment, not for posterity. It is reasonable to concentrate on writings or fragments revealing something about his basic attitudes. Ever since his first jottings Dürrenmatt has retained a connection between the world and his dramaturgy (cf. p. 203 above). His early plays grow out of World War II; since the middle 1960's there has been an additional emphasis on moral and social issues in his practice and theory. The title word "critical" means in fact "socially critical"; it has little to do with aesthetic criticism. On the other hand, "dramaturgic thinking" includes a strong element of criticism, especially against the state.[20] "Dramaturgic" and

[19] Jenny, *Theater heute*, Feb. 1966.
[20] "To think dramaturgically. Central is criticism. A 'critical theater for a critical democracy' " (Melchinger, *NZZ*, Sept. 1, 1968). A

401

"critical": by placing these words side by side Dürrenmatt possibly emphasized their firm connection in his vocabulary, or was implying that there are writings *both* dramaturgic *and* critical in this anthology—in addition to a few dramaturgic writings in the more limited, non-social, technical sense of the word.

Dürrenmatt's reflections on the dramaturgic possibilities of Switzerland form a kind of "Swiss Interlude," opus two. He is after exemplary and parabolic elements; he wants to avoid what is too specific, too local (DK 234). These are general principles followed in his thinking in "models." True to his reputation as a public nuisance, he uses festive occasions to make polemical speeches constructed with considerable rhetorical skill. These speeches certainly include controversial elements; for example, when receiving the literary prize of the city of Berne in 1969, Dürrenmatt transferred the money to three critics of the state. This action was taken as "a hit below the belt" by the bestower of the prize.[21] However, I only know Dürrenmatt's contributions to these polemics, and this is not enough for a more detailed discussion.

Turning from Switzerland to his study, from a view of society to his personal dramaturgy, Dürrenmatt paused to sketch a picture of the contemporary theatrical situation. His experiences in Basle influenced a few of his speeches; so did the crisis in the subsidized theater of the German-speaking countries in those years. Dürrenmatt's remedy for the artistic and organizational ailments is simple enough: one should try to achieve fewer and better performances. Demanding sixty-three premières within two years from the Basle City Theater condemned the company to mediocrity. Repeating the rhetorical formula "it is senseless," Dürrenmatt also argued against supporting plays fit for the amateurs, the

clear distinction between what "belongs to the state, what to the individual" is mentioned by Schmid as a traditional Swiss ideal (*Unbehagen im Kleinstaat*, p. 241).

[21] Quoted from a Berne newspaper by Melchinger, "Ein Kommentar," *Theater heute*, Dec. 1969.

cinema, or television, not for the professional stage, and against one-sided political tendencies. "The theater is not unambiguous, it is ambiguous. . . . The thinking of the theater, though critical, remains a theatrical way of thinking. The message of the theater, though it aims at politics, and it must aim at politics, remains a message of the theater. Becoming conscious of this turns it into a critical theater" (DK 30–31).

The theater is ambiguous: a border line is drawn against over-facile attitudes adopted on the stage, against simple propaganda. Dürrenmatt demands attitudes, albeit ambiguous ones; politics albeit analytical, non-emotional, rational politics. A principle behind quite a lot of his plays is given a programmatic shape. Dürrenmatt does not write "agit prop" plays.

Dramaturgic and Critical Writings includes an essay in which Dürrenmatt comes close to presenting a coherent view of dramaturgy. Its promising title is "Aspects of Dramaturgic Thinking," its disappointing subtitle "A Fragment." And a fragment it remains, a collection of interesting points, thus reminding us of some of Dürrenmatt's plays: the reader does not know for sure how to connect these points with one another and with points outside the fragment. A subdivision headed "Dramaturgy—with a Purpose" aims at portraying one of three alternative schools of playwriting. It uses Schiller and Brecht as its examples—then drifts into a two-page quotation and a five-page discussion of Schiller's use of verse and chorus. Dürrenmatt's examples and conclusions are out of balance.[22] Yet the equation between these two classics leads to notable results, too.

In an earlier comparison between Schiller and Brecht Dürrenmatt called them rebels and 'sentimental' dramatists

[22] A still more scattered and unbalanced sketch for a basic dramaturgy is a series of six articles published by Dürrenmatt in the *Sonntags Journal/Zürcher Woche* ("Gedanken über das Theater," April–July, 1970).

(TS 220–23; pp. 217–20 above). Now he remarks that both create an alienated, non-naturalistic, idealistic world on the stage (DK 214). Both start with an idea, with a purpose. Communist Brecht also starts from the general, from the society (DK 216), as the Good Shepherd Game does. And Dürrenmatt? Where is his starting-point?[23] According to our interpretation Dürrenmatt would be glad to accept the alienated worlds of the theater, provided that they were not clearly oriented toward a purpose, a premeditated idea, but were based on conflicts between the particular and the general, between freedom and justice, between chaos and order. He understands Schiller's and Brecht's positions, yet does not follow their example. He concludes this subdivision by remarking that we do not know what kind of theater is expected by the people of our scientific age, thus refuting one of Brecht's favorite ideas.

Dürrenmatt's next subdivision is headed "Dramaturgy Starting from the Individual." He discusses Ionesco and Beckett; the heading implies that absurdism is an artistic reaction within the Wolf Game. Ionesco's maxim that the theater can only be theater and his aversion to the theater as "ideology, allegory, politics, lecture, essay or literature" (DK 219), are accepted by Dürrenmatt only in a qualified sense, only as polemics against naturalism. The thinking of the theater "remains a theatrical way of thinking": yet the world created on the stage refers to and comments on another world, on reality. "The theater is not the world, it signifies

[23] There are several suggestions in Melchinger's interesting interview with Dürrenmatt (*NZZ*, Sept. 1, 1968). A playwright starting from unresolvable conflicts (e.g., Dürrenmatt), not from the individual or from the society, knows that "there is no pure causality, because chance exists; yet he cannot understand either why everything should be absurd." His theater is "not absurd, but paradox." A play is ambiguous because it is varied by the spectators, actors, and production proceedings, because the language of art deviates from the unequivocal language of politics, and because "the world is too complex to be presented" as simple. Fantasy and artistic inventions are means of criticism "leading to the cruellest truth: that of the paradox." Cf. Esslin, *Brief Chronicles*, p. 122.

the world, whether this is changeable or only visible" (DK
220). Ionesco's idea about revealing and heightening the
means of the theater leads to the grotesque and to the primitive theater, surviving today in the figure of the clown. Dürrenmatt calls Ionesco's and Beckett's characters "clowns
without masks" and "ultimate people in ultimate situations."
From "mythical semigods through kings and noblemen,
through bourgeois heroes," through Woyzeck, to the clowns
of absurdism: the downhill road of the hero in Western
drama. "The individual appears reduced to mere existence,
stripped of character, dismissed from every social function"
(DK 222–23). Man's existential ego has been objectified,
the first person brought to the stage, an old dramaturgic rule
thus outwitted—with greater artistic success by Beckett than
by Ionesco.

Again, Dürrenmatt has his reservations. Count Übelohe
and Matthäi, Möbius and Schwitter can perhaps be called
clowns with a character and social function. Dürrenmatt's
men of courage are certainly also men of character. In this
phase of his essay Dürrenmatt places a playful gesture of
evasion in a four-page footnote: "Attention: do not reveal
your dramaturgy, or you will have to stick to it" (DK 226).
Which does not prevent him from completing his "fragment"
with a "sketch": "Dramaturgy Starting from the Stuff." He
is employing a method of triangulation. Having defined the
positions of Brecht and Ionesco, of dramaturgies starting
with a purpose and from the individual, he launches a dramaturgy of a third kind, of his own. The possibilities inherent
in the materials of a play are thought over, a method we know
from Dürrenmatt's practice as a playwright and as the writer
of *Justice and Human Rights*.[24] There are dramatists "who
discover in the very stuff the objective motif of drama, turning it into a symbol of reality (not into an allegory), into a

---

[24] "I think that writing is an intensive business starting from the
'stuff,' " Dürrenmatt once said. "I do not feel obligated to any poetic
art. I feel obligated only to the stuff . . . only to the theater" (interview with Sauter, *Sinn und Form*, 1966, pp. 1226–27).

simile that is in essence not unambiguous but ambiguous, that does not put forward one problem but several" (DK 229–30). And, in an effort to round off his fragment, Dürrenmatt returns to Schiller, to *Wilhelm Tell*, and to an old Dürrenmattian concept: "the stuff becomes decisive, the artistic invention that discovers or creates the stuff" (DK 231).

This is how far it is legitimate to interpret and complete Dürrenmatt's fragment. He does not define his own position in greater detail, he only uses Brecht and Ionesco as the buoys through which he sails into the open sea, as he once sailed between Schiller and Brecht in his Mannheim lecture. Or, to modify his own metaphor, he escapes "between the legs of the dinosaur into freedom" (DK 236). The claustrophobic tightness of a dramaturgic theory can hold him no more than the just state of Babylon was able to arrest Akki. Yet there is in him a zest to theorize and dispute, to interpret and explain: he cannot help himself, an inborn polemist that he is.

The realization of this paradox leaves Dürrenmatt's critics the task of pondering over his plays, stories, and treatises, of playing again the games of chess, as he demands. In the case of the postscripts to his plays included in *Dramaturgic and Critical Writings* this has been done in the preceding chapters. In the case of *Justice and Human Rights*, Dürrenmatt's most remarkable essay of the late 1960's and early 1970's, it should be noted that it was not launched by its companion piece *The Fall*, a novel, as effectively as *Problems of the Theater* was by *The Visit*, a tragicomedy of considerable and immediate impact. In the case of other treatises it remains to be stated that *Dramaturgisches und Kritisches* is oriented more toward the external world and less toward Dürrenmatt's personal working methods than the first volume of his "Writings and Lectures on the Theater." He has grown more cautious in constructing his own "basic dramaturgy." A key he has offered to his readers and critics more than once is the word "paradox."

406

We do not know whether Dürrenmatt's fragment will ever be completed. Judging by *Urfaust* and *Woyzeck*, he is not even quite certain any more whether "comedy alone is suitable for us" (FP 33). What he is still certain about is that he wants to face the challenge of reality with humor, with "the enjoyment of a comedian" by continuing to create new similes of the world (DK 280–82). It is a matter of secondary importance whether these similes will be plays or prose, adaptations or essays, comedies, tragicomedies, or comitragedies. His abundance now takes the form of a wide range of literary genres. In his political pentalogy, in these five dissimilar volumes linked by certain recurrent ideas about the state, Dürrenmatt showed his versatility.

Connections is the last volume in Dürrenmatt's pentalogy. It does not fall neatly into any known literary category. Its origins are in an essay on "Israel's Right to Live" (DK 109–16), in Dürrenmatt's public appeal for Israel during the 1973 Yom Kippur war, and in his interest in the state. He calls the book "an essay" and "a sketch" (eine Konzeption); it grew from a lecture delivered in three places in Israel. To begin with, the lecture was nineteen pages; after each delivery followed by a discussion, Dürrenmatt revised his script, kept rewriting it and, when safely at home, over the next two years. The result is a book of 240 pages, a mixture of an historical-political essay, a travel book, and a novel.

Dürrenmatt tells us about the consecutive phases of his work in the essay itself. It is, however, difficult for the reader to distinguish among sequences written before, during, and after this "passage to Israel." *Connections* begins and develops as a lecture, grows long and detailed, digresses from its main subject, finds itself in dead ends, has a touch of prose fiction, returns to philosophical arguments, changes into a travel book—and bursts into a novel-like, Kafkaesque story.[25]

---

[25] There are in *Connections* "cascades of thoughts and associations" taking us by surprise, "wildly, violently, hardly tamed, carrying us away, leaping from one theme to another" (A. Cattani, *NZZ*, Aug. 27, 1976).

It is as good a showcase as any for Dürrenmatt's versatility within the covers of a single book.

A return to abundance? Possibly; yet the material itself seems to have led Dürrenmatt into this kind of treatment. Israel is, of course, a name charged with political dynamite; Dürrenmatt's sympathy is with the Israelis, yet he takes the many implications of his subject as a challenge, trying to approach it from various angles—historical, religious, philosophical, and political viewpoints. A critic of the state, he starts by inquiring the necessity of the state of Israel. His thinking is dramaturgic; he tries to capture conflicts with the help of language (Z 14–15). Finally he has to admit that Israel is too enormous a subject to be treated by means of his customary dramaturgic thinking alone. This is, I think, how *Connections* arrived at its final shape of a literary hybrid.

In Part One of *Connections*, the emphasis is on history and religion. Dürrenmatt speaks more openly about his own personal views of religion that he has done for quite a while. What he wants to retain are Christ's words; faith is for him "something subjective and thus existential" (Z 17–18). In *Justice and Human Rights* he operated with a pair of contrasts: the existential and general concepts of man. Now the antithesis of "existential" is "ideological"; before long, the latter word comes to mean "propagandistic," if not "distorting" in his language. We should not generalize our private religious feelings: this process leads to institutionalized religion, to the power of various churches, to conflict between ideologies, to gross intolerance.

The history of the Jews cannot be separated from religion. Dürrenmatt refuses to interpret the Near East only in terms of political conflict. As a state, Israel is a special case, a shelter for a persecuted nation, for "a social and religious community" that "owes its three thousand years of survival to the permanence of its culture" (Z 29). Dürrenmatt, though a critic of the state, is ready to see this state as a necessity. Jewish spirit is not nationalistic, "but theologically defined and thus dialectic" (Z 30–31). Following Kant, Dürrenmatt calls dialectics "a method in thinking that tries to reach knowledge independently from experience"; the most important and far-reaching result of Jewish dialectics is the idea of God as a creator (Z 31–32). He builds a simplified model about the birth of three world religions, all connected with the Jews. As founders of these religions he chooses Paul, Mohammed, and Marx.

Judaism and Christianity allow man a certain amount of freedom, in contrast to the strict determinism of Islam and Marxism. Dürrenmatt has found the focal quadrangle of his essay; these are the four religions among which he finds connections and dissimilarities. As before, most markedly in *Justice and Human Rights*, he characterizes Marxism as a fanatic religion; it is based on an outdated, mechanical view of the world. He sees the age of enlightenment as a step forward toward tolerance; it helped the Jews to be accepted by the Christians, and so enabled them to contribute to Western civilization. And, in the concluding pages of Part One, Dürrenmatt makes Hitler look like the hero in one of his novels. Against all calculations, Nazi terrorism brought about the birth of the Jewish state.

On the other hand, Israel was founded as a safeguard against those incalculable elements in life that made Hitler possible. In an interesting sentence Dürrenmatt states that politics make things happen arbitrarily, "through breakdowns and by chance" (Z 25). In the headline of an interview from 1970 he says, quite categorically: "I am interested only in politics."[26] Elsewhere in *Connections* we read: "Chaos obviously corresponds with reality better than order" (Z 109). The world of politics, governed as it is by breakdowns and chance: is it the chaotic element that fascinates Dürrenmatt in politics? Have we found an explanation for Dürrenmatt's political orientation since the late 1960's? Breakdowns,

---

[26] *Theaternachrichten*, Düsseldorfer Schauspielhaus, Dec. 1970.

chance, conflicts between order and chaos: these are concepts operative in his world. He needs frameworks for his grotesqueries; he has been in search of them in politics, not only because this has been modish but because of the conspicuously high rate of breakdowns in that sphere of life. *Connections* indeed: not only among four world religions, between the existential and the ideological, between history and the present day, but also among our host of various Dürrenmatts.

In Part Two another speaker takes the floor: Dürrenmatt the amateur Orientalist. *An Angel Comes to Babylon, Romulus, Donkey's Shadow, Hercules,* an abortive plan to write a novel placed in the Byzantine Empire: the Mediterranean Sea takes a central position on the map of his imagination. Now he inserts an outline history of Islam (Z 85–106). He emphasizes turning-points, decisive battles, cruel and grotesque individual fates; there is prehaps a connection as far back as to the battle-filled history books of his youth. His primary aim is to present Judaism and Islam as related religions, the Jews and the Arabs as potential friends and neighbors. Christians are more heavily guilty of persecuting the Jews than Muslims are. "From an historical point of view, the Arab is not at all the archenemy of the Jews" (Z 113).

Dürrenmatt is in Israel on a peace mission. He underscores his message with the story of two unorthodox theologians thrown into prison by the caliph in 760: Abu Chanifa, a Moslem; Anan ben David, a Rabbi. Living among rats in a dark prison vault they have to share, these two refuse to eat from the same bowl. There are torturers visiting prisoners not far from their vault: suddenly we are in the world of Dürrenmatt's early prose, in *The City.* The two theologians enter upon a competition in piety and humbleness, until each acknowledges the strength of religious conviction in his companion.

This is the beginning of an interminable discussion. The

Moslem and the Rabbi start eating from the same bowl. Both sing praises to the same majestic God, "incalculable in his grace and in his hatred, in his inexplicable injustice" (Z 124). They pray to a God reigning over Dürrenmatt's canon; they say their prayers so loudly that the torturers are frightened away. There is a ray of light forcing its way into the prison vault and into Dürrenmatt's essay. We have forgotten "the Arabic-Jewish Renaissance," ended in 1258, a period of relative peace and mutual tolerance in the Near East. It has "almost become a fairy tale, often full of blood, often grotesque, as everything in the history of the world, often unreally real in a curious way, a hope for today, perhaps a chance for tomorrow" (Z 125).

After this digression into fiction, back to facts and philosophy. Part Three repeats and modifies the conciliatory attitude adopted in Part Two. Ideologies vie in abusing the language; as his concrete example, Dürrenmatt analyzes the various connotations given to the German word "das Volk" in Judaism, Nazism, and Marxism (Z 141–46). The discussion, not easily transferable into English, leads to parallels among the religious, scientific, and political usages of language. After one more fling at the "dishonesty of Marxism" (Z 160), Dürrenmatt is ready to translate his story about peaceful coexistence between a Rabbi and a Moslem into the language of daily politics. The "chance for tomorrow" is that there is room enough for both a Jewish and a Palestinian state, with Jerusalem as the capital of both. "This seems utopian. The future is always utopian" (Z 163). What Israel needs is "wisdom and patience" (Z 167).

Dürrenmatt the idealist has taken the floor. His role in *Connections* is less prominent than the above summary shows; it has been impossible to do justice to all the reservations and realistic observations he presents. Yet, interestingly enough, Dürrenmatt is not satisfied with his plea for conciliation either. He changes the pace and style of his prose. In the

411

first three parts of the book, his half-page sentences proceed in neatly arranged and balanced cadences. This language is neither easily speakable nor effortlessly comprehensible; it has connections with the traditional essay style in German. Now, with about one quarter of the book left to go, the verbs take over. Concepts are replaced by observations, history by everyday life in Israel, Dürrenmatt the philosopher by a traveling writer. The lecture is finished. The travel book may begin.

A self-portrait of Dürrenmatt's enters his prose. The first person in *Connections* is a more directly self-confessional alter ego than anything we have met before—with the possible exception of "Dokument," that short piece of childhood memories.[27] Dürrenmatt goes astray when looking for the old part of Jerusalem; he senses the hostility and indifference of the people he meets. It is as if he had only gone along the border line of reality in his essay, without reaching it— just as he walked along the endlessly long city wall without finding a gateway (Z 185).

Dürrenmatt looks out of the window of his airplane, and meets the reality of Israel. The God he has spoken about, the God of the Jews, Christians, and Muslims, is in fact identical with "the experience of the desert" (Z 186). Faith means being perturbed (Z 187). "I feel my lecture more and more unreal, more grotesque, an erroneous abstraction leading to the approximate, too simple for reality." When revised, the lecture remains "a wild battlefield of my powerlessness" (Z 193–95). On his return flight to Switzerland he is pained by pictures from his memory, of nameless strangers in the streets, of a visit to a kibbutz, of being received by the president of the state. He is an outsider, an onlooker, his conscience is bad because he has never possessed the presence of mind shown by his endangered friends (Z 201). He feels guilty of being safe.

And he closes *Connections* with a return to Kafkaesque

[27] Dieter Fringeli emphasizes the personal and self-confessional character of the essay (*Basler Nachrichten*, March 24, 1976).

prose fiction, a somehow definite and final homecoming.[28] Abu Chanifa and Anan ben David, those two crystallizations of the Arabic-Jewish conflict, never die. Their discussion about God goes on and on, always as intensively, until they change into the holy books of their religions. They have been thrown into prison in Bagdad in 760; centuries later the whim of a caliph releases Anan ben David. Dressed in rags, old as the world, this Rabbi wanders for centuries through Dürrenmatt's dimly-lit fairy-tale prose. He is perhaps seen in Granada during the days of the inquisition, perhaps in Auschwitz: a Wandering Jew. At last his travels bring him back to Bagdad, where a strange sense of being at home leads him to the prison. He is chased by a dog, an echo from *The City*.[29]

Abu Chanifa lives in his vault in a long-forgotten part of the Bagdad prison. Anan ben David somehow finds his way into the vault, and there follows a violent fight in the dark between the two ancient men, until the rats recognize the newcomer. The discussion is resumed; these two have now changed into Yahweh and Allah.

What happened to Dürrenmatt in Israel? On the early pages of *Connections* he starts a journey toward himself (Z 14). Somewhat later he does his best to purge politics from myths (Z 48); still, at the end of the entire volume he himself modifies the myth of the Wandering Jew. His story speaks for peace, for cooperation, for mutual understanding, for rational politics; yet it is based on a myth. How is it that this exactly calculating writer is brought to the opposite of his acknowledged aim? A breakdown caused by chance?

No, I do not think so. Rather, Dürrenmatt finds himself. Perhaps we should try to see the matter from the viewpoint

[28] Jean Amery chooses this "parable of two heretics" as "one of the most moving parts of the book" (*Frankfurter Rundschau*, Juni, 1976).

[29] Ernst Müller, calling *Connections* "one of Dürrenmatt's most personal books," finds the final story "reminiscent of his early expressionistic prose" (*Berner Tagblatt*, Apr. 10–11, 1976).

of his audiences. Three gatherings of people assemble in various parts of Israel to listen to a lecture by a well-known Western intellectual from neutral Switzerland. These congregations have recovered from two wars within a few years' time, and may well feel threatened by repeated acts of terrorism. What does our lecturer do? He starts a long-winded and abstract religious-historical-philosophical-semantic discussion with hairbreadth distinctions on the necessity of the state of Israel, the corner of the earth these listeners live in. For them, it is a necessary and concrete reality.

A grotesquely incongruous situation, is it not? Dürrenmatt does not report on the discussions that followed his lecture in Israel; he only records his own dissatisfaction. The reader of *Connections* does not know how much of the three spoken versions is included in the printed book. Yet something like the speech situation reconstructed above must have taken place, otherwise the form and contents of Dürrenmatt's Part Four would not make any sense at all. His lecture tour made him face a basic dilemma, the dichotomy between the concreteness of life in Jerusalem or at Neuenburg, and his abstract or phantastic lines of thought. He was forced to test a conception of his with reality. His conception did not stand the test. He was honest and brave enough to admit his failure. Even more, he published a logbook of his odyssey.[30]

The abstract distinctions in Part Three, as it still stands, may have been especially difficult for the listeners to swallow. The aberrations of political language could be described with a more modest display of polemical acumen than Dürrenmatt does. Fiction and reality, language and the referent: personal problems for a writer. Is not Dürrenmatt, with his refined philosophical equipment, slightly out of context in the insensitive and irrational world of power politics, in spite of his interest in chance and breakdowns? With due respect to Kant and "Jewish dialectics," is it, after all, possible to base one's

[30] Hermann Levin Goldschmidt applauds Dürrenmatt's openness of mind: the book is impressive because the writer is still looking for his final message (*Zürichsee-Zeitung*, March 21, 1976).

conception of Israel on "knowledge independent of experience?"

Dürrenmatt the novelist answers in the negative. His last effort to make his philosophical and empirical levels meet (Z 215–16) amounts to a plea that is rhetorical rather than convincing. In the essaistic Part One of *A Dangerous Game* Dürrenmatt looks for stories that would reflect the average tribulations of modern man; in Part Four of his latest essay he gives glimpses of the average tribulations of people in Jerusalem and elsewhere in Israel. These glimpses are feasible elements in a work of art. So are the two variations of Dürrenmatt's Oriental story.

Where did they come from? Opus One, the concluding sequence in Part Two, has mainly an illustrative function. Opus Two grows into an independent, symbolic fairy tale. It runs parallel with an earlier sequence in *Connections*: Dürrenmatt strays in the labyrinth of houses in Old Jerusalem, his Anan ben David wanders in Bagdad. Reality and its reflection in fiction: why should not a storyteller of Dürrenmatt's caliber go ahead and tell his stories?—and without the accompanying abstractions?

In several of his previous works, in *Justice and Human Rights, The Fall*, and *Dramaturgic and Critical Writings*, Dürrenmatt had utilized model-like, abstract basic structures. Simplifying models or dramaturgic thinking were not means powerful enough to tame the stuff he met in Israel. This encounter with a resilient and disobedient material helped and forced him to adopt his old glorious role of a storyteller. He also seems to be on a return flight not only from the Near East but also from the far left.

I cannot help experiencing *Connections* as a transitional work. As in *The Anabaptists*, Dürrenmatt harks back, this time to his early prose, to Kafka, to his mother's biblical stories, to the world of religion—yet he sees his memories from a distance of time. He perhaps even returns to his old ideal of "men of courage," now exhorting both himself and

415

his readers to endure this world of political absurdity and injustice with wisdom and patience. In the cluster of his five political prose works, *Connections* takes a middle position. If it were to be placed into any single literary category I should call it a piece of journalism: interesting and stimulating with its lines of thought and political arguments rather than consistently well-written. It does not reach the level of *Justice* and *The Fall*; it is above the average level of his *Dramaturgic and Critical Writings*, well above *Sentences from America*.

What next? A new original play he worked on in the summer of 1975? He knows exactly what it will be like, according to his *Interview with Heinz Ludwig Arnold*, a journalist (G 65). The interview was taped in March, 1975, published in 1976 (85 pages), and quoted here and there above, mostly in the footnotes. Dürrenmatt also received the International Writers' Prize of the Welsh Arts Council in 1976, and spent part of the year in Wales, within a small cultural sphere next door to a bigger one—just as the Swiss live side by side with the Germans, speaking their language with a marked accent.

Or will his next book be *Stuffs*: On My Work as a Writer, as promised on the jacket of *The Partaker*? Will he look forward or backward in time? In a curious way, due to the heterogeneity of his latest works, he is in a position similar to that of the young and inexperienced writer of *It Is Written* thirty years ago. Anything might follow. Dürrenmatt will continue his intellectual decathlon.

Conclusion

DÜRRENMATT AND THE STAGE

‖‖

In young Friedrich Dürrenmatt there is abundance everywhere. His first play, *It Is Written*, a lavish and chaotic social panorama, consists of static scenic images loosely bound together. There is an overdose of parody and of individual fates, expressionistic drunkenness with words and monologues, there are elements of the absolute grotesque in a richly bubbling mixture. A whole world is built up on the stage. A community gathers in meetings and choruses; an executioner is introduced in a broadly conceived crowd scene. On the other hand, man is set against the sky: the play is written by a painter and budding poet—and by a student of Kierkegaard, Barth, and Kafka. Parodist and meditator, comedian and tragedian, storyteller and a meteor demolishing conventions, all of these and others meet in happy discord. Dürrenmatt's first stage language speaks in shrill, powerful, and contradictory tones.

Anything might have followed; all kinds of plays did follow. Yet there were surprisingly many elements of focal significance already present in *It Is Written*. These elements can be approached through the scenic means of expression, scenic images and units of the play. Scenic images are characteristic expressions in a style. This is our remaining task: observations on Dürrenmatt's stage language[1] in various plays will be summarized and connected with his characterization, with his love of the grotesque, with his polemical inclinations, and with certain dominant conflicts in the world of his creation. These prevail between chaos and order, between abun-

---

[1] There is an overall summary of this theater language in my earlier study of Dürrenmatt, published in *Tapa puhua*, 1963, pp. 144–50.

417

dance and coherence. Glances at Dürrenmatt's novels and theoretical writings will help us to define his position in the total pattern of modern drama.

Man against a distant sky:[2] there is a metaphysical dimension in young Dürrenmatt, with an emphasis on God as an alien and cruel power. Death in the hands of an executioner: a vividly grotesque and unpathetic image. Crowd and chorus scenes: Dürrenmatt's social nightmares depict an individual in the middle of a hostile crowd. His metaphysical nightmares bring his characters into a cold and stony world of death. Prosaist Dürrenmatt had started with Kafkaesque exercises and short stories, yet found a personal manner of expression in ghostly hilarity. Grotesque scenic images were to replace the dynamic verbal images of his prose. Dürrenmatt's early and lasting interest in doubled figures and in a Jekyll-and-Hyde theme may have its roots in an effort to dramatize conflicts between man's good and evil potentialities and thus in Dürrenmatt's early religiosity. Or in his lyrical inspiration: it was natural to go from self-centered lyricism to a dialogue between an individual and his double. There are cases like this in the early prose, in stage and radio plays. On the other hand, there are also identical twins among Dürrenmatt's doubled figures. An exact replica of a character makes it lose its individuality, turning it into a grotesque marionette.

As early as in *The Blind Man* Dürrenmatt brought to the stage his alternative dramaturgic model, a case study. A paradoxical contrast to the first, this play is schematic and compact rather than abundant. A fresco for a world theater was followed by a charcoal drawing, a single scenic image stretched beyond its durability. The story is built around a basic paradox and a dominant role, while secondary characters represent ideological viewpoints in conflict with the blind faith of the Duke. Figures of this type helped Dürrenmatt "to investigate what happens when certain ideas collide

---

[2] According to Deschner, heaven as a background makes it possible to see man's behavior "as a comedy of errors, not as an ultimate absurdity" ("F.D's Experiments with Man," p. 194).

418

with people who really take them seriously" (FP 162), as Bodo von Übelohe puts it.[3] These investigations were continued.

Dürrenmatt avoids giving unambiguous answers. The scenic evidence presented in the early chapters of this study and summarized above seems to indicate that he has no unambiguous answers to his religious questions either. The focal scenic images in his two early plays are too self-contradictory and grimly grotesque to allow us to crystallize his religious views into any single faith or statement, paradoxical or straightforward. These contradictions cannot be ignored. Dürrenmatt is a religious writer in a specific sense: he has been preoccupied with God, he does not exclude the possibility of His existence. Knipperdollinck and the Duke really take God seriously. Since *The Blind Man*, Dürrenmatt has not brought religion downstage. Religion is a private, not a public matter, he states in *Connections*.

Romulus the Great is a mature synthesis of several trends. It is both coherent and abundant; it places a case study in surroundings of high social significance. An individual appears in the midst of his antagonists in the key scenic images; the setting, with a host of chickens and the busts of former Roman emperors, is used as the background to cleverly interwoven action. The play is a counter-sketch to a thriller: it employs surprise twists and entrances, it reaches a grotesque balance between everyday life and Armageddon, between a Shavian discursive comedy and farcical interludes, between a parody of *Julius Caesar* and an ideological dispute about the aftermath of World War II. Repetitions, short scenes of pantomime, and shifts from one style to another are used in a purposeful way. From the point of view of scenic means and units, the most remarkable new feature is that abundance is turned into action.

Megalo- and monomaniacs have appeared in Dürrenmatt since his earliest plays. In *Romulus* he develops a charming

[3] The collision between ideas and people is emphasized as "the basic structure" of Dürrenmatt's comedy by Steiner, "Die Komödie Ds," *Der Deutschunterricht*, *15*, 6, Dec. 1963, p. 94.

and dangerous protagonist, a sovereign polemicist and political philosopher in the guise of a clown. When that attire is removed, we see a judge over an entire world. *It Is Written* showed how an order was smashed, *The Blind Man* affirmed the paradoxical order of blind faith at any price; *Romulus the Great* points out that chance may nullify careful, deeply personal calculations and world orders. The play is Dürrenmatt's first genuine tragicomedy and one of his major works. Several interacting scenic images create a coordinated total impression.

Surprise twists in the plot are a major asset in *Romulus*; in *The Marriage of Mr. Mississippi* there is an over-indulgence in them. Dürrenmatt assembles a museum of European history to function as his setting. The violence inhabiting our living-rooms is a result of conflicts between fanatical believers in various truths, he asserts. For a playwright interested in describing conflicts rather than solving problems there are enticing possibilities hidden in collisions between representatives of various formulas of thought. The conflicts take place on an ideological or philosophical, not on a psychological, level. As a rule, Dürrenmatt has shown little interest in relations between fully conceived human beings, e.g., in tensions between members of a family.[4] An illusion of reality is for him a means toward an end, toward making the conflicts described believable in terms of the stage. He approaches reality from the unreal, realism from Kafkaism, the grotesque from the macabre, not from its everyday elements. How to concretize, not how to abstract, is a burning artistic problem for Dürrenmatt.[5]

[4] The family plays a conspicuously small role on Dürrenmatt's stage. In *The Visit*, *Romulus*, *The Physicists*, or *The Meteor*, family relationships are shuffled aside, as matters of minor importance, rather than developed. The family has a somewhat more central position in *Frank V*, mainly as a concretization of the generation conflict.

[5] Syberberg speaks of two contrary tendencies in Dürrenmatt, one leading to "a superabundance of concrete details," the other to "an abstraction of the concrete into a model case" ("Zum Drama F.Ds," p. 121).

420

This can be seen most clearly when there is a gap between the concrete and abstract levels of a play. *Mississippi* is such a script. Yet the play had its significance for Dürrenmatt's total development by bringing his name before a German-speaking and a world audience. The play discussed contemporary problems in modern surroundings and took a step toward case studies treated as compressionistic problem plays.

An Angel Comes to Babylon is Dürrenmatt's most abundant, even if not most successful play. The dialogue is both witty and poetic, the characters include a charming rogue, a comic angel, an ingenue, and several monomaniacs. There are one heavenly and two worldly settings; as in *Mississippi*, Dürrenmatt plays with a conglomerate and anachronistic picture of various ages. Short pantomimes and quick movements to and from the stage create a contrast with the static basic situation. It is appropriate that this fairy tale confused by lavish artistic inventions is finished with a Song of Songs to freedom. Valedictory poetry is a Dürrenmattian scenic unit: a parallel to his free-flying scenic images and artistic inventions. Between God's and man's rigid orders there is a narrow route of escape through which Dürrenmatt's man of courage and a heaven-sent gift direct their route to a promised land of ambiguity and abundance.

Behind their backs they leave many a claustrophobic vision. A fundamental motivation for Dürrenmatt's grotesqueries is a paradoxical tension between anxiety and relief, between fear and laughter. At his best as an artist he is able to find an expression for this tension, already present in his reminiscence of his childhood, in its contrast between an anguished village milieu and a wide and wild world of fairy tales. In Dürrenmatt's stories we meet claustrophobic houses, hospitals, and asylums. An individual may be enclosed by a circle of people, or by the walls of a building. Beyond these walls and behind the settings of novels extend idyllic Swiss landscapes with quiet farm-houses, forests, mountains, and abrupt changes of lighting. Authentic landscapes are drawn with a few strokes of the brush. Grotesquely enough, these surroundings are battlefields for nihilists and men of order. In the reflective passages and dialogues of his novels Dürrenmatt gives shape to the conflict between chaos and order in a straightforward manner. He sees life as a mixture of chaos and order, of senselessness and sense. He criticizes his nihilists who rely on the omnipresence of chance—and his idealists who rely on the all-powerful force of human reason. Chance is "what limits man," especially Dürrenmatt's detached, coolly calculating characters like Matthäi in *The Pledge.*

There are absurd elements in our life. Absurdity gives a dimension of depth to a great many of Dürrenmatt's works. He sometimes finds a faultless artistic equivalent to this theme: in *A Dangerous Game,* in *The Pledge,* two examples of the absolute grotesque in prose, both coherent and well-mastered. The latter novel, "A Requiem for the Detective Story," gives chance a prominent role as a theme. Using and overusing chance in a similar function and as a dramaturgic factor led Dürrenmatt to failures, too, especially in the 1960's.

A Dangerous Game also includes the most spectacular occurrence of a very Dürrenmattian scenic unit, here embedded in narrative prose. Traps' festive last meal is a sustained dramatization of a grotesque contrast. It is used as a structural factor in an example of the absolute grotesque climaxing in a senseless suicide. Here we are, Dürrenmatt's last meals say, happily consuming the good things of this earth; in the next moment we shall be dying. This combination of an enjoyment in life and of the closeness of death is not the only collision between extremes in this remarkably compact story. *A Dangerous Game* is also a comitragedy, a countersketch to tragedy in prose, and a grotesque meeting-place between the everyday and the macabre, an anachronistic conception of justice and modern amorality, play-acting and reality, order and chaos. The balance of Dürrenmatt's prose during the 1950's shows stylistic achievements of a high standard. There is wizardry in his grotesque atmospheres, there are scenes placed against wider backgrounds as if they were stratified scenic images. The molds of detective, trial, and love-story and of stage tragedy are filled up with Dürrenmatt's own molten metal.

Dürrenmatt's eight radio plays include both intimate case studies and social panoramas. They range from ancient Greece to science fiction, from parodies of heroics to moral probing, and from early and clumsy metaphysical studies to a slick bagatelle. His radio style is free and spacious; experiences with this medium probably encouraged him to incorporate short sketch-like scenes and stylized milieus into his stage plays. Theatricalistic settings outlined with a light hand belong to *The Visit*, Dürrenmatt's masterpiece, the most perfect embodiment of his theory of a grotesque, colorful, and anxious tragicomedy, a theory formulated in *Problems of the Theater*, a widely read and poignant essay. *The Visit* is a synthesis of everything he had written.

Dürrenmatt's complex personality includes both a born storyteller and a moralist. *The Visit* is a play in which these two basic roles unite, leaving nothing unused. A shocking and consistent story describes the fateful collision between a meteor and a community: an order is smashed, there follows a phase of chaos, until a new, thoroughly evil order is built on the ruins. Dürrenmatt approaches the everyday life of his Guellen from the atmosphere of nightmare. The commonplace, the other half of the grotesque, is depicted with amusement and a sure sense of tragicomedy. If there are cracks or gaps in the foundations of Dürrenmatt's plays, it is due to his impatience in cementing his ideas together rather than to any lack of wild or unreal artistic invention. Guellen and *The Visit* stand solidly together; there is no question of a crack.

A great many scenic units and means are used with distinction. *The Visit* is Dürrenmatt's crowd play; there are several climactic chorus scenes combining a powerful emotional impact with an ironical or coolly detached intellectual element.

A guilty individual is placed in the middle of nightmarish crowds, and this freely constructed trial story leads to a ritual murder. There are doubled gangsters and eunuchs, grotesque and theatricalistic forest scenes, and a rich stage picture in which the past becomes the present. Instead of a last meal, Dürrematt's tragicomic protagonist enjoys a last drive in a car, a ritual scene placing him against the sky and in harmony with his surroundings. Parallel action is utilized in a way that reminds one of the montage techniques of film. The coordinated scenic images of this play speak a language that seems to be Dürrenmattian par excellence. He plays games with the stage and on it. He is a comedian and a fantast; his dramatic idiom has startling ingredients in it. A caprice, an artistic invention, a sudden improvisatory idea catches fire on his stage and fills it with action, with a stratified scenic image including both parodical and serious, playful and anxious elements. Yet the story dominates its parts. A central invention is used to build up an entire world of tragicomedy not departing from our common world. The artistic miracle of *The Visit* consists in a writer gaining control over his experimental materials.

The Visit is both a social panorama and a case study. Ill, a tainted non-hero, acquires the dimensions of a man of courage in the middle of a model-like community. Yet his self-sacrifice does not save Guellen; it confirms Claire's evil order, it condemns the town to moral depravity. This makes *The Visit* into a counter-sketch to tragedy and into an example of the absolute grotesque: it expresses an unresolvable conflict not to be submitted to any artistic or philosophical considerations. Human justice is terrifying; this is the beginning and end of *The Visit*.

Dürrenmatt's career up to *The Visit* makes sense: an uphill road. What after the culmination? It was easier for him to attain a world reputation than to sustain it. The total pattern gets mixed. There is a middle group of four original plays first performed in 1959–66. Of these, *The Physicists*

424

is clearly the most significant: Dürrenmatt's best compressionist play, a culmination of a second line of development. This line is a contrast to that of his wide social panoramas, to his world theater.

Our present-day world is not brought to the stage in *The Physicists*. Yet it is compellingly present behind the walls of Dürrenmatt's asylum. Violence and a blissful harmony are contrasted in a living-room which contains remnants from more peaceful periods in the history of mankind. The play is a claustrophobic thriller with elements of a horror farce; its plot includes a maximum number of twists within a limited area and span of time. Dürrenmatt's vision of the dangers of nuclear physics encompasses recent developments, present-day disputes, and a dark view of the future. The efforts of Möbius, a man of courage, are futile; the forces of chaos win an out-and-out victory.

Ever since his first play, Dürrenmatt has used all kinds of dramaturgic formulas and given them his own whimsical twist. Now he fabricates a formula of his own. Chance is to give "the worst possible turn" to a tightly knit action, thus frustrating the exact plans of calculating characters. His entire dramaturgy of chance reveals his determined effort to retain some space for the richness of his ideas, for his artistic inventions—in the middle of a world governed by science, on a stage governed by consistent formulas of dramaturgy. "The worst possible turn": a concept expressing Dürrenmatt's fears and his extremism. The newly conceived formula works in *The Physicists*; a terrifying chance existing also in reality is introduced in a convincing way. The story remains in control over the separate artistic inventions, the foreground events and the background vision are in balance, though the play is not by any means easy to interpret on the stage, because of its heterogeneous elements.

Dürrenmatt is now starting to eliminate his abundance. His first target is language: his dialogue is becoming more and more stark, mostly or merely functional. There are passages of verbal poetry in *The Physicists*; yet the play relies even

425

more heavily on a poetry of the theater, on the setting and lights, on music, on silent action, on stage situations, on a string of scenic images. *The Physicists* was a world-wide success; it spoke a contemporary and personal language of the stage about matters of importance.

There are more alarming signs in Dürrenmatt's other middle plays. A writer of vitally and playfully grotesque tragicomedies and novels has drifted toward thin story-lines based on paradoxes. There is a youthful feature in Dürrenmatt, in his brisk reliance on sudden and abundant artistic invention, on parodies and witticisms. This characteristic does not necessarily draw any advantage from a growing experience. Dürrenmatt starts running into difficulties in welding together his improvisatory ideas and his stories, his foreground events and thought constructions.

Polemicist Dürrenmatt theorizes quite a lot about developing his stories to a logical conclusion. Yet this may well be an inadvertent confession of a limitation in his creative work. His imagination functions piecemeal, he proceeds situation by situation; he creates isolated, highly effective, and characteristic scenic images with ease. It is more laborious for him to follow a total strategy when constructing a play; his successes in this field are splendid exceptions. As early as in the late 1950's he was losing contact with the everyday element and the mixture of feelings presupposed by the grotesque, and falling into monotonously macabre tones of voice. Three middle plays leave a sporadic impression, for these and other reasons.

Frank V is a banking "opera" close to Brecht's *Threepenny Opera*. This monotonous collection of separate songs and scenes includes an overdose of ambiguous parody, which is an excellent spice but a poor dish. The stage version of *Hercules*, a piece of Swiss cheese and another effort along the lines of cabaret theater, was not more successful. *The Meteor* consists of a loose string of scenic images, in spite of its ambitious effort to be a compressionistic problem play. Chance is manipulated; the story with its repeated resurrections meant for Dürrenmatt something that cannot be read from the text. Wolfgang Schwitter is evidence of a curious dichotomy in Dürrenmatt's relation to his numerous monomaniacs. He expresses his horror at their powerful one-sidedness, yet keeps criticizing them with a kind of involuntary absorption. They include the criminals of his detective stories and a flock of semi- or totally parodical stage heroes. Writing counter-sketches to heroics is a compulsion for Dürrenmatt, ever since the war-like books and games of his youth.

In the 1960's Dürrenmatt's characterization became gradually cooler. The men of courage have disappeared. What is left is a hero-like clown offering the spectator not the opportunity of identification but an intellectual insight into a moral conflict. Fear through criticism. This amounts to demanding a great deal of the spectator.

There were Herculean labors connected with Dürrenmatt's efforts to build up entire worlds of tragicomedy on the stage. He did not always succeed in widening the sphere around his paradoxical stories; a short cut found during the late 1960's was to enter a world created by someone else and give it a twist. After seven meager years there began a new period of plenty marked mostly by adaptations. Dürrenmatt's working methods grew out of his own earlier habits of rewriting his scripts and of creating counter-sketches; he was supported by a German tradition of producing and revising the classics. Remarkably enough, five out of his six adaptations are plays of the panoramic world theater and only one is compressionistic.

Dürrenmatt's adaptations do not use only his personal idiom. They are rather free translations from one stage language to another. Most of Dürrenmatt's scenic means and images retain umbilical cords to their mother, to the source text. Dürrenmatt's individuality is most conspicuous when no cords exist, when he indulges in his wild artistic inventions: the head of Austria in a soup-tureen, Faust M.D. drawing earthworms from Mephisto's abdomen. Keeping this res-

427

ervation in mind, one can delineate a picture of Dürrenmatt's total development during this period. He was both turning backward in time and trying to be contemporary. He returned to historical surroundings, prevalent in his first three plays; he adapted his own firstling. In the 1950's he had experienced absurdism as a competing movement in drama; now there were documentary plays appearing all around him. Dürrenmatt started using classics as his documentary materials, as it were.

He practiced with his own script. *The Anabaptists* is doubtless a more mature sample of dramatic craftsmanship than *It Is Written*. Yet cutting language down to a stark level, a leading principle for dramaturge Dürrenmatt, has not only been for the good of his adaptations and original plays. In its setting and action *The Anabaptists* remains colorful; its characterization includes a drastic alienation effect in turning Bockelson into a professional actor, and this reshaping both narrows the play down and scatters its constellation of characters. Its final scenic image makes an appeal for a more sensible world order. The world of the play is one of politics, no longer one of religion.

Play Strindberg: a further step toward asceticism. Dürrenmatt cut away not only all vacillating elements from the dialogue but also what he called "plush": a sense of period, the roundness of characterization. There was a marked tendency to dethrone stage heroes in the 1950's, and Dürrenmatt shared it. Man was seen as a marionette of alien powers, incapable of personal deeds and of individual guilt.[6] An after-effect of this leveling trend was harmful in the case of Strindberg's subjectivism: Dürrenmatt eliminated the play's dimension of depth. Paradoxically enough, this operation took place during a period restating the value of the individual on the stage. The crisp dialogue did not leave the actors any space

---

[6] Referring to Dürrenmatt and *Problems of the Theater*, Mayer describes irresponsibility and a division into separate roles as typically German phenomena in the 1960's. One is "family father" and "official," "friend of music" and "club mate," never a responsible individual, "a total man" (*Zur deutschen Literatur der Zeit*, pp. 342–43).

428

to breathe; all that was communicated was a desperate boxing match between man and wife.

König Johann continued along the lines of *The Anabaptists.* Both Shakespeare's original and Dürrenmatt's adaptation are political plays: English patriotism was replaced by an appeal for peace and internationalism. A modern outsider and the voice of reason entered the medieval world of princes and papal legates; these men were stripped and revealed as dangerous clowns. In its effort to outline a sociological chart of feudalism the play approached a modification of the epic theater. In this adaptation, probably his best, Dürrenmatt mastered the difficult problems of diction well. He achieved a stratified style in the dialogue and on the stage: there were harshly ironic contrasts and anachronisms. His additions sometimes reached the level of a laconic poetry of lamentation. With changes in the setting and with his own comic inventions Dürrenmatt stamped the work with a style of his own.

The failure of *Titus Andronicus* was partly compensated for by two adaptations of German classics. Dürrenmatt also directed the world premières of both, enlarging the sphere of asceticism to cover the visual elements, too. Against simple and monotonous backgrounds he staged two uneven tragedies which were accused of dryness, though enlivened by some surprising inventions and cabaret tricks. The only textual additions in *Urfaust* were a song by Goethe and passages from a documentary book; in *Woyzeck* Dürrenmatt extended the customary puzzle play of a Büchnerian adapter quite considerably by concocting speeches, as well as scenes, from the various manuscript versions of the play. Yet *Woyzeck* is a faithful adaptation, not a counter-sketch. Büchner's cool criticism of science and his concise verbal and stage poetry harmonized with Dürrenmatt's aspirations early in the 1970's. The days of the absolute grotesque are over for him.[7]

[7] The critical studies emphasizing the role of the grotesque in Dürrenmatt mostly date back to the early 1960's. There are contributions, e.g., by Klarmann (1960), Grimm and Oberle (1962), Jauslin, Sander and Waldmann (1964) quoted above.

429

CONCLUSION

Instead of the inexplicable elements in life his characters now face explicable political circumstances. Those in power, the princes in *The Anabaptists* and *König Johann*, the learned in *Urfaust* and *Woyzeck*, are guilty of the senselessness and tragedy of life. Dürrenmatt loses a part of his previous metaphysical depth and general validity; he gains in modishness, and moves toward a dramaturgic thinking in models not yet defined by him in an indisputable way. A model attempts to represent something outside its own limits: it incorporates a dimension of depth of a new kind. Though the history of drama in these years has still to be written, it is possible to say that the golden age of the absolute grotesque seems to cover roughly a decade, marked by *Waiting for Godot* in 1953, and *Marat/Sade* in 1964. The latter play, certainly open to contradictory interpretations, initiates a new orientation toward politics. Grotesque tragicomedies and absurdism remain a possibility of the modern theater, in revivals and new plays, but they no longer represent the prevalent style.

From abundance to asceticism: this line of development is confirmed by Dürrenmatt's latest original plays before 1977. The grotesque is a self-contradictory phenomenon; eliminating part of his characteristic richness led Dürrenmatt away from all forms of the grotesque, not only from its absolute variant. The everyday elements have been retreating. The particular worlds of *Frank V*, with its gangster democracy; of *The Meteor*, with its repeated resurrections; of *Portrait of a Planet*, with its end of the earth; and of *The Partaker*, with its Murder Inc. run by the state—these worlds have only tenuous connections with the world of the audience. Dürrenmatt's tone of voice takes a turn toward the monotonously macabre. He no longer reaches even the outer fringes of realism. His more and more extreme efforts to find grotesque elements in our streamlined technological world tend to grow artificial. It is easier to found a world on abundance than on a single paradox.

430

"His theater, not reality, is grotesque" (M 41). This is a self-mocking remark of Durrenmatt's from *The Meteor.* Yet both so-called reality and the theater include their grotesque elements; those inherent in the chaos of life can be given an artistic shape on the stage.[8] This presupposes a paradoxical kind of equilibrium: a balance of conflict. The self-contradictory elements in the grotesque, the conflicts between the comic and the tragic, the ludicrous and the fearsome, the everyday and the apocalyptic, the relieving and the depressing, should be balanced in one way or another. They can probably coexist in various proportions; the grotesque is too young an aspirant to the position of an aesthetic category to allow of precise definitions. Yet eliminating the other half of the grotesque causes the balance to totter.

This is what takes place in some of Dürrenmatt's adaptations and in both of his latest plays. They are only praised for their inventive details, not for their total conception. An essentially grotesque moment probably cannot last long; remarkably many masterpieces of absurdism are one-act plays. The grotesque centers on a single scenic image, or a limited number of them. It does so in *The Visit* and in *The Physicists*: these plays include a few interacting scenic images bound together by a strong story line. These images are effective within the framework of a quieter development, against "non-grotesque" scenes and sequences. There are no contrasting diminuendo sequences in *Titus Andronicus, Portrait of a Planet*, and *The Partaker*. Dürrenmatt's extremism results in the one-sidedly fearsome. Everything is emphasized, accordingly nothing is.

Portrait and *The Partaker* are also marred by the banality of their materials. Dürrenmatt's experiment with collage techniques led him to adapt newspaper articles; his series of cosmic and worldly visions is probably a throw-away product,

[8] Syberberg finds an artist's efforts to form chaos as such valuable: "For every artistic shape wins through its mere existence a victory over a world stuff, no matter how chaotic" (p. 144).

a stage collage too intimately bound to the passing moment to last. Reaching an intellectual control of grotesque materials also implies that the unresolvable conflict found must prevail within a theme relevant for us as people of this late age. On the other hand, *The Partaker* manifests an unrealistically high reliance on the actors to elevate melodramatic ingredients. This is what is left of Dürrenmatt's abundance: a belief in the richness of the actor's craft.

The Dürrenmatt of the late 1960's or early 1970's did not produce any climactic play. A kind of synthesis is achieved in two books belonging to other literary genres. It is possible to speculate that the new stage of development reached in the early 1970's will lead to a culmination later on; yet the artistic standard of Dürrenmatt's plays from 1970 and 1973 does not give rise to any high hopes. *Justice and Human Rights*, a long essay, and *The Fall*, a short novel, are clearly his most significant works since *The Physicists*. Both build critical models of the state, thus continuing a long line of development in Dürrenmatt. Romulus denies the right of the state to sacrifice a human being for the common good; Ill sacrifices himself to no purpose. An individual in the middle of a hostile crowd: this archetypal social nightmare of Dürrenmatt's is now given a new shape in which an abstract and anonymous state machinery represents the crowd. The essay is an effort to visualize that machinery with the help of two dramaturgic models; the novel shows the effect of the state on a power group at the very top of society.

Justice invites the readers to enter the study or mind of storyteller Dürrenmatt. Various possibilities of dramaturgic thinking are developed in a search for a feasible story. Throughout his canon Dürrenmatt is interested in the paradoxical and baffling possibilities of his inventive tales rather than in their characters; his best artistic achievements, however, reach a balance between the story and characterization. A basic feature occurring in all of Dürrenmatt's major characters is a belief in certain formulas of thought. Man is for him an animal producing interpretations of the world. "Man establishes all the time fictions in which he believes until he recognizes them as fictions and lets them fall in order to build up new ones, only to see through them once more. Yet those scales with which man measures himself and confronts himself and his reality, sometimes prevent the world from becoming too inhuman" (DK 127). *Justice* analyzes two such fictions, called the Wolf Game and the Good Shepherd Game. Both are unsatisfactory. Politics is an impossible art. Yet these and other fictions attain a precarious balance between justice and human rights, between the existential and general concepts of man, between chaos and order. This is all there is to prevent inhumanity from taking over.

The Fall is a grotesque novel. While failing to retain the importance of grotesquerie in his two latest plays, Dürrenmatt has kept it in the foreground of his novel, a compressionistic thriller. There is an everyday element balancing the macabre; the fearsome is made ludicrous. The only safe place is a claustrophobic and ascetic room shadowed by power politics. The people filling that room speak, gesticulate, and act, and Dürrenmatt's precise observations on their behavior keep the novel concrete, in spite of its ambition to be a model, too. A, a powerful individual, faces a collective body with its shifting frontiers and psychological turning-points, not an anonymous crowd. There are ritual elements and a parallel to *The Visit* in the concluding scenes of the novel. The entire series of events is caused by chance and by the very nature of the political power system, not by any inexplicable phenomenon in life. Although grotesque, the novel is not an absolute grotesque.

Dürrenmatt's expansive potentialities have led him to journalistic activities, too. He is a public figure in Switzerland. There are pieces of varying standard and significance among the treatises and lectures gathered together in *Dramaturgic and Critical Writings*, Dürrenmatt's second anthology of this kind. *Connections*, a many-faceted political essay on Israel, seems to mark a turning-point toward storytelling, toward a fruitful encounter between reality and Dürrenmatt's

CONCLUSION

remarkable powers of imagination: an honest, impressive, and uneven book. Sketching a portrait of Dürrenmatt as a Swiss debater (or as a stage director) is a task to be left to his would-be biographers. His views on the craft of playwriting need, however, a concluding remark. *Problems of the Theater*, a coherent essay, remains his best piece of work in this field. His experiences as a practicing dramaturge and controversial playwright since the middle 1950's have made him too cautious to outline a definite dramaturgic program. In a defensive mood he emphasizes that the worlds created on the stage are independent constructions of a playwright's fantasy, yet admits that these worlds have to retain a connection with reality. He expects a critic to play a game of chess with him, with any playwright—a game following the opening move made by the writer.

This sounds a fair enough demand, provided that the critic can bring his own conception of reality into the game. Art is a meeting-place between the two imaginations of the artifex and of the receiver. If the critic does not bring his intellect and skill, his experiences and personal qualities to his task, he has nothing to judge by. These abilities are needed; there is a long road from the opening to the endgame.

Dürrenmatt is a representative of a late age in drama. He is a European playwright, conscious of the literary and theatrical heritage in Switzerland and Germany. He knows that the openings available to him as a modern dramatist have been studied before. More than that: throughout his career he has kept creating contrasts and tensions, occasionally also harmonies, between his own ideas and the artistic formulas he has found in his cultural milieu. He is a child of his age and a rebel against it. The molds filled by Dürrenmatt with his own metal include those of tragedy and comedy, of detective story and thriller, of compressionism and social panorama, of epic theater and cabaret.

The artistic sense of this procedure can be justified in a variety of ways. One is to speak about the parodistic gro-

434

tesque as a Dürrenmattian tone of voice, another to use the widely relevant term of 'counter-sketch.' An artist of our late age wins his freedom from the supremacy of ready-made artistic shapes by parodying them (FP 37). Freedom for his own creative achievements. Furthermore: how to justify a story? What kinds of stories are feasible and significant? These are key problems for theorizing storyteller Dürrenmatt. One of his practical answers is to place his own story into a tense relation with earlier stories and with the expectations of his audiences. These expectations include archetypes and myths of our age—as far as we possess such things. Everyone expects the discursive Shavian comedy of *Romulus* to end as a discursive comedy, too; it does not. One hopes against all reason that Ill's self-sacrifice will save Guellen; it does not.

Dürrenmatt's plays have not only a beginning, middle, and end but also a kind of shadow structure behind the actual stage events. So do his novels: it is against all the rules of the game that detective Matthäi loses his fight. The expression 'story line' implies that a story is something thin. It is Dürrenmatt's ambition, not always fulfilled, to thicken that thin line until it covers a whole world, a particular world of tragicomedy. The limited area of the stage is filled with two stories, one told, the other figuring as a shadow, as a potentiality, in the minds of the spectators. Dürrenmatt aims at a stratified stage language. One of his strategies is to write counter-sketches.

Another is to construct grotesque scenic images. There are all kinds of contrasts present on Dürrenmatt's stage: parody and seriousness, past and present, individual and crowd, man and heaven, fear and laughter, the terrible and the everyday —all these and other pairs of contrasts are presented simultaneously, as ingredients in self-contradictory, grotesque scenic images. Dürrenmatt is an experimental playwright: he has written in a great many different styles dictated by the inherent qualities of his "stuff." It is thus not an easy undertaking to describe a typically Dürrenmattian scenic image, to go beyond listing those pairs of contrasts, beyond revealing those conflicts. Representative examples might include Ill's execution surrounded by Guelleners, with the news media ironically close at hand; Möbius as poor King Solomon reciting his final autobiographical statement with its cool poetry of the stars; Traps hanging from the window frame. These moments crystallize the absolute grotesque and visualize Dürrenmatt's two recurrent nightmares: an individual amidst a hostile crowd or against an empty sky. They are memorable words in Dürrenmatt's stage language or his prose.

They also belong to a series of interacting scenic images or sequences of narrative prose. Dürrenmatt's best works are combinations of abundance and coherence; some of his most conspicuous failures are anthologies of separate artistic inventions loosely bound together, or, on the other hand, plays abstracted to skeletons. It has not been easy for him to submit his thousand and one artistic inventions to a controlling central idea, his improvisatory scenic whims to a strong story. Taking his career in chronological order, we can speak of three Dürrenmatts; the three parts of this study reflect this division. A writer of wildly poetic and scattered stories and plays, a young student of Kafka and Kierkegaard; a master of the grotesque, a creator of playfully abundant, loose or compact tragicomedies and novels; a stage routinist and dramaturge losing contact with the everyday and eliminating his abundance in favor of asceticism. *Angel* was over-rich; *The Partaker* fails in building a stage world around its thin and paradoxical story line.

Dürrenmatt's scenic images have been seen from two viewpoints both in the above summary and throughout this study. They are analyzable particles of a play; they build up its characteristic texture. A scholar using scenic images as his analytic tools combines the roles of a nuclear physicist and a chemist. We can take a single scenic image and read its artistic qualities; we can scrutinize the interaction between several images within a play. Now, having completed my second overall study on a modern playwright, I am convinced of the usefulness of the scenic image as a tool for a scholar. Plays are written for the stage; this basic fact cannot be denied. Yet the fact as such is not enough; we need a framework to organize the impressions left by a theater performance and/or scenic reading of a play. The scenic image provides such a framework. A feature found with its help may characterize the playwright even in other respects.

Everywhere in Dürrenmatt we meet contrasts: between abundance and coherence, wild artistic inventions and artistic formulas, chance and consequence, practice and theory, relief and anxiety. Between chaos and order. The first halves in these pairs speak of freedom, of movement, of shapelessness; the latter, of an effort to find order. Whatever field of human thought we pick out, there are hidden and open conflicts and ambiguities in his works: religion, philosophy, science, sociology, politics, history, classical literature.

"To write is to keep Judgment Day over one's head," Ibsen once said.[9] "Over man's head," Dürrenmatt the storyteller might say. He makes a persistent effort in his works to judge the various fictions man has kept creating for himself. Judging is for him a terrible and/or tragicomic event. Faithful to his polemical inclinations[10] and to his extremism, he has given these conflicts a sharp form; he has heightened rather than mitigated. This has led him both to embarrassing errors and to valiant deeds, to powerful scenic images and plays with unresolvable conflicts.

A high degree of *Problemträchtigkeit*, density of problems, is usually taken as a merit in modern literary research. Judged by this criterion Dürrenmatt is a remarkable artist. He belongs to a German and central European stage tradition in

---

[9] *Samlede dikterverker, VI*, p. 422.

[10] Brock-Sulzer has formulated a precise description of Dürrenmatt's polemical quality: "He is both heavy and quick. It generally takes time to move weighty masses. In Dürrenmatt these move as quickly as the light ones. This is what makes his art dangerous for him and for us. It is more difficult to tame its momentum than that of others. Its stroke is harder. A bear-like power is combined with the quickness of an intellectual in him, and not always in a peaceful manner" (*Die Tat*, Feb. 2, 1954; *Frisch und D.*, p. 124).

which the various modifications of theatricalism have been more strongly emphasized than realism.[11] As a young writer he received impulses from Aristophanes and Brecht, from Wedekind, Nestroy, and Wilder. As a mature writer he has fought for the independence of his stage worlds, not for their truth to everyday reality. His work has continued through several periods in post-war drama: the rule-books of aesthetics have been rewritten more than once.

Growing from the aftermath of World War II, Dürrenmatt's work ran parallel with absurdism, yet kept within the limits of grotesque tragicomedy. He is a leading representative of this genre in both practice and theory. Admitting that chance and senselessness have a role in life, Dürrenmatt refuses to base his whole vision of the world and concept of art on absurdity. In the 1960's he turned toward politics, yet remained faithful to his belief in his task as a detector of conflicts, not as a solver of problems. He believes neither in the ultimate absurdity of life, nor in easy changes to be achieved through political action. He is comparable with Max Frisch in his readiness to construct stage models and to take social attitudes,[12] though not along the lines of party politics. Dürrenmatt's place in the total pattern of postwar drama is in the middle, outside the fields of absurdism and the epic theater. He is, of course, something more than a

[11] A theatricalistic independence of the illusion of reality has been seen as a specifically modern phenomenon by a great many scholars, among them Klarmann: "The modern theatre . . . establishes the reality of illusion. . . . Brecht, Anouilh, Genet, Georges Schehadé, Max Frisch are all fully aware of the splendid autonomy of the stage. And of these it is difficult to imagine a greater display of theatrical pyrotechnics than those unleased by Dürrenmatt" ("F.D. and the Tragic Sense of Comedy," *TDR*, *4*, 4, May 1960, p. 78).

[12] It is easier for the Swiss to esteem Dürrenmatt, an "unpolished fellow countryman," than Frisch, a rebel against Switzerland (Bänziger, p. 204). Both have dealt with national subjects. Witz mentions it as a double task to prove that modern Swiss literature has both a special national character and great international significance (Mariacher and Witz, eds., *Bestand und Versuch*, 1964, p. 8). Dürrenmatt's work certainly has.

central European court jester.[13] He is an author *sui generis*. There is no other pen like his in the wide world of literature. The 1950's, Dürrenmatt's most fertile creative period, belongs to an irritating no man's land. It is not distant enough in time to be taken as the legitimate territory of the historian; it is not recent enough to be covered by the words "present" or "our time." Photographs of Dürrenmatt's premières give those years a kind of historical aura: this is what was meant by the grotesque then, before the theater of cruelty. In our eyes the atmosphere is both 'right' and 'wrong,' both modern and slightly outmoded. There are too many things belonging to the scenery or props on the stage; the setting lacks the streamlined abstractness of a somewhat later style of staging and of theater architecture. These details belong to the theatrical world in which Dürrenmatt made his greatest impact, and to those years when he struck his vein of gold. *The Visit* made him a ruling prince of the stage. His fight for this position against generations of usurpers includes both victories and defeats.

Friedrich Dürrenmatt in his fifties is far from an "endgame." His customary abundance now takes the form of various literary genres, of a wide field of activities. Dramaturge, playwright, novelist, journalist, public speaker: he has hardly said his last word in any of these fields. A vision above, based on *Dramaturgic and Critical Writings*, showed him sailing to freedom between the buoys dedicated to Brecht and Ionesco. Curiously enough, the simile of the ship occurs in one of the earliest jottings of young Dürrenmatt. Let it be so: his route has brought and will bring him to the wide and troubled waters of free winds, of wild artistic inventions, of submarines and a sky full of stars, of laughing sunshine and tempests, of grotesque animals and fairy-tale figures hidden in the depth of oceans.

[13] According to Reich-Ranicki, Dürrenmatt was still taken "with a strange reserve" in 1967: "People endure or praise him, without trusting him. . . . He is not taken quite in earnest" (*Literatur der kleinen Schritte*, pp. 250–51).

Appendix

A LIST OF WORKS

||||||||||||||||||||||||||||||||||||||||||||||||||||||||||||||||||||||||||||||||||||||||||||||||||||||||||||||||||

This chronological list of Dürrenmatt's works discussed in this study is based on corresponding catalogues published by Brock-Sulzer (*Friedrich Dürrenmatt*, pp. 268–71), Bänziger (*Frisch und D.*, pp. 254–55, 264–67) and Peppard (*F.D.*, pp. 13–15). Additional information has been sought in Hansel's *F.D.-Bibliographie*, in *Reclams Hörspielführer*, ed. by Schwitzke, in playbills and newspaper reviews, and from Dürrenmatt's publisher, Verlag der Arche, Zurich.

Title	Year written	First production	First printing
The City	1943–52		1952
It Is Written	1946	Zurich, Apr. 19, 1947	1947
The Double	1946	NR/BR, 1960	1960
The Blind Man	1947	Basle, Jan. 10, 1948	1960
Romulus the Great	1948	Basle, Apr. 25, 1949	1958
The Judge and His Hangman	1950		1950
The Marriage of Mr. Mississippi	1950	Munich, March 26, 1952	1952
The Quarry	1951		1951
The Case of the Donkey's Shadow	1951	Studio Bern, 1951	1956
Nocturnal Conversation with a Despised Person	1951	Munich, July 25, 1952	1957
Stranitzky and the National Hero	1952	NWR-Hamburg, 1952	1953
An Angel Comes to Babylon	1948–53	Munich, Dec. 22, 1953	1954
Hercules and the Augean Stables (radio version)	1954	NWR-Hamburg, 1954	1954
Operation Vega	1954	BR/SR/NR, 1955	1958
Problems of the Theater	1954		1955
Once a Greek . . .	1955		1955

441

Title	Year written	First production	First printing
The Visit	1955	Zurich, Jan. 29, 1956	1956
Die Panne (radio play)	1956	BR/SR, 1956	1961
A Dangerous Game	1956		1956
Episode on an Autumn Evening	1956	NR, 1957	1957
The Pledge	1957		1958
Frank V	1958	Zurich, March 19, 1959	1960
The Physicists	1959–61	Zurich, Feb. 20, 1962	1962
Hercules and the Augean Stables (stage version)	1962	Zurich, March 20, 1963	1963
Writings on the Theater	1947–65		1966
The Meteor	1959, 1965	Zurich, Jan. 20, 1966	1966
The Anabaptists	1966	Zurich, March 16, 1967	1967
König Johann	1968	Basle, Sept. 18, 1968	1968
Justice and Human Rights	1968		1969
Play Strindberg	1968–69	Basle, Feb. 8, 1969	1969
Sentences from America	1969–70		1970
Urfaust	1969–70	Zurich, Oct. 22, 1970	
Titus Andronicus	1969–70	Düsseldorf, Dec. 12, 1970	1970
Portrait of a Planet	1969–70	Düsseldorf, Nov. 10, 1970	1971
The Fall	1966, 1971		1971
Woyzeck	1971–72	Zurich, Feb. 17, 1972	
Dramaturgic and Critical Writings	1966–71		1972
The Partaker	1959, 1972	Zurich, March 8, 1973	1976
Connections	1974–75		1976
Interview with Heinz Ludwig Arnold	1975		1976

Abbreviations of radio networks:

BR = Bayerischer Rundfunk (Radio Bavaria)
NR = Norddeutscher Rundfunk (Radio Germany North)
NWR = Nordwestdeutscher Rundfunk (Radio Germany North-West)
SR = Süddeutscher Rundfunk (Radio Germany South)

Bibliography

Allgöver, Walter. Review in the *Basler Nachrichten*, Jan. 11, 1948.

Alvarez, A. Reviews in the *New Statesman*, Oct. 10, 1959, and July 2, 1960.

Amery, Jean. Review in the *Frankfurter Rundschau*, Juni, 1976.

Ammann, Hans J. "Theaterarbeit. Zur Entstehung von 'Play Strindberg,'" *Neue Zürcher Zeitung*, June 15, 1969.

Angermeyer, Hans Christoph. *Zuschauer im Drama*. Brecht—Dürrenmatt—Handke. Frankfurt/Main: Athenäum Verlag, 1971.

Arnold, Armin. *Friedrich Dürrenmatt*. Berlin: Colloquium Verlag, 1969.

————. *Die Literatur des Expressionismus*. Stuttgart: W. Kohlhammer Verlag, 1966.

Askew, Melvin W. "Dürrenmatt's *The Visit of the Old Lady*," *Tulane Drama Review*, 5, 4 (June 1961).

Bachmann, Dieter. "Enttäuschte Erwartung," *Die Weltwoche*, March 14, 1973.

————. " 'Mitmacher sind wir alle,' " *Die Weltwoche*, March 7, 1973.

Bänziger, Hans. "Dürrenmattiana," *Neue Zürcher Zeitung*, June 6, 1970.

————. *Frisch und Dürrenmatt*. 5th rev. ed.; Bern und München: Francke Verlag 1967 (1960).

————. "Schweizer Literaturbrief," *Merkur*, *11*, 10 (Oct. 1957).

Barraclough, Clifford A. "Nestroy, the Political Satirist," *Monatshefte für deutschen Unterricht*, *52*, 5 (Oct. 1960).

Baschung, Urs J. "Zu Friedrich Dürrenmatts 'Der Tunnel,' " *Schweizer Rundschau*, *68*, 10–11 (Oct.–Nov. 1969).

Basler Theater. Playbill of *König Johann*, 1968–69.

Baumann, Gerhart. *Georg Büchner*. Göttingen: Vandenhoeck & Ruprecht, 1961.

Bayer, Hans. Review in the *Stuttgarter Nachrichten*, March 20, 1967.

Beckmann, Heinz. Review in the *Rheinischer Merkur*, March 26, 1967.

BIBLIOGRAPHY

Beissel, Henry. "Between Two Nightmares: The German Theatre After World War II," *Seminar, 1,* 2 (Fall 1965).

Benedikt, Michael, and Wellwarth, George E. (eds.). *Postwar German Theatre.* London and Melbourne: Macmillan, 1968.

Bernhard, Roberto. *Allemanisch-welsche Sprachsorgen und Kulturfragen.* Mit Beiträgen von Friedrich Dürrenmatt (reprinted in DK) und Albert Richli. Frauenfeld: Verlag Huber, 1968.

Bichsel, Peter. *Des Schweizers Schweiz.* Zürich: Die Arche, 1969.

Bienek, Horst. *Werkstattgespräche mit Schriftstellern.* München: Hanser, 1962.

Binder, Wolfgang. *Das Bild des Menschen in der modernen deutschen Literatur.* Zürich: Artemis Verlag, 1969.

Bloch, Peter André. "Dürrenmatts Plan zur Bearbeitung von Shakespeares *Troilus und Cressida,*" *Jahrbuch der deutschen Shakespeare-Gesellschaft West,* 1970.

Blum, Ruth. "Ist Friedrich Dürrenmatt ein christlicher Schriftsteller?" *Reformatio, 8,* 8 (Sept. 1959).

Boesch, Walter. Reviews in the *Tages-Anzeiger,* March 21, 1959, and Sept. 20, 1968.

Bondy, François. "Gute Hirten—untereinander." *Die Weltwoche,* Aug. 27, 1971.

————. Review in the *Süddeutsche Zeitung,* Oct. 26, 1970.

de Boor, Helmut, and Newald, Richard (eds.). *Geschichte der deutschen Literatur,* vi: 1, München: C. H. Bech'sche Verlagsbuchhandlung, 1957.

Boyd, Ursel D. "Die Funktion des Grotesken als Symbol der Gnade in Dürrenmatts dramatischem Werk," Ph.D. dissertation, University of Maryland, 1964.

Braun, Karlheinz (ed.). *Deutsches Theater der Gegenwart,* i. Nachwort von Henning Rischbieter. Frankfurt/Main: Suhrkamp, 1967.

Brentano, Bernardo von. *Schöne Literatur und öffentliche Meinung.* Wiesbaden: Limes Verlag, 1962.

Briggen, Hansjürg. Review in the *Zolliker Bote,* March 23, 1967.

Brock, Erich. "Basler Stadttheater. Friedrich Dürrenmatt: 'Der Blinde,'" *Schweizer Monatshefte, 27,* 1947.

Brock-Sulzer, Elisabeth. "Darf man lachen? Wie der 'Meteor' einschlug," *Theater heute, 7,* 3 (March 1966).

444

Brock-Sulzer, Elisabeth. "Dürrenmatt am Scheideweg?" *Schweizerische Theaterzeitung, 18*, 4 (Apr. 1963).

———. *Dürrenmatt in unserer Zeit.* Eine Werkinterpretation nach Selbstzeugnissen. Basel: Friedrich Reinhardt Verlag, 1968.

———. "Dürrenmatt's 'Meteor' in Zürich," *Schweizerische Theaterzeitung, 21*, 2 (Feb. 1966).

———. "Friedrich Dürrenmatt," *Der Monat, 15*, 5 (May 1963).

———. *Friedrich Dürrenmatt.* Stationen seines Werkes. 2d rev. ed.; Zürich: Die Arche, 1964 (1960).

———. "Der neue Dürrenmatt," *Schweizersche Theaterzeitung, 22*, 4 (Apr. 1967).

———. Reviews in the *Frankfurter Allgemeine Zeitung*, March 22, 1963, Jan. 24, 1966, and March 20, 1967; in *Die Tat*, Apr. 24, 1947, Dec. 12, 1949, Feb. 2, 1954, March 23, 1959, March 23, 1963, Jan. 23, 1966, March 20 and 21, 1967, Sept. 23, 1968, Feb. 12, 1969, Oct. 26, 1970, March 29, 1971, Feb. 21, 1972, and March 12, 1973.

Brües, Otto. *Gut gebrüllt, Löwe.* Emsdetten: Verlag Lechte, 1967.

Brunner, Hans Heinrich. "Aber wie?" *Kirchenbote, 53*, 4 (Apr. 1967).

Brunner, Karl. "Middle-Class Attitudes in Shakespeare's Histories," *Shakespeare Survey, 6*. Cambridge: University Press, 1953.

Brustein, Robert. "Portrait of a Warning," *The Observer*, Feb. 4, 1973.

———. *The Theatre of Revolt.* London: Methuen & Co., 1965.

Bucher, Werner, and Ammann, Georges. *Schweizer Schriftsteller im Gespräch*, I. Basle: Friedrich Reinhardt Verlag, 1970.

Büchner, Georg. *Complete Plays and Prose.* Translated and with an Introduction by Carl Richard Mueller. New York: Hill and Wang, 1963.

———. *Sämtliche Werke und Briefe*, I-II. Historical-critical edition by Werner R. Lehmann. Hamburg: Christian Wegner Verlag, 1967, 1971.

———. *Woyzeck*, Dichtung und Wirklichkeit. Edited by Hans Mayer. Frankfurt/M—Berlin: Ullstein Bücher, 1963.

445

BIBLIOGRAPHY

Büchner, Georg. *Woyzeck.* Texte und Dokumente. Critical edition by Egon Krause. Frankfurt am Main: Insel Verlag, 1969.

Bullough, Geoffrey. *Narrative and Dramatic Sources of Shakespeare,* IV. London: Routledge and Kegan Paul, New York: Columbia University Press, 1962.

Buschkiel, Jürgen. Reviews in *Die Welt,* Feb. 11, 1962, Sept. 20, 1968, and Oct. 27, 1970.

Calgari, Guido. *Die Vier Literaturen der Schweiz.* Olten und Freiburg im Breisgau: Walter-Verlag, 1966 (1958).

Campbell, Lily B. *Shakespeare's Histories.* San Marino, Calif.: The Huntington Library, 1963 (1947).

Canaris, Volker. Review in *Die Zeit,* Nov. 20, 1970.

Carew, Rivers. "The Plays of Friedrich Dürrenmatt," *The Dublin Magazine,* 4, 1 (Spring 1965).

Carlsson, Anni. *Die deutsche Buchkritik von der Reformation bis zur Gegenwart.* Bern und München: Francke Verlag, 1969.

Cattani, A. Review in the *Neue Zürcher Zeitung,* Aug. 27, 1976.

Chiari, J. *Landmarks of Contemporary Drama.* London: Herbert Jenkins, 1965.

Daiber, Hans. *Deutsches Theater seit 1945.* Stuttgart: Philipp Reclam jun., 1976.

————. Review in the *Handelsblatt Deutsche Wirtschaftszeitung,* Dec. 24, 1968.

Daviau, Donald G. "Justice in the works of Friedrich Dürrenmatt," *Kentucky Foreign Language Quarterly,* 9, 4 (1962).

Dennis, Nigel. "Fun with Fission," *Encounter,* 114, March 1963.

Deschner, Margareta Neovius. "Dürrenmatt's 'Die Wiedertäufer': What the Dramatist Has Learned," *The German Quarterly,* 44, 2 (March 1971).

————. "Friedrich Dürrenmatt's Experiments with Man: An Analysis of His First Five Plays," Ph.D. dissertation, University of Colorado, 1966.

Die deutsche Bühne, 2–8 (29–35), 1958–64. Statistics of the yearly repertoire of German theater companies.

Deutsches Theater heute. An anthology from the periodical *Theater heute.* Velber bei Hannover: Friedrich Verlag, 1967.

446

Dick, E. S. "Dürrenmatts 'Der Besuch der alten Dame,' " *Zeitschrift für deutsche Philologie, 87*, 4 (Oct. 1968).

Dietrich, Margret. *Das moderne Drama*. Strömungen, Gestalten, Motive. Stuttgart: Alfred Kröner Verlag, 1961.

Diller, Edward. "Dürrenmatt's Use of the Stage as a Dramatic Element," *Symposium, 20*, 3 (Fall 1966).

———. "Friedrich Dürrenmatt's Chaos and Calvinism," *Monatshefte, 63*, 1 (Spring 1971).

———. "Friedrich Dürrenmatt's Theological Concept of History," *The German Quarterly, 40*, 1 (Jan. 1967).

———. "Friedrich Dürrenmatt's 'Weihnachten': A Short, Short, Revealing Story," *Studies in Short Fiction, 3*, 2 (Winter 1966).

———. "Human Dignity in a Materialistic Society: Friedrich Dürrenmatt and Bertolt Brecht," *Modern Language Quarterly, 25*, 4 (Dec. 1964).

Drese, Claus Helmut. "Friedrich Dürrenmatt," *Eckart, 28*, 4 (1959).

Dürrenmatt, Friedrich. *Der Besuch der alten Dame*. Oper in drei Akten (composed by Gottfried von Einem). London: Boosey & Hawkes, 1970.

———. *Der Blinde*. Ein Drama. Zürich: Verlag der Arche, 1960.

———. *A Dangerous Game* (Die Panne). Transl. by Richard and Clara Winston. London: Jonathan Cape, 1960. Title in the U.S.: *Traps*. New York: Alfred A. Knopf, 1960.

———. *Dramaturgisches und Kritisches*. Theater-Schriften und Reden II. Zürich: Verlag der Arche, 1972.

———. *Die Ehe des Herrn Mississippi*. Bühnenfassung und Drehbuch. Zürich: Verlag der Arche, 1966. Druck- und Bühnenrechte der Bühnenfassung: Europa Verlag, Zürich.

———. *Episode on an Autumn Evening* (Abendstunde im Spätherbst). Transl. by Myron B. Gubitz. *Switzerland Today, 1*, 1 (June 1967).

———. *Es steht geschrieben*. Ein Drama. Zürich: Verlag der Arche, 1959 (1947).

———. *Four Plays*. Transl. by Gerhard Nellhaus (*Problems of the Theater* and *Romulus the Great*), Michael Bullock (*The Marriage of Mr. Mississippi*), William McElwee (*An Angel Comes to Babylon*), and James Kirkup (*The Physicists*). London: Jonathan Cape, 1964.

447

BIBLIOGRAPHY

Dürrenmatt, Friedrich. *Frank der Fünfte*. Oper einer Privatbank, Musik von Paul Burkhard. Zürich: Verlag der Arche, 1960.

————. *Frank der Fünfte*. Eine Komödie, mit Musik von Paul Burkhard. Bochum version. Zürich: Verlag der Arche, 1964.

————. "Friedrich Dürrenmatt über seine Komödie 'Der Meteor,'" an interview, *Neue Zürcher Nachrichten*, Feb. 28, 1966.

————. "Gedanken über das Theater," a series of six articles, *Sonntags Journal/Zürcher Woche*, Apr. 18–19—July 11–12, 1970.

————. *Gesammelte Hörspiele*. Zürich: Verlag der Arche, 1961 (1954).

————. Goethes *Urfaust*, szenische Fassung. Archives of Schauspielhaus Zürich: world première Oct. 22, 1970.

————. *Grieche sucht Griechin*. Eine Prosakomödie. Frankfurt/M—Berlin: Ullstein, 1963 (1955).

————. *Die Heimat im Plakat*. Ein Buch für Schweizer Kinder. Zürich: Diogenes Verlag, 1963.

————. *Herkules und der Stall des Augias*. Eine Komödie. Zürich: Verlag der Arche, 1963.

————. *The Judge and His Hangman* (Der Richter und sein Henker). Transl. by Cyrus Brooks. London: Penguin Books, 1969 (1954).

————. *Komödien* I. Zürich: Verlag der Arche, 1961 (1957).

————. *Komödien* II *und frühe Stücke*. Zürich: Verlag der Arche, 1964.

————. *König Johann*. Nach Shakespeare. Zürich: Verlag der Arche, 1968.

————. *Der Meteor*. Eine Komödie in zwei Akten. Zürich: Verlag der Arche, 1966.

————. "Mich interessiert nur die Politik," an interview, *Theaternachrichten*, Düsseldorfer Schauspielhaus, Dec. 1970.

————. *Der Mitmacher*. Acting edition. Basel: Reiss AG, 1973. Copyright by Verlag der Arche, 1973.

————. *Monstervortrag über Gerechtigkeit und Recht nebst einem helvetischen Zwischenspiel*. Zürich: Verlag der Arche, 1969.

————. *Once a Greek* . . . (Grieche sucht Griechin). Transl. by Richard and Clara Winston. London: Jonathan Cape, 1966 (1965).

448

BIBLIOGRAPHY

Dürrenmatt, Friedrich. *Die Panne*. Eine noch mögliche Ge-
schichte. Zürich: Verlag der Arche, 1959 (1956).
————. *Die Panne* and *Der Tunnel*. Ed. with an introduction by
F. J. Alexander. London: Oxford University Press, 1967.
(1956, 1952).
————. *Die Physiker*. Eine Komödie in zwei Akten. Zürich:
Verlag der Arche, 1962.
————. *Play Strindberg*. Totentanz nach August Strindberg.
Zürich: Verlag der Arche, 1969.
————. *The Pledge* (Das Versprechen). Transl. by Richard
and Clara Winston. London: Penguin Books, 1964 (1959).
————. *Porträt eines Planeten*. Zürich: Verlag der Arche, 1971.
————. *The Quarry* (Der Verdacht). Transl. by Eva H. Mor-
reale. London: Jonathan Cape, 1962.
————. *Der Richter und sein Henker*. Einsiedeln: Benziger,
1957 (1950).
————. *Sätze aus Amerika*. Zürich: Verlag der Arche, 1970.
————. *Die Stadt*. Prosa i–iv. Zürich: Verlag der Arche, 1962
(1952).
————. *Der Sturz*. Zürich: Verlag der Arche, 1971.
————. *Theater-Schriften und Reden*. Zürich: Verlag der
Arche, 1966.
————. *Titus Andronicus*. Eine Komödie nach Shakespeare.
Zürich: Verlag der Arche, 1970.
————. " 'Der Ur-Herkules,' " playbill, Schauspielhaus Zürich,
1962–63.
————. *Der Verdacht*. Roman. Einsiedeln-Zürich: Benziger,
1967 (1951).
————. *Der Verdacht*. Ed. by Leonard Forster. London: Har-
rap, 1965.
————. *The Visit* (Der Besuch der alten Dame). A tragi-com-
edy. Transl. by Patrick Bowles. London: Jonathan Cape,
1968 (1962).
————. *Die Wiedertäufer*. Eine Komödie in zwei Teilen. Zü-
rich: Verlag der Arche, 1967.
————. *Woyzeck*. A stage director's book in the archives of
Schauspielhaus Zürich: world première Feb. 17, 1972.
————. *Zusammenhänge*. Essay über Israel. Eine Konzeption.
Zürich: Verlag der Arche, 1976.

BIBLIOGRAPHY

Dürrenmatt, Peter. *Schweizer Geschichte.* Zürich: Schweizer Verlagshaus AG, 1963.

Durzak, Manfred. *Dürrenmatt, Frisch, Weiss.* Stuttgart: Philipp Reclam jun., 1972.

————, ed. *Die deutsche Literatur der Gegenwart.* Stuttgart: Philipp Reclam jun., 1971.

Duwe, Wilhelm. *Deutsche Dichtung des 20. Jahrhunderts,* II. Zürich: Orell Füssli, 1962.

————. *Die Kunst und ihr Anti von Daba bis heute.* Berlin: Erich Schmidt Verlag, 1967.

Edschmid, Kasimir. *Lebendiger Expressionismus.* München/Wien/Basel: Verlag Kurt Desch, 1964.

Ehinger, Hans. "Zwischen Bern, Basel und Zürich," *Die Deutsche Bühne, 3* (*30*), 7–8, (July–Aug., 1959).

Ellestad, Everett M. "Friedrich Dürrenmatt's *Mausefalle,*" *The German Quarterly, 43,* 4 (Nov. 1970).

Ellwood, William R. "Preliminary Notes on the German Dramaturg and the American Theater," *Modern Drama, 13,* 3 (Dec. 1970).

Elsner, Hans. Review in the *Kurier,* Wien, March 22, 1967.

Emmel, Hildegard. *Das Gericht in der deutschen Literatur des 20. Jahrhunderts.* Bern und München: Francke Verlag, 1963.

Esslin, Martin. *Brief Chronicles.* London: Temple Smith, 1970.

————. Review in *The Guardian,* Jan. 10, 1963.

————. *The Theatre of the Absurd.* London: Eyre & Spottiswoode, 1962.

Fechter, Paul. *Das europäische Drama,* III. Mannheim: Bibliographisches Institut, 1958.

Fehr, Karl. Review in *Der Landbote,* Winterthur, Feb. 18, 1966.

Fehse, Willi. *Von Goethe bis Grass.* Biografische Portraits zur Literatur. Bielefeld: Verlag Ernst und Werner Gieseking, 1963.

Fickert, Kurt J. "The Curtain Speech in Dürrenmatt's *The Physicists,*" *Modern Drama, 14,* 1 (May 1970).

Flora, Paul. *Veduten und Figuren.* Vorwort von Friedrich Dürrenmatt. Zürich: Diogenes Verlag, 1968.

Frank, Armin P. *Das Hörspiel.* Heidelberg: Carl Winter, Universitätsverlag, 1963.

450

Franz, Hertha und Egon. "Zu Dürrenmatts Komödie 'Der Meteor,' " *Zeitschrift für deutsche Philologie*, 87, 4 (Fall 1968).

Franzen, Erich. "Das Drama zwischen Utopie und Wirklichkeit," *Merkur*, *14*, 8 (Aug. 1960).

————. *Formen des modernen Dramas*. 2d ed. München: C. H. Beck, 1970 (1961).

Friedmann, Hermann and Mann, Otto (eds.). *Deutsche Literatur im 20. Jahrhundert*, I, Strukturen. 4th rev. ed. Heidelberg: Wolfgang Rothe Verlag, 1961 (1954).

Fringeli, Dieter. Review in the *Basler Nachrichten*, March 24, 1976.

Frisch, Max. "On the Nature of the Theatre," excerpts from the diary, transl. by Carl Richard Mueller. *Tulane Drama Review*, *6*, 3 (March 1962).

————. "Romulus der Grosse. Zur Komödie von Friedrich Dürrenmatt," playbill, Schauspielhaus Zürich, 1949–50.

Frischauer, Paul. *Die Welt der Bühne als Bühne der Welt*, II. Hamburg: Marion von Schröder Verlag, 1967.

Gabriel, Cola. "Basler Stadttheater. Friedrich Dürrenmatt: 'Romulus der Grosse,' " *Schweizer Monatshefte*, *29*, 2 (June 1949).

Garten, H. F. *Modern German Drama*. London: Methuen, 1964 (1959).

Gascoigne, Bamber. "Fable and Fiction," *The Spectator*, Jan. 18, 1963.

Gasser, Manuel. "Moritat in Weltformat," *Weltwoche*, Jan. 28, 1966.

Gassner, John. *Form and Idea in the Modern Theatre*. New York: Holt, Rinehart & Winston, 1956.

————, and Quinn, Edward (eds.). *The Reader's Encyclopedia of World Drama*. New York: Thomas Y. Crowell, 1969.

Geissler, Rolf (ed.). *Zur Interpretation des modernen Dramas*. Brecht—Dürrenmatt—Frisch. Frankfurt am Main, Berlin, Bonn: Verlag Moritz Diesterweg, 1961.

Gellert, Roger. Review in the *New Statesman*, Jan. 18, 1963.

Gillis, William. "Dürrenmatt and the Detectives," *The German Quarterly*, *35*, 1 (Jan. 1962).

Ginsberg, Ernst. "Romulus der Grosse," playbill, Schauspielhaus Zürich, 1949–50.

451

BIBLIOGRAPHY

Goethe, Johann Wolfgang von. *Faust und Urfaust. Bremen*: Carl Schönemann Verlag, 1962.

————. *Urfaust.* Stuttgart: Reclam, 1962.

Goldschmidt, Hermann Levin. Review in the *Zürichsee-Zeitung,* March 21, 1976.

Goldschmit, Rudolf. Review in *Der Tagesspiegel,* Berlin, Oct. 28, 1960.

Gontrum, Peter B. "Ritter, Tod und Teufel: Protagonists and Antagonists in the Prose Works of Friedrich Dürrenmatt," *Seminar, 1,* 2 (Fall 1965).

Grack, Günther. Review in *Der Tagesspiegel,* Berlin, Jan. 18, 1970.

Gregor, Ulrich. "Verfilmtes Theater," *Theater heute, 2,* 8 (Aug. 1961).

Grene, David, and Lattimore, Richmond (eds.). *Greek Tragedies,* I. Chicago and London: The University of Chicago Press, 1963.

Grenzmann, Wilhelm. *Dichtung und Glaube.* 5th rev. ed. Frankfurt/M.—Bonn: Athenäum Verlag, 1964 (1950).

Greul, Heinz. *Bretter, die die Zeit bedeuten.* Köln und Berlin: Kiepenheuer & Witsch, 1967.

Grimm, Reinhold (ed.). *Episches Theater.* Köln/Berlin: Kiepenheuer & Witsch, 1966.

————, Jäggi, Willy, and Oesch, Hans (eds.). *Der unbequeme Dürrenmatt.* Mit Beiträgen von Gottfried Benn, Elisabeth Brock-Sulzer, Fritz Buri, Reinhold Grimm, Hans Mayer und Werner Oberle. Basel/Stuttgart: Basilius Presse, 1962.

————, Jäggi, Willy, and Oesch, Hans (eds.). *Sinn oder Unsinn?* Das Groteske im modernen Drama. Basel/Stuttgart: Basilius Presse, 1962.

Gross, Alexander. "The Theatre of the Manure," *Encore, 12,* 2, 1965.

Grut, Mario. Review in the *Aftonbladet,* Stockholm, Sept. 26, 1969.

Guth, Hans, P. "Dürrenmatt's *Visit*: The Play behind the Play," *Symposium, 16,* 2 (Summer 1962).

Guthke, Karl S. *Geschichte und Poetik der deutschen Tragikomödie.* Göttingen: Vandenhoeck & Ruprecht, 1961.

————. *Modern Tragicomedy.* New York: Random House, 1966.

Haller, Hans Rudolf. "Zeit der Dürre," *TV-Radio-Zeitung*, Apr. 4–10, 1971.

Hallikainen, Pertti (ed.). *Kirjallisuudentutkijain seuran vuosikirja 24* (Annuaire des historiens de la littérature). Helsinki: SKS, 1969.

Hallingberg, Gunnar. *Radiodramat*. Stockholm: Sveriges Radios Förlag, 1967.

Hammer, John F. "Friedrich Dürrenmatt and the Tragedy of Bertolt Brecht," *Modern Drama, 12*, 2 (Sept. 1969).

Hansel, Johannes. *Friedrich Dürrenmatt–Bibliographie*. Bad Homburg v.d.H./Berlin/Zürich: Verlag Gehlen, 1968.

Hatfield, Henry. *Goethe*. Cambridge, Mass.: Harvard University Press, 1964.

Heidsieck, Arnold. *Das Groteske und das Absurde im modernen Drama*. Stuttgart: W. Kohlhammer, 1969.

Heilman, Robert Bechtold. *The Iceman, the Arsonist, and the Troubled Agent*. London: George Allen & Unwin (Seattle: University of Washington Press), 1973.

————. "The Lure of the Demonic: James and Dürrenmatt," *Comparative Literature, 13*, 4 (Fall 1961).

————. "Tragic Elements in a Dürrenmatt Comedy," *Modern Drama, 10*, 1 (May 1967).

Helbling, Hanno. Review in the *Neue Zürcher Zeitung*, March 20, 1959.

Hemberger, Armin. "Dürrenmatt über Dichtung," *Der Deutschunterricht, 21*, 2 (March–Apr. 1969).

Henel, Heinrich. "Szenisches und panoramisches Theater," *Neue Rundschau, 74*, 2 (1963).

Hensel, Georg. *Spielplan*, II. Berlin: Propyläen Verlag, 1966.

Hill, R. F. "The Composition of *Titus Andronicus*," *Shakespeare Survey, 10*, 1957.

Hillard, Gustaf. "Theater in dieser Zeit," *Merkur, 10*, 6 (June 1956).

Hilty, Hans Rudolf. Reviews in the *Volksrecht*, Jan. 22, 1966, and March 23, 1967.

Hinchliffe, Arnold P. *The Absurd*. London: Methuen & Co., 1969.

Holdheim, W. Wolfgang. *Der Justizirrtum als literarische Problematik*. Berlin: Walter de Gruyter & Co., 1969.

453

Holenstein, Carl. Reviews in the *Neue Zürcher Nachrichten*, Sept. 21, 1968, Nov. 11, 1970, and March 30, 1971.

Holm, Hans Axel. Review in the *Dagens Nyheter*, Stockholm, Sept. 26, 1969.

Holm, Ingvar. *Drama på scen*. Stockholm: Bonniers, 1969.

Holz, Hans Heinz. Review in the *Frankfurter Rundschau*, March 21, 1968.

Holzapfel, Robert. "The Divine Plan Behind the Plays of Friedrich Dürrenmatt," *Modern Drama, 8*, 3 (Dec. 1965).

Hope-Wallace, Philip. Review in *The Guardian*, Jan. 10, 1963.

Horst, Karl August. "Humoristische Brechung und Trickmechanik," *Merkur, 10*, 8 (Aug. 1956).

————. "Notizen zu Max Frisch und Friedrich Dürrenmatt," *Merkur, 8*, 6 (June 1954).

Hornung, Peter. "Auf der Suche nach dem dritten Ort," *Weltstimmen, 26*, 6 (June 1957).

Hortenbach, Jenny C. "Biblical Echoes in Dürrenmatt's 'Der Besuch der Alten Dame,' " *Monatshefte für deutschen Unterricht, 57*, 4 (April–May 1965).

Hübner, Paul. Review in the *Rheinische Post*, Dec. 23, 1968.

Huder, Walther. "Friedrich Dürrenmatt oder die Wiedergeburt der Blasphemie," *Welt und Wort, 24*, 10 (Oct. 1969).

Ibsen, Henrik. *Samlede dikterverker*, vi. Standardutgave, 5th ed. Oslo: Gyldendalske Bokhandel, 1922.

Isler, Manuel. Reviews in the *National-Zeitung*, Apr. 14, 1964, and Jan. 24, 1966.

Jacobi, Hansres. Reviews in the *Neue Zürcher Zeitung*, Sept. 19, 1968, Nov. 12, 1970, Dec. 15, 1970; in the *Tagesspiegel*, Berlin, March 10, 1973.

Jacobi, Johannes. Reviews in *Die Zeit*, Feb. 18, 1966, and Feb. 14, 1969.

Jäggi, W. "Auch Basel spielt Dürrenmatt," *Schweizerische Theaterzeitung, 14*, 4 (Apr. 1959).

————. Review in the *Basler Volksblatt*, Jan. 12, 1948.

Jauslin, Christian Markus. *Friedrich Dürrenmatt*. Zur Struktur seiner Dramen. Zürich: Juris-Verlag, 1964.

Jenkins, Harold. "Shakespeare's History Plays: 1900–1951," *Shakespeare Survey, 6*, 1953.

Jennings, Lee B. "Gottfried Keller and the Grotesque," *Monatshefte für deutschen Unterricht, 50*, 1 (Jan. 1958).

Jennings, Lee B. *The Ludicrous Demon*. Berkeley and Los Angeles: University of California Press, 1963.

Jenny, Urs. *Friedrich Dürrenmatt*. Velber bei Hannover: Friedrich Verlag, 1965.

————. "Das kleinste Risiko mit dem grössten Effekt," *Theater heute*, *8*, 4 (Apr. 1967).

————. "Vom Komödienzufall und Komödientod," *Du*, *26*, 4 (Apr. 1966).

————. "Lazarus, der Fürchterliche," *Theater heute*, *7*, 2 (Feb. 1966).

————. Reviews in *Die Zeit*, Jan. 28, 1966; in the *Süddeutsche Zeitung*, Nov. 25, 1967, and Feb. 10, 1969.

————. "Überlebensgross Herr Schwitter," *Theater heute*, *7*, 3 (March 1966).

Jens, Walter. *Statt einer Literaturgeschichte*. 5th rev. ed. Pfullingen: Neske, 1962 (1957).

Johann, Ernst. *Georg Büchner*. Reinbek dei Hamburg: Rowohlt, 1958.

————, and Junker, Jörg. *Deutsche Kulturgeschichte der letzten hundert Jahre*. München: Nymphenburger Verlagshandlung, 1970.

Jonas, Klaus, W. "Die Dürrenmatt-Literatur (1947–1967)," *Börsenblatt für den Deutschen Buchhandel*, *24*, 59 (July 23, 1968).

Kaiser, Joachim. "Grenzen des modernen Dramas," *Theater heute*, *5*, 12 (Dec. 1964).

————. Reviews in the *Süddeutsche Zeitung*, March 22, 1963, Jan. 22–23, 1966, Feb. 14, 1966, March 18, 1967, and Sept. 20, 1968.

————. "Die Welt als Irrenhaus," *Theater heute*, *3*, 4 (Apr. 1962).

Karasek, Hellmuth. Reviews in the *Deutsche Zeitung und Wirtschafts-Zeitung*, Stuttgart, March 22, 1963; in the *Stuttgarter Zeitung*, Jan. 24, 1966, and March 18, 1967.

Karsch, Walther. Review in the *Tagesspiegel*, Nov. 30, 1971.

Kayser, Wolfgang (ed.). *Deutsche Literatur in unserer Zeit*. 4th rev. ed. Göttingen: Vandenhoek und Ruprecht 1966 (1959).

————. *Das Groteske*. Seine Gestaltung in Malerei und Dichtung. Oldenburg und Hamburg: Gerhard Stallin Verlag, 1957.

BIBLIOGRAPHY

Keller, Iso. Review in the *Neue Zürcher Nachrichten*, Jan. 22, 1966.

Kerr, Walter. Review in the *New York Herald Tribune*, Oct. 24, 1964.

Kesting, Marianne. *Das epische Theater.* Stuttgart: W. Kohlhammer, 1959.

————. *Panorama des zeitgenössischen Theaters.* München: R. Piper & Co. Verlag, 1962

Kieser, Rolf. "Gegenwartsliteratur der deutschen Schweiz," *The German Quarterly, 41*, 1 (Jan. 1968).

Kilchenmann, Ruth J. *Die Kurzgeschichte. Formen und Entwicklung.* Stuttgart: W. Kohlhammer, 1967.

Kirchberger, Lida. " 'Kleider machen Leute' and Dürrenmatt's 'Panne,' " *Monatshefte für deutschen Unterricht, 52*, 1.

Kitchin, Laurence, *Drama in the Sixties.* London: Faber and Faber, 1966.

Klarmann, Adolf D. "Friedrich Dürrenmatt and the Tragic Sense of Comedy," *Tulane Drama Review, 4,*4 (May 1960).

Knapp, Gerhard P. (ed.). *Friedrich Dürrenmatt.* Studien zu seinem Werk. Heidelberg: Lothar Stiehm Verlag, 1976.

Koebner, Thomas (ed.). *Tendenzen der deutschen Literatur seit 1945.* Stuttgart: Alfred Kröner Verlag, 1971.

Korn, Karl. Review in the *Frankfurter Allgemeine Zeitung*, March 23, 1959.

Kott, Jan. *Theatre Notebook 1947–1967.* London: Methuen & Co., 1968.

Kranz, Gisbert. *Christliche Literatur der Gegenwart.* Anschaffenburg: Paul Pattloch Verlag, 1961.

Krautkrämer, Horst-Walter. "Das deutsche Hörspiel 1945–1961," Ph.D. dissertation, Heidelberg: Ruprecht-Karl-Universität, 1962.

Krättli, Anton. "Nackter Hamlet und Welttheater," *Schweizer Monatshefte, 51*, 2 (May 1971).

Krywalski, Diether. "Säkularisiertes Mysterienspiel?" *Stimmen der Zeit, 92*, 5 (May 1967).

Kuczynski, Jürgen. "Friedrich Dürrenmatt—Humanist I–II," *Neue Deutsche Literatur, 12*, 8–9 (Aug.–Sept. 1964).

Kühne, Erich. "Satire und groteske Dramatik," *Weimarer Beiträge, 12*, 4 (1966).

Kurzweil, Baruch Benedikt. "Betrachtungen zum Werk Friedrich Dürrenmatts," *Neue Zürcher Zeitung*, March 24, 1963.

Kux, Ernst. "Der Meteor schlägt ein," *Epoca*, Apr. 1966.

L., J. v. "Dürrenmatts 'Meteor' in London," *Die Weltwoche*, Aug. 26, 1966.

Leber, Hugo. "Gewandelte Perspektiven—Vielgestaltigkeit der Formen," *Welt und Wort, 24,* 10 (Oct. 1969).

————. Reviews in the *National-Zeitung,* March 10, 1972; in the *Tages-Anzeiger,* Zürich, Jan. 22, 1966, and March 18, 1967.

————. "Strindberg—Playground für Friedrich Dürrenmatt," *Die Weltwoche,* Feb. 14, 1969.

Lefcourt, Charles R. "Dürrenmatt's *Güllen* and Twain's *Hadleyburg:* the Corruption of Two Towns," *Revue des Langues Vivantes, 33,* 3 (Summer 1967).

Leiser, Erwin. "Den fromme nihilisten," *Bonniers Litterära Magasin, 25,* 2 (Feb. 1956).

Lengborn, Thorbjörn. *Schriftsteller und Gesellschaft in der Schweiz.* Frankfurt am Main: Athenäum Verlag, 1972.

Linder, Hans R. "Der Aussenseiter und das politische Spiel," *National-Zeitung,* Sept. 19, 1968.

Linder, Heinz-Peter. "Die schweizerische Gegenwart im modernen Roman der Deutschen Schweiz," Ph.D. dissertation, University of Bern, 1957.

Litten, Rainer. "König Johann." An interview with Dürrenmatt. *Tages-Anzeiger,* Sept. 14, 1968.

Loetscher, Hugo. "Das Engagement im Welttheater," playbill, *Die Wiedertäufer,* Schauspielhaus Zürich, 1966–67. Also published in *Die Weltwoche,* March 17, 1967.

————. "Requiem auf den Kriminalroman?" *Du, 18,* 12, (Dec. 1958).

———— (ed.). *Varlin.* Texte von Friedrich Dürrenmatt (reprinted in DK) et alii. Zürich: Verlag der Arche, 1969.

————. "Von der Unmöglichkeit zu sterben," playbill, *Der Meteor,* Schauspielhaus Zürich, 1965–66.

————. "Zu Frank V.—Oper einer Privatbank," playbill, Schauspielhaus Zürich, 1958–59.

Loram, Ian C. " 'Der Besuch der alten Dame' and 'The Visit,' " *Monatshefte für deutschen Unterricht, 53,* 1 (Jan. 1961).

Lucas, Lore. *Dialogstrukturen und ihre szenischen Elemente im deutschsprachigen Drama des 20. Jahrhunderts*. Bonn: H. Bouvier u. Co. Verlag, 1969.

Luft, Friedrich. Reviews in *Die Welt*, Feb. 23, 1962, March 22, 1963, Jan. 22, 1966, March 18, 1967, Nov. 29, 1971, and March 12, 1973.

Lüthy, Herbert. *Die Schweiz als Antithese*. Zürich: Verlag der Arche, 1969.

Lutz-Odermatt, Hedwig. "Totentanz 1966," *Schweizer Rundschau, 65*, 2 (Feb. 1966).

Madler, Herbert Peter. "Dürrenmatts mutiger Mensch," *Hochland, 62*, 1 (Jan. 1970), reprinted in *Schweizer Rundschau, 69*, 5 (Sept.–Oct. 1970).

Mann, Otto. *Geschichte des deutschen Dramas*. Stuttgart: Alfred Kröner Verlag, 1960.

Mariacher, Bruno und Witz, Friedrich (eds.). *Bestand und Versuch*. Schweizer Schrifttum der Gegenwart. Zürich und Stuttgart: Artemis Verlag, 1964.

Marti, Kurt. *Die Schweiz und ihre Schriftsteller—die Schriftsteller und ihre Schweiz*. Zürich: EVZ-Verlag, 1966.

Marxer, Peter. "Literarische Humor," *Volkshochschule*, Zürich, March 1963.

Massberg, Uwe. "Der gespaltene Mensch," *Der Deutschunterricht, 17*, 6 (Dec. 1965).

Mayen, Veronika. "Das Problem des Todes im Werk Friedrich Dürrenmatts," Ph.D. dissertation, University of Hamburg, 1966.

Mayer, Hans. "Aus einem Interview," playbill, *Der Meteor*, Schauspielhaus Zürich, 1965–66.

————. *Dürrenmatt und Frisch*. Anmerkungen. Pfullingen: Verlag Günther Neske, 1963.

————. "Friedrich Dürrenmatt," *Zeitschrift für deutsche Philologie, 87*, 4 (Fall 1968).

————. "Komödie, Trauerspiel, deutsche Misere," *Theater heute, 7*, 3 (March 1966).

————. *Zur deutschen Literatur der Zeit*. Zusammenhänge, Schriftsteller, Bücher. Reinbek bei Hamburg: Rowohlt, 1967.

Meier, Peter. Reviews in the *Tages-Anzeiger*, Oct. 24, 1970, March 27, 1971, and Feb. 19, 1972.

Mehlin, Urs. "Claus Bremer, . . . Friedrich Dürrenmatt, *Titus*

Andronicus, . . . ," *Deutsche Shakespeare-Gesellschaft West,* Jahrbuch, 1972.

Melchinger, Siegfried. *Drama zwischen Shaw und Brecht.* Bremen: Schünemann, 1957.

————. "Dürrenmatts Gangster-Oper," *Stuttgarter Zeitung,* March 21, 1959.

————. "Dürrenmatts Salto Mortale," *Theater heute,* 7, 3 (March 1966).

————. "Grimmiger Dürrenmatt," *Theater heute, 9,* 10 (Oct. 1968).

————. "Ein Kommentar: Das Unfeine an Herrn Dürrenmatt", *Theater heute, 10,* 12 (Dec. 1969).

————. "Was hat der bitterböse Friedrich mit Strindberg nun gemacht . . . ," *Theater heute, 10,* 3 (March 1969).

————. "Wie schreibt man böse, wenn man gut lebt?" *Theater heute, 9,* 9 (Sept. 1968), abridged in the *Neue Zürcher Zeitung,* Sept. 1, 1968.

Mittenzwei, Werner. *Gestaltung und Gestalten im modernen Drama.* 2d ed. Berlin und Weimar: Aufbau-Verlag, 1969 (1964).

———— (ed.). *Theater in der Zeitenwende,* I–II. Berlin: Henschelverlag, 1972.

Moritz, Karl. "Friedrich Dürrenmatt: Der Tunnel," *Der Deutschunterricht, 12,* 6 (Dec. 1960).

Morley, Michael. "Dürrenmatt's Dialogue with Brecht," *Modern Drama, 15,* 2 (Sept. 1971).

Moser, Hansueli W. "Die Dinge so zeigen, wie sie wirklich sind," *Abend-Zeitung,* Basel, Sept. 18, 1968.

————. "Dürrenmatt und Düggelin, Leiter am Basler Theater," *Schweizer Heim,* Zürich, Oct. 9, 1968.

————. "Experiment Basler Theater," *Sie und Er,* Sept. 12, 1968.

Muhres, Michael. "Dürrenmatts Begriff der Verantwortung," Ph.D. dissertation, Goethe-Universität, Frankfurt/Main, 1974.

Müller, Ernst. Review in the *Berner Tagblatt,* Apr. 10–11, 1976.

Müller, Joachim. "Max Frisch und Friedrich Dürrenmatt als Dramatiker der Gegenwart," *Universitas, 17,* 7 (July 1962).

————. "Verantwortung des Dramas für unsere Zeit—Bert Brecht und Friedrich Dürrenmatt," *Universitas, 20,* 12 (Dec. 1965).

BIBLIOGRAPHY

Munk, Eric. "Junge Schweizer Dramatiker," *Die deutsche Bühne, 8*, 7–8 (July–Aug. 1964).

Murdoch, Brian. "Dürrenmatt's *Physicists* and the Tragic Tradition," *Modern Drama, 14*, 3 (Dec. 1970).

Nadel, Norman. Review in the *New York World-Telegram and Sun*, Oct. 14, 1964.

Neukirchen, Alfons. Reviews in the *Düssseldorfer Nachrichten*, Dec. 23, 1968, and Dec. 14, 1970.

Neumann, G., Schröder, J., and Karnick, M. *Dürrenmatt, Frisch, Weiss*. München: Wilhelm Fink Verlag, 1969.

Niemi, Irmeli. *Nykydraaman ihmiskuva*. Helsinki: Tammi, 1969.

Nonnenmann, Klaus (ed.). *Schriftsteller der Gegenwart*. Olten und Freiburg im Breisgau: Walter-Verlag AG, 1963.

Oeri, Georgine. Review in *Die Weltwoche*, Apr. 24, 1947.

Ollén, Gunnar. *Strindbergs dramatik*. 3d rev. ed. Stockholm: Prisma, 1966.

Patterson, Michael. *German Theatre Today*. London: Pitman Publishing, 1976.

Pawlowa, N. "Theater und Wirklichkeit: Über das Schaffen von Friedrich Dürrenmatt," *Kunst und Literatur, 14*, 1 (Jan. 1966).

Penzoldt, Günther. *Georg Büchner*. Velber bei Hannover: Friedrich Verlag, 1965.

Peppard, Murray B. *Friedrich Dürrenmatt*. New York: Twayne Publishers, 1969.

Peter, Max. "Der Einfall und seine Folgen." *Schaffhauser Nachrichten*, Apr. 14, 1967.

Pfefferkorn, Eli. "Dürrenmatt's Mass Play," *Modern Drama, 12*, 1 (May 1969).

Pfeiffer, John R. "Windows, Detectives and Justice in Dürrenmatt's Detective Stories," *Revue des Langues Vivantes, 33*, 5 (1967).

Phelps, Leland R. "Dürrenmatts *Die Ehe des Herrn Mississippi*," *Modern Drama, 8*, 2 (Sept. 1965).

Picker, Henry (ed.). *Hitlers Tischgespräche*. Bonn: Athenäum-Verlag, 1951.

Plunien, Eo. Reviews in *Die Welt*, Dec. 23, 1968, and Dec. 14, 1970.

Pongs, Hermann. *Romanschaffen im Umbruch der Zeit*. 4th rev. ed. Tübingen: Verlag der deutschen Hochschullehrerzeitung, 1963 (1952).

Prang, Helmut. *Geschichte des Lustspiels*. Stuttgart: Alfred Kröner Verlag, 1968.

Price, Antony. "The Freedom of the German Repertoire," *Modern Drama, 13*, 3 (Dec. 1970).

Profitlich, Ulrich. *Friedrich Dürrenmatt*. Stuttgart: W. Kohlhammer, 1973.

Quandt, Volker. "Rollen-Relationen in Dürrenmatts Dramatik," Lunds universitet, Sverige, 1970.

Rasch, Wolfdietrich. *Zur deutschen Literatur seit der Jahrhundertwende*. Stuttgart: J. B. Metzlersche Verlagsbuchhandlung, 1967.

Read, Herbert. *Vuosisatamme maalaustaiteen historia*. (A Concise History of Modern Painting). Helsinki: Otava, 1960 (1959).

Reed, Eugene E. "Dürrenmatt's 'Der Besuch der alten Dame': A Study in the Grotesque," *Monatschrift für deutschen Unterricht, 53*, 1 (Jan. 1961).

———. "The Image of the Unimaginable," *Revue des Langues Vivantes, 27* (1961).

Reich-Ranicki, Marcel. *Literatur der kleinen Schritte*. München: R. Piper & Co., 1967.

Reske, Hermann. *Faust—Eine Einführung*. Stuttgart: W. Kohlhammer, 1971.

Riess, Curt. *Theaterdämmerung oder Das Klo auf der Bühne*. Hamburg: Hoffman und Camps, 1970.

Rischbieter, Henning. "Dürrenmatts dünnste Stück," *Theater heute, 1*, 3 (Nov. 1960).

———. "Der neue Dürrenmatt," *Theater heute, 4*, 5 (May 1963).

Rogoff, Gordon. "Mr. Duerrenmatt Buys New Shoes," *Tulane Drama Review, 3*, 1 (Oct. 1958).

Ross, Werner. "Zimmerschlachten," *Merkur, 23*, 10, (Oct. 1969).

Rubinstein, Hilde. "Der Schaukampf des Friedrich Dürrenmatt," *Frankfurter Hefte, 25*, 3 (March 1970).

Rüedi, Peter. "Get Strindberg," *Zürcher Woche*, Feb. 14, 1969.

Rühle, Günther. Reviews in the *Frankfurter Allgemeine Zeitung*, March 8, 1965, March 23, 1967, Sept. 20, 1968, Oct. 26, 1970, March 29, 1971, and Feb. 22, 1972.

Rumler, Fritz. "Mit Strindberg in den Boxring," *Der Spiegel*, Feb. 3, 1969.

BIBLIOGRAPHY

Saarikivi, Sakari. *Aikamme maalaustaide*, Porvoo/Helsinki: WSOY, 1961.

Salmony, George. "Der Meteor verglüht," *Epoca*, Apr. 1966.

―――. Review in the *Abendzeitung*, Nov. 25, 1967.

Sander, Volkmar. "Form und Groteske," *Germanisch-Romanische Monatsschrift*, Neue Folge, *14*, 3 (1964).

Sauter. "Gespräch mit Friedrich Dürrenmatt," *Sinn und Form*, *18*, 4 (1966).

Schaub, Martin. Review in the *Handelsblatt*, Düsseldorf, March 22, 1967.

Schlocker, Georges. Review in the *Handelsblatt, Düsseldorf*, Jan. 26, 1966.

Schmid, Karl. *Unbehagen im Kleinstaat*. Zürich und Stuttgart: Artemis Verlag, 1963.

―――. "Zur Uraufführung von *Es steht geschrieben*," playbill, Schauspielhaus Zürich, 1946–47.

Schmidt, Aurel. "Ein Stück Theaterarbeit," *National-Zeitung*, Feb. 6, 1969.

―――. Review in the *National-Zeitung*, Feb. 10, 1969.

Schnabel, Dieter. Review in *Die Welt*, Dec. 27, 1968.

Schneider, Peter. *Die Fragwürdigkeit des Rechts im Werk von Friedrich Dürrenmatt*. Karlsruhe: C. F. Müller, 1967.

Schondorff, Joachim (ed.). *Herakles*. Complete text of eight plays. Preface by Walter H. Sokel. München—Wien: Langen-Müller, 1964.

Schorno, Paul. Reviews in the *Basler Volksblatt*, Nov. 23, 1970, and *Neue Zürcher Nachrichten*, March 10, 1973.

Schultz, Uwe. Review in the *Christ und Welt*, Nov. 20, 1970.

Schulz, Klaus. "Die Dramatischen Experimente Friedrich Dürrenmatts," *Deutsche Rundschau*, *84*, 7 (July 1958).

Schumacher, Ernst. *Bertolt Brechts 'Leben des Galilei' und andere Stücke*. Berlin: Henschelverlag, 1968.

―――. "Der Dichter als sein Henker," *Sinn und Form, 18* (1966), Sonderheft I.

Schwab-Felisch, Hans. Reviews in the *Frankfurter Allgemeine Zeitung*, Dec. 24, 1968, and Dec. 14, 1970.

Schweizer, Eduard. "Zu Friedrich Dürrenmatts 'Besuch der alten Dame,' " *Reformatio*, *5*, 3 (March 1956).

Schweizer Theaterbuch. Contributions by Paul Kopp, Elisabeth Brock-Sulzer, Geo-H. Blanc, Carlo Castelli and Edmund Stadler. Zürich: Atlantis Verlag, 1964.

462

Schwitzke, Heinz (ed.). *Reclams Hörspielführer.* Stuttgart: Philipp Reclam, 1969.

Searle, Ronald. *Weil noch das Lämpchen glüht.* Preface by Friedrich Dürrenmatt (reprinted in TS). 2d enlarged ed. Zürich: Diogenes Verlag, 1955 (1952).

Seidmann, Peter. "Modern Swiss Drama: Frisch and Dürrenmatt," *Books Abroad, 34,* 2 (Spring 1960).

Seiler, A. J. Review in the *National-Zeitung,* March 26, 1963.

Shaefer, Albert (ed.). *Das Menschenbild in der Dichtung.* München: Verlag C. H. Beck, 1965.

Shakespeare, William. *King John.* The New Arden edition, by E.A.J. Honigmann. London: Methuen & Co; Cambridge, Mass.: Harvard University Press, 1962 (1954).

―――. *Shakespeares Dramatische Werke,* I, V. Transl. by August Wilhelm von Schlegel and Ludwig Tieck, ed. by Alois Brandl. Leipzig und Wien: Bibliographisches Institut, 1897.

―――. *Titus Andronicus.* The New Arden edition, by J. C. Maxwell. London: Methuen & Co; Cambridge, Mass.: Harvard University Press, 1961 (1953).

Sharp, Sister Corona. "Dürrenmatt and the Spirit of Play," *University of Toronto Quarterly, 34,* 1 (Oct. 1969).

―――. "Dürrenmatt's *Play Strindberg,*" *Modern Drama, 14,* 3 (Dec. 1970).

Sierig, Hartmut. *Narren und Totentänzer.* Hamburg: Agentur des Rauhen Hauses, 1968.

Simon, John. "Theatre Chronicle," *The Hudson Review, 15,* 2 (Summer 1962).

Spencer, T.J.B. "Shakespeare and the Elizabethan Romans," *Shakespeare Survey, 10,* 1957.

Spinner, Wilfried. "Aergernis Dürrenmatt," *Neue Zürcher Zeitung,* Feb. 28, 1966.

Spycher, Peter. *Friedrich Dürrenmatt. Das erzählerische Werk.* Frauenfeld und Stuttgart: Verlag Huber, 1972.

Stamm, Rudolf. "King John—König Johann," *Deutsche Shakespeare-Gesellschaft West,* Jahrbuch 1970. Heidelberg: Quelle & Meyer.

Stange, C. R. Review in the *Basler Nachrichten,* Sept. 19, 1968.

Steffen, Hans (ed.). *Das deutsche Lustspiel,* II. Göttingen: Vandenhoeck & Ruprecht, 1969.

BIBLIOGRAPHY

Steiner, Jacob. "Die Komödie Dürrenmatts," *Der Deutschunter-richt, 15*, 6 (Dec. 1963).

Stickelberger, Rudolf. "Ein Dichter begräbt seinen Film," *Reformatio, 7*, 10 (Oct. 1958).

———. "Frank V.," Dürrenmatts jüngstes Werk," *Reformatio, 8*, 4 (April 1959).

———. "Weltsensation des Theaters?" *Reformatio, 11*, 3 (March 1962).

Stoll, E. E. *Art and Artifice in Shakespeare.* New York: Barnes & Noble, 1951 (Cambridge: Cambridge University Press, 1933).

Strelka, Joseph. *Brecht, Horváth, Dürrenmatt.* Wien–Hannover–Bern: Forum Verlag, 1962.

Strindberg, August. *Skrifter av August Strindberg,* XII. Stockholm: Albert Bonniers Förlag, 1957.

Stumm, Reinhardt. Review in the *Basler Nachrichten,* Feb. 10, 1969.

Suter, Gody. "Ausweglosigkeit mit biederem Ausweg," *Die Weltwoche,* March 29, 1963.

Syberberg, Hans-Jürgen. "Zum Drama Friedrich Dürrenmatts," Ph.D. dissertation, München: Ludwig-Maximilians-Universität, 1963.

Taëni, Rainer. *Drama nach Brecht.* Basel: Basilius Presse, 1968.

Tank, Kurt Lothar. Reviews in the *Sonntagsblatt,* Hamburg, March 26, 1967, and Apr. 9, 1967.

Taubman, Howard. Review in the *New York Times,* Oct. 14, 1964.

Terry, Thomas. Review in the *Tagesspiegel,* Feb. 23, 1972.

Theater. Meinungen und Erfahrungen von Therese Giehse et al. Affoltem a. A.: Achren Verlag, 1945.

Thiel, Heinz. Review in the *Abendzeitung,* March 30, 1971.

Thomson, Philip. *The Grotesque.* London: Methuen & Co., 1972.

Thorn, Fritz. " 'Meteor' in London," *Süddeutsche Zeitung,* Aug. 3, 1966.

Thurner, Felix. Review in the *Luzerner Neueste Nachrichten,* March 22, 1967.

The Times, Nov. 15, 1968: an anonymous review of *König Johann.*

Tiusanen, Timo. *O'Neill's Scenic Images.* Princeton, New Jersey: Princeton University Press, 1968.

464

Tiusanen, Timo. *Tapa puhua.* Helsinki: Kirjayhtymä, 1963.

Tozzoli, Gian Paolo. "Gefahren und Chancen für den schweizer Autor," *Welt und Wort, 24,* 10 (Oct. 1969).

Trewin, J. C. (ed.). *Plays of the Year, 32,* 1966. Includes *The Dance of Death,* I-II, by August Strindberg, transl. by Norman Ginsbury. London: Elek Books, 1967.

Tschechoslowakei 1968. Speeches by Peter Bichsel, Friedrich Dürrenmatt (reprinted in DK), Max Frisch, Günther Grass, Kurt Marti, and a letter by Heinrich Böll. Zürich: Verlag der Arche, 1968.

Tynan, Kenneth. "Prophetic Satire in the Madhouse," *The Observer,* Jan. 13, 1963.

Uhlig, Gudrun (ed.). *Autor, Werk, und Kritik,* II. München: Max Hueber Verlag, 1969.

Usmiani, Renate. "Friedrich Dürrenmatt as Wolfgang Schwitter," *Modern Drama, 11,* 2 (Sept. 1968).

―――. "The invisible Theater: The Rise of Radio Drama in Germany after 1945," *Modern Drama, 14,* 3 (Dec. 1970).

Vellinghausen, Albert Schulze. "Stinkend, Feydeau." *Theater heute, 7,* 3 (March 1966).

Vidal, Gore. "Comment: Turn left, or right, to more vivacious matters," *Esquire,* May 1962.

Vielhaber, Gerd. Review in the *National-Zeitung,* Dec. 16, 1970.

Voser, Hans Ulrich. "Friedrich Dürrenmatt, das 'enfant terrible,'" *Ex Libris, 13,* 7 (July 1958).

Voser, Irma. Reviews in the *Neue Zürcher Zeitung,* Feb. 23, 1962, March 22, 1963, Jan. 21, 1966, March 18, 1967, Oct. 20, 1970, March 27, 1971, and March 10, 1973.

Waith, Eugene M. "The Metamorphosis of Violence in *Titus Andronicus,*" *Shakespeare Survey, 10,* 1957.

Waldmann, Günter. "Dürrenmatts paradoxes Theater," *Wirkendes Wort, 14,* 1 (1964).

Watts, Richard Jr. Review in the *New York Post,* Oct. 14, 1964.

Weber, Dietrich (ed.). *Deutsche Literatur seit 1945 in Einzeldarstellungen.* Stuttgart: Alfred Kröner Verlag, 1968.

Weber, Werner. Reviews in the *Neue Zürcher Zeitung,* Jan. 12, 1948, June 19, 1962, and May 2, 1971.

Wehrli, Max. "Gut christlich. Wie der 'Meteor' einschlug," *Theater heute, 7,* 3 (March 1966).

Weibel, Kurt. "Der gläubige Dürrenmatt," *TV-Radio-Zeitung,* Feb. 12–18, 1966.

BIBLIOGRAPHY

Weibel, Kurt. "Letztes Destillat," *TV-Radio-Zeitung*, March 18–24, 1973.

———. "Urfaust—gedürrt oder Der dürre Geist der Richter," *TV-Radio-Zeitung*, Nov. 1–7, 1970.

Weigel, Hans. *Lern dieses Volk der Hirten kennen*. München: Deutscher Taschenbuch Verlag, 1968 (1962).

Weimar, Karl S. "The Scientist and Society: A Study of three Modern Plays," *Modern Language Quarterly*, *27*, 4 (Dec. 1966).

Wellwarth, George E. "Friedrich Dürrenmatt and Max Frisch: Two Views of the Drama," *Tulane Drama Review*, *6*, 3 (March 1962).

———. *The Theater of Protest and Paradox*. Rev. ed. New York: New York University Press, 1971 (1964).

Welti, Jakob. Reviews in the *Neue Zürcher Zeitung*, Apr. 21, 1947, and Dec. 12, 1949.

Wendt, Ernst. "Mit dem Irrsinn leben?" *Theater heute*, *3*, 12 (Dec. 1962).

Westecker, Wilhelm. Review in the *Christ und Welt*, Stuttgart, April 16, 1959.

Wilbert-Collins, Elly. *Four Contemporary German-Swiss Authors*: Dürrenmatt, Frisch, Walser, Zollinger. A Bibliography. Bern: Francke Verlag, 1967.

Wieland, Christoph Martin. *Geschichte der Abderiten*. With a postscript by Karl Hans Büchner. Stuttgart: Reclam-Verlag, 1958.

von Wiese, Benno (ed.). *Das deutsche Drama*, II. Düsseldorf: August Bagel Verlag, 1968 (1958).

Williams, Raymond. *Drama from Ibsen to Brecht*. Rev. ed. of *Drama from Ibsen to Eliot*. London: Chatto & Windus, 1968 (1952).

Wolff-Windegg, Philipp. Reviews in the *Basler Nachrichten*, March 1, 1961, Feb. 23, 1962, March 21, 1963, Apr. 13, 1964, and Oct. 6, 1969.

Wollenberger, Werner. "Der Besuch der kalten Dame," *Zürcher Woche*, Nov. 6, 1964.

———. "Kongress der Mörder," *Zürcher Woche*, Sept. 25, 1968.

———. "Die Mistkäfer-Komödie," *Zürcher Woche*, March 29, 1963.

Wollenberger, Werner. "Der totale Dürrenmatt," *Zürcher Woche*, March 23, 1967.

———. "Wer stirbt, hat mehr vom Leben," *Zürcher Woche*, Jan. 28, 1966.

Wyrsch, Peter. "Die Dürrenmatt-Story," *Schweizer Illustrierte*, *52*, 12–17 (March 18.–Apr. 22, 1963).

Zbinden, Hans. *Schweizer Literatur in Europäischer Sicht*. Zürich und Stuttgart: Artemis Verlag, 1964.

———. "Zur Situation der Literatur in der Schweiz," *Welt und Wort*, *24*, 10 (Oct. 1969).

Zimmermann, Werner. *Deutsche Prosadichtung unseres Jahrhunderts*, II. Düsseldorf: Pädagogischer Verlag Schwann, 1969.

Zimmermann, Willy. Review in the *Neue Zürcher Nachrichten*, Apr. 21, 1947.

Züfle, Manfred. "Friedrich Dürrenmatt," "Zu den Bühnengestalten Friedrich Dürrenmatts," *Schweizer Rundschau*, *66*, 1–2 (Jan.–Feb. 1967). Reprinted from *Christ auf der Bühne*, Einsiedeln/Zürich/Köln: Benziger & Co. 1967.

ADDENDA

Busch, Eberhard. *Karl Barth*. London: SCM Press Ltd., 1976.

Dürrenmatt, Friedrich. *Gespräch mit Heinz Ludwig Arnold*. Zürich: Verlag der Arche, 1976.

———. *Der Mitmacher*. Ein Komplex: Text der Komödie, Dramaturgie, Erfahrungen, Berichte, Erzählungen. Zürich: Verlag der Arche, 1976.

———. *Writings on Theatre and Drama*. Transl. with an introduction by H. M. Waidson. A selection of twenty-two essays from TS and DK, including a new translation of *Problems of the Theater*. London: Jonathan Cape, 1976.

Hayman, Ronald (ed.). *The German Theatre*. London: Oswald Wolff, 1975.

Index

||||||||||||||||||||||||||||||||||||||||||||||||||||||||||||||||||||||||||||||||||||||||||||||||||||||||||

469

INDEX

artistic invention (*cont.*)
103, 209, 283, 297, 321, 336,
340ff, 352, 354n, 363, 374,
385, 421, 423–25ff, 429, 436–
37; as a starting-point for an
entire work, 73, 110, 124–25,
146, 206, 251, 288, 304–306,
329ff, 365
Arx, Cäsar von, 47
asceticism, 428, 429–30, 433,
436
Askew, Melvin W., 239n
astronomy, 194, 366
atheism, 48
atomic bomb, 43, 124, 191–93,
204–205, 211, 266–70, 279,
384
avant-gardism, 108
Axer, Erwin, 369n

Bach, Johann Sebastian, 322
Bachmann, Dieter, 377n
Balance of Terror, 275
ballad, 354
Bänziger, Hans, 26, 41; *Frisch
und Dürrenmatt*, in notes: 3,
12–13, 44, 47–48, 50, 55, 61,
82, 95, 107, 112, 115, 118,
125, 132, 135, 143–44, 180,
186, 196–99, 232, 243, 260,
263, 271, 278, 288, 301, 437–
38
Bark, Joachim, 40n
baroque, 44, 65, 68
Barraclough, Clifford A., 44n
Barth, Karl, 53–55, 417
Baschung, Urs J., 39
Basle City Theater, The, 20, 60–
61, 322, 337n, 402
Bastard, the (*King John*), 338–
45, 363n
Baudissin, Wolf von, 347n
Baumann, Gerhart, 363n
Beckett, Samuel, 23n, 33n, 184;
Endgame, 274, 319, 405;
Krapp's Last Tape, 191n;
Waiting for Godot, 430
Beckmann, Heinz, 318n
Beethoven, Ludwig von, 269

Beissel, Henry, 46n, 299n
Bergemann, Fritz, 357n, 359–60,
362
Bergman, Ingrid, 251n
Beria, Lavrenty Pavlovich, 392n
Bernhard, Roberto, 130n
Beutler, Ernst, 355n
Bible, The, 88, 311, 327n, 367,
369
Bichsel, Peter, 12n, 383n
Bienek, Horst, 21n, 107n, 225n,
256n
Black Power, 349
Blind Man, The, 43, 61–69, 73,
77, 89, 100, 110, 111n, 140,
241, 245, 265, 418, 419, 420;
characterization, 61–67, 83,
87, 105, 162, 183, 313
Blum, Ruth, 10n, 104n
Boesch, Walter, 258n
Bondy, François, 356n, 398n
de Boor, Helmut, 354n
Borchert, Wolfgang, 46
Bosch, Hieronymus, 17, 47, 68
Braun, Karlheinz, 91n
Brecht, Bertolt, 3, 11, 17, 26,
44–45, 47ff, 58, 65n, 69, 90n,
99n, 121, 182, 186, 217–20,
221–22, 247, 256, 263n, 264,
285n, 319–20, 348, 403–406,
438, 439; *Arturo Ui*, 313n;
Baal, 50; *The Caucasian Chalk
Circle*, 115n; *Galileo Galilei*,
220n, 286; *The Good Person
of Szechwan*, 122n; *Mutter
Courage*, 56, 339; *The Three-
penny Opera*, 117, 260–61,
310, 349n, 426
Brentano, Bernardo von, 12n
Briggen, Hansjürg, 320n
Brock, Erich, 63n, 68n
Brock-Sulzer, Elisabeth, 26;
"Dürrenmatt and the Sources"
(in *Der unbequeme Dürrenmatt*), 33n, 58n, 190n, 194n,
214n; *Dürrenmatt in unserer
Zeit*, 88n, 173n, 229n; *Friedrich Dürrenmatt*, 26, 35, 77,
260, 292; in notes: 37, 49, 55,

470

66, 73, 79, 86, 95–96, 102, 110, 121, 124, 131, 135, 137, 141, 143, 147–48, 152, 160, 169, 174, 179, 183, 186, 188, 196, 200, 238, 240–41, 258, 268, 273, 276, 279, 290; "Friedrich Dürrenmatt" (article in *Der Monat*), 9, 44n, 259n; preface to TS, 5n, 7n, 26, 203n, 221n; reviews: 297; in notes: 52, 88, 113, 299, 313, 316, 356, 361, 369, 371, 376, 437; (ed.), *Schweizer Theaterbuch*, 46, 47n
Brook, Peter, 251n, 269n
Brooks, Cyrus, 129n
Brown, Kenneth, 276n
Brueghel, Pieter, 17, 47, 68, 310
Brunner, Hans Heinrich, 316n
Büchner, Georg, 16, 322, 337; *Woyzeck*, 32n, 209. See also separate entry for *Woyzeck*
Bulganin, Nikolay Aleksandrovich, 392n
Bullough, Geoffrey, 337n, 338n
Bunuel, Luis, 10
Buri, Fritz, 9, 10n, 32, 55n, 118n
Burkhard, Paul, 255, 259–60, 269n
Busch, Eberhard, 54n
Buschkiel, Jürgen, 334n, 345n, 355n
Button, The, see Comedy

cabaret, 46–47, 69, 219, 370; as an element in Dürrenmatt, 49, 76ff, 89–90, 199, 243, 258, 287–89, 291, 307, 349–50, 363, 426, 429, 434
Calderon, 229n
Calgari, Guido, 46n, 289n
Caligula, 76n
Calvinism, 51
Campbell, Lily B., 337n, 338n
Camus, Albert, 142; *The Plague*, 187n
Canaris, Volker, 373n

Caracalla, 76
Carew, Rivers, 102n, 248n, 249n
caricature, 96, 102, 194, 264, 292–93, 305, 343, 392n
Carlsson, Anni, 17n, 207n, 210n
Case of the Donkey's Shadow, The, 180–84, 186–88, 190, 201, 228, 241, 252, 310, 410
Catholicism, 10, 27, 48, 59, 106
Cattani, A., 407
Cervantes, Miguel de, 205
chance: as a dramaturgic concept, 85–86, 103, 114, 122–24, 241, 257, 278n, 281–83, 286, 289–90, 294–95, 298–99, 301, 306–307, 316n, 341, 344–45, 364n, 375, 380, 404n, 409–10, 413–14, 420, 425–26, 437–38; in novels, 131–33, 140, 148, 162ff, 171–75, 394–97, 400–401, 422, 433
Chandler, Raymond, 128n
changeability of the world, 218–20, 247, 405
chaos: as a contrast to order, 59, 127, 130–31, 148, 165, 171–73, 175, 210–12, 246–50, 264n, 279, 382, 387, 404, 409–410, 417, 422–23, 433, 437; within a work of art, 68, 265; within the world, 74–75, 142, 158, 162, 275n, 279, 282, 390, 425, 431
characterization: in adaptations, 314–17, 320, 331–33, 338, 342–46, 348, 350n, 356, 428–29; in early plays, 48–49, 58–59, 63, 80, 88, 95ff, 102–103, 108, 111, 119–20, 419–20; in late works, 392–94, 397–98, 405, 432–33; in middle plays, 233–37, 240–43, 280–81, 284–85, 300–302, 305–307, 427
Chekhov, Anton, 19
Chesterton, G. K., 128n
Chiari, J., 278n
chorus, 125, 160–61, 312, 403, 417–18; in middle plays, 258, 288, 299; in radio plays, 185,

127, 147, 161–62, 190, 194, 245, 260, 283, 425, 434, 437; as an object of criticism, 75, 101, 105, 112, 125, 420
Forster, Leonard, 138n
Frank, Armin P., 176n, 177, 180n, 181n, 194n, 199n
Frank V, 219, *255–65*, 266–69, 272, 281, 286, 291, 306, 310, 330, 337, 377, 420n, 426, 430
freedom, 132–33, 193, 196, 204, 214–15, 220, 260–62, 276, 283, 382–85, 390, 404, 406, 421, 435, 437, 439
Friedmann, Hermann, 112n
Frisch, Max, 3, 14n, 46, 65n, 77n, 109, 176, 337n, 438n; *Andorra*, 266; *Biedermann*, 180n; *Graf Öderland*, 102; "On the Nature of Theatre," 64n; *Tagebuch 1946–49*, 11, 33; *Stiller*, 207
Fry, Christopher, 48
Furzewa, Jekaterina Aleksejevna, 392n

gallows humor, 163, 235, 302
Garten, H. F., 11n, 50n, 101n, 114n, 121n, 284n
Gassner, John, 319n
Gassner, Manuel, 301n
Geissler, Rolf, 44n, 82n, 114n
Genet, Jean, 438n
gestalt psychology, 23
Giehse, Therese, 46
Ginsberg, Ernst, 46, 61, 91
Ginsbury, Norman, 323n
Glauser, Friedrich, 128n
Göchhausen, Luise von, 353n
Goebbels, Joseph, 277n
Goering, Hermann, 277n
Goethe, Johann Wolfgang von, 57, 265n, 322, 337; *Faust*, 378n; *Urfaust*, 347, *352–56*, 357, 359, 429; *see also* separate entry for *Urfaust*
Gogol, Nikolai, 205
Goldschmidt, Rudolf, 262n

Gontrum, Peter B., 139n, 141n, 153n, 175n
"Good Shepherd Game," 381–89, 391–94, 398–400, 404, 433
Grabbe, Christian Dietrich, 84n
grace, 110–12, 118, 122–25, 143, 146–48f, 151, 238, 246f, 256, 272, 298
Grack, Günther, 334n
Grass, Günther, 300, 337n
Greek tragedy, 188, 225, 244, 245n
Greene, Graham, 55, 128
Gregor, Ulrich, 108n
Greul, Heinz, 46n
Grimm, Reinhold, 14–15, 429n; *Der unbequeme Dürrenmatt* (ed.), 14; in notes: 7, 10, 32, 58, 101, 111, 118, 119, 145, 148, 155, 160, 240, 258; (ed.), *Episches Theater*, 49n; (ed.), *Sinn oder Unsinn?*, 16n, 178n
grotesque, the, 4, *14–22*, 34, 36, 141, 162–65, 186, 211–13, 237, 355, 439; as a Dürrenmattian feature, 42–43, 107, 127, 171, 194–95, 203, 204–205, 229, 245n, 269, 296, 300, 320, 352, 373–74, 377–78, 417, 419, 430–32; in characterization, 62, 100, 106, 116–17, 128, 178n, 224, 234, 241, 270, 281, 356, 392n, 394, 405, 418; in novels, 130, 134–36, 145, 155, 157, 160n, 170–72, 173–75, 226n, 397, 421–23, 433, 410–12; in scenic images, 51, 53, 56, 66–67, 104, 119, 125, 183–84, 197, 199, 200–201, 232–33, 243–44, 285, 340, 372, 418, 435–37; in tragicomedies, 215, 222–23, 246–47, 268, 274, 307, 326–29, 426, 430, 438; stylistic concept, 48, 58, 77, 180, 292–93, 294, 339, 345–46, 349, 363. *See also* absolute grotesque, parodic grotesque.
Grut, Mario, 334n

Library of Congress Cataloging in Publication Data

Tiusanen, Timo.
Dürrenmatt: a study in plays, prose, theory.

Bibliography: p.
Includes index.
1. Dürrenmatt, Friedrich—Criticism and interpretation.
PT2607.U493Z89   832'.9'14   76–45915
ISBN 0–691–06332–X